SLEUTHING C. S. LEWIS

Also by Kathryn Lindskoog

C. S. Lewis: Mere Christian
The Lion of Judah in Never-Never Land
Up from Eden
Loving Touches
The Gift of Dreams
A Child's Garden of Christian Verses
Around the Year with C. S. Lewis and His Friends
How To Grow a Young Reader: Books from All Ages for Readers of All Ages
The C. S. Lewis Hoax
Creative Writing for People Who Can't Not Write
Fakes, Frauds and Other Malarkey
Light in the Shadowlands
Finding the Landlord: A Guidebook to C. S. Lewis's Pilgrim's Regress
Light Showers
Journey into Narnia
Dante's Divine Comedy, Journey to Joy: Inferno
Dante's Divine Comedy, Journey to Joy: Purgatory
Dante's Divine Comedy, Journey to Joy: Paradise
Words to the Wise: Collected Essays
Surprised by C. S. Lewis, George MacDonald, and Dante

SLEUTHING C. S. LEWIS

MORE LIGHT IN THE SHADOWLANDS

By Kathryn Lindskoog

Mercer
University
Press
2001

ISBN 0-86554-741-6 (hardcover)
ISBN 0-86554-730-0 (paperback)
MUP/H557/P215

© 2001 Mercer University Press
6316 Peake Road
Macon, Georgia 31210-3960
All rights reserved

First Edition.

∞The paper used in this publication meets the minimum
requirements of American National Standard for
Information Sciences—Permanence of Paper for Printed
Library Materials, ANSI Z39.48-1992.

Library of Congress Cataloging-in-Publication Data

Lindskoog, Kathryn Ann.
Sleuthing C.S. Lewis: more Light in the Shadowlands/by Kathryn Lindskoog.
p. cm.
Rev. and expanded version of: Light in the Shadowlands. 1994.
Includes bibliographical references and index.
ISBN 0-86554-730-0
1. Lewis, C. S. (Clive Staples), 1898-1963—Authorship. 2. Christianity and
literature—England—History—20th century. 3. Executors and administrators— Great
Britain. 4. Authors, English—20th century--Biography. 5. Christian literature,
English—Authorship. 6. Literary forgeries and mystifications. 7. Christian
Biography—England. I. Lindskoog, Kathryn Ann. Light in the Shadowlands. II. Title.

PR6023.E926 Z7797 2001
823'.912--dc21
                                                                    [B]2001018014

To Perry Bramlett,
who spreads light through
C. S. Lewis for the Local Church Interstate Ministries

Truth is mighty and will prevail.
There is nothing the matter with this, except that it ain't so.
Mark Twain

With him is strength and wisdom:
the deceived and the deceiver are his.
He discovereth deep things out of darkness,
and bringeth out to light the shadow of death.
Job 12:16, 22 [KJV]

CONTENTS

Foreword by Joe R. Christopher ix
Introduction by Robert Ellwood xi
Preface xiii
Acknowledgments xv

1. Re-Packaging C. S. Lewis
   No End in Sight After All? 1
2. Shining Some Light on the *Dark Tower*
   Not a Lost Lewis Novel After All? 13
3. Throwing Water on the Bonfire Story
   Not a Literary Rescue After All? 41
4. Seeing Through "Through Joy and Beyond"
   Not the Film of a Lifetime After All? 56
5. Strange Visions and Revisions
   Not Real Rhymes or Reasons After All? 75
6. Forms of Things Unknown
   Not What Lewis Had in Mind After All? 103
7. The Most Substantial People
   Not a Flimsy Fiction After All? 125
8. Will the Real Mrs. Lewis Stand Up
   Not Really Not Really Married After All? 142
9. Forging a Friendship
   Not a Genuinely Copied Signature After All? 164
10. They Fall Together
    Not a Stolen Manuscript After All? 186
11. The Business of Heaven
    Not Unworldly Wisdom After All? 221
12. Battle for the Dark Tower
    Not a Contest After All? 251

Appendices   293

1. Afterword by John Bremer   293
2. Facts about Forgery   302
3. The Mistress of C. S. Lewis by John Bremer   312
4. Stealing the King's Ring   322
5. A. N. Wilson Errata   337
6. Lewis Petition and Signatories   346
7. The Portland Statement   353
8. Letter to *La Paz*   356
9. The Julius Grant Report   364
10. The Nancy Cole Report   368
11. Who Owns C. S. Lewis?   387
12. Three Letters from C. S. Lewis   392
13. Chronology   397

Index   407

FOREWORD

When I wrote a foreword for Kathryn Lindskoog's *The C. S. Lewis Hoax*, I asked of Lewis's publishers and his main editor, in essence, "Is it not time for answers to be given?" I did not think that six years later at the time of *Light in the Shadowlands* and now, seven years later, the situation would be nearly the same as before. There is still no responsible answer from Walter Hooper, the main editor of Lewis's works since his death; and Kathryn Lindskoog keeps asking questions, keeps finding more pieces of evidence, and keeps reporting new complications and developments.

Lindskoog published "Some Questions about C. S. Lewis Scholarship" in 1978, raising mainly biographical questions about Hooper's various claims, such as a lengthy friendship in England with Lewis. In the 1987 edition of her *C. S. Lewis: Mere Christian*, she questioned the authorship of "The Dark Tower" fragment, which had been written as if by Lewis. The next year, in *The C. S. Lewis Hoax*, she brought together these and other problems; although much of the book was about Hooper. There were parts in the book that raised questions about the publishing and media industry related to Lewis. In 1989 she began her small journal, *The Lewis Legacy*, still being published, which has discussed a variety of topics through the years. However, when Walter Hooper gave a manuscript of "The Dark Tower" to the Bodleian Library in Oxford, in what looked like C. S. Lewis's handwriting, the arguments in Lindskoog's journal often turned to questions of forgery. A full account of her journal is not necessary, for the main arguments, as refined issue after issue, appeared in *Light in the Shadowlands* in 1994 and now, with further revision and extension, in this book.

In my experience in discussions with those who side with Walter Hooper, some refuse to put their responses in writing because they do not want Lindskoog to add their names to her journal and subsequent book. Some dismiss her arguments as having been disproved, and some tell me what a friendly man Hooper is. One has attacked Lindskoog for jumping to conclusions without evidence. The reader of this book can judge the latter charge. Those who say her charges have been disproved usually refer to the report by Nancy Cole (see Appendix 10). The situation Lindskoog got herself into that has most hurt her reputation was her attempt to convince Stephen Schofield that forgeries could fool him; this episode exploded on her when he took one of her "spoofs" (her term, in "A Hoaxer's Epilogue" to her *Fakes, Frauds, and Other Malarkey*) to a newspaper as authentic news. Her account of this incident is in the last chapter of this book. But however one gauges this episode, it does not affect any arguments for which she provides evidence, for it is factual evidence that will decide the issues in the long run.

I wrote in my original foreword, "Can any of Lindskoog's arguments be dismissed? Perhaps some can. But their power is in their accumulative weight. I do not think, overall, that they can be dismissed. Any *ad hominem* attack on Lindskoog will not eliminate her textual and historical arguments." I believe this is still true concerning this much extended version of the first book on these topics. Lindskoog has clarified her organization at points, reshaped emphases occasionally, and now presents twelve chapters; the first version had eight and the second had ten. (The appendices have gone from two to eight to thirteen.) And finally her material has an index—a much needed guide to her discussions!

In addition to the material I have touched on above, this book is an indictment of a financial industry based on Lewis's books, his name, and his prestige. C. S. Lewis wrote his books to serve God; others have used them—perhaps sometimes naively, sometimes less naively—to serve their vanity or other more peculiar ends, but mainly—so Lindskoog reports—to serve Mammon.

—Joe R. Christopher
Co-editor of *C. S. Lewis: An Annotated Checklist of Writings about Him and His Works*
Author of *C. S. Lewis,* Twayne's English Authors Series
Compiler of *Chad Walsh Reviews C. S. Lewis*

INTRODUCTION

It is an honor to be asked to introduce this important work by Kathryn Lindskoog. She is a friend of some thirty-five years, and one of the most courageous women I know. For some time she has been engaged in an unceasing struggle to present to the world certain propositions about the literary legacy of the great C. S. Lewis which she believes to be true, but which have proved highly unwelcome in powerful quarters. Like such other determined women as Lucretia Mott and Florence Nightingale, in her struggle she has had to fight against two sets of relentless adversaries, one without and the other embedded in her own flesh.

As she has engaged in her battle for truth as she believes it must be told, she has suffered from multiple sclerosis which has kept her increasingly confined and weakened. Often the struggle to use her keyboard in bed despite great pain and fatigue has demanded every ounce of energy, and the temptation to give it all up must have been overwhelming, but she has persevered. At the same time, she has suffered demeaning slurs and rebukes, or worse has been given the silent treatment, from those in the multi-million dollar C. S. Lewis "industry" who ought to take her well-documented case more seriously.

I am not a scholar in the issues dealt with in this book, and cannot vouch for the truth of all of Kathryn Lindskoog's assertions, though I usually find myself persuaded as she painstakingly pulls all her evidence together. I do profoundly believe, however, that she is right to state them and that she must be heard.

Some might say that the way of charity would require silence in such matters as these, where words can cause hurt and acrimony. I do not so think, and neither does Kathryn.

To her, truth is important, and on weighty matters love can only follow in *its* service, not that of falsehood. Otherwise there would be no love shown to those whose reputations have been harmed, and rightful rewards pilfered, by plausible and articulate religious entrepreneurs—many there are in this world—whose master is other than truth. The way of truth even when unpleasant was the way of the prophets, of he who was greatest of them, and of Lewis himself, that most scrupulously honest of men in whose name much that is otherwise has apparently been done.

Let Kathryn's claims be tested; so far they have been stonewalled, denied, and ridiculed. They have been condemned without due process by self-credentialed judges and juries in shadowy, Kafkaesque proceedings at which Kathryn was allowed no rebuttal or even the right to be present, and though they have gotten out press releases have never published full reports.

(One can hardly imagine procedures more distasteful to Lewis's own academic or political principles. He loved a good, fair, honest debate; he had a visceral hatred of anything that smacked of elitism or highhandedness. He also had no great regard for the straightforwardness of the print media. For all this see *That Hideous Strength,* which may contain veiled prophecies of its author's own postmortem fate in this world.)

But despite all efforts to undercut them by means fair and foul, Kathryn's charges have not been refuted. With the appearance of this trenchant new version of a brave writer's *J'accuse,* it is time for a reckoning.

Robert S. Ellwood
Emeritus Professor of Religion
University of Southern California

PREFACE

As the second millennium begins, C. S. Lewis is more famous and popular than ever; the C. S. Lewis industry is richer than ever; and the C. S. Lewis fraud is bigger than ever.

Twenty-eight years ago, in 1973, C. S. Lewis's brother Warren died; and in 1975 I read shocking statements in his diary. For eleven years I kept discovering more and more evidence of a relentless literary deception. In my dismay, in 1986 I wrote to my friend Clyde Kilby. (Dr. Kilby was known as the dean of American C. S. Lewis studies.)

On 11 September 1986, Dr. Kilby answered, "Why don't you write the whole thing up?" Early in October I called him in response, and he came in from his garden to talk with me. He was bright and healthy. Two weeks later he died in his sleep.

I followed Dr. Kilby's final suggestion, and two years later I published my findings in *The C. S. Lewis Hoax*. Six years later, I revealed much more in *Light in the Shadowlands*; and now, seven years later, I offer *Sleuthing C. S. Lewis: More Light in the Shadowlands*.

By now most of Lewis's personal friends and early readers have passed from these mortal Shadowlands into the vivid world ahead that Lewis described at the end of the last book he ever wrote, *Letters to Malcolm*.

"And once again, after who knows what aeons of silence and the dark, the birds will sing and the waters flow, and lights and shadows move across the hills, and the faces of our friends laugh upon us with amazed recognition.

"Guesses, of course, only guesses. If they are not true, something better will be."

In the meantime, old fables and new falsehoods abound here in the Shadowlands. As Albert Camus said, truth can be hard to look at, like bright light; but falsehood is a beautiful twilight. (Lewis warned about an evil twilight city in *The Great Divorce*.) This book is needed now, like a bright lamp-post in Narnia, to cast more light into dim shadows. Where C. S. Lewis and most of his friends are now, no lamps are needed.

ACKNOWLEDGMENTS

There have been a series of landmark contributions to this book. In 1975 a librarian named Barbara Griffin showed me telltale revelations in Warren Lewis's diary. In 1978 Clarence Walhout, editor of the journal *Christianity & Literature*, courageously published my first inquiry into posthumous C. S. Lewis affairs. In 1986 Carla Faust Jones contacted me about her computer analysis of *The Dark Tower*. In 1988 leaders of Multnomah Press took the risk of publishing *The C. S. Lewis Hoax.* In 1991 A. Q. Morton tested some posthumous C. S. Lewis literature for me, thanks to a donation from Professor Don Cregier of the University of Prince Edward Island. In 1994 Questar Publishers asked me to update and expand *The C. S. Lewis Hoax,* creating *Light in the Shadowlands.* That year Dean Picton underwrote the cost of someone hand-copying otherwise unavailable Lewis documents I needed. In both 1988 and 1994 I had the good fortune of working with book editor Rod Morris. And in 2000 Marc Jolley of Mercer University Press decided that it was time for this greatly updated, expanded account of the matter.

People are at times unsympathetic to my investigation have contributed highly valuable information anyway. The staffs of the Marion E. Wade Center at Wheaton College, the Department of Western Manuscripts at the Bodleian Library in Oxford, and the Southern Historical Collection of the University of North Carolina at Chapel Hill did so. Nicolas Barker, Deputy Keeper of the British Library, did so. Editors or contributors to *C. S. L.: Bulletin of the New York C. S. Lewis Society, Mythlore, Mythprint, The Lamp-Post of the Southern California C. S. Lewis Society,* and *Newsletter of the Salinas Valley C. S. Lewis Society* have all done the same.

For fifteen years, Stephen Schofield published a rich array of Lewis lore in his *Canadian C. S. Lewis Journal.* With zestful determination, he once managed to wheel me into Duke Humfrey's Library at the Bodleian, which was not easily accessible for nonambulatory researchers. There we sat in the very stall where Lewis used to read, examining Lewis letters and papers. Mr. Schofield took me to the Kilns, where its owners Mr. and Mrs. J. W. Thirsk entertained us. He also took me to meet five of Lewis's delightful friends: John Wain of Oxford, Mary Neylan of Godstone, Mr. and Mrs. James Dundas-Grant of Woking, and Ruth Pitter of Long Crendon. Miss Pitter shared an afternoon of memories and poetry with me, enriching me with the glorious mind that gave C. S. Lewis joy.

I also owe a debt of gratitude to Leonard and Molly Miller, who opened their home to my husband and me and our son Peter one sunny morning. Later, Douglas Gresham favored us with the pleasure of a visit on his way home from a trip around the world.

Before publication of *The C. S. Lewis Hoax* the following people responded to the project with information or encouragement: Pauline Baynes, K. L. Billingsley, Frederick Buechner, Joe R. Christopher, Arthur C. Clarke, Robert and Gracia Fay Ellwood, William Geiger, Douglas R. Gilbert, Richard Lancelyn Green, Roger Lancelyn Green, Dom Bede Griffiths, Virginia Hearn, James Houston, Madeleine L'Engle, Ian McMurdo, Joan Ostling, Richard Pierard, Faith Sand, George Sayer, Sheldon Vanauken, Carolyn Vash, Walter Wangerin, and Patrick Wynne.

Last, but far from least, the following people have helped in a variety of great and small ways: Michael Aeschliman, Lloyd Alexander, Chimene Bateman, David Baumann, Robert Bayliss, Ralph Blair, Paul Blattner, Fay Blix, Mary Borhek, Perry Bramlett, John Bremer, Jonathan Brewer, Algis Budrys, Sharon Cregier, Lawrence Crumb, John Docherty, Lyle Dorsett, Loring Ellis, Robert O. Evans, Jillian Farringdon, Alastair Fowler, Larry Gilman, George Gorniak, Fred Graham, Mary Ellen Gresham, Brenda Griffing, Douglas Hackleman, John Haynes, Walter Hearn, Ranelda Hunsicker, Matt Jacobson, Burton Janes, Carolyn Keefe, Martha Kilby, Ursula Le Guin, Michael Logsdon, James Long, Linette Martin, Wayne Martindale, Bruce McAllister, Paul McCusker, Gilbert Meilaender, David Nelson, Gary Oliver, Nancy-Lou Patterson, H. Boone Porter, Tim Powers, Jason Pratt, Larry Repass, A. L. Rowse, Wendell Wagner, Martin Ward, John West, Richard Wilbur, Terri Williams, Doreen Anderson Wood, W. R. Wortman, and Charles Wrong. To the many others who also aided or encouraged me in my efforts, I offer heartfelt appreciation.

1

RE-PACKAGING C. S. LEWIS

NO END IN SIGHT AFTER ALL?

"It's an industry, you see." This was C. S. Lewis's rueful comment about serious literature less than a year before he died.[1]

Now C. S. Lewis is a literary industry himself. It is estimated that 200 million of his books have sold so far. It is particularly ironic in light of the fact that when he died some people said his prominence and popularity would quickly fade away; the opposite, of course, was true.[2] Careers and fortunes, as well as frauds, grow out of his popularity. What has happened to Lewis since his death is an amazing saga of fakery, fraud, and forgery.

Lewis was a scrupulously honest and humble man. It is not his fault that those who like to celebrate his thinking and writing are often accused of worshipping him. In 1984 British author Humphrey Carpenter set the tone for this in *The Spectator*.

...that Lewis was God. This notion has always been hovering on the edge of what are referred to in Wheaton, Illinois, and points west as "C. S. Lewis Studies." (Wheaton, Illinois, is where Lewis's letters and manuscripts have been lovingly collected; it is also the *alma mater* of

---

[1] A conversation recorded on 4 December 1962, and published as "Unreal Estates" in *Of Other Worlds* by C. S. Lewis (London: Bles, 1966) 93.

[2] "And perhaps, like Kierkegaard, Lewis will become popular only long after the age he rebelled against has passed away. His popularity is only minimal in an age which demands originality above all." Peter Kreeft, C. S. *Lewis: A Critical Essay* (Grand Rapids: Eerdmans, 1969) 42.

Dr. Billy Graham.) But now it comes out in the open. Mrs. Kathryn Lindskoog, a doyenne of "Lewis criticism"...writes of Lewis: "Being with him was a bit of heaven, and I hope that heaven will include a bit of being with him." Not surprisingly, given this identification of Lewis with the Deity, Mrs. Lindskoog was "giddy with awe" when she actually sat on a sofa next to him.[3]

A few months after Carpenter's sarcastic article, an event took place that may seem to confirm his charge: an eight-foot tall C. S. Lewis stained glass window was dedicated in St. Luke's Episcopal Church of Monrovia, California.[4] Actually, the window is one of several tributes in that church to outstanding teachers and workers in Christendom. Ten years later, a C. S. Lewis window was installed in St. David's Church in Denton, Texas.[5] These tributes are an accurate reflection of the enthusiastic love that part of the American public has for C. S. Lewis today. Whether that love is inordinate or not is a matter of opinion.

In 1993 the head of a C. S. Lewis Centre in London sniffed in *The Observer*, "Lewis was an inspiration to us, but we do not worship at his shrine as some American groups do. We're not groupies or hagiographers."[6] Thus, in the opinion of some critics, the Lewis mementos at Wheaton College, including a large wardrobe closet made by his grandfather, are religious relics at a "St. Lewis" shrine.

But if America has a Lewis shrine, England has a Lewis sanctuary. In 1980 seven and a half acres of Lewis's Oxford property, where he swam, boated, and even ice-skated on his woodland pond, were purchased by the Berkshire, Buckinghamshire & Oxfordshire Naturalists' Trust. A sign at the entrance gate says "In 1980 the Reserve became a memorial to Henry Stephen

---

[3]Humphrey Carpenter, "Giddy with Awe," *The Spectator* (March 1984): 31.

[4]John Dart, "C. S. Lewis Honored in Church Window," *Los Angeles Times* (20 October 1984) 2:12. Dart describes the image of Lewis with academic gown, open book, and smoking pipe in hand.

[5] The cover of the 14 May 1995 issue of *The Living Church* showed the set of four stained-glass narthex windows depicting "Saint Hilda of Whitby, Abbess," "The Venerable Bede, Historian," "John Donne, Preacher & Poet," and "C. S. Lewis, Scholar & Churchman."

[6] Andrew Walker, head of the C. S. Lewis Centre for Religion and Modernity, as quoted in *The Observer*, 28 November 1993.

and C. S. Lewis and will remain a place of sanctuary for Aslan, the hobbits and all natural wildlife on the Reserve." In 1994 the reserve became a place for schools to study nature and wildlife conservation.[7]

Holy Trinity Church in Headington Quarry, where Lewis is buried in the churchyard, did not make much of him before 1990; but in 1991 it installed two clear windows with frosted glass designs of Narnia that were donated for the small sanctuary, and on 6 March 1994 the BBC broadcast a program there. The Reverend Canon Christopher Hewetson said the church had had a "yes but" feeling about Lewis in the past, but Lewis brought in such a stream of visitors that "we are forced now to improve our connection" with him.

In 1984 Lewis's red brick house, the Kilns, was purchased by a partnership of American Lewis enthusiasts recruited by a California entrepreneur. They bought it in good condition for $120,000, intending to use it for a Lewis museum and their own private hostel. After a couple of years, leaders of the project informed shareholders that the partnership was defunct; the investors automatically became donors. Although the house declined into a run-down dormitory for men in Oxford, it thrived as a perennially charming cottage in evocative American fundraising appeals. Year after year, new donors have contributed to the heartwarming idea of the Kilns. Meanwhile, the far more picturesque (and brickless) "Kilns" in the 1993 film "Shadowlands" was not like the real Kilns after all.

There are three separate C. S. Lewis Institutes.[8] A variety of Lewis conferences are held every year: in 1998 they were set in Belfast Ireland; Oxford and Cambridge, England; Queens, New York; Wheaton, Illinois; Seattle,

---

[7] The property now distinguished by Lewis's 33-year residence was long used as a quarry for a brick company. Removal of clay had created the pond that Lewis treasured. Lewis enjoyed the fact that according to local tradition the poet Shelley used to sail toy boats on this quarry pond.

[8] The C. S. Lewis Institute for Summer Studies in Washington, D. C. was founded in 1976 by James M. Houston, also founder and former Chancellor of Regent College in Vancouver, B.C. Seattle Pacific University in Washington has been offering a summer C. S. Lewis Institute since 1978. The third C. S. Lewis Institute, launched in 1988 by California fundraiser Stanley Mattson, holds triennial conferences in England.

Washington; and Valyermo, California.[9] Independent C. S. Lewis societies meet all year in places as far-flung as Oxford, Toronto, New York, Tulsa, Los Angeles, Portland and Japan. According to British journalists who repeat a wild estimate from Dr. Andrew Walker of King's College, London, there are 500 C. S. Lewis societies in the United States. Perry Bramlett[10] gives a more sober estimate of over 200 Lewis Societies and reading groups worldwide. According to Bramlett, over 100 seminaries, church schools, colleges, and high schools in the U. S. have built courses of study (literary and religious) around the works of Lewis, and over 200 U. S. master's theses and doctoral dissertations have been written about Lewis and his works so far.

Ever since 1969, the New York C. S. Lewis Society has issued a monthly bulletin; there are also three separate Lewis quarterlies on the West Coast (there have been five), plus a handsome journal devoted primarily to Lewis and Tolkien. These collected journals and newsletters total many thousands of pages now, yet no one ever runs out of new material.

Macmillan, Cahill, Tyndale, and Collins have produced and marketed several handsome C. S. Lewis calendars. Not surprisingly, some Lewis aficionados have produced their own. The possibilities for Lewis calendars seem endless.

The proliferation of the Internet in the 1990s coincided with the proliferation of public interest in C. S. Lewis. As a result, when the twenty-first century began there were hundreds of C. S. Lewis offerings on the Internet. There are C. S. Lewis-centered web sites, link pages, email groups, online journals, booksellers, and chat rooms. One can find pictures of Lewis and his locales, along with various illustrations of his books. There are excellent essays, articles, and reviews for the taking, along with the entire text of Lewis's first book, which is now in the public domain.

---

[9] Over 400 participants attended the centenary conference in Illinois. Over 800 participants, most from the U. S., attended the tandem centenary conferences in England.

[10] The Reverend Perry C. Bramlett of Louisville, Kentucky, is a Lewis specialist who has developed an extraordinary fulltime interdenominational ministry called "C. S. Lewis for the Local Church Interstate Ministries." He presents a variety of lessons, sermons, seminars, book studies, and displays of Lewisiana at schools, churches, and retreats. His Internet site is www.win.net/~pbramlett.

Centennial Lewis observances, conferences, and publications abounded in 1998. In Belfast a statue was erected in his honor and a plaque was mounted at his birthplace. At Magdalen College in Oxford a stone plaque was mounted on the wall at Addison's Walk. In 2000 HarperCollins unveiled a lavish Narnia Internet site for children as part of its marketing plan. A flood of new editions and adaptations of books by and about Lewis hit the market, along with Narnia paper dolls and a Narnia cookbook; and many new books about Lewis were released. There was also a rash of articles about Lewis, and he was discussed on many radio programs. On public television's "Religion and Ethics Newsweekly" a segment was devoted to Lewis, and he was selected as one of the twenty-five most influential religious leaders of the twentieth Century. "Jack: A Musical Portrait of C. S. Lewis in Music and Words," a new Broadway-style musical review about C. S. Lewis, premiered in Great Britain. A £3.5 million laser dance spectacular inspired by "Riverdance" premiered also, featuring Joss Ackland as C. S. Lewis. And the Royal Shakespeare Company launched a lavish musical adaptation of *The Lion, the Witch and the Wardrobe*.[11]

As of this writing, there is at least one Lewis documentary on the horizon, and possibly three. In 1997 Carol Hatcher began work on a PBS documentary called "C. S. Lewis: An Examined Life," and in 1998 she began production. (At first she was told to desist because the Lewis literary estate was reserving that privilege for themselves, but that was resolved and she forged ahead.) Zondervan Publishing House expects to release a coffee-table book as a companion to Hatcher's documentary, along with a "ChurchSource" study guide and video. As if one PBS Lewis documentary were not blessing enough, a second one, "To Know We Are Not Alone," was also in production in 2000

---

[11] An original cast recording of music from this production was marketed on a CD. Selections included 1. The Professor's House - (instrumental) 2. Always Winter Now (Mr Tumnus) 3. Back Through the Wardrobe (instrumental) 4. Misery Me (Lucy) 5. Turkish Delight (The White Witch, Grumpskin & Edmund) 6. Swiggle Down the Lot (The Beavers & Children) 7. Wrong will be Right (Mr Beaver) 8. The Witch's Castle (instrumental) 9. Christmas is Here (Father Christmas) 10. The Thaw (instrumental) 11. Come to the Table (company) 12. Aslan's Bargain with the White Witch (instrumental) 13. Come to the Carnival (The White Witch & Company) 14. The Lion Leaps (Aslan, Lucy, Susan and the Lion's chorus) 15. The Spite of the Spell (company) 16. The Coronation at Cair Paravel (company) 17. The White Stag (instrumental) 18. Finale: Long Live the Mountains (company).

in hopes of a 2001 broadcast. This one is from the Crouse Entertainment Group, with Chip Duncan as writer/producer and Ben Kingsley as narrator. Nothing has been announced yet about a documentary from the Lewis literary estate, but there are hints that there will be one from the BBC.

Since his death in 1963, about forty[12] more Lewis books have been added to the thirty-seven that were already published. Some of these posthumous volumes are anthologies that collect and recollect, arrange, and rearrange his previously published work, and some are just picture-book simplifications of Narnia extracts; but others present writing never before available. (The following were not originally intended for publication: seven collections of personal letters with more to come, lecture notes, childhood stories and drawings, and a diary.) All the posthumous publications have been tightly controlled and rationed out year by year.

It was reasonable to assume that no further Lewis essays were going to surface. But Perry Bramlett discovered one in 2000 that no other Lewis experts had ever heard of. In 1944 it was published in *In Our Tongues*, a 128-page collection of Christian essays. Lewis's five paragraph evangelistic piece "All or Nothing" is one of thirty-two essays there, half by "serving chaplains" and a quarter by "broadcasters." (Lewis's had appeared earlier in an obscure publication called *Think*.)[13]

Year after year, decade after decade, Lewis's old stand-bys keep coming out in new editions—with new prefaces, new covers, new illustrations, new comments, and always with staggering sales. Almost all of Lewis's original thirty-nine books are still in print. According to Bramlett, from the early 1940s until 1989 sales of books by Lewis in English averaged over one million per year. Since 1989 that figure has increased to one and half million copies per year, with some estimates going as high as two million. But according to United Media, that estimate is much too low.

In a news release from New York on 13 June 2000, United Media announced its licensing partnership with the recently formed C. S. Lewis Company. The partnership includes a worldwide licensing and

---

[12] Because of overlapping, there are various ways to count Lewis's posthumous books.

[13] A close paraphrase of "All or Nothing" appears in my book *Surprised by C. S. Lewis, George MacDonald, and Dante* (Macon GA: Mercer University Press, 2001).

merchandising program for a new series of books to be based on the world of Narnia and scheduled for release in the fall of 2002 from HarperCollins Children's Books. "The licensing program will feature products in the plush, toys, gift, stationery, interactive and apparel categories focusing on mid and upper tier retailers. This is the first time that any licensed merchandise will be produced for this classic fantasy series. 'We are very pleased to have entered into this licensing partnership with United Media,' stated Simon Adley, C. S. Lewis Company. 'United Media has always been recognized as a leader in brand-building and also for its reputation in establishing these same brands as long term entertainment properties driven by content and quality.' The licensing program surrounding these editions will primarily target the young adult and adult gift purchaser in upper tier retailers. Since its debut in 1950, the series has sold over 60 million copies worldwide and upwards of 3 million copies each year with 20% annual sales growth each of the last two years."[14]

Before this development, the Narnian Chronicles alone brought in at least $2 million a year and in 1990 the Macmillan Company reportedly paid Britain's giant publishing conglomerate HarperCollins $3 million for permission to continue publishing the Chronicles in the U. S. However, that was evidently not enough. U. S. rights to the series had reverted to the Lewis Estate in 1987, and the estate sold them to HarperCollins. In spite of Macmillan's long, desperate struggle to retain the books, the legal case was finally settled in favor of HarperCollins before going to trial. Although Collins originally published only five of the seven books in England and none of them in the U. S., HarperCollins now owns the entire worldwide English-language rights to Narnia.[15]

More than 170 books by Lewis in about 30 languages other than English have been published so far, ranging from Afrikaans to Swedish. Lewis books have long been available in French, German, Italian, Japanese, Russian

---

[14] United Media, an E.W. Scripps Company, also licenses and/or syndicates a variety of cartoon properties including Peanuts, Raggedy Ann and Andy, Miffy, Dilbert, Rainbow Fish, Nancy and Sluggo, Get Fuzzy and Fido Dido.

[15] According to a 1998 article in the *Daily Telegraph*, total sales of the Narnian Chronicles totaled 16 million then; but neither the publishers nor the estate have ever been willing to answer inquiries about sales totals of Lewis books through the years. This seems to be standard practice in the publishing industry.

(including the Narnian Chronicles in one volume), and Spanish; now some are also available in Chinese, Hungarian, Turkish, Polish, Romanian, Slovene, and Estonian. (According to one of the Estonian translators, Aldo Randmaa, several titles have come out in Estonian since the fall of the Soviet Union; but at one time an Estonian *Screwtape Letters* was printed in Finland and distributed underground in Estonian churches.)

Lewis is one of the most quotable writers who ever lived. Six volumes of his selected quotations have been published so far. Whenever fair-use rules don't apply, the minimum permissions charge from his two main United States publishers, Macmillan and Harcourt Brace Jovanovich, was $25. In 1986 I had to pay HarperCollins £15 to quote the well-known opening sentence of the Narnian story *Voyage of the Dawn Treader*, "There was a boy named Eustace Clarence Scrubb, and he almost deserved it."[16] It was a high price, and the sentence almost deserved it.

In 1980 a cloistered Carmelite nun in Flemington, New Jersey, wrote an eighth chronicle of Narnia, telling what happened to Susan, and called it *The Centaur's Cavern*.[17] (C. S. Lewis sometimes encouraged readers to invent new tales of Narnia.[18]) It was so good that she soon found a Protestant publisher who wanted to bring it out. The altruistic plan was to make it extremely clear that this was *not* by C. S. Lewis, and to donate all profits to the work of Mother Teresa. One of Lewis's personal friends, the well-known author Sheldon Vanauken, endorsed the project; and everyone involved felt sure that Lewis would have approved. But those in control of the Lewis Estate

---

[16] I used this sentence on the 7 August page in my book of days, *Around the Year with C. S. Lewis and His Friends* (C. R. Gibson, 1986). "Eustace Scrubb, a character in C. S. Lewis's third Chronicle of Narnia, began keeping a diary on board "The Dawn Treader" on this day. 'There was a boy called Eustace Clarence Scrubb, and he almost deserved it.' —C. S. Lewis's famous opening sentence in *The Voyage of the Dawn Treader*."

[17] On 22 January 1957 C. S. Lewis wrote to a boy named Martin: "The books don't tell us what happened to Susan. She is left alive in this world at the end, having then turned into a rather silly, conceited young woman. But there is plenty of time for her to mend, and perhaps she will get to Aslan's country in the end—in her own way." Lyle W. Dorsett and Marjorie Lamp Mead, eds., *Letters to Children* (New York: MacMillan, 1985) 67.

[18] "And why not write stories for yourself to fill up the gaps in Narnian history?" Letter to a girl named Denise, 8 September 1962. Lyle W. Dorsett and Marjorie Lamp Mead, eds., *Letters to Children* (New York: Macmillan, 1985) 104.

turned the nun down. Narnia was private property, and no creative nuns were allowed to trespass in the name of charity.[19] One company purchased the right to market a cheap board game, however; and another company bought the right to market a Narnia video game that sold for $40.

Much original C. S. Lewis music and drama has been created, but permission for professional or amateur production is usually denied. Even when free performances of members' works have been prepared for local schools and churches, the Lewis Estate has usually refused permission and warned that such infringement of copyright is illegal. No wonder Sparrow Records, Inc., paid a heavy financial fine for releasing original songs about Narnia by the group called Second Chapter of Acts, and the David C. Cook company was forced to shred thousands of full-color posters—a beautiful Aslan by Joe DeVelasco and an illustrated map of Narnia by Sylvia Smith.[20]

An extremely talented California couple composed and produced a tape called *Dawn Treader Suite* made up of distinctive synthesizer compositions for each of the major sections of *The Voyage of the Dawn Treader*. They paid a printer to make hundreds of handsome inserts they had designed. Their songs had no lyrics and they assumed that no one would object to below-cost or free distribution of the tape. But when one of the custodians of the Lewis Estate saw their Internet announcement, he threatened them with a lawsuit for using the words *Dawn Treader* in their title, and words like Dark Island for individual sections. The Lewis Estate did not want them to distribute music celebrating a book by Lewis. The couple consulted a copyright lawyer who advised them that they were innocent of copyright infringement and would most likely win a court case, but that the monetary cost of fighting powerful corporate lawyers would be extremely high. So they sadly packed away all the tapes they had prepared as joyful gifts for the public.

In the 1970s professional Atlanta actor and playwright Tom Key delighted audiences with his impersonation of Lewis in "An Evening with C. S. Lewis," a one-man show. He paid a fee to the Lewis Estate for every performance, but

---

[19] The right to issue new books about Narnia was evidently being reserved for whoever might offer high enough financial gain to the owners of the Lewis Estate.

[20] In 2000 a senior communications major at Walla Walla College in Washington rather easily obtained permission for his stage play "The Great Divorce." He realizes how fortunate he is. He owns the copyright for his play and scheduled its first performance for spring 2001.

the estate suddenly withdrew permission and abruptly ended that phase of Key's career. After a long hiatus, he is sometimes allowed to present his show again. (In 2000 the English-born, Nashville-based actor David Payne was allowed to tour the U. S. with his one-man show "After Shadowlands," based on Lewis's *A Grief Observed.*)

Fortunately, no one has to gain permission to write or teach about C. S. Lewis. Books about Lewis and his books freely abound; the total is over 150, and most Lewis-watchers lost count long ago. There are six adult Lewis biographies plus three picture books about him, four Lewis biographies for children, a biography of his wife, three books about his marriage, and selections from his brother's diary.[21]

There are several books about Lewis's fiction in general and over ten separate books in English about the Narnian chronicles alone. Five separate books about Lewis have been written in Japan, and the most handsome Japanese study of Narnia comes with a slipcover and ribbon marker. There are several books telling what Lewis believed about various topics, four anthologies of essays about Lewis by people who knew him, and plenty of others by people who didn't. There are two large Lewis encyclopedias and one small one, in addition to one concise guide to the Lewis landmarks in Ireland and England. There are also two Irish books devoted to his roots in Ulster. In contrast, there are several books that devote their sections on Lewis to attacking him, and one entire book called *The Skeleton in the Wardrobe* that psychoanalyzes Lewis and sounds the alarm about how dangerous he is. (The public has also been warned against him in newspaper articles by major writers A. N. Wilson and Phillip Pullman, as well as others.)

In spite of these scattered warnings, Lewis's 1994 popularity surge accelerated by the Academy Award nominee "Shadowlands" has not yet abated. There are three separate films, four videotapes, and one highly successful international stage play about Lewis's life so far. The stage play,

---

[21] At this point David Bratman observed in *Mythprint,* "Adults should not disdain children's books: they can be fine sources for brief introductions on a topic. Unfortunately, none of the children's biographies of Lewis can be recommended with any enthusiasm: they are all unbalanced or inaccurate. The most easily available currently, *The Man Who Created Narnia* by Michael Coren (Eerdmans, hardcover), is riddled with factual errors, in particular distorting the story of Lewis's changing religious beliefs."

Shadowlands, was first performed in London in 1989, then spread abroad; in March 2000 it opened in the Rakvere Theatre in Estonia, coordinated with the release of *Surprised by Joy* in Estonian.

Four televised films of Narnia are available on videotape so far, and a Narnia film for theaters has long been a possibility at Paramount.[22] Dramatic adaptations of all seven Narnia stories are sold in audio cassettes. Cassettes of Lewis's recorded radio talks about the four loves, John Bunyan, and Charles Williams are always popular; and readings from his books by John Cleese, Michael York, Ian Richardson, Claire Bloom, and Sir Michael Hordern have sold widely. The newest of these at the time of this writing was Michael York's $24 four-hour reading of *The Lion, the Witch and the Wardrobe*, released before Christmas 2000. There is even a videotape for sale about Douglas Gresham, one of Lewis's stepsons.

Lewis was a man who cherished his privacy, yet few publicity-hungry writers have been so accessible and so popular in life and in death. Few are the center of so much attention. To other authors, Lewis's literary fortune seems like an author's best dream come true. But in fact his situation is also every honest author's worst nightmare come true.

C. S. Lewis's literary legacy is increasingly defiled by fraud, forgery, and falsehood. Such a fate is ironic in light of Clyde S. Kilby's astute tribute to him shortly after his death: "a man who had won, inside and deep, a battle

---

[22] The Emmy-award-winning animated version of *The Lion, the Witch and the Wardrobe* that aired in the 1970s is still available from the Episcopal Radio-TV Foundation. It was reportedly viewed in 40% of American homes and in 63% of the homes with children between six and eleven years of age. Walter Cronkite stated, "In a dramatic and compelling way these classics present human values often lacking in today's television: loyalty, courage, caring, responsibility, truthfulness and compassion. Produced with care for these values, *The Chronicles of Narnia* can, and I believe will, become the classics in television that they are in literature."

Ironically, delightful parts of the first section of the film were lifted from Rapture Rep, an altruistic Orange County, California lay ministry which had created a superb musical version of the story. (They had to pay a fee every time they gave their free performances at churches, hospitals, or Christian camps.) An unsmiling stranger showed up at several of their performances, and when the cartoon version premiered on TV a few months later, his motive was clear. It is a shame he did not thank them for what he copied.

against pose, evasion, expedience, and the ever-so-little lie and who wished with all his heart to honor truth in every idea passing through his mind."[23]

Besides his passionate defense of truth and battle against lies, Lewis is noted for his saving sense of humor. At some level he might laugh at the pious pomposity of the cynical C. S. Lewis industry and encourage us to do the same. But first we need the facts; then we can laugh or cry. In spite of an almost ludicrous amount of detail about C. S. Lewis available to his admirers and his enemies, the powerful Lewis industry itself is shrouded in secrecy.

> The way to learn more is to let in more light, not to continue a shroud of secrecy.
> —*Hershel Shanks, editor of Biblical Archaeology Review*

---

[23] Clyde S. Kilby, *The Christian World of C. S. Lewis* (Grand Rapids: Eerdmans, 1964) 5.

2

SHINING SOME LIGHT ON THE DARK TOWER

NOT A LOST LEWIS NOVEL AFTER ALL

In 1977 *Time* magazine devoted a page to C. S. Lewis and reported, "In May, Harcourt Brace Jovanovich released a fantasy, *The Dark Tower*, that Lewis never finished."[1] Now it seems that Lewis never started it. The most far-fetched fantasy of 1977 may have been the idea that Lewis was the author of *The Dark Tower*.[2] The mystery surrounding this semi-obscene book is far more interesting than the bumbling fantasy within it.[3]

---

[1] "C. S. Lewis Goes Marching On," *Time* (5 December 1977): 92.

[2] The title *The Dark Tower* is a reference to Robert Browning's strange poem "Childe Roland to the Dark Tower Came." Browning said the poem came to him in a dream, and he wrote all 204 lines in one day. He did not say what he thought the nightmarish dream signified. Browning's title came from an unexplained line in *King Lear*: "Child Rowland to the dark tower came."

[3] Two coincidences link C. S. Lewis to Browning's *Dark Tower*. Lewis's deep affection for wartime evacuee Jill "June" Flewett prompted him to pay her way through drama school. (Her stage name was Jill Raymond.) In 1950 she had the female lead in Louis MacNeice's radio play "The Dark Tower," in which Roland was played by young Richard Burton. (Shortly thereafter, she married the grandson of Sigmund Freud and has been known as Jill Freud from that time on.)

In 1941-42 and 1945-47 Lewis served as tutor for Oxford undergraduate Derek Brewer, author of "The Tutor: A Portrait" in *C. S. Lewis at the Breakfast Table*. On 26 January 1984 Brewer gave an inaugural speech at the University of Cambridge

Lewis wrote three excellent interplanetary novels between 1937 and 1944. According to J. R. R. Tolkien, C. S. Lewis said to him one day, "Tollers, there is too little of what we really like in stories. I am afraid we shall have to try and write some ourselves." They agreed that Lewis would write of space travel and Tolkien would write of time travel.[4]

The two men were experienced readers of science fiction, but complete amateurs at writing it. Tolkien began to write a novel about the destruction of Atlantis; but his publisher told him that it would not be appealing enough to justify publication, and he never finished it. Lewis forged ahead and finished his space novel, but then encountered difficulty in getting any publisher to accept it. After it was published in 1938 the reception was moderate until Lewis skyrocketed to popularity with his *Screwtape Letters* in 1942. From then on most Lewis fiction sold well.

This first space novel by Lewis, *Out of the Silent Planet,* told how a philology professor, much like J. R. R. Tolkien, was kidnapped by scoundrels and sent to Mars on their space ship. Through his surprising adventures there, the professor, Elwin Ransom, began to grow into a wise man and a hero in touch with the true meaning of the universe.

Not all science-fiction enthusiasts enjoy *Out of the Silent Planet,* partly because it includes nothing about technology or science and is in reality a moral and religious fantasy. But many agree with Marjorie Nicolson, author of the historical study *Voyages to the Moon.* She declared at the end of her book, "*Out of the Silent Planet* is to me the most beautiful of all cosmic voyages and in some ways the most moving..."[5]

In the second of the series, *Perelandra* (1943), Ransom left the earth for Venus and entered into the cosmic struggle between good and evil there. In this book Lewis dispensed with a spaceship altogether and transported Ransom in a mysterious white coffin-like box. *Perelandra* is a spiritual thriller with scenes of breathtaking beauty. It has been the favorite Lewis book of many Lewis readers, and was reportedly his own favorite of all his books until he wrote *Till We Have Faces.*

(where C. S. Lewis taught from 1955 to 1963) titled "Childe Roland to the dark tower came: an approach to English studies."

[4] Humphrey Carpenter, *Tolkien* (Boston: Houghton Mifflin, 1977) 170.

[5] As quoted by Roger Lancelyn Green in *C. S. Lewis: A Biography,* 165.

The third book of the trilogy, *That Hideous Strength* (1945), engaged Ransom in a struggle against cosmic evil on earth. Merlin came back to life to help; and, quite literally, hell broke loose and the heavens came down to earth. For all the outer tumult and cataclysm, the main adventure was inner again.[6]

Needless to say, those who love this trilogy have often wished that Lewis had written a tetralogy instead. Twenty-one years after *That Hideous Strength* was published, they were told they had not wished in vain. There *was* a fourth Lewis novel about Ransom's adventures.[7]

In 1966 editor Walter Hooper quietly mentioned in his preface to the new Lewis anthology *Of Other Worlds* that this unknown novel existed. "Lewis wrote another romance (unpublished) about Dr. Ransom which falls chronologically between *Out of the Silent Planet* and *Perelandra*." I asked Hooper for details, but he didn't give any. After many months, I finally asked Clyde Kilby of Wheaton College in Illinois "Do you know anything about it?" This prompted Kilby to write to his friend Warren Lewis, because as Lewis's devoted brother, living companion, personal secretary, and heir, Warren should know. On 23 January 1968 Kilby's inquiry prompted Warren to write a note to Hooper exclaiming that he knew of no such story by his brother: "Clyde does not, nor do I...Do you know of any such work?" No answer at all came back from Hooper to Warren to Kilby to me.

On 13 July a self-proclaimed Lewis addict named Frank Charles wrote to Warren that his nose whiffled and his mouth watered at the merest sniff of a possibility that there was another Ransom book lying around. So on 15 July

---

[6] The opening of *That Hideous Strength* is written in what appears to be Lewis's handwriting on page 68 of a notebook of Walter Hooper's that he placed in the Bodleian Library in 1989. In this version of the opening the name of the heroine is Jane Ruddock instead of Jane Studdock. Because this notebook also contains a story purportedly written by Lewis in the 1920s in ink that reportedly did not exist until the 1950s, the content of the notebook is suspect. See Joe R. Christopher's "A Catalogue, Two Notebooks, and an Exercise Book," *Mythprint* (April 1994): 2-4.

[7] On page 154 of *Clive Staples Lewis, A Dramatic Life,* William Griffin recorded as if it were factual what he imagined to be an event in Lewis's life in the summer of 1938: "Buoyed by the good reviews his space journey was getting, Lewis decided that he would try a time journey. 'If there is to be any more space-traveling, it would have to be time-traveling as well...!' That was the last sentence of *Out of the Silent Planet,* and from that he developed the first sentence of a work tentatively entitled *The Dark Tower."*

1968 the bewildered Warren tried Hooper again: "What the dickens is all this about an unpublished Ransom novel?"[8]

Warren evidently gave up, and Hooper maintained a discreet silence until after Warren's death in 1973. In 1977 Hooper claimed on page 92 of *The Dark Tower* that he had showed the Dark Tower manuscript to Warren in 1964: "After an unavailing search for more pages, I showed this fragment to Major Lewis, Owen Barfield, and Roger Lancelyn Green..."

Green disagreed. He told me that he didn't get to see the original manuscript in 1964 or at any other time. Green had been a friend of C. S. Lewis for seventeen years, and he was accustomed to reading Lewis's handwriting. Yet all he ever saw of *The Dark Tower* was a typed copy that Hooper gave to him so he could describe the story in their Lewis biography. So far as I can ascertain, no one saw the handwritten manuscript before 1980, when Hooper placed it in his private cache in the Bodleian Library in Oxford for his own use. When I was viewing the C. S. Lewis document collection in the Bodleian Library in June 1984, librarian Dennis Porter explained that, of course, I would not be allowed to see Hooper's Dark Tower manuscript.[9]

(The late MacDonald Harris pointed out in his 1990 novel *Hemingway's Suitcase* that a literary forger writes a story first; then he concocts a scenario about where he got the manuscript of the story and forges the manuscript itself.)[10] Harris responded to my report on *The Dark Tower* in my 1988 book *The C. S. Lewis Hoax* with interest:

---

[8] This correspondence is located in the Walter McGehee Hooper collection (#4236) that Hooper sold to the archives of the University of North Carolina Library at Chapel Hill in 1980. The complete set of 1200 items was available on microfilm through interlibrary loan until October 1992, when it was suddenly restricted to researchers at Chapel Hill approved by Walter Hooper. No items written by Hooper or other living people may be read at all anymore, and the items that may be read by favored researchers may not be copied.

[9] In 1989, right after publication of the C. S. Lewis Hoax, Hooper donated the manuscript to the Bodleian and pretended it had been available to researchers there since 1980. On 26 May 1989 he wrote to a correspondent In Oregon that it had been In the Bodleian for at least ten years, but that I had not bothered to examine it.

[10] As Ernest Hemingway buffs know, in 1922 his wife Hadley put his early stories into a small suitcase and went to meet him. On the way, the suitcase was stolen. Sixty-five years later, California novelist MacDonald Harris thought of a "merry prank": faking twenty Hemingway stories about Nick Adams, putting them on old paper in an old suitcase—and then publishing them, with himself as editor. "In some ways, I regret

> The parallels to Hemingway's stolen suitcase, and to Nils-Frederick's forgeries in my novel...are fascinating. The best of luck on your crusade.

Soon after Warren died, co-author Walter Hooper put the finishing touches on the Green/Hooper biography, and eager readers were soon devouring Green's description. He announced that the fourth novel was, in fact, only part of a novel. After eight years of suspense, that belated announcement was a severe disappointment. But Green's evaluation of the fragment was at least as disappointing as the news that the novel was only half written. He did not praise it.[11]

Green began his review by noting that no one from the past, not even Lewis's brother, had ever seen or heard of this aborted manuscript while Lewis was alive. Furthermore, Lewis never mentioned the project in any of his letters to friends. This was unlike Lewis's behavior when he wrote the other three Ransom novels, which his friends were well aware of when he wrote them.

Green summarized the plot. C. S. Lewis tells the story this time, as an active participant in the story. (In the other three Ransom novels Lewis merely related events that had occurred in the life of his friend Ransom.) The story begins in the Cambridge rooms of Dr. Orfieu, with his assistant Scudamour, C. S. Lewis, Ransom, and MacPhee there. MacPhee is an

---

not having done that. It would have made me a celebrity overnight...And it would be an immensely satisfying trick to play on the world."

Instead, Harris turned his idea into *Hemingway's Suitcase,* a novel that tackles egotistical writers, fatuous English professors, the crass world of publishing, and the possibilities of forgery. The problem for Harris's Hemingway forger is that if he wrote his stories, they are almost worthless; and if Hemingway wrote them, they automatically belong to the literary estate. So he can't collect the royalties.

MacDonald Harris was the pen name of Donald Heiney, founder of the writing program at the University of California at Irvine. Harris/Heiney said, "Any person who is a professional writer has to be somewhat cynical about the publishing industry." Harris was highly imaginative, but he did not have his clever forger gain control of the Hemingway literary estate in order to bring out his bogus Hemingway tales.

[11] Roger Lancelyn Green and Walter Hooper. *C. S. Lewis, A Biography* (London: Collins, 1974) 166-69.

instructor from Manchester University who appears as a far more interesting and lifelike character in *That Hideous Strength*.

Green doesn't bother to mention any of the glaring contradictions and subtle inconsistencies sprinkled throughout the aborted story. For example, the second sentence of the novel says, "There were four of us in Orfieu's study." Then the author immediately names five. In the fifth sentence the character named Lewis says "I had been mixed up with that [*Silent Planet*] affair;" but that's an odd claim because the Lewis character merely heard Ransom's story and wrote it for him in *Out of the Silent Planet*. One of the five characters, MacPhee, is identified in the twelfth sentence as "the Scot." "'Go on, go on,' said the Scot." But in *That Hideous Strength* MacPhee is repeatedly identified as an Ulsterman. (Ulster is a section of Ireland.) He is an Ulsterman who speaks the Ulster-Scots dialect. According to James O'Fee, "To a typical Ulsterman, or a Belfastman like C. S. Lewis, Ulster-Scots speech is distinctive and faintly comic...Lewis illustrates this in *That Hideous Strength* by giving MacPhee amusing expletives such as 'forbye' [meaning 'as well']."

This group of five looks into a "chronoscope" (a small curtain of brain material called the "Z substance" hung in front of a light bulb), which shows with three-dimensional realism what is transpiring in some other time—not necessarily past or present, and most likely another time system parallel to ours.

The friends look into a Dark Tower, a duplicate of the University Library building at Cambridge[12] in which a sinister man sits and waits for ordinary humans to come to him to be transformed. The man has an oozing growth on his forehead like an oversized red thorn, and he plunges it into the spines of his semi-naked victims, turning them into zombies. Scudamour's double

---

[12] In contrast to fanciful depictions of the Dark Tower on book covers, the architecture of the actual 156-foot building in Cambridge is blocky and commonplace. Ironically, the genuine "Dark Tower" library building contains a copy of *The Dark Tower and Other Stories*. Thus the genuine Cambridge tower building contains a genuine copy of the counterfeit Lewis *Tower*, which of course contains the genuine Cambridge tower and a counterfeit tower. This building also contains a copy of Derek Brewer's lecture about Browning's Dark Tower poem. (Only people acquainted with Hooper's *Dark Tower* would connect Browning's mysterious Dark Tower with the library building that holds it.) Furthermore, this building also contains a copy of *The C. S. Lewis Hoax* and 33 other titles with the subjects "Literary forgeries and mystifications."

appears in the pictures, and this double grows a sting on its forehead. Then the double of Scudamour's fiancée Camilla appears and is about to be stabbed in the spine by him. The real Scudamour breaks the chronoscope in a fit of rage, and thus accidentally trades bodies with his double, acquiring the sting on his forehead and finding himself in Othertime.

From that point on, the last quarter of the manuscript consists of Scudamour describing his adventures in Othertime. The last section is "an over-long and laboured account" of Othertime mathematics and science that Scudamour reads about in a library inside the tower. The story breaks off in mid-sentence at that point, before getting back to its characters.

According to Green, there is no clue to the real content of the book. The slowness of the connecting links and sheer lifelessness of Scudamour's investigations suggest to Green that Lewis discarded the book because he had no idea what should happen next.

Hoping that Green was unduly grim about the quality of the fourth novel, those who read his description wanted to see for themselves. Three years later, in 1977, Collins in England and Harcourt Brace Jovanovich in the United States published *The Dark Tower and Other Stories*. (All but one of its other stories was already available in *Of Other Worlds*.) The attraction of this volume was the mysterious *Dark Tower* fragment pictured on the cover. The book is in public and private libraries everywhere, and new editions are still selling. But that does not mean that it is being enjoyed or that it is often read all the way through.

On 7 July 1986 Lewis's friend Sheldon Vanauken wrote to me, "I dislike TDT, wish it had been burnt if his, and would be glad to have it proved a fraud." On 31 January 1987 Lewis's friend Charles Wrong wrote, "I have to confess I started it but didn't finish it. I think it's the only Lewis book of which this is true." On 12 June 1987 Lewis's friend Dom Bede Griffiths wrote, "I have got a copy of *The Dark Tower*, but I have not read it. It didn't attract me." These are common reactions.

In contrast, Walter Hooper insists that many readers like *The Dark Tower* and are glad to have it. In 1992 he revealed for the first time that one of its admirers was the American astronaut Dr. Joseph Kerwin, who became an astronaut as a result of reading Lewis's space trilogy. (An odd claim in light of the fact that Lewis was strongly opposed to space probes.)

As published, the Dark Tower story is preceded and followed by ten pages of enthusiastic notes by Walter Hooper. The original manuscript is described as yellow with age. (It consists of 62 pages of lined paper measuring 8" by 13". Pages 11 and 49 are missing, and the last page is numbered 64. Lewis's handwriting is clearly legible.[13]

Hooper claims that Lewis linked the last sentence of *Out of the Silent Planet* to the plot of *The Dark Tower*. But in the last sentence of *Out of the Silent Planet* Ransom assumes that with the destruction of the earth's only spaceship, people would have to travel back in time to use that spaceship in a sequel.[14] In fact, no one goes back in time in *The Dark Tower*, and there is no hint of a spaceship or interplanetary travel or time travel; instead, there is transference from one dimension to another. Therefore Hooper's claim that the end of *Out of the Silent Planet* points toward *The Dark Tower* makes no sense. Furthermore, at the end of the penultimate chapter of *Out of the Silent Planet* Lewis says that momentous events occurring before its publication had rendered it a prologue to the more important story yet to come. This seems to point to the profundities of *Perelandra*, not the aimlessness of *The Dark Tower*.

Hooper also points out that one character in *The Dark Tower* stresses that they were living in 1938, which shows that Lewis wrote *The Dark Tower* in 1938 or 1939. (That is remarkably convenient. None of Lewis's other novels offer tips about exactly when they were written.)

Hooper offers a peculiar disclaimer: although "it would be madness to put such literature on a level with Scripture, and unwisdom to mistake it for the advancement of an ethical theorem," it is a pleasure to offer it as good holiday fiction for entertainment. It should not be compared with Lewis's other interplanetary novels. Even Lewis did not believe it attained that level of perfection. In fact, Hooper remarks, Lewis probably did not remember that he had written it.

---

[13] For a description of the Dark Tower document see Joe R. Christopher's "A Visit to 'The Dark Tower'" *Mythprint* (March 1993): 3-4. Christopher points out that there are manuscript corrections in pencil, which shows that whoever wrote it went back over it.

[14] Lewis surprises his readers by sending Ransom off to Perelandra in a magical kind of coffin rather than a spaceship.

In their biography, Green had claimed that no one else remembered the story either; but in his *Dark Tower* notes, Walter Hooper corrects Green. According to Hooper, Lewis's friend Gervase Mathew had heard Lewis read the first four chapters of this novel aloud at an Inklings meeting in 1939 or 1940. Some of the unnamed friends who allegedly heard it along with Mathew complained to Lewis that the sting seemed to have unpleasant sexual connotations that Lewis did not intend. Mathew and Lewis discussed the novel again as they strolled around Addison's Walk at Magdalen College.

Unfortunately for skeptics, Gervase Mathew was dead by the time *The Dark Tower* was published. Aside from Hooper's word, there is no evidence that the dying Mathew remembered hearing Lewis read *The Dark Tower*. Furthermore, according to Humphrey Carpenter on page 186 of *The Inklings*, there is no record of Mathew ever attending any Inklings meetings before 1946.[15]

If Lewis had really been warned by friends wiser than he that the sexual symbolism of the sting was too obvious in the first four chapters, why would he go ahead and use it even more graphically in chapter five? There, Scudamour gained relief by stinging his hand in a startling parody of masturbation.

The Dark Tower has troubled many readers from the beginning. On the night of 6 December 1974 Christian Hardie,[16] sister of Lewis's typist Barbara Wall and wife of Colin Hardie, read a typed copy of the story and stayed up after midnight to finish it. Then she felt haunted by it. She said she felt the story was a vision of Hell or a vision of the diabolic level of the subconscious.[17]

---

[15] In a 3 February 1940 letter to Warren and a 21 December 1941 letter to Dom Bede Griffiths Lewis listed categories of current Inklings, and Mathew, a Dominican monk, was not in either list. These letters can be read in *Letters of C. S. Lewis*.

[16] Christian Hardie's sister typed C. S. Lewis's manuscripts for him in the 1940s. In 1945 he dedicated *The Great Divorce* to her: "To Barbara Wall, Best and most long-suffering of scribes."

[17] In the 1974 Hooper/Green biography Colin Hardie found that he had been confused with his brother, a friend of Lewis's in the 1920s. Colin Hardie only claimed to be a "very marginal" member of the Inklings, and only after about 1945. He first met Walter Hooper on 17 June 1963, and in 1974 Hooper gave him a typescript of the Dark Tower typescript for comment. He read it at his home, Rackham Cottage, Greatham, Pulborough, Sussex, and sent Hooper his response on 7 December. Unlike

In 1977 another woman reacted similarly. "Nobody who draws upon deep unconscious material can be blamed for getting swamped by it at times; and this is one of Lewis's nearest approaches to a venture into the outer (or inner?) dark." She mentioned the embarrassingly naive sexual overtones. That was Ursula Le Guin, reviewing *The Dark Tower* in the 16 April issue of *The New Republic*.[18]

Le Guin does not describe the embarrassingly naive sexual overtones that she dislikes, but alert readers will see what she means. The erection of the Dark Tower in Othertime is key. Gangs of semi-naked young men rush about energetically every day from sunrise to sunset, making a constant racket, doing such chores as climbing the scaffolding and sawing stones. (They wear nothing but short red kilts.) They are typically fine, muscular fellows, bronzed from the open air, and not very intelligent—but open and friendly looking. "Nor will you understand how we loved that young man," Lewis says about the first one he sees, who is pierced from behind.

In spite of the erection noise outdoors, inside the Dark Tower people are living quietly as if the building had been completed years ago. This contradiction is not mentioned or explained. The only function of the handsome, semi-naked young "builders" is to become bearers and thrusters of the male stings or else to be pierced by the stings of other men.

Inside the unfinished tower there is a very large oblong room with many doors, where twelve or fifteen retired stinging men sit on the floor and play every day with little boxes and jars and bowls, bottles, tubes, packets, and tiny spoons. Envious of younger men, they whisper together and try all kinds of nostrums, diets, and exercises in the futile hope of regaining their ability to sting people. In this world we would call that a senile obsession with aphrodisiacs.

---

his wife, he said he found it enthralling: "CSL must have had the outcome of the story clearly in mind..." He predicted (wrongly) that its incompleteness would add to its interest. Hardie was impressed by Hooper's claim that he was then supervising the Lewis research of two doctoral candidates, and he invited Hooper to come to Sussex to tell him about it. He concluded with the news that Gervase Mathew had been ill.

[18] Ursula LeGuin, "The Dark Tower," *Dancing at the Edge of the World* (New York: Grove Press, 1989).

Le Guin's review was followed by Alastair Fowler's in *The Times Literary Supplement* [19]: "'The Dark Tower' is the least literary of all Lewis's fictions. Certainly it is the farthest from allegory and even from paraphrasable meaning. Consciously or unconsciously it approaches an area of mysteriously strong negative feelings and conflicts, untouched elsewhere in his work."

One year after *Dark Tower* publication, at the April 1978 meeting of the New York C. S. Lewis Society, science fiction expert and Lewis admirer Richard Hodgens delivered a paper on it. He began by saying "Many [writers] would try to suppress a scrap as embarrassing as this one." He explained, "*The Dark Tower* is not a fragment, but a tissue of fragments that could not be reconciled."[20] He concluded by describing four different stories entangled in *The Dark Tower*, none original, but all potentially satisfactory if they had been written separately and skillfully by Lewis. At their best, however, they could never have been as good as the stories that Lewis actually wrote. Hodgens pointed out wistfully that chapter 7 is a new beginning for a far better Lewis story than what was in the first six chapters. It would have been a story without the nastiness.[21]

In 1979, in *The Literary Legacy of C. S. Lewis*, Chad Walsh exclaimed that it is hard to imagine a book less like its predecessor. *Out of the Silent Planet* had plausible characters, color, vivid scenes, and strong aspects of goodness as well as evil. In *The Dark Tower* the characters are dull and colorless. There are long paragraphs of pseudoscientific jargon. The tale is unpleasant, rather morbid, and without any apparent meaning.

In 1981, in *C. S. Lewis: The Art of Enchantment*, Donald Glover also emphasized the sharp contrast between *Out of the Silent Planet* and *The Dark Tower*. In the latter the interest seems to be more scientific and mechanical

---

[19] Fowler, *The Times Literary Supplement*, (1 July 1977): 795.

[20] As an active member of the New York C. S. Lewis Society, Hodgens must have been well aware of the bizarre ten-page article by Hooper's admirer Charles Brady praising *The Dark Tower* in *CSL*, Issue 95. Brady said, "Even in its incomplete state, far from being a torso merely, *The Dark Tower* is the crown jewel of this present collection." Without mentioning Brady, Hodgens courteously sought to set the record straight. (Brady's article diverged into many byways, including seven paragraphs about the notorious homosexual Count Robert de Montesquiou, who on 10 August 1901 "had been out skylarking with his invert associates, and skylarking 'in drag' at that...").

[21] Reported in issue 102 of *CSL*, the bulletin of the New York C. S. Lewis Society.

than imaginative. It is stiff and slow in narration, thin in descriptive matter, and heavy with "information."

In 1981, in Unger's *C. S. Lewis*, Margaret Hannay voiced some of these same criticisms, adding the problem of the overly obvious and unpleasant sexual implications of the sting. Hannay also pointed out that the control of the Big Brain over those who have been stung is remarkably similar to the control that IT exercised over its victims in Madeleine L'Engle's classic children's book *A Wrinkle in Time*. L'Engle, on the other hand, could not have been influenced by *The Dark Tower*, because she published her fantasy in 1962, and she could not have seen *The Dark Tower* until 1977. Hannay did not consider the far-fetched possibility that *The Dark Tower* was really written after 1962, when *A Wrinkle in Time* won the Newbery Award and became an instant favorite with the reading public.

In the spring 1989 issue of the *Canadian C. S. Lewis Journal*, George Sayer stated, "Truly *The Dark Tower* is badly written and quite unworthy of Lewis."

If one wanted to guess at a date of composition for *The Dark Tower* after Lewis's death in 1963, it would make sense to set it sometime between the 1966 announcement of a fourth Ransom novel (not identified as a fragment) and Hooper's little-known announcement in *Mythlore* in 1970 that the story was a 64-page fragment.[22] (Of course it could have been altered at any time until Hooper invited people to read it in typescript in 1974.) With such a scenario in mind, it is worth looking at the similarity between the zombie accounts in the two books.

In *A Wrinkle in Time* L'Engle wrote, "As they approached the end of the room their steps slowed. Before them was a platform. On the platform was a chair, and on the chair was a man."[23] Something about the man was intensely cold and dark.

---

[22] "Yes, there is a fragment of a fourth Ransom novel: 64 folio pages, which are in my possession. I do not know if Lewis ever completed the book or not. I have not yet decided what to do with it, but I don't feel that the time for publishing the fragment is yet come. I have been working on an edition of the Boxen Stories for the last few years, but there are some people who do not feel that they should be published, at least not now." *Mythlore* (6 Autumn 1970): 26.

[23] Madeleine L'Engle, *A Wrinkle in Time* (New York: Farrar, Straus and Giroux, 1962; Dell Edition, 1973) 120.

In *The Dark Tower*, one reads that there was a dais at the front of the room. By it there was a chair, and on it sat the Man. He was singularly unattractive, with a mass of black hair that was dead black, with the blackness of a coal cellar (31).

Standing before the seated man in *A Wrinkle in Time*, Charles Wallace was taken over by the man's power; and then he gave his sister a smile that was not his smile. When he was told to go, he started to walk in a strange mechanical manner. He walked out of the room with a jerky rhythm and did not look back to see if the others were coming (137). He had a marionette's walk (138). He moved jerkily (139).

Standing before the seated Man in *The Dark Tower*, a beautiful young man was taken over by the power of the Man; and then his face wore a fixed grin. When he was to go, he did not look behind him at the one who had stung him. He strutted with sharp, jerky movements, as if marching strangely to some abominable music. All individuals left that room with a permanent clockwork swagger (35). C. S. Lewis, the narrator in the story, said that he and his friends called these slaves "Jerkies." (Such flippancy seems unlike Lewis.)

Perhaps someone who had read *A Wrinkle in Time* wrote *The Dark Tower* as an apocryphal C. S. Lewis story. This is what some Lewis admirers are tempted to think.

In addition to the 1962 book *A Wrinkle in Time*, three films could have influenced the mid-1960s writer of an apocryphal Ransom novel. This information is from Wendell Wagner. Story elements that would have been highly inventive from Lewis in the 1930s were not in the 1960s.

First is the popular 1953 film *Invaders from Mars*, with scenes in which a giant brain controls people by planting something in their necks. This could have inspired the Big Brain in *The Dark Tower* and the Sting thrust into people's spines to turn them into robots.

In the 1963 French film *La Jetée* travel in outer space has become impossible after a nuclear war, and experimenters investigate time travel as an alternative. A man is forced to undergo mental time travel while a group of four or five experimenters observe him. This bears a resemblance to four or five experimenters observing an unwilling time traveller in *The Dark Tower*. Furthermore, the rationale for time travel in this film is exactly the one proposed by Walter Hooper in his preface to *The Dark Tower*.

In the 1964 film *The Time Travelers*, some experimenters have built what they think is a window on the future, but it turns out to be a door into the future instead. One of the experimenters steps through it into a very dark era and finds that he can't get back.

Assuming that its similarity to popular sci-fi films is coincidental (an unjustified assumption), how could C. S. Lewis's 1938 novel about time travel copy a scene from Madeleine L'Engle's book that wasn't published until 1962? L'Engle herself has been disturbed by the seeming likeness between *The Dark Tower* and her Camazotz scenes in *A Wrinkle in Time*. She says she cannot account for the similarity. But she wrote her book as an affirmation of a God of particularity and love, and *The Dark Tower* has no such affirmation.[24]

The almost unrelieved nastiness of the book seems a blemish on Lewis's character, and the vastly inferior writing (produced between *Out of the Silent Planet* and *The Problem of Pain*) seems a blemish on his otherwise stable intellect. In fact, *The Dark Tower* never seems to rise above Scudamour's belief, "Some filthy sort of something going on alongside the ordinary world and all mixed up with it" (48). The sentence strikes some readers as an ominous summary of the whole *Dark Tower* affair. In the 1993 edition of *The Encyclopedia of Science Fiction*, editor Peter Nicholls mentioned the *Dark Tower* problem and noted, "What there can be no doubt of is that the works assembled by Hooper have affected readers as being both sexually poisonous and egregiously amateur."

Sheldon Vanauken once playfully proposed a scenario that would absolve Lewis of responsibility for *The Dark Tower* and account for most of the circumstances. (He was not serious.) Perhaps around 1950, after Lewis's space trilogy was familiar to the public, one of Lewis's students or correspondents tried writing a fourth book for the series. He used MacPhee and Ransom from *That Hideous Strength* and added Lewis himself as a character. Lewis kept the unfinished attempt among his papers, unidentified.

According to this scenario, after Lewis's death Walter Hooper found the manuscript among papers he saved from a bonfire; because the penmanship resembled that of C. S. Lewis, he mistook it for Lewis's handwriting. Later, shortly before the death of Lewis's old friend Gervase Mathew, this seriously ill man mistakenly thought he recalled Lewis reading the story aloud in 1939.

---

[24] In a letter to Kathryn Lindskoog dated 18 February 1987.

As far-fetched as this scenario is, it strikes concerned readers as far more likely than the idea that C. S. Lewis wrote *The Dark Tower*. However, the scenario leaves out *A Wrinkle in Time* and the three 1960s sci-fi films.

Ironically, a similar scenario turned out to be true for a lost Sherlock Holmes story discovered by Adrian Conan Doyle in a chest of his father's papers in 1942. Richard Lancelyn Green, son of C. S. Lewis's friend and biographer Roger Lancelyn Green, in his 1985 book The Further Adventures of Sherlock Holmes, now describes the whole affair.[25]

In 1911 a Holmes enthusiast named Arthur Whitaker submitted his story "The Man Who Was Wanted" to Arthur Conan Doyle, who paid him ten guineas for it and filed it as a possible source of story ideas for future use. In 1942 Adrian came across it and announced the discovery to an eager world of Holmes readers. Adrian gave the impression that the manuscript was in his father's handwriting, although in fact it was in typescript. He allowed his father's biographer Hesketh Pearson to quote from the story in his 1943 volume about Conan Doyle; this foreshadowed biographer Green being allowed to introduce *The Dark Tower* in his 1974 volume about C. S. Lewis. It didn't occur to Green or Pearson to doubt the authenticity of the inferior stories.

The apocryphal Conan Doyle story was published with fanfare in *Cosmopolitan* in the United States in August 1948, and published in the *Sunday Dispatch* in England in January 1949. The editor explained that Conan Doyle and his family realized that this story was not up to his usual standard, but that the family now yielded to public pressure to publish it anyway. This was meant to forestall criticism, but it didn't work.

Some serious Sherlock Holmes experts didn't believe that the story was genuine Conan Doyle and said so in print. One suspected Adrian of concocting it, one suspected Adrian and his brother Dennis of constructing it from notes left by their father, and another suspected that it was by an American forger. In fact, the real writer of the story had tried to identify himself in 1945, when he happened to discover the mistake in Pearson's biography of Conan Doyle, but to no avail.

When Whitaker realized that his old story was now published in its entirety under the name of Conan Doyle, he wrote to the Conan Doyle sons

---

[25] Published by Penguin Books in 1985. See pages 13-19.

about it in January 1949. To his surprise, he received an angry reply from Adrian threatening to sue him for casting aspersion on the manuscript. Indeed, Adrian turned the matter over to Vertue, Son & Churcher, solicitors for the Conan Doyle estate. He seemed eager for a fight.

Whitaker called in his own solicitors, provided them with his 1911 letter from Conan Doyle about the manuscript, and promptly settled the matter; then he promptly died. If he had died one year sooner, "The Man Who Was Wanted" might have remained in the Conan Doyle corpus until this day. It lasted there for seven years.

So far *The Dark Tower* has been included in the Lewis corpus for almost thirty years, and no one has come forth and confessed to writing it yet. Hope for that grows fainter every year.

In 1986 Carla Faust Jones, a graduate student of Corbin Scott Carnell at the University of Florida decided to use the Literary Detective computer program for a statistical analysis of the prose in *The Dark Tower, Out of the Silent Planet, Perelandra*, and *That Hideous Strength*. She found differences between *The Dark Tower* and the other three in letter and letter-pair frequencies, which showed that *The Dark Tower* was a divergence from Lewis's normal vocabulary. Jim Tankard, author of the program, confirmed her results.[26]

In response to a letter from Jones with her news, I promptly began investigating *The Dark Tower* and writing *The C. S. Lewis Hoax*. I sent copies of the manuscript to some of Lewis's friends and asked for their opinions. Then I asked for permission to quote them on the cover.[27] George

---

[26] "The Literary Detective Computer Analysis of Stylistic Differences Between 'The Dark Tower' and C. S. Lewis' Deep Space Trilogy," *Mythlore* 57 (Spring 1989):11-15. As Jones explains, she entered passages from all four novels into the computer program, which tallied the incidence of certain letter combinations. This kind of analysis is strictly alphabetical and numerical, and has nothing to do with artistry or meaning. It measures just one aspect of vocabulary. Results were conclusive. Although Lewis supposedly wrote *Dark Tower* after *Out of the Silent Planet* and before *Perelandra*, those two correlate with each other and *Dark Tower* does not correlate with either of them.

[27] I did the same with a few others. Douglas R. Gilbert, coauthor of *C. S. Lewis, Images of His World*, contributed "Explosive material, light approach, spirit of charity." Philip Yancey contributed "I spent the afternoon reading it instead of working. Fascinating! I'm very glad you pursued it." Frederick Buechner contributed "I read *The C. S. Lewis Hoax* with horrified fascination. It is a profoundly unedifying

Sayer contributed, "Quite astonishing reading." Sheldon Vanauken said, "Clear, compelling. The time has come for such a book." Dom Bede Griffiths said, "It reads like a detective story and is as exciting as Sherlock Holmes." Richard Lancelyn Green said, "My father has read the book with interest, and while not agreeing with every particular, feels that Jack Lewis and his brother would have approved of it. It is an intriguing study of the danger of being over-zealous toward an author, of which I am perhaps also guilty." (Green is a Sherlock Holmes enthusiast.)

Jones sent me her feeling about the import of her study on 10 December 1987: "I'm certainly excited about all of this and am rather astounded that I was able to participate in such a literary mystery. Little did I know what was beginning when I placed a rose on Lewis's grave in 1977."

In 1988 Arthur C. Clarke, who was C. S. Lewis's favorite science-fiction author, learned about the *Dark Tower* problem and said, "I would like to see justice done, and this is certainly an intriguing case." Eight years later, on 26 January 1995, Clarke was receiving an honorary D. Litt. from the University of Liverpool and brought up C. S. Lewis early in his acceptance speech. Brandishing a copy of *Light in the Shadowlands*, Clarke challenged his colleagues in full academic regalia to take the "extraordinary book" seriously.[28]

Clarke explained, "[The] thesis is that C. S. Lewis' posthumous books are at least partly forged. If you don't take this seriously, let me quote a testimonial from an authority you will all admire: 'A fascinating piece of detective work, which may serve to free C. S. Lewis from the shadows of a misogyny and arrogance which it appears may have been cast upon him...I finished it liking Lewis, as man and artist, better than I had ever done before...The book's temperate tone and elegant illustrations make it a pleasure to read,' Ursula Le Guin."

---

story and yet for the sake of C. S. Lewis and his canon an important one to tell." Walter Wangerin contributed "A straight face for the scholarly, but a constant, deep chuckle for Lewis himself. Good!"

[28] A videotape of the Arthur C. Clarke Honorary Degree Ceremony ceremony is available in appropriate format from the University of Liverpool. Contact its Central Television and Photographic Service, Chatham Building, P. O. Box 147, Liverpool L69 3BX (Telephone 0151 794 2662, Fax 0151 794 2221).

"Though I only met Lewis once," he continued, "I had an extensive correspondence with him, which is now in the Bodleian Library. And I used to see Joy Gresham almost every week at our 'White Horse' get-togethers, so I—and millions of others—would like to know if there is indeed a 'Lewisgate' scandal. What about commissioning a probe...?" According to observer Peter Wright, Clarke's academic audience rustled nervously.

In 1990 James Long, a consulting engineer who formerly taught at Cal Tech, devised his own computer study. He selected eighteen content items, then checked *The Dark Tower, Perelandra,* and *That Hideous Strength* for correlation. He counted the lines containing items such as derogatory remarks, scenery, or technical explanations, and then made percentage comparisons. He found that *Perelandra* and *That Hideous Strength* score significantly closer to each other than to *The Dark Tower.* In fact, he found that 19.08 percent of *The Dark Tower* is given over to six science topics; in *Perelandra* and *That Hideous Strength* the amount is 0.00 percent.

Readers who don't want to use computers to compare pieces of literature can compare them in their own brains instead, as C. S. Lewis would have done. One can look for style, content, character, and ethical or religious beliefs. In the second part of Long's study, he looked for the latter and found significant conflicts between the author of *The Dark Tower* and Lewis concerning inner rings, Freudianism, moral standards, and whether or not niceness guarantees salvation.[29]

There seems to be a blatant Americanism on the fifth page of the first chapter. There the character named Orfieu says to the character named Ransom, "When you get a mental picture of a little boy called Ransom in an English public school you at once name it 'memory' because you know you *are* Ransom and were at an English public school." Because the term "public school" has opposite meanings in America and England, Americans preface the term with the word "English" when referring to what Americans would call a private school. Needless to say, the English have no need to do so. It is hard to believe that in England in 1939 Lewis would have used the inappropriate American locution "English public school." (The sentence in

---

[29] James Long, Ph.D. (with Mary V. Borhek), "An Engineer Analyzes *The Dark Tower*" *The Lewis Legacy* 58 (Autumn 1993): 12-14.

question was eventually tested statistically and did not match the statistical pattern of Lewis's writing.)

It is easy to compile lists of sentences illustrating characteristics of the author of *The Dark Tower*. For example, when the plot lags the author apparently tries to add drama by giving good men inexplicably foul tempers or violent impulses:

"Why the hell doesn't Orfieu come back?" said I [C. S. Lewis himself], and realized I was shouting. (36)

Orfieu said nothing, but knocked out his pipe on the frame of his deck-chair so violently that it broke, then flung it away with a curse. MacPhee gave one of his gutteral growls...There was rank hatred in the air. "What the devil is the matter with you both?" said MacPhee. (38)

It was MacPhee who released the bomb...when he suddenly swore and then stood up. (44)

...an Orfieu I had not yet seen for he was in a towering rage. He wanted to know where—where the hell—we'd all been and why we'd left him to face the music. (61)

He felt that he must smash something—preferably the Stingingman, but at any rate something—or go mad. In other words, he "saw red." (62)

Scudamour felt a quite old-fashioned desire to hit the man hard in the face. (76)

Sentence-by-sentence examination of *The Dark Tower* will cause most honest readers to conclude, "Much of this does not seem like Lewis's writing to me."

Lewis's sentences are noted for their grace and vitality. Yet *The Dark Tower* includes wordy sentences like this one: "What followed has effaced it, for destiny chose this night to pitchfork us brutally, and with no gentle gradations, into something so shocking that, if I had not had the business of recording it always before my mind, it would by now perhaps have been dropped out of my consciousness altogether." It was never by writing such turgid prose that Lewis achieved his vigorous style.

Lewis had an attitude toward sexuality that was neither prudish nor sniggering; it could most simply be called a "clean-minded" approach, including awe, humor, and humility about temptation. He did not avoid or stress sex in his writing. Yet in *The Dark Tower* he supposedly wrote, "During the whole of our stay in College with Orfieu, his aged colleague Knellie (Cyril Knellie, the now almost forgotten author of *Erotici Graeci Minimi, Table Talk of a Famous Courtesan*, and *Lesbos: A Masque)* was a great trial to us."

To begin with, Knellie's surname is evidently meant to be cute. According to slang dictionaries, the homosexual term "Nellie" originated in America. The 1965 *Lavender Lexicon* defines it: "Nellie/Nelly: An effeminate, affected homosexual who makes public display of his homosexuality." This description fits Knellie perfectly. In the 1972 *Queen's Vernacular* "Nelly" is defined as "outrageously effeminate; coy, silly." According to the 1984 edition of Eric Partridge's *Dictionary of Slang and Unconventional English*, "Nellie" was not adopted into British English until after World War II. It seems highly unlikely that Lewis would have injected any post-war slang from America into a British novel in 1939.

The *Oxford English Dictionary* traces the term no farther back than to 1961 and provides this 1973 use "There is a tendency among homophile groups to deplore gays who play visible roles—the queens and the nellies." Because that is its exact use in *The Dark Tower* and Lewis was not a homophile (or homophobe), inclusion of this word strongly suggests that an anonymous person wrote the story in the 1960s rather than C. S Lewis in 1939.

Cyril Knellie combines a senile, spinsterish personality with an unquenchable appetite for filth. He plays no part in the plot and seems to be included simply because the author enjoys writing about him. It is unlike Lewis to afflict his readers with such entertainment.[30]

---

[30] In *That Hideous Strength* Lewis included an extremely revolting villain called Fairy Hardcastle, but she is in no way the literary equivalent of Cyril Knellie.

Lewis, for all his humor and humility, had personal reserve appropriate to an Oxford don. Yet if he wrote *The Dark Tower* he put into his own mouth as a character in the story the following sentence: "On the strength of having been at my old college—some time in the nineties—[Knellie] addressed me as Lu-Lu, a sobriquet I particularly dislike." If Lewis had foolishly invented a character named Knellie who called him Lu-Lu, he might have been mocked about it from then on. Aside from Lu-Lu, Lewis would particularly dislike in his own prose the phrase "a sobriquet I particularly dislike." He never used words that could give the impression of prissy fastidiousness. He would have been apt to write simply, "I loathe that name."

One odd sentence cannot prove a point, but perhaps dozens of them can. *The Dark Tower* has dozens of inept sentences that are odd indeed. Here are a few of them in chronological order, with criticisms that C. S. Lewis might be apt to make if he read them:

The jibe recalled Orfieu to the real purpose of our meeting, and after a few moments of keen but not unkindly chaff between the two philosophers we settled ourselves to listen again. (19.)
Stodgy narrative.

"Um—well perhaps," said Orfieu. (20.)
"All right, all right," said Orfieu with a smile. (25.)
Slow dialogue.

I think that all of us, even MacPhee, were a bit excited by now, and we urged Orfieu to go on with his demonstration. (25.)
Plodding style.

"Is it in the future or the past?" I queried. (27.)
Amateurish verb choice.

Knellie's surname is an inside joke for a few readers, but Fairy's nickname should be obvious to all readers. Knellie is a harmless old fool, but Fairy is a malevolent monster who enjoys sexual sadism. Knellie's eccentric personality is insignificant to the plot, but Fairy's grotesque form of predatory evil (not her homosexual orientation) is central to the plot.

We blinked in the sudden inrush of daylight and there was a general shifting of positions and intaking of breath...(28.)
Awkward repetition (in, in, in).

We realized afresh that behind certain windows, not fifty yards away, humanity was opening a door that had been sealed from the beginning, and that a train of consequences incalculable for good or evil was on foot. (29.)
Mixed metaphors.

It was hard and horny, but not like a bone. It was red, like most of the things in a man, and apparently lubricated by some kind of saliva. (33.)
Accidental vulgarity.

"You don't like them?" he queried. (37.)
Amateurish verb repeated.

To us, of course, the whole Othertime world was absolutely silent: in reality, what between the bands and the noise of the workmen, it must have been dinning with sound. (40.)

Superfluous words what *and* with sound.

Everything was dark but by the light of a single taper I could see...(41.)
Self contradiction.

I remember Ransom saying, "That young fellow may blow up any moment." (44.)
Inappropriate dialogue.

At this point it will be convenient if my narrative turns to Scudamour. (61.)
Awkward transitional sentence.

As he stood thus, with clenched hands, fighting down the riot of his senses, he took in his surroundings without much immediate attention. (63.)
Purple prose and pedestrian prose.

At this time he did not, of course, understand the linguistic situation which I have just described. (65.)
Wordiness and awkward transition.

Presumably the body which Scudamour now animated had not fed for some time, and he found himself turning to his meal with alacrity. (79.)
Circuitous and stilted style.

"I don't believe a word of it!" ejaculated Scudamour suddenly...(87.)
Suggestive verb choice with superfluous adverb.

Most of these sentence weaknesses are flaws that might occur in the prose of ordinary writers. But they are completely out of character for C. S. Lewis, who was no ordinary writer.

Defenders of *The Dark Tower*'s authenticity sometimes admit that the prose is inept but explain it by claiming that as a writer Lewis doesn't belong on a pedestal in the first place. George J. Marlin made that claim in the fall 1989 issue of *Reflections*, in which he said that suspicions about forgery are utter nonsense. "Perhaps C. S. Lewis had a bad day."

Other defenders of *The Dark Tower*'s authenticity assume that Lewis had to polish and rewrite his fiction before it was fit for publication. "To have a valid basis of comparison one would have to set 'The Dark Tower' along side the original draft of another of Lewis's novels, *not* the final product."[31]

But editor Hooper disagrees. On page xvii of the preface to his 1982 collection of Lewis essays titled *On Stories*, he states emphatically: "Except for his academic works, Lewis never wrote more than a single draft of his novels, which indeed suggests that the stories were worked out in his head before he

---

[31] John Rateliff, "The Kathryn Lindskoog Hoax: Screwtape Redux" *Mythlore 58.* (Summer 1989): 54.

put pen to paper." Because those who defend *The Dark Tower's* authenticity trust Hooper's claims, it seems that they should explain themselves on this point.

John Lawlor, a student and friend of Lewis's, bore testimony to the Lewis's expeditious writing habit in his 1999 book *C. S. Lewis: Memories and Reflections*. "He once told me that he was what might be called a 'first–time' writer, in the sense that we speak of first–time gifts in a games–player—no hesitation, the stroke delivered with perfect immediacy. 'I write one draft,' he used to say; 'then I read it through and correct it; and then if I don't like it, away it goes into the wastepaper basket.'"

Another defense of *The Dark Tower* is recognition of Lewis's voice; it just "sounds" like Lewis to some people. In his 4000-word article *"The Dark Tower: A Challenge to Lewis Scholars"*[32] Larry Gilman lists ten of the close parallels between *The Dark Tower* and Lewis's genuine works of fiction. (For example, the Stingingman's performance of a series of obscene acts for no apparent purpose other than to disconcert Ransom and the other chronoscope watchers closely resembles the Un-man's performance [in chapter 10 of *Perelandra*] of a "whole repertory of obscenities" for Ransom to see.) "I noticed that *Tower* contains scraps of dialogue, character interaction, and philosophy that recall portions of Lewis's later books very closely—at times, almost word for word. If *Tower* is by Lewis, it seems to often anticipate his later writings with wonderful particularity; if not, it bears the fingerprints of a forger who seems to have written with Lewis's books spread open before him, sampling them..."

In Gilman's opinion, *The Dark Tower* is bad enough to be by a clever imitator and good enough to be by C. S. Lewis in a severe funk. But *The Dark Tower* presents more serious problems than its inferior literary quality. Most importantly, it has no provenance (no known history), and there is evidence that no one ever heard of it while Lewis was alive. Secondly, it is dissimilar to Lewis's other writing in style, beliefs, and sexual orientation. Third, it anachronistically echoes the 1962 children's classic *A Wrinkle in Time*. Fourth, it contains a palpable Americanism, the term "an English public school." Fifth, there is post-1950 ink on the 1938 manuscript. Sixth, two completely different kinds of statistical analysis, the Literary Detective

---

[32] *The Lewis Legacy 84 (Spring 2000).*

Program and Cusum Analysis, both show that *The Dark Tower* does not match the invisible linguistic patterns of other Ransom novels. And seventh, in 1998 both HarperCollins and C. S. Lewis Pte Ltd[33] (publisher and copyright owners of *The Dark Tower*) suddenly, without any explanation, abandoned their claim that Lewis wrote it in 1938 and dated the story at about 1958—an insupportable date in light of the *Dark Tower* portrayal of MacPhee as a Scot.[34]

For people who once took *The Dark Tower* seriously and now decide that it must be a hoax, MacPhee's words on page 45 take on a special meaning. There, the skeptical MacPhee scolds Orfieu for trying to get him to believe in the chronoscope. "...you can have your joke—but I'm not going to stay here and be hoaxed any longer." The author, whoever he is, has said it for us.

In 1986 Roger Lancelyn Green, then sixty-eight years old, had never yet doubted that *The Dark Tower* was written by C. S. Lewis (according to a letter dated September 30). Then at the beginning of June, 1987, he read an early draft of this book at one sitting and changed his mind. His only general criticism was that the complicated final chapter about Lewis juvenilia (see Appendix 4), was anti-climactic; he thought (correctly) that the previous chapter would make a better ending. He said he found little to fault and much that he agreed with. He sent his thanks and appreciation on 6 June. On 8 October he died.

Ironically, it was Roger Lancelyn Green who once entertained C. S. Lewis with the account of an earlier science fiction hoax. In 1957 Lewis thanked Green for a copy of Green's new book *Into Other Worlds*. The book tells about Lewis's own "scientifiction" and is subtitled *Space Flights in Fiction from Lucian to Lewis*. What interested Lewis most in Green's book was the century-old story of the famous Lunar Hoax.[35]

---

[33] Pte Ltd means Private Trade Entity, Limited.

[34] Dr. Philip Robinson of the Ulster Folk Museum, Holywood, County Down, is an expert on Ulster-Scots who has published an "Ulster-Scots Dialect Grammar." Dr. Robinson is also a Lewis buff, and he writes: "I can say with conviction that there is no possibility whatsoever that Lewis would have characterized his MacPhee in *The Dark Tower* as a Scotsman *after* writing *That Hideous Strength.*"

[35] Roger Lancelyn Green and Walter Hooper, *C. S. Lewis: A Biography* (London: Collins, 1974) 163.

In 1853 the New York *Sun* ran a series of scientific articles reprinted from the Edinburgh *Journal of Science*, a journal that never existed. The articles were alleged reports from the British astronomer Sir John Herschel, who had gone to the Cape of Good Hope to try out a powerful new telescope. Herschel's amazing descriptions of the moon fascinated readers. He described in colorful detail what he saw of oceans, beaches, plants, and even animals. Public excitement mounted with each new installment.

The fourth installment from Herschel described furry, bat-winged people who live on the moon. On the day that report was published, the *Sun* boasted the largest circulation of any paper in the world—19,360. Other papers were frantic and copied the articles from the *Sun*, claiming that they got them directly from the *Journal of Science*. A committee of suspicious scientists from Yale University hastened to New York to inspect the *Journal of Science* material; but the *Sun* shunted them in their search for the missing document, and they finally gave up. At last, after three weeks, the *Sun* confessed its hoax.

An account of this great Lunar Hoax can be read in Curtis MacDougall's *Hoaxes*, first published in 1940 by Constable in England and by Lewis's publisher Macmillan in the United States, and since then published by Dover Publications.[36]

C. S. Lewis thought the *Sun's* description of the moon's land and sea was remarkably well written, and he thought the hoax was good fun. It would no doubt have seemed incredible to Lewis that only nine years later he would be dead and a new book titled *Of Other Worlds* (Green's title was *Into Other Worlds*) would link his own interplanetary novels to what seems to be a new hoax. This new hoax would not aim at selling about 20,000 newspapers; it would aim at selling perhaps 200,000 copies of a new book—a book of science fiction purportedly written by C. S. Lewis.

But what about the yellowed, sixty-four-page manuscript in Lewis's own handwriting? Doesn't it prove that *The Dark Tower* is genuine? In 1989, a few months after *The C. S. Lewis Hoax* challenged the authenticity of *The Dark Tower*, Hooper quietly donated that valuable document to the Bodleian and implied falsely that it had always been available for viewing. Four years later he was still complaining about his American critics not trekking to the

---

[36] Curtis D. MacDougall, *Hoaxes* (New York: Dover, 1958) 229-31.

Bodleian: "It continues to surprise me that none of those who say the manuscript is a forgery will go to look at it."[37]

This struck me as a bit disingenuous, because by the time Hooper donated this curious document to the Bodleian, I was a housebound invalid unable to return there to see it.[38] But when Lyle Dorsett, second curator of the Marion E. Wade Center, was in England in 1989 he went to look at it one day. Unprepared visitors are turned away from the Bodleian Library, primarily because of the difficulty of finding a qualified sponsor to sign the form required for a pass,[39] but Dorsett had a pass and signed right in. To his surprise, he was told that someone was already using the Dark Tower manuscript. Undaunted by the coincidence, he left and returned hours later. Again, it was not available. His one day in Oxford was over, and he didn't get to see the mysterious manuscript after all.

An amazing *Dark Tower* double coincidence or good-natured prank occurred the next year, in 1990. That is when Joe Haldeman, a Hugo and Nebula Award-winning author, published his fantasy about forgery titled *The Hemingway Hoax.*[40] I wonder if Haldeman knew about MacDonald Harris's 1990 novel *Hemingway's Suitcase* and if he knew about *The C. S. Lewis Hoax* and *The Dark Tower.* His book seems to combine elements of all three.[41]

Haldeman's story is about a literature professor who is a Hemingway scholar. "In some ways he's an absolute nut about Hemingway. Obsessed, I mean. It's not good for him." The professor succumbs to the temptation to forge an unfinished Hemingway novel.

---

[37] *The Canadian C. S. Lewis Journal* 79 (Summer 1992): 18.

[38] "Donated" documents belong to the Bodleian and may be read by researchers. "Deposited" documents are stored in the Bodleian but are reserved for the use of their owners or those researchers who are granted access by the owners.

[39] The niece of Arthur C. Clarke went to the Bodleian once to look at the C. S. Lewis letters that her uncle had donated to the collection, and she was turned away because she had no pass.

[40] Joe Haldeman, *The Hemingway Hoax* (New York: William Morrow and Company, 1990; Avon Books, 1991).

[41] To add to the coincidence, there is a copy of Haldeman's *Hemingway Hoax* in the Cambridge University Library (along with *The Dark Tower* and *The C. S. Lewis Hoax*).

In the middle of page 15 of Haldeman's story someone says, "Just use good judgment. That Ransom guy..." The name *Ransom* was a slip of the tongue, the speaker quickly explains; he meant to say *Manson*. Is Haldeman winking at us? Like *The Dark Tower,* his story turns into a sinister fantasy about parallel time realities, where things are almost identical but also extremely different.

Like MacDonald Harris, Haldeman explains very clearly what is involved in forging an unfinished novel by a great writer: "The problem divided itself into three parts: writing the novel fragment, forging the manuscript,[42] and devising a suitable story about how one had uncovered the manuscript."

First, the unknown novel. Second, the mysterious manuscript. And third, the story of the great manuscript bonfire. The bonfire story is the subject of chapter three.

> There is no worse robber than a bad book.
> —*Italian Proverb*

---

[42] When I visited Walter Hooper in Oxford on 27 December 1975, I asked him what he was working on, and he answered that he was working on Lewis's unpublished Ransom novel. (With his permission, I taped the visit; and so I have his exact words.) As one can see by comparing the published story with the clear handwritten manuscript that Hooper donated later to the Bodleian Library, he did no editing at all on the text. In 1974 Hooper was showing a typed copy to people, so what work was he doing on it in 1975? I suspect that in 1975 he was forging the manuscript on appropriate paper in what looks like Lewis's handwriting.

3

THROWING WATER ON
THE BONFIRE STORY

NOT A LITERARY RESCUE AFTER ALL?

The Lewis bonfire story is both heartrending and heartwarming.[1] Disaster
followed disaster when C. S. Lewis died. Within two months his disconsolate
brother, "the Major," went on an erratic housecleaning binge and dumped
out pile after pile of precious Lewis papers and manuscripts. Relentlessly, he
passed bushels of papers on to Fred Paxford, the old gardener, to be thrown on
a hungry bonfire in the orchard.

All day long flames licked the sheaves of paper covered with Lewis's small,
tidy penmanship; all the white pages curled, and browned, and charred, and
turned to fine white ash. Smoke rose through the bare branches of
surrounding trees hour after hour, drifting away toward the winter sky.
Flakes of ash sometimes swirled up in a gust of breeze like ghosts of the words
and ideas that Lewis had laboriously entrusted to paper with his old fashioned
broad-nibbed pen. Sounds of crackling flame and rushing air were the last
sounds those words would ever make; and their many meanings all became
just one meaning: *Lost*. It has been claimed that some of the pages that burned

---

[1] Walter Hooper told the bonfire story in his introductions to *The Dark Tower*,
They Stand Together, and *Boxen*. He told it in the 1977 April and August issues of the
bulletin *CSL*. And he has told it in *Alumni Review* of the University of North
Carolina in March 1980 (pp. 14-15) and Summer 1987 (pp. 31-32). He also told it in
his 1984 recorded interview with Charles Glaise.

contained Lewis's continuation of his autobiography *Surprised by Joy,* telling the story of the second half of his life.[2] No one ever got to read it.

Faithful Paxford, straining and shuffling a bit, silently heaved another batch of pages onto the fire. After thirty-three years of tending the grounds of the Lewis home, he sorely missed "the Boss." First, the real boss, Mrs. Moore, had died of old age in 1951. Then before long Joy Gresham, an American, arrived on the scene and became Mrs. Lewis. But she didn't last long; she was soon dead of cancer. And now, three years later, the Boss himself was dead. Only the Major was left here now, with neighbors Len and Molly Miller to look after him. The American stepsons might come home for brief visits. How short life's good years seem when we look back, Paxford probably reflected sadly. And the days are short in January in England. Sundown before 5:00 P.M. Six hours of burning done already, and a small mountain of paper still left for tomorrow's flames.

The second day was like the first. Morning, afternoon, and evening, Fred Paxford dutifully tended the Major's fire in the orchard, burning mountains of papers and manuscripts whose value will never be known. When night fell, fuel for several more hours was left. On the third morning Paxford started the bonfire again. But he got an idea. This time he begged the Major for permission to set aside a large quantity of notebooks and manuscripts that might be of special value. Paxford had got the idea of showing them to an American who had just moved to Oxford and was living temporarily in a spare room at Keble College.[3] The Major relented; Paxford could save one pile of papers for Walter Hooper, but only until sundown. If Hooper did not arrive before then and carry them away, they would have to be burned at sundown.

Before long, Walter Hooper got a peculiar feeling that he must visit the Lewis home that very day, no matter what. Not knowing why, he went there in the afternoon. As he was walking up the drive, Fred Paxford came to meet him and steered him to the fire in the orchard. The pile of notebooks and manuscripts that had appealed to Paxford was right there waiting for him.

---

[2] Walter Hooper, "Reflections of an Editor," *CSL* (August 1977): 1-2.

[3] According to one of Walter Hooper's alternative accounts of the manuscript rescue (tape-recorded during his visit to Portland, Oregon, in 1979), it was Warren Lewis rather than Paxford who thought of the idea that Hooper would like to have the manuscripts.

Did he want it? Hooper says it took all of his strength and energy to drag the huge pile back to his room by means of two large trunks and a city bus.[4] He got back just in time for supper.

As soon as possible after supper, Hooper rushed to his room to examine his windfall. Among many other things, he found a blue notebook full of poems, a yellowed manuscript of a science fiction novel about a dark tower,[5] and some of Lewis's childhood writing and drawing. Although he was living with Lewis's good friends Austin and Kay Farrer, he didn't show them the "pile of scorched manuscripts," as he referred to them later.[6] He hardly told anyone about the rescue. Readers and audiences were unaware of it for over ten years.[7]

According to Hooper's published accounts, the Major never admitted to himself or others what he had done.[8] As a lifelong bachelor who was devoted to his famous brother and who cherished every scrap of Lewis data, this

---

[4] Hooper was thirty-two years old and not at all physically weak or slender. His accounts about the luggage that he borrowed from Warren Lewis have varied from one or two trunks to "enough suitcases." "There were so many manuscripts that I didn't think I could take them all back to Oxford. Finally, I asked Major Lewis if he had a suitcase I could borrow. But I couldn't get all of them in there, so I asked Major Lewis if I could leave the rest and come out the next day. He said 'No, no. Whatever you leave goes on the bonfire.' So I found enough suitcases to drag all the manuscripts to the bus and take them to Oxford." From a recorded interview of Walter Hooper by Charles Glaize in August 1984. According to the calculations of Martin Ward, a fit and healthy young man can carry a 110-pound bag of coal with ease, which is the equivalent of twenty reams of standard paper. This suggests that Hooper rescued over 9,000 manuscript pages from the bonfire.

[5] In Hooper's 1979 interview with John Dart, religion editor of the *Los Angeles Times,* Dart understood him to say that he had discovered the Dark Tower manuscript stuck in a drawer.

[6] Walter Hooper, "Reflections of an Editor," *CSL* (August 1977): 3.

[7] In a taped question-and-answer session on 9 March 1979 Hooper said, "Nearly everything that I have published was destined for the bonfire."

[8] At least once, Hooper has claimed that Warren admitted he had burned his brother's papers in a bonfire. On 5 April 1979, in McFarland Auditorium on the Southern Methodist University campus in Dallas, Hooper claimed to possess a letter from Warren in which he mentioned the bonfire and reaffirmed his gift of the manuscripts to Hooper. Research reveals, however, that there is no such letter in the collected letters from Warren to Hooper that Hooper has placed in the Southern Historical Collection of the University of North Carolina at Chapel Hill.

sensitive and sentimental man could not face the fact of his own destructiveness.[9]

In March 1964, less than two months after the alleged three-day bonfire, Major Lewis was himself again and advertising in England and the United States for any letters from C. S. Lewis that people could contribute to the book of Lewis letters that he was working on. In April he was responding clearly and in detail to people who wanted to contribute.[10]

After the book of letters came out in 1967, the Major wrote to me:

---

[9] John Rateliff attested to Warren's destructiveness on page 55 of *Mythlore 58:* "...it is a matter of public record that in the mid-1930s when [Warren] had completed his edition of *The Lewis Papers,* a ten-volume selection from family archives (including, among other things, Lewis' correspondence with his father), he destroyed all the originals, so that today only the transcribed excerpts survive." But that commonly repeated story is not true. Walter Hooper's claim on page 42 of *They Stand Together* (1979) that Warren Lewis destroyed the original Lewis family papers is often used as evidence that Warren might have burned C. S. Lewis's papers in 1964 as Hooper claims; but we have Warren Lewis's written word that he did *not* destroy the Lewis family papers. In letters to Walter Hooper on 1 April 1967 and 14 March 1968, Warren Lewis stated clearly that C. S. Lewis, not he, destroyed those papers in 1936.

[10] The following is the text of Warren Lewis's letter to me:

The Kilns, Kiln Lane
Headington Quarry, Oxford
24th April 1964
Dear Mrs. Lindskoog,
I am most grateful to you for your kindness in sending me the copy of my brother's letter to you, which is interesting, and which I think I can use. Now as regards your questions:—
(1) I have no recordings of his voice, and so far as I know, the only people who might have them would be the British Broadcasting Co. I believe when one broadcasts for them, a tape is made of the broadcast.
(2) My brother had been ailing for some considerable time with a kidney complaint, but what actually finished him was a stroke.
(3) He married in 1956, but I don't know the exact date. His wife died on 13th June [sic] 1960.
(4) There are two stepsons who may I think be described as semi-adult. The elder is 20 and the other one over 18. There is nothing private about these facts. With all good wishes, & thanks.
Yours sincerely,
W. H. Lewis

I am glad that you enjoyed the 'Letters.' Putting them together was an interesting but sad task for me. I was much touched by the extraordinarily generous response from America to my appeal for material, and particularly from those who sent photostats, saying they would not trust the originals out of their possession.

I am glad you liked the photos. Personally, I always fight rather shy of this kind of book if I find it is not illustrated.[11]

After reading my review of his book, he wrote again:

Many thanks for sending me your very interesting and understanding article on my collection of the C. S. L. letters—and your overflattering reference to 'the highly gifted writer' who did the arranging of them! Most of us produce books these days to help pay our taxes, but in this case I felt that firstly, such a collection was a debt owing to my brother's memory, and secondly that letters which had been of such value to their recipients might easily benefit a larger circle. In the latter object I am proud to say that I've been successful, and letters have poured in from all quarters thanking me for having published. He himself would have enjoyed your well written tribute.

As regards the length of the book, don't blame me, but the publisher who for commercial reasons cut out all the material I had supplied for the first fifteen years of my brother's life—a mistake, I thought, for when I read a book of this sort it is the childhood and boyish years which always seem to me the most interesting.[12]

In 1966 Warren Lewis began to formally bequeath his precious collection of Lewis papers and manuscripts to Dr. Clyde S. Kilby's collection at Wheaton College in Illinois, now called the Marion E. Wade Center, for public use. (Kilby had started the collection in 1965 by freely donating his seventeen letters from C. S. Lewis.) On 18 March 1968 Warren assured Hooper that he would gladly will to the Bodleian any Lewis papers that current law restricted to England, but that he would prefer to see them all go

---

[11] Letter from W. H. Lewis to me, 3 February 1967.
[12] Letter from W. H. Lewis to me, 13 July 1967.

to America for a variety of reasons. For one, he thought the papers would be safer in America. "And for another, I think that American scholarship—the *best* of it—is now turning out better work than we are doing in England. (Though to be sure a lot of it is phoney hackwork.)" Needless to say, Warren's concern for the preservation and use of the papers seems at variance with Hooper's explanation of the bonfire in his Preface to *The Dark Tower:* "The Lewis brothers felt little of that veneration for manuscripts so typical of many of us..."[13]

The Major died in 1973, and in the 1974 biography of C. S. Lewis Walter Hooper finally allowed the world to find out about the Dark Tower fragment, although he was not yet ready to tell who had it or where he got it. (The biography not only failed to mention the juvenilia rescued from the same fire, but also explicitly denied the existence of such juvenilia.[14] Hooper was to reveal the existence of rescued juvenilia later.) On 16 August 1975, guest of honor Hooper told the bonfire story to an enthralled audience in California,[15] and in 1977 he published it in his preface to *The Dark Tower*

---

[13] In his 2 March 1977 address in London launching *The Dark Tower*, Hooper made a peculiar claim: "Lewis normally destroyed his own manuscripts, out of a desire, as he put it, not to have the proud owner of a first edition one-upped by someone saying 'Well, *I* have the original manuscript....'" Mary Kirkpatrick, "A Lewis Evening in London", *CSL* (April 1977). C. S. Lewis was not a collector of first editions and was not noted for having an interest in other people's competitive book collecting.

[14] On page 24 of their biography, Green and Hooper say, "And unfortunately none of the early stories of 'knights-in-armor' (even if the knights were dressed animals) seem to have survived, though there are a few early attempts at verse concerning 'Knights and Ladyes'." For the facts, see Appendix 4.

[15] The speech was given in 1975 at Mythcon VI, held on the campus of Scripps College at Claremont, California. When Hooper read the text of the speech afterward as transcribed from a tape for publication in *Mythlore*, he deleted the passage about the bonfire. It seems that after he tried it out on his California audience he decided to save it for more strategic use.

In 1975 Hooper supposedly saved another part of the Lewis legacy from flames. He wrote to Dr. Arthur Lynip of Westmont College in California that Mr. and Mrs. J. W. Thirsk, who had bought the Kilns in 1974, intended to chop up Lewis's wardrobe "for firewood," to make room for a built-in closet. That wardrobe was apparently the prototype for the magic wardrobe in the Narnian Chronicles, and Dr. Lynip obtained it for Westmont College. But Mr. Thirsk, a University librarian, and Mrs. Thirsk, a University instructor, definitely cared about Lewis. In 1984 they proudly showed me the Lewis brothers' huge, healthy rosebush full of little pink blooms. In the sitting room

and told it to enthralled audiences in both London and New York.[16] He said "The story of Major Lewis's bonfire...is such an essential episode in the part I have played in Lewis studies that I see no way of leaving it out." Asked about his account of the fire in 1994, Hooper insisted, "I remember it and Owen Barfield remembers it."

(But in 1996 Hooper published his 940-page compendium *C. S. Lewis, Companion and Guide,* and left the bonfire story out; perhaps at that point he saw no way of leaving it in because it was discredited, or perhaps his editor made that decision.)

Shortly after the bonfire story was published in *The Dark Tower,* I consulted Len Miller and Fred Paxford, who were appalled. "As regards Walter Hooper's story about a bonfire, I am still in touch with Paxford and went to see him yesterday," Len Miller wrote to me. "He says it is all lies."[17]

Two weeks later, in his next letter, he added, "I am afraid anything Hooper says should be taken with a large pinch of salt."[18]

According to Miller and Paxford, early in 1964 the Major had Paxford burn some worthless papers that he and Lewis's lawyer Owen Barfield had carefully sorted out. But those papers were not literature, and they did not make a three-day fire. Moreover, Fred Paxford did not ask for permission to set anything aside for the American bachelor. He simply burned the trash and was done with it. It boggled his mind to be told fourteen years later that he

---

we browsed in their copy of Kilby's *Images of His World,* including the page (64) that shows that very room. They were delighted when I gave them a copy of my book *The Lion of Judah in Never-Never Land.* The house looked immaculate and had been greatly improved during the decade of Thirsk ownership. Best of all, both their children had grown up in the Kilns knowing the Narnia books.

[16] The London speech was presented on 2 March 1977 at Church House Westminster, at an event organized by Nigel Sustins upon the occasion of publication of *The Dark Tower.* About 150 people attended, and speakers included Walter Hooper, Owen Barfield, Roger Lancelyn Green, Priscilla Tolkien, and actor Robert Eddison. In Mary Kirkpatrick's report "A Lewis Evening in London," (page 1 of the April 1977 issue of *CSL*), she noted that Hooper said he saved "a small mountain" of papers from the bonfire. The New York speech was presented on 13 August 1977 at a C. S. Lewis Weekend on the campus of Albertus Magnus College in New Haven, Connecticut. It was then published as "Reflections of an Editor" in the August 1977 issue of *CSL.*

[17] Letter from Leonard Miller to me, 26 October 1977.

[18] Letter from Leonard Miller to me, 10 November 1977.

had been the hero who rescued a pile of valuable manuscripts. Nonsense, he answered.

In a letter to me postmarked 9 December 1977 and written from 5 The Square, Churchill, OXON, F. W. Paxford said, "In all my failings, one is that I am much too independent. So it cuts out begging the Major, much less Walter Hooper anyway. To me, the whole thing sounds phoney and I cannot see the Major burning any papers that were important."

It is often said that dour, honest Fred Paxford inspired C. S. Lewis to invent Puddleglum, the Marshwiggle, in *The Silver Chair* of the Narnian Chronicles. It happens that Puddleglum's finest hour came when he broke the magic spell caused by a sweet-smelling fire; he stamped it out with his bare feet and woke everyone up. This is one of the high points in the Narnian Chronicles. Perhaps Paxford's flat-footed denial of the enchanting bonfire story gives him more in common with Puddleglum than anyone could have foreseen.

When I published Paxford's denial in an article in *Christianity & Literature*, a small journal for American instructors of literature, it created almost as much heat as the famous bonfire. Furious letters came in from two leaders of the New York C. S. Lewis Society. Eugene McGovern protested "a slander," "preposterous scenario," and "tasteless probing" into things that are "none of Lindskoog's business." He said my essay moved from the realm of the useless to that of the obnoxious. James Como, a professor of rhetoric, called the article "back-fence gossip" and said "I very nearly expected her to provide an O. E. D. [Oxford English Dictionary] treatment of 'bonfire', which (come to think of it) would have been an improvement upon the many distortions of fact and of context with which she assails us." Owen Barfield also wrote in, protesting my "mass of inaccurate statements, ingenious speculations, and waspish innuendo." But one of the letters seemed positive. It came from a scientist in England. The editor of *Christianity & Literature* was much interested and published it in the Winter 1979 issue.[19]

The bonfire letter was typed on official letterhead stationery of the Physical Chemistry Laboratory of Oxford University, on South Parks Road, Oxford OX1 30Z. The letterhead includes the traditional Oxford shield with three crowns surrounding an open book with the Latin inscription *Dominus*

---

[19] *Christianity & Literature*, (Winter 1979): 12-13.

Illuminatio Mea ("the Lord is my light"). The letter was dated 20 November 1978. It began with the title *Carbon Particle Analysis: A Fresh Dimension to the Lewis Bonfire:* A contribution to the productive dialogue from Anthony Marchington, B.A. (Oxon), of the Physical Chemistry Laboratory, Oxford, England. Marchington states:

> "Far be it from me to involve myself in an ongoing situation of debate, but I wish simply to report here, without any malice or prejudice, the results of scientific research carried out here in Oxford over the last three years which, I believe, goes a long way in answering the question: "Did the bonfire of C. S. Lewis's papers which Hooper claims to have witnessed ever actually occur?" and if so, "Do the remains of this bonfire under chemical analysis account for all the papers which Hooper claims were destroyed?"[20]

A collaborative research project between the University departments of Chemistry and Archeology has recently given birth to a new method of dating sites of pyrolitic residue. The minute details of this research needn't be explained here, but in order to interpret the results a short description must be given.

Basically, during a bonfire fine particulate carbon along with refractory ash and minerals are deposited about the site. Much of the surface material is then dispersed by the elements but a representative insoluble sample remains indefinitely at various depths in the soil. The carbon trapped as fine particles in this ash has been the subject of our research. Firstly, its chemical analysis can tell us what sort of material was originally burned: e.g. wood, paper, leather etc. This sort of analysis is now standard practice. Secondly, however, our work at Oxford has shown that computer structural data analysis of particle sizes can yield both date and average temperature of such a bonfire. Of our many recent successes I can quote the application of this technique to earth excavated from a place close to the main lectern in the old Coventry Cathedral, England. As a result we were able to pinpoint the remains of what was most likely the Cathedral Bible and calculated the date of its burning as between May and December 1940. The night of the Coventry Blitz when the

---

[20] As soon as I read the opening of the letter I felt sure it was a spoof, and so I read the rest with great amusement and curiosity about the writer's motives.

Old Cathedral was destroyed was, in fact, 14 November 1940. Encouraged by such results and others we are at present applying this new method to many such fires of historical interest.

This letter goes on to say that some of Marchington's research workers went to Hooper's apartment to discuss plans for analysis of the Lewis bonfire over tea, and Hooper's response to the project was "Professional scientists ought to have better things to do than rummaging around in soot." In fact, his opinion was published in the University newspaper.

Marchington goes on to describe the process of obtaining soil samples from about a third of an acre around the site of the reported bonfire and transporting thirteen hundred pounds—over a half-ton—of soil from Lewis's orchard to the laboratory. There the soil was examined with standard methods such as Light Interferometry, Ultra Violet Spectroscopy, and Combustion Elemental Analysis. This analysis proved that there had not been a significant bonfire of any sort in that area for at least eight hundred years.

The letter is signed by Anthony F. Marchington, Hulme Exhibitioner and Charitable Foundation Scholar, Brasenose College, Oxford. In a note at the bottom of the page, he says, "As with all my publications, a copy of this article has been given to my academic supervisor, Dr. Stephen C. F. Moore (Brasenose College) and to Dr. T. G. Earp (Malvern) to whom I am greatly indebted."

Although some readers were immensely impressed with this research, a little transatlantic detective work revealed that Marchington's "academic supervisor, Dr. Stephen C. F. Moore" was in fact just a young science student. More important, many readers agreed with my first impression, that the letter was a silly batch of ficto-science, not real science at all.[21]

---

[21] The following letter from Dr. Walter R. Hearn to me on 10 March 1988 offers information about Anthony Marchington's bonfire letter and his subsequent career.

"I have read the letter by Anthony F. Marchington published in *Christianity & Literature* Vol. 28 (Winter 1979) 2:12-13, concerning chemical examination of residues from bonfires. In your book manuscript you add that the Marchington letter was on official stationery of the Physical Chemistry Laboratory of Oxford University. Although the letter is in the form of a report from that laboratory, I think it has all the earmarks of a practical joke.

"Without personal experience in forensic or archaeological chemistry, I can imagine that spectroscopy or other techniques might enable one to distinguish ashes

Furthermore, without the help of Light Interferometry or Ultra Violet Spectroscopy—just an ordinary magnifying glass—I discovered that although Marchington's letter was typed on official stationery of Oxford University's Physical Chemistry Laboratory, it was not typed there. It was typed on Walter Hooper's own home typewriter. The minute irregularities in the letter configurations make that indisputable. Marchington's letter was typed on the same machine that Walter Hooper used for his own typing for years.[22]

The fact that Marchington pretended in his letter that he did not know Hooper and sent researchers to Hooper's apartment to discuss the project with

---

from certain kinds of incompletely combusted materials. The claims of the letter and the wording of the accompanying footnotes, however, leave me totally skeptical about this report's authenticity. The idea that 'computer structural data analysis of particle sizes' could yield 'both date and average temperature' of a bonfire sounds preposterous to me. Reporting that the date of burning of the Coventry Cathedral bible was pinpointed to within six months by such a technique I suspect is the author's way of making sure that only the most gullible readers will be taken in by his hoax.

"At any rate, no mention of such methods is made in two symposia on the chemistry of archaeology published by the American Chemical Society in 1973 and 1977, or in a standard work by Zvi Goffer, *Archaeological Chemistry: A Sourcebook on the Applications of Chemistry to Archaeology* (New York: John Wiley and Sons, 1980). There is no record in Chemical Abstracts that the promised paper by 'Marchington, Pigot-Churchhouse and Wizard' was ever published.

"Anthony F. Marchington is indeed a real person with training in physical chemistry and computers, however. He has published a number of technical papers, first with William Graham Richards and co-workers at the Physical Chemistry Laboratory at Oxford. He began with a study of the inductive effect in molecules and ions, using computer calculations. He used computer graphics of visualization of three-dimensional structures in studies of enzyme-substrate interactions at Oxford and then for the design of new fungicides at the Jealotts Hill Reseatch Station of Imperial Chemical Industries Plant Protection Division in Bracknell/Berkshire, UK RG12 6EY. His name appears on a British patent for such compounds (assigned to ICI), and in 1984 he published a review of computer graphics in the design of triazole fungicides."

Dr. Hearn has a bachelor's degree in chemistry from Rice University and a Ph. D. in biochemistry from the University of Illinois. He served on the biochemistry faculties of the medical schools of Yale and Baylor Universities and then of Iowa State University, which he left in 1972. He now lives in Berkeley, California and until recently edited the *Newsletter of the American Scientific Affiliation.*

[22] The editor of *Christianity & Literature* gave me a clear photocopy of Marchington's bonfire letter. I have on hand samples of Hooper's typing from 1973, 1979, and 1980 (about twenty pages).

him takes on a new light when one guesses that Marchington was typing that very letter in Hooper's tiny apartment, probably chuckling.

There can be no question. The Marchington "Lewis Bonfire" letter was some kind of prank. To this day I do not know why Anthony "Tony" Marchington wrote it. Friends of mine suggested that he might have expected me to take the letter seriously and stake my reputation on it; then he could have exposed my gullibility and discredited me by explaining his joke. If so, the joke was on him, because I realized before the end of the long first sentence that the letter was a prank. I enjoyed it. I wrote to him later, but he didn't answer.

Shortly after publication of the letter, Robert G. Collmer, Dean of Graduate Studies at Baylor University, "saw that it had the characteristics of a put-on" and wondered if Anthony Marchington really existed. Collmer telephoned him at Brasenose College, and the two spoke briefly; "but he did not divulge any other details nor did he imply that he had written a joke." In the summer of 1989 Marchington told an acquaintance that he still remembered getting the phone call from America a decade earlier.[23]

Sixteen years after publication of the Marchington letter, Walter Hooper publicly admitted that it was typed by his living partner and co-author on Hooper's own typewriter. His comment was "What's wrong with that?"[24]

There is as much fantasy in Marchington's bonfire letter as there is in *The Dark Tower,* and there also seems to be as much time travel in Hooper's bonfire account as there is in *The Dark Tower.* According to Hooper's account in *The Dark Tower,* Warren's fire took place sometime in January 1964, when Hooper was living briefly at Keble College and not visiting the Kilns regularly. When Hooper rescued the huge pile of manuscripts, he asked Warren for the suitcases in which he dragged them to his room in Keble College. Hooper also says he spent three weeks in January working on the collected C. S. Lewis letters with Warren in the Kilns before Warren took a trip alone to Ireland. Both men used their own typewriters.[25]

---

[23] By this time Marchington was a successful scientist.

[24] Quoted in "The Highjacking of C. S. Lewis," a 4000-word article in the October 1994 issue of *Heterodoxy* by journalist K. L. Billingsley.

[25] Walter Hooper, "Introduction," *Letters of C. S. Lewis,* ed. W.H. Lewis, Revised and Enlarged edition edited by Walter Hooper (London: Collins Fount, 1988) 13.

But Warren and Hooper never met until mid-February, long after Hooper had moved away from Keble College to a room in Oxford's Wycliffe Hall. Hooper wrote from there to Warren on 4 February, offering to come to Ireland to accompany him home. Warren answered on 8 February, declining Hooper's offer.[26] Warren went on to say that when he returned from Ireland on about 18 February he intended to start work on a collection of C. S. Lewis letters, which he described. He said he was glad that Hooper was comfortably installed at Wycliffe Hall: "I look forward to meeting you."[27] He added that in his last weeks C. S. Lewis had often wanted Hooper's company. (Lewis knew Hooper as an enthusiastic graduate student.) The complete bonfire scenario presents a puzzle worthy of the cleverest science fiction/fantasy authors. If the bonfire took place in January, when Hooper was at Keble College, the two men had not yet met. Warren hadn't even told Hooper about the letter project in January, much less worked on it with him; and he couldn't have given Hooper a pile of scorched manuscripts or the suitcases to carry them in. (If Hooper carried Lewis papers away from the Kilns in January 1964, who gave him permission to do so?) On the other hand, if the bonfire took place in the second half of February, after Warren met Hooper, Hooper was no longer at Keble College; and Warren would have already taken his trip to Ireland that came after their three weeks of working together but before their first meeting. Given this tangle of contradictions, it seems that the only possible time for the manuscript bonfire is in Othertime, in a parallel universe.[28]

---

[26] Hooper placed Warren's letter of 8 February 1964 in his collection of papers in the University of North Carolina library at Chapel Hill.

[27] In context it impossible to read this as meaning anything other than a first meeting.

[28] Both Walter Hooper and Owen Barfield vouch for the three-day manuscript bonfire, but they don't tell the January dates when it occurred. They don't even tell the week. Even if Hooper made no notes at the time (in print he refers to 1963, 1966, and 1978 entries in his diary), pinpointing the week of the historic bonfire should be easy enough for him.

The first of January fell on a Wednesday in 1964. If Hooper met Warren on Saturday, 4 January, he might have started typing with him in the Kilns on Monday, 6 January. According to Hooper, they typed together for three weeks; then Warren started drinking and left for Ireland. Judging from Hooper's 4 February letter, Warren probably left no later than Monday, 27 January.

It appears that people who believe *The Dark Tower* to be authentic have to choose between a January fire without Warren or a February fire without Keble College, because the bonfire story is Hooper's only foundation for the tottering *Tower*. On the other hand, if *The Dark Tower* was not written by Lewis and was not rescued from a three-day bonfire by Paxford and Hooper,[29] then *The Dark Tower* and the bonfire story and the bonfire letter look like parts of an audacious hoax.[30]

Who could have written *The Dark Tower*? It seems like a hodgepodge by more than one writer. Anthony Marchington is an Oxford scientist to this day (Managing Director of Oxford Molecular), he is interested in the origin of *The Dark Tower*, and he tricked *Christianity & Literature* with a scientific spoof. Furthermore, he was about eight years old when Madeleine L'Engle published her children's classic *A Wrinkle in Time*, and so he could have read it then. That could account for unconscious copying of L'Engle's automaton scene.

Surely Hooper can remember whether the bonfire took place during his first days in England, before he started typing in the Kilns—or on the weekend of 27 January, after he stopped typing at the Kilns. The bonfire probably didn't happen during the three weeks when he was typing in the Kilns, because he says he had no reason to visit there during the three-day bonfire.

[29] In a 1994 telephone interview, Lewis's friend Sheldon Vanauken said of the bonfire story "I don't believe it." K. L. Billingsley, "The Highjacking of C. S. Lewis," *Heterodoxy*, (October 1996).

[30] The following manuscript bonfire calculations were made by James Long:

As a conservative estimate, let's start with the fire burning only five hours a day for the three days. Further, let's assume that Fred Paxford was lazy and burned only two big armloads of paper per hour. The standard box of copy paper contains 5000 sheets and can be considered a big armload. This indicates to me that at least 150,000 sheets of C. S. Lewis manuscripts were burnt in the bonfire. If these pages had been produced uniformly over C. S. Lewis' adult life starting at age 20, he averaged nine and a half sheets of bonfire paper per day. Since C. S. Lewis was frugal with paper, often using both sides, he would have had to fill up to 19 sides per day for the future bonfire.

Despite his full-time academic load, heavy correspondence, constant reading, family chores, and writing for publication, let's assume that on the average Lewis devoted four hours of additional time each day to manuscripts that would end up on the bonfire. This means that C. S. Lewis wrote out about five pages per hour for the bonfire, at the rate of about 20 words per minute. This is an astronomical show of stamina. If Lewis had to occasionally pause to think, the actual handwriting speed would be even higher.

There is a peculiar coincidence that could possibly have inspired Marchington and Hooper to create the Dark Tower hoax. Lewis's family and some of his friends called him Jack. Jack Lewis was also the name of the American author of a clever science fiction story titled "Who's Cribbing?" It consists of a dozen (imaginary) letters between the American Jack Lewis and his (imaginary) science fiction editors.

In this fantasy, every time Jack Lewis submitted an original new story to an editor, it was returned with word that it was copied exactly from some story published long ago by Todd Thromberry, an obscure electronics expert who had died in 1941. Thromberry's stories had been ahead of their time (in more ways than one) and were little known and hard to find.

In the fantasy, Jack Lewis finally gathered all the letters about his stories, titled them "Who's Cribbing?" and sent them in with his bizarre theory that Thromberry had cracked the time-space barrier, was copying Lewis's stories from a different time cycle, and thus published them long before Lewis wrote them. In the fantasy, Lewis's editor answered that in 1940 Thromberry had already published this very set of letters as a story titled "Who's Cribbing?"

In the real world, Madeleine L'Engle's *A Wrinkle in Time* was distributed widely in 1962, and Jack Lewis's "Who's Cribbing?" was distributed widely in Isaac Asimov's *Fifty Short Science Fiction Tales* in 1963. Perhaps those two fantasies inspired Hooper and Marchington to write their own fantasy about cracking the time-space barrier and to playfully attribute it to their own Jack Lewis.

How did clever young Anthony Marchington get involved in C. S. Lewis affairs in the first place, and what else has he written? That is the subject of chapter 4.

Very few things happen at the right time, and the rest do not happen at all.
The conscientious historian will correct these defects.
—*Herodotus*

4

SEEING THROUGH "THROUGH JOY AND BEYOND"

NOT THE FILM OF A LIFETIME AFTER ALL?

Anthony Marchington, the Lewis bonfire jokester, entered Brasenose College in 1973. When he wrote his letter about soot analysis for *Christianity & Literature* he was still an anonymous university student. He had been living with his close friend Walter Hooper near the Eagle and Child (Bird and Baby) pub in Oxford, in a tiny upstairs apartment at 19 Beaumont Street.[1] There, Marchington studied science, and Hooper managed the C. S. Lewis estate.

But Marchington and Hooper collaborated on projects of mutual interest. One of the collaborations was probably the article that Hooper co-authored with a friend and published in *Oxford* magazine under the single pen name Walter Churchington. It defended the tradition of excluding females from the all-male colleges.[2]

The collaboration that would eventually make Marchington a public figure in the United States began with a telephone call back in September 1977. Walter Hooper's Illinois friend Bob O'Donnell called Hooper with a

---

[1] On 26 April 1978, Walter Hooper wrote in his Editor's Note that he shared his home with Anthony Marchington and that Marchington was his helper (C. S. Lewis, *They Stand Together* (New York: Macmillan, 1979) 45.

[2] Sheldon Vanauken read the article and wrote to Churchington in agreement. To his surprise, he got a letter from Walter Hooper revealing that he and a friend had published it under this pseudonym.

request. He wanted permission from the C. S. Lewis estate to make a C. S. Lewis film. O'Donnell was not the first or last to have that wish; but he had the inside track and permission was granted.[3]

O'Donnell was the actor who played the unscrupulous Commander in "The Gospel Blimp," a widely circulated rental film based upon Joseph Bayly's satirical book with the same name.[4] The long-term popularity of that film in evangelical churches was impressive. It seemed obvious that a film about C. S. Lewis might appeal to that market as well as to Episcopal churches and to colleges and seminaries; best of all, it might be aired on television.

O'Donnell and Hooper hatched a bold plan. O'Donnell would serve as producer and director, and Hooper would serve as both author and on-camera narrator.[5] Peter Ustinov would be hired to read all the passages of

---

[3] Chad Walsh, an ordained Episcopal priest, was the first published C. S. Lewis authority. He was extremely friendly and helpful to Hooper, beginning in 1962. He wrote a recommendation for Hooper to be ordained to the priesthood in 1964. He repeatedly opened his vacation home in Vermont to Hooper. But he differed with Hooper by liking Clyde Kilby, liking the Lewis collection at Wheaton College, and believing that the Lewis marriage was consummated.

In April 1977 Walsh ended a letter to Hooper: "I hope all goes well with you, beloved friend." But already in 1977 Hooper had been corresponding negatively with James Como about Walsh. From what Hooper told him, Como decided that Walsh was a terribly erratic man, obviously up to something. He advised Hooper to get his ammunition ready.

When Robert Baylis, owner of the Logos bookstore in Berkeley, set out to make a C. S. Lewis film focused on Dr. Kilby and the C. S. Lewis collection at Wheaton College, the C. S. Lewis Estate galvanized to block him.

Chad Walsh was invited to speak in both O'Donnell's and Baylis's films in 1978. On 24 April 1978 he wrote to O'Donnell, "The more I think about it, the more it seems to me that my job is to write and lecture about Lewis and to cooperate with any legitimate Lewis projects that come along, not identifying myself exclusively with any faction or project. I should simply be available to all for whatever I can contribute."

On 3 May O'Donnell sent some kind of warning to Walsh about potential ille-gality involved in a Baylis interview. Walsh responded meekly on 9 May, agreeing that it was the task of the Trustees to cooperate with one project and to refuse cooperation with another. (Walsh himself was dependent upon Hooper for the use of Lewis quo-tations in some of his work.) "I want to remain simply a scholar." The Baylis film project was forcibly cancelled, and Walsh wasn't used in O'Donnell's film after all.

[4] On 1 February 1978, Joseph Bayly remarked in regard to some behind-the-scenes business in Lewis affairs, "In this as in so many things, I feel that the cause of Christ really suffers because people are unwilling to 'stick their necks out'."

[5] *Through Joy and Beyond,* xi.

literature used in the film. As Hooper tells it, he immediately consulted Marchington about the project and included him as co-author of the script and as assistant producer.[6] (Near the time of the filming, Marchington bought himself a steamroller. Always colorful, in 1996 he would be featured in the business section of the *Oxford Mail* as "the millionaire boss of the drug design firm Oxford Molecular," because he was buying for restoration The Flying Scotsman, the first steam locomotive to go more than 100 miles per hour.[7] And in 1998 he and his brother were to achieve notoriety in an Oxford Molecular maneuver that allegedly netted them millions at the expense of biotech investors.)[8]

In March 1978, Bob O'Donnell arrived to arrange for a summer film crew. In May a bit of preliminary filming was done. In June, Hooper and Marchington completed the script, and in July they began filming full-time. In August, Bob O'Donnell and some helpers flew to Palermo, Sicily, to meet Peter Ustinov for his readings. In the fall the film was edited in Illinois, and the distributor, Gospel Films, was preparing major publicity.

Anachronistic as it may seem, in the 8 July 1983 issue of *National Review*, H. N. Kelley devoted almost a page to publicity for the four-year old film, beginning, "Bob O'Donnell is a man who believes in putting his money where his heart is. He sank five years [sic] and vast quantities of his own money into producing a documentary film on the life of C. S. Lewis, entitled *Through Joy and Beyond*, simply, he says, 'to help get people interested in reading Lewis.'"[9] Kelley ended his article with the claim that when Walter Hooper toured the United States to answer questions about C. S. Lewis, he found to his surprise that his heavily evangelical audiences were not much

---

[6] Ibid., xii. Hooper does not say why he chose the athletic young science student to serve as coauthor and film producer.

[7] *The Oxford Mail*, (27 February 1996): 14.

[8] "Marchington Infuriates City" was the headline of an article in the 10 November 1998 issue of *Pharmeceutical Marketing*. "After just a year in the business, Allan Marchington walks away with £4.5m, while shareholders of Oxford have seen their investment slump this year from over 280p to a low of 44p."

[9] H. N. Kelley, "The Lewis Tapes," *National Review* (8 July 1983): 834, 836. Kelley, referring to Hooper's centrality in the film, comments, "Father Hooper, of course, knows Lewis as no one else possibly could. He was his secretary, lived with him, attended the famous Inklings meetings with him, talked endlessly with Lewis as he reminisced in his final days."

interested in Lewis's life and beliefs, but wanted to know instead about his smoking and drinking habits.[10]

Kelley was wrong about the evangelical questions, and he was wrong about the year of the tour, which he placed in 1982. But he was right that there was a tour. The film premiered in "A Visit with C. S. Lewis" seminars in twenty cities around the United States in February, March, and April of 1979. Full-page ads appeared in magazines, handsome full-color brochures were sent to homes, large full-color posters were mailed out, and a special half-hour preview film was given to television broadcasters. Newspapers were contacted personally and urged to interview Hooper. In the publicity and in the film itself, Anthony Marchington's name was placed right next to Walter Hooper's as co-author.

The entire film turned out to be two and a half-hours long and comes in three reels, only two of which were used in the seminars. The first reel is called "The Formative Years," and in it Hooper covers Lewis's childhood and youth until shortly after the World War I. The second reel is called "The Informed Years," and in it Hooper covers the rest of Lewis's life. The third reel is called "Jack Remembered" and features Hooper introducing a few of Lewis's many friends—Dr. Robert Havard, John and Priscilla Tolkien, Pauline Baynes, and Owen Barfield. And, of course, Anthony Marchington!

Viewers all over the United States have met Anthony Marchington at the end of "Jack Remembered." He appears as the president of a small men's dining club in the Oxford tradition (it is not clear whether this is a real club or a fictitious one), where the members wear tuxedos and enjoy formal British dining. Hooper explains that the men have enjoyed a seven-course dinner with dessert and "fruits as to the season." Then Anthony Marchington introduces the after-dinner speaker, Martin Moynihan, who reminisces very briefly about C. S. Lewis.

Moynihan appears to be remarkably lubricated, although that may have been part of the script. He mentions expansively that there has been only one real epic—*Beowulf*. He laughs. Then he regales his listeners with an anecdote demonstrating C. S. Lewis's genius in philosophical discourse:

---

[10] Two of the key elements in Kelley's essay appear decade after decade in popular writing about Lewis: chronological confusion, and the idea that Hooper has had to defend Lewis from the twin dangers of oblivion and evangelical distortion.

[A man] turned on Lewis and said, "Well, what do you mean by God?" and Lewis didn't turn to waffle; he didn't turn aside; he strove on. He said, "God is a self-subsistent being, creator of all that is, independent of all things." I was enormously impressed.

During this speech, the young men puff on big cigars and sip port. Anthony Marchington sits at the speaker's left, puffing dutifully. He looks as if he is in his mid-twenties, with rather long, thick, curly brown hair, which he tugs on at times. He tends to slump at the table. To his left is Walter Hooper, in his late forties, leaning on the table with an intensely appreciative expression, also making a show of his cigar. Lingering close-ups of some of the other club members, apparently personal friends of Marchington, give the impression that they were more interested in the film than in the speech. One of them has a face twinkling with silent laughter. Could one of these young men be Marchington's "academic supervisor Dr. Stephen C. F. Moore"? The men puff and sip with an air of bemused bonhomie.

When Sheldon Vanauken—author of *A Severe Mercy*, personal friend of C. S. Lewis, and lover of Oxford—heard about this scene, he wrote to me, "It sounds very odd indeed to me. I myself belonged to a dining club at Oxford. One of the first things I learned there was that one never, never smokes with port wine. Cigars would kill the port. With the fruit, one drinks port. Then coffee and cigars or pipes."

Perhaps the cigars were only symbolic and the dinner a fiction anyway. It was a rather curious way to end the film, but an unexpected opportunity to see and hear the author of the Lewis Bonfire letter, co-author of the film itself, and—just possibly—co-author of *The Dark Tower*.

The 1991 videocassette version of *Through Joy and Beyond* distributed by The Bridgestone Group includes only the first two reels and abridges them at that. But anyone who wants to see Anthony Marchington without buying a copy of the third reel of the film can find his picture on page 79 of the book made from the film, *Through Joy and Beyond* (Macmillan, 1982).[11] Mar-

---

[11] For a more contemporary photo, see the 1992 Hilary Issue of *Oxford Today: The University Magazine*, which includes a 1992 photo of Dr. Tony Marchington, now Director of Oxford Molecular. He is shown with Prime Minister John Major at the opening of the Magdalene Centre at the Oxford Science Park. He appears quite stout.

chington was named as co-author on the front of the book until the last minute, when his name was removed from the cover.[12]

Two years after publication of the book, Walter Hooper says, he was summoned to Rome so that Pope John Paul II could talk with him about C. S. Lewis, and he had his photo taken while presenting a copy of *Through Joy and Beyond* to the Pope. Hooper's account of this meeting appeared in the February 1987 issue of *The Chesterton Review*. He discovered that the Pope was very much like C. S. Lewis, and talking to him was like talking to Lewis. First, the Pope asked Hooper, "Do you still love your old friend, C. S. Lewis?" Then he told Hooper that editing Lewis's books was Hooper's *apostolate* (mission). "Our Wal-ter Hoo-per—you are doing very good WORK!"

At the beginning and end of the conversation, Hooper knelt and kissed the Pope's ring. Both times, a miracle took place, although bystanders would not realize it. The first miracle was dramatically obvious to both Hooper and the Pope, and bound them in a mystical way. The Pope whispered to Hooper, "I understand." The second miracle, in which Hooper gladly took into himself some intense suffering of the Pope's, was known to Hooper alone—and to God—until Hooper decided to tell the world in 1987.

In Hooper's account, it seems that Pope John Paul II has endorsed Hooper's career in Lewis affairs, and it seems that God has supported the Pope's endorsement—with miracles before and after. Needless to say, questioning the accuracy of Hooper's account would seem indelicate at best, and sacrilegious at worst. It puts doubters in an awkward position.[13]

The book that Hooper gave the Pope is worth having, although it includes meandering bathos like this: "But people come and go, yet on a warm Trinity evening the quad will still have that sweetness about it and the cloisters still whisper to the same cool fragrance. But, be that as it may; if there were great rejoicings in Heaven that particular evening as Lewis crossed the quad to begin his now regular chapel attendances, you can be sure that all this would have maintained its usual quiet discretion."

---

[12] The original cover design for *Through Joy and Beyond* was pictured on the inside of the front cover of the Advent issue of *The Anglican Digest in* 1982. Marchington evidently left Lewis studies as abruptly in 1982 as he had entered in 1978.

[13] Hooper joined the Roman Catholic Church in 1988. Allegations that C. S. Lewis was in the process of becoming a Roman Catholic are discussed in Chapter 5.

The film upon which the book is based is pleasant and interesting, although not highly professional. But there are a few minor errors and some significant distortions in the film.

Minor errors include using large hydrangeas to illustrate what Lewis said about delicate currant blossoms;[14] using what Lewis said about Malvern to describe Surrey; placing Lewis's famous' atheism letter after instead of before his service in the trenches of World War I;[15] making Warren Lewis into a Major before World War I; the idea that Lewis enjoyed his heavy burden of correspondence; the idea that Lewis had to constantly deny to readers that he had ever traveled in outer space; the idea that children's literature is the particular branch of literature in which few authors attain more than a transitory or esoteric fame; and the idea that Lewis could get from Magdalen College to his home at Headington Quarry three miles away by taking Addison's Walk (a one-mile circular walk at Magdalen College). These suggestions are surprising, but they can be shrugged off as the result of hasty production.

There is an inappropriate choirboy sequence in the film. Of all the interesting people and places that could have been included and weren't, seven minutes (almost one-eighth of "The Informed Years") is devoted to a boys' choir singing in the chapel at Magdalen College. Hooper indicates that as soon as Lewis came to believe in God he started attending Evensong and listening to the boys. But Lewis said that he attended morning rather than evening chapel; and he made it clear that whenever he went to worship, he did not

---

[14] In Warren Lewis's diary entry on 21 March 1967 (in *Brothers and Friends,* page 272), he explained what flowering currants meant to the brothers. "The flowering currant is now out in several places, and this is always one of the highlights of my year. Enjoyment of it and the wallflower are the earliest aesthetic experiences of my life—dating back to long before we left Dundela Villas. I can still remember the thrill of joy with which I used to greet the arrival of both, a thrill that one never experiences once childhood is past; and which is perhaps the purest one ever receives. Is it I wonder wholly fanciful to think that this thrill is a dim recollection of having just come from a better world?"

[15] Whether he meant it or not, in 1998 Douglas Gresham seemed to perpetuate this chronological error. "However, he pursued a career at the university, after his tutor Kirkpatrick, and he took a triple first at Oxford when he was a very young man. He fought in the First World War as a volunteer in the Somerset Light Infantry and had some horrific experiences" (from Douglas Gresham's lecture "C S Lewis and Contemporary Culture" at the University of Tennessee, 16 April 1998).

enjoy church music. The film indicates the opposite. Some viewers find the lingering close-up of one boy's face, then another's, irritating and distracting. When I saw the film in Pasadena in 1979 and in Costa Mesa in 1987, I heard several complaints that the choirboy portraits were too close or too long for comfort. I believe C. S. Lewis would agree on both counts; any hint of aesthetic pederasty is out of place in a C. S. Lewis film.[16] In *The C. S. Lewis Hoax* I pressed this point. Two years later, the entire choirboy sequence was deleted from the videocassette version.

Unfortunately, no one deleted Hooper's popular fable about Lewis and his army friend Paddy Moore pledging to each other that if only one of them returned from France alive, he would care for his friend's parent for life. This claim is supposed to account for Lewis living with the ignorant, self-centered, possessive Mrs. Moore for over thirty years. Barfield's and Hooper's attempts to portray her as a pleasant companion don't fit the facts we get from directly from C. S. Lewis and Warren.

The two-way promise would not have made any sense. C. S. Lewis's father Albert, a successful Belfast attorney, was a widower with two sons and many other relatives. He was moody, eccentric, and set in his ways. He certainly would not have wanted a young stranger with a dependent mother and sister in tow "rescuing" him. The idea is ridiculous, and C. S. Lewis would not have entertained it for a moment.

Sixty years before Hooper announced the two-way promise, Mrs. Moore announced a one-way promise. In a letter to C. S. Lewis's father Albert, Mrs. Moore claimed that his son had promised Paddy that he would care for her after the war if Paddy didn't come back. Albert thought that was not an adequate explanation for what was going on. He was right.

In retrospect, two historical facts undermine Mrs. Moore's story of a unilateral promise. First, according to both C. S. Lewis and Warren, she often spoke untruth. Second, C. S. Lewis never told anyone of such a promise, although it would have cleared the air. Only once did Warren dare to ask

---

[16]"People commonly talk as if every other evil were more tolerable than this [pederasty]. But why? Because those of us who do not share the vice feel for it a certain nausea, as we do, say, for necrophily?" C. S. Lewis, *Surprised by Joy* (London: Geoffrey Bles, 1955) 107.

Lewis why he lived with Mrs. Moore, and he was told to mind his own business.[17]

There was no particular affinity between Lewis and Paddy Moore; they paired off because they were put together alphabetically.[18] They were not close friends. Furthermore, if Lewis really had made a promise to take Paddy's place in caring for Mrs. Moore, that would hardly have obligated him to live under her domestic tyranny until she died. No one thinks that Paddy Moore would have lived on with her as an adult. He did not get along with her.[19]

Albert Lewis called his son's relationship with Mrs. Moore an affair, and he was heartsick because, this woman old enough to be Jack's mother, was exploiting him. Lewis's behavior confirmed his father's fears. On 30 July 1966 Warren received a letter from his cousin Ruth Hamilton Parker.[20] She reflected upon Albert Lewis and her parents discussing the exasperating misfortune of Mrs. Moore's entry into C. S. Lewis's life: "Dear me, how they talked and talked. Uncle A. wanted to know if Jack had been killed would he have been adopted by the Moore boy."[21]

C. S. Lewis never dedicated a book to Mrs. Moore. In his autobiography, he mentioned Paddy Moore but left out Mrs. Moore entirely. Instead of acknowledging her existence, he confessed that at the end of the World War I there came a huge, complex episode in his life that he could not divulge.[22] He greatly regretted it, and it taught him to avoid unbridled emotionalism the rest of his life. This is not how someone thanks a devoted foster-mother or speaks of fulfilling a promise to a deceased friend.

Moreover, the sanitized story was contradicted all along by the attitude of Mrs. Moore's daughter. Instead of enjoying memories of her famous "foster brother," Maureen Moore Blake, Lady Dunbar of Hempriggs, detested the

---

[17] Roger Lancelyn Green and Walter Hooper, *C. S. Lewis: A Biography* (London: Collins, 1974) 66.

[18] Warren Lewis, *Letters of C. S. Lewis* (New York: Harcourt, Brace & World, 1966) 8.

[19] Warren Lewis, *Brothers and Friends*, 233.

[20] C. S. Lewis's last cousin, Ruth Hamilton Parker, died in Edinburgh on 4 December 1995, aged 95. She and her husband had lived in Holywood near Belfast, but as a widow she moved to Edinburgh to be near her daughter.

[21] Warren Lewis, *Brothers and Friends*, 264.

[22] C. S. Lewis, *Surprised by Joy*, 188.

subject. By her own account, she seldom looked back on her Oxford days or talked about them. She wouldn't answer questions. When she inherited the Kilns in 1973, she was intensely eager to sell it and put her life there farther behind her. In 1978 she curtly refused to take any part in the film *Through Joy and Beyond*. She told Hooper that she found the raking over of Jack's domestic history both embarrassing and distasteful. (She might have had a similar response to learn that her private letters to Hooper were available to everyone in the United States on microfilm from his collected papers at the University of North Carolina at Chapel Hill.)

I was publicly excoriated in 1988 for daring to claim in *The C. S. Lewis Hoax* that Lewis's relationship to Janie Moore was originally sexual.[23] But after Maureen Moore's death in 1997, her friend George Sayer revealed in the new paperback edition of his Lewis biography what she had indicated about the reality of the sexual relationship to him.[24]

Lewis stayed with Mrs. Moore and allowed himself no new romance so long as she lived, evidently as an extreme form of *noblesse oblige* after the end of his affair with her.[25] It was no misguided dedication to the memory of her son Paddy that bound him to the chaos of Mrs. Moore for over thirty years. In

---

[23] When asked about the idea at the 1995 summer workshop of the Southern California C. S. Lewis Society at Valyermo, Douglas Gresham replied "Hogwash!" in language so strong that *Lamppost* editor James Prothero had to resort to a euphemism to report it. Gresham cited Lewis's two-way promise to Paddy Moore and his honorable character.

[24] Maureen Moore died on 14 February 1997. The 1997 paperback edition of George Sayer's biography *Jack: A Life of C. S. Lewis* (Wheaton IL: Crossway, 1994) has a new introduction. It begins, "Eight years have passed since the first edition of this book was published. I have written this introduction to take into account some new information about C. S. Lewis that has come into my possession, and to refute certain false and misleading allegations that have been written about him."

"I have had to alter my opinion of Lewis's relationship with Mrs. Moore. In chapter eight of this book I wrote that I was uncertain about whether they were lovers. Now after conversations with Mrs. Moore's daughter, Maureen, and a consideration of the way in which their bedrooms were arranged at the Kilns, I am quite certain that they were."

[25] Roger Lancelyn Green mentioned in his essay ("In the Evening" in *C. S. Lewis at the Breakfast Table* [James Como, ed., New York: Macmillan, 1979] 212) that the unnamed daughter of the head of an unnamed Oxford College reportedly spoke of Lewis (occasion and decade unknown) as an awkward suitor. This allegation is so vague that it appears to be entirely insubstantial.

my opinion, he was living out Tennyson's description of Galahad in *The Idylls of the King*:

> His honour rooted in dishonour stood
> And faith unfaithful kept him falsely true

(This refers to Galahad honorably foregoing a love match with Elaine because of his disastrous love affair with Guinevere.)[26] Lewis quoted those two lines in *Arthurian Torso* in 1948, when he was still thrall to Mrs. Moore's needs and wants.

Ever since reading what struck me as Warren's discrete hints about Jack's domestic history,[27] I suspected that Lewis and Mrs. Moore first lived together as lovers.[28] But when I asked Hooper about it on 19 August 1971, he said that Warren would be horrified by my question. He pointed out that Mrs. Moore was about forty-seven when she and Lewis set up housekeeping. I backed off and began quietly accumulating evidence about their relationship as it became available. Meanwhile, Hooper fostered a legend about Lewis's virginity and lack of normal youthful heterosexuality that spread far and wide.

Realizing how dangerous this situation was for Lewis's reputation; I published my conclusions in 1988 in *The C. S. Lewis Hoax*, seventeen years after my inquiry to Hooper. I hoped to mitigate the damage to Lewis's name that was bound to occur when someone hostile to Lewis demolished the pious legend in order to defame him. Not surprisingly, I stood alone; no one publicly agreed with me. Two years later, in the very book that lampooned my *Hoax* scholarship, A. N. Wilson did just what I dreaded.

The very next year, in his introduction to *All My Road Before Me*, Hooper reversed himself completely and announced as if it were his own idea, "The notion of sexual intimacy between the two must be regarded as likely." In

---

[26] On 4 May 1915 Lewis began the first of what became a series of 27 letters to Arthur Greeves with "Dear Galahad." There is no record of what particular significance this nickname had to the two teenaged boys, but it may have had a sexual connotation.

[27] W. H. Lewis, *Letters of C. S. Lewis* (New York: Harcourt Brace and World, Inc., 1960) 12-13.

[28] See Appendix 3, "The Mistress of C. S. Lewis," by John Bremer.

1994 Humphrey Carpenter announced in *The Sunday Times* of London: "Certainly we know that, from his student days at Oxford until her death shortly before Joy Gresham came into his life, Lewis shared a home with Mrs. Janie Moore, the mother of a schoolfriend [sic] who had been killed in the World War One. Wilson produces convincing evidence that Lewis slept with her during the early years of their menage..."[29]

I couldn't help thinking of a certain observation made by William James: "Any new theory first is attacked as absurd; then it is admitted to be true, but obvious and insignificant; finally it seems to be important, so important that its adversaries claim that they themselves discovered it."[30]

The second major misrepresentation in the film is about the second woman who lived with C. S. Lewis, his wife Joy. She received only two minutes of attention. "It was in 1952 that Lewis first met Joy Davidman. She had ambitions as a writer and had long admired Lewis." In fact, she had more than ambitions as a writer; she had prizes and books to her credit.

The film goes on to say that Joy left her husband and two young sons behind in New York while she spent a year in England. Upon her return, the film says, her husband divorced her. More accurately, she left her husband and sons in the care of her cousin while she stayed in England for six months. C. S. Lewis advised her to divorce her husband, whom she described to him as unfaithful, alcoholic, and sometimes violent. She delayed filing, and her husband did it for her so he could marry his mistress, her cousin, as soon as possible.

The film claims that although Lewis married Joy, he never considered consummating the marriage. There is so much evidence to the contrary that this opinion is untenable. Both C. S. Lewis and Joy Lewis indicated that the marriage was consummated.[31] Douglas Gresham once commented, "I never

---

[29] Humphrey Carpenter, "Of more than academic interest," *The Sunday Times*, (27 February 1994) 9:2-4.

[30] In 1995 Oxford University Press published a scathing 24-page attack upon C. S. Lewis by someone named John Goldthwaite in a $30 book titled *The Natural History of Make-Believe: A Guide to the Principal Works of Britain, Europe, and America.* Among other false charges, Goldthwaite claims on page 232, "For the next thirty years of his life [Lewis] would live with [Mrs. Moore] secretly as a lover..."

[31] Joy described her married sex life to her brother, Howard Davidman, as explained in *And God Came In* by Lyle Dorsett. See also Chad Walsh's 13 February

got a doctor to do a medical examination on my mother to find out if the marriage was consummated. But knowing my mother...you can be sure it was."[32] (For more about the marriage, see Chapter 6.)

The treatment of Warren Lewis in this film is also unbalanced. "As for Warnie, he was fast sliding into serious alcoholism." It is true that Major Lewis was an alcoholic most of his adult life. But so little is said about him in the film that the additional statement "Much of the time Warnie was away—drunk—in Ireland" tips the scales too far. Not a word is said about Warren being a devout Christian, a successful author, and C. S. Lewis's personal secretary.[33]

Hooper tells about his own relationship to C. S. Lewis near the end of "The Informed Years": "In fact, I first met him early in 1963; and as we grew more intimate he asked me to become his companion-secretary and I moved here to the Kilns." But according to William Griffin's biography *Clive Staples Lewis: A Dramatic Life,* Hooper first met C. S. Lewis on 7 June 1963. And whatever Hooper means by "intimate," he had a room at Exeter College through the first week in August, spent the third week in Cambridge, and left England during the fourth week.[34]

The droll anecdotes that Hooper tells about himself and C. S. Lewis in the film take up about three minutes and give an excellent example of his skill as a winsome storyteller. He is a talented raconteur who radiates humility and cheer.

1978 letter to Walter Hooper in the Chapel Hill collection. C. S. Lewis indicated that the marriage was consummated in his 20 December 1961 letter to Dom Bede Griffiths.

[32] Douglas Gresham, "Video Interview, 4 June 1982," Marion E. Wade Center, 24-25.

[33] Warren Lewis was still functioning as Lewis's secretary in 1963 except for his sadly extended summer vacation in Ireland. On 12 May 1969 he looked back at his records and wrote to Hooper: "Your file number for 1963 was 63/358. Now assuming that Jack's correspondence was running at the average, this number would have come into use around the end of June; in other words, you were in touch with Jack *by letter* within five months of his death. In point of fact, so far from being here for a year, I am told on good authority that you were here for approximately the whole month of August, after which you returned to the States."

[34] Hooper's nights at the Kilns in August 1963 were so few that Leonard Miller was unaware of them. He wrote in a letter to me early in 1978, "Hooper never lived at the Kilns whilst C. S. Lewis was alive. During that period he lodged somewhere in Oxford. But I don't know where." (The place was Exeter College.)

In the summer of 1987 Hooper addressed a C. S. Lewis and G. K. Chesterton conference in Seattle, Washington, and received a standing ovation. Charles Wrong, a member of the audience who was once a student of Lewis's, wrote to me on 20 July 1987, "My two friends regard him as a kind of Tartuffe....I don't know what to think myself, and it's a mercy I'm not likely to be called on to make a judgment. His style as a speaker is enormously effective: self deprecating, soft-spoken, with a masterly light touch."

Walter Hooper had exercised this same storytelling skill before large audiences in his 1979 tour. Dr. W. R. Wortman of Baylor University recalls driving with friends and students to the 5 April presentation at McFarland Auditorium on the Southern Methodist University campus in Dallas:

> After the film, Reverend Walter Hooper invited the audience to participate in a question and answer session. There were microphones at the head of each of the several aisles. Members of the audience who wished to ask a question walked to the microphone in the nearest aisle and waited for a turn to address a question to Reverend Hooper on stage.
>
> One of my stalwart young men, when his turn came, asked about the "bonfire at which you discovered all those manuscripts." In midsentence and before his question could be completed, his microphone went dead. A muscular young man in black slacks and a black jersey stepped out from behind the curtain, arms folded across his chest, and announced that if questions could not be limited to the material in the film and the lecture for the evening, he would close the question and answer session. My student resumed his seat and the session continued.

It is clear that Hooper had the mistaken idea that people were conspiring to sabotage his film tour. By the end of the year he was confiding in Barbara Reynolds of Cambridge, who had just been named managing editor of the Wade Center's new Anglo-American literary journal, *Seven*. (The two editors under her at that time were Wheaton's Beatrice Batson and Clyde Kilby.) She first wrote to Hooper in October 1979, mentioning that she had recently seen all three reels of his film in Wheaton, Illinois.

On 13 November Hooper sent her a letter headed PRIVATE AND CONFIDENTIAL, which he promptly placed in his public collection in the library of the University of North Carolina at Chapel Hill. In that letter he told Dr. Reynolds that he wanted to protect her from possible hurt (presumably because she was obligated to deal with Kilby) but felt it was necessary to put before her "the salient facts" about Kilby. In 1965, he said, Kilby wrote to him demanding for Wheaton College the manuscripts that C. S. Lewis and Warren had given to Hooper. [35] In 1974 Kilby was infuriated when the Green/Hooper biography of Lewis was published; he told Barfield that he alone should write a biography of Lewis. He took some ladies from Wheaton to England and wrote letters to Lewis associates announcing that he was having to re-write the Green/Hooper biography. Many of those people sent Kilby's letters on to Hooper.

After that, according to Hooper, Kilby bombarded Owen Barfield for years with the demand that the Bodleian should "surrender" its Lewis collection to Wheaton College. Of course Barfield could not give the Bodleian collection to Kilby if he wanted to, but Kilby was unrelenting. Hooper suffered great pain for Kilby (presumably for his demented condition) and worried about the stress Kilby was causing Barfield.

Next, Hooper told Reynolds, one of Kilby's former pupils named Kathryn Lindskoog published a twenty-page article attacking him in *Christianity & Literature*. He and Barfield knew without doubt that Kilby supplied the "fuel" for Lindskoog's attack although he didn't write it for her. (I was never a pupil of Kilby's, never attended Wheaton College, didn't get my information from him, and meant my 1978 article as an inquiry, not an attack.)

Lindskoog made it clear to Gospel Films that if they tried to show *Through Joy and Beyond* in the United States she would do all she could to undermine it. She fulfilled her threat by calling newspapers all over the country with a set of questions designed to embarrass Hooper. Then she attacked Hooper in the *Los Angeles Times, Christian Century,* and other periodicals. In the mean-

---

[35] It is a fact that both Warren Lewis and Clyde Kilby suspected Hooper of appropriating or trying to appropriate some Lewis papers that Warren willed to the Wade Center. The records do not yet reveal whether or not Kilby ever contacted Hooper about missing Lewis papers in an attempt to secure them for the Wade Center.

time, Kilby was also behind Stephen Schofield's attacks upon Hooper in the *Canadian C. S. Lewis Journal*. (Needless to say, I was in no way opposed to Hooper's film tour, never contacted Gospel Films, and never contacted any newspapers. And I know for a fact that Kilby had nothing to do with Schofield's editorializing about Hooper.)

On 20 November Hooper wrote to Chad Walsh of Beloit College that I was trying to destroy his film tour, which had cost investors something like $300,000. In this account Hooper said that I had called newspapers around the country with questions for them to ask Hooper, and many of the reporters called Macmillan in New York to ask why they should do such a thing. Then I wrote to Barfield threatening to hold him responsible unless he denied having anything to do with Hooper saying in the film that Warren was an alcoholic. Hooper had no intention of answering any of my and Schofield's ravings. Clyde Kilby was behind it all. (Needless to say, I never called any newspapers, and I didn't write to Barfield about the film. Furthermore, it was Hooper who once told me to keep Warren's alcoholism secret, not vice versa. I have his letter.)

According to Hooper, Stephen Schofield was set on controversy with such a vengeance that one of Hooper's New York publishers was thinking of suing him. Schofield was doing all he could to undermine the authority of one of the trustees—Hooper. (In fact, Schofield was awkwardly but earnestly appealing to Hooper, not trying to undermine his authority.)[36]

---

[36] On 9 December 1977 Walter Hooper had written to me about allegedly bizarre behavior of Sheldon Vanauken, whose book *A Severe Mercy* was published in England in November. Hooper said that Vanauken became so angry about the estate for owning copyright on his letters from Lewis that Hooper thought he might be going soft in the head. Vanauken told Barfield that he intended to destroy Hooper. Vanauken claimed illogically that Lewis didn't want any of his writing copyrighted. In his long rage he wrote letters abusing Hooper to everyone he could think of, knowing that as a Christian Hooper would not retaliate. He blamed Hooper for copyright laws. Although Vanauken caused Hooper much heartache, Hooper gave him everything he wanted and more. Hooper hoped I would not be embarrassed that he shared this private hurt with me.

This account and similar accounts to Reynolds and Walsh about Kilby and me in Hooper's Chapel Hill collection, in addition to the Hooper/Como correspondence about Walsh, seem to show a pattern of perceived victimization (by enraged, mentally deranged adversaries) or else habitual victim impersonation.

On 22 December Chad Walsh sent Hooper a kind reply noting the psychological and sociological fact that literary executors are often distrusted and resented by research scholars. He said he didn't know me personally and was genuinely puzzled by the vehement way in which she was (reportedly) operating. But he was acquainted with Clyde Kilby and doubted that Kilby was providing fuel to attackers. He believed that Kilby would welcome any attempt at rapprochement.[37]

I had quietly attended Hooper's film presentation at the Pasadena Civic Auditorium in California on 12 March 1979. I was fascinated by the fact that on stage Hooper intentionally gave people the impression that he was a stranger here. He referred to his audience as "you Americans," acted bewildered by American geography, and marveled at the American love for gadgets like the "wireless." He even remarked about the American custom of taking showers. No one would have guessed that he had already visited California four years earlier or that he was thirty-two years old when he first visited England; most people assumed he was born there.[38]

Hooper began to seem English long before the film. In 1973 author Robert Ellwood, a professor of religion at the University of Southern California and an ordained Episcopal priest, was in England on a sabbatical and went with his wife Gracia Fay Ellwood, an author interested in Tolkien and Lewis, to meet the forty-two-year-old Walter Hooper. As she told me later, Hooper seemed uninformed about American education; therefore, Dr. Ellwood took much time to explain the American school system to him.[39] Hooper seemed to

---

[37] In February and March of 1977 Walter Hooper and James Como exchanged letters discussing allegedly erratic behavior of Chad Walsh. Como advised Hooper to prepare his ammunition for possible future use. These letters are in the Chapel Hill collection.

[38] Although many Americans assume that Hooper's strong British accent is appropriate for a resident of Oxford, there are others who claim that it is a uniquely contrived accent and not a natural linguistic blending.

[39] Ironically, Walter Hooper, a product of American public schools, professed ignorance of them in 1973; but Douglas Gresham, a product of English boarding schools, professed understanding of American schools in 1998. He said "If you do not get Christianity back into your universities, back into your primary schools, back into your secondary schools...[America] is doomed. Now you say 'the crisis in the [American] public school systems.' I say which one? The whole system is in crisis. It is imploding on itself" (from Douglas Gresham's lecture "C S Lewis and Contemporary

the Ellwoods to be interested and grateful. After they got back to the United States, they learned to their chagrin that Hooper was really as American as they were.[40]

Hooper obviously enjoys meeting people and enjoys drama. In 1991 he gently condoned in print personal misrepresentations and the leading of double lives: "None of us is either this or that; rather we and all 'ordinary' people we meet and know are many things at once, full of shading and nuance."[41]

Perhaps Hooper pretended to be English in order to be more like Lewis. Perhaps he pretended that Lewis never had sexual intercourse with Joy in order to qualify Lewis for sainthood. And perhaps Hooper pretended that Lewis didn't have wandering thoughts during church in order to make him even more saintly.

In the film *Through Joy and Beyond* Hooper slightly altered the origin of Lewis's *Screwtape Letters*. In the film, Hooper stands in Lewis's parish churchyard and declares, "It was here, following an 8 A.M. Communion service, that the book which brought him international fame was conceived. Writing to his brother Warren, he said, 'After the service was over, I was struck by an idea for a book.'"

But Lewis did not conceive of the book in the churchyard after the 8 A.M. service. In his letter to Warren he makes that quite clear. On that fateful Sunday he had gone to midday church service, and he wrote to Warren, "Before the service was over—one could wish these things came more seasonably—I was struck by an idea for a book."

Culture" at the University of Tennessee, at Chattanooga, 16 April 1998). Both Hooper and Gresham identify themselves as key managers of the Lewis literary estate.

[40] In 1989 Gracia Fay Ellwood reflected on this experience in *Mythlore 59*: "Is this incident so important? I don' t think it cancels out Walter's graciousness to us; but it leaves me feeling confused. How can a person be good to others and yet manipulate them at the same time? Is the confusion involved the same as that described by Scott Peck in his disturbing book *People of the Lie*?

"I don't know, but I believe that a willingness to deceive and manipulate is, except in life-threatening situations, a cause for tears. It means that the manipulator is profoundly crippled in his/her ability to love, to relate to others 'not as a means only, but always as an end also.' This latter is the kind of emotional discipline in relationships that Lewis valued, and for good reason."

[41] Walter Hooper, "Introduction," *All My Road Before Me* (San Diego: Harcourt Brace Jovanovich, 1991) 9.

It is a minor change, but minor changes add up.[42]

The Screwtape Letters received much attention in *Through Joy and Beyond,* and the special edition produced by Lord and King was displayed in the film itself, and then sold in the lobby after the seminar. An order blank for the Lord and King version accompanied the film when it was rented, and that version was distributed nationwide in bookstores. But some of it is not what Lewis really wrote. That is the subject of chapter 5.

I don't want to tell you any half-truths unless they are completely accurate.

—*Boxing manager Dennis Rappaport*

---

[42] Strange as it seems, in 1979 Hooper gave a contrasting account in his essay on the flap of the dustjacket of the gift edition of *Screwtape* published by Collins and illustrated by Papas. There he said, "In fact the idea of the book came to C. S. Lewis while taking Communion in his parish church in Headington Quarry, Oxford, on 14 July 1940. Writing to his brother a few days after..." But the letter to his brother was completed on the very day of the church service, 21 July, and Lewis does not say that the idea came to him while he was in the act of taking Communion. Some of Hooper's confusing inaccuracies like this are probably due to misreadings and carelessness rather than serving a purpose.

5

STRANGE VISIONS AND REVISIONS

NOT REAL RHYMES OR REASONS
AFTER ALL?

Ever since C. S. Lewis's death, strange things have been happening to his books. Although it began earlier, the strangeness first became clear in the Lord and King edition of *The Screwtape Letters*. *The Screwtape Letters* was Hooper's third foray into Screwtape territory.

His first foray was writing and publishing an unfortunate Screwtape letter of his own.[1] His second foray was his description of *The Screwtape Letters* in *C. S. Lewis: A Biography* (1974); there Hooper claimed that C. S. Lewis got his idea for *Screwtape* after the 8 A.M. communion he attended on 15 July 1940. That timing is wrong in four ways; it is the wrong week, the wrong day of the week (15 July was a Monday), the wrong time of day, and the wrong location. Inaccuracies like this are regrettable, but understandable;

---

[1] Hooper's first known foray into Screwtape territory apparently took place during his 1965-1967 tenure as college chaplain at Wadham College. He wrote a Screwtape letter and published it under the title "Hell and Immortality" in an undated periodical called *Breakthrough*. (A copy exists in the Wade Center.) Screwtape complains about a wise college chaplain (apparently Hooper) who praises alcohol and is "quite amused when, on Sunday mornings, he sees little puddles of vomit scattered here and there, tokens of Freshmen who overdrank the night before." The chaplain's good spirit frustrates Screwtape. Then Screwtape gloats about "the Cult of the Anti-Hero." "There is a long, long descent from a knight in shining armour to the feckless anti-hero squeezing pimples in front of a looking-glass."

to err is human.[2] In his special Lord and King edition, however, Hooper switched the birth of Lewis's *Screwtape* idea from 15 July to 14 July (although in his letter Lewis said he stayed home with the flu that Sunday), and moved the whole story from England to the United States!

The Devil In the Details

Hooper's introduction to that 1976 edition of *The Screwtape Letters* states mysteriously that "some papers" recently "came to light" which tell how Lewis got the idea for the book. As a matter of fact, Warren Lewis willed all his letters and papers to the Marion E. Wade Center for research purposes, and the Wade Center gave copies to the Bodleian Library in Oxford. This is how the "papers came to light"—as an intentional gift to the public from Warren Lewis. Sometimes simple facts seem mysterious because they are dramatized, and great mysteries are glossed over as if they were simple facts.

Unfortunately, mystification about the letter's coming to light and confusion about what the letter says are the least of the problems in this edition. And this edition came out in six different forms at once: (1) a $40 autographed book (not autographed by Lewis, of course), advertised as bound in real leather; (2) a $15 hardback book; (3) a large $5 paperback book; (4) a small $1.75 paperback book (later $3.50 from Spire); (5) a $25 phonograph album; (6) a $50 album of six cassette tapes.

The surprising thing about all six products is that they appear to offer *The Screwtape Letters* as Lewis wrote it. There is no warning on the covers or title pages that some of Lewis's words (and meanings) have been changed. In the small paperback, the most popular of the items, readers have to read more than eight solid pages of introduction before they get to the key fact buried in the middle of a paragraph on the ninth page, that Walter Hooper and Owen Barfield have allowed "slight alterations" in the text.

Few readers will take time to read the entire introduction in the first place, and those who do won't know the audacity of the changes that have

---

[2] The confusion that began with these inaccuracies persists into the 21st century. Not one biography or study of Lewis includes the correct date; they vary from 14 July (Griffin), and 20 July (Glover) to autumn 1942 (Glaspey). In 2000 dramatist David Payne announced in conjuction with his Screwtape-based play that the idea came to Lewis in 1940 on 30 July.

been made. (To add to the confusion, in 1982 Macmillan brought out a new edition of *The Screwtape Letters* that states boldly on the cover "Revised Edition"—and it is not revised at all. It is in Lewis's own words throughout.)

The most wrenching change in the Lord and King version is that World War II bombing was moved from England to the United States. The British Museum is changed to the Metropolitan Library. German leaders are changed to Enemy leaders;[3] but because in this book the term "Enemy" stands for God, this means that German leaders have been turned into God's leaders.

In Letter Eleven the attitude of "the English" to humor is changed to the attitude of "the modern generation." The verb "twits" is changed to "kids," and "a comical fellow" is changed to "a comic." "English" seriousness about humor is changed to "modern" seriousness about humor—a purported trend that Lewis himself never noted. Television is brought in.

In Letter Sixteen Lewis's reference to Jacques Maritain is replaced by a reference to none other than C. S. Lewis himself. The French Roman Catholic philosopher might be surprised to see himself turned into Lewis, but surely Lewis's amazement would be greater. (In the 1930s Lewis said of Maritain and T. S. Eliot, that there was no sector of religious opinion with which he felt less sympathy.) Popping C. S. Lewis into his own book is a bit of drollery that reminds me of his uncomfortable presence in *The Dark Tower*.

In Letter Seventeen the English are changed into Americans, thus indicating that Lewis thought Americans were especially given to the theory that vigorous athletic activity contributes to chastity.

Lord and King Associates copyrighted these changes in the text in 1976, and "no part thereof may be reproduced or transmitted in any form, or by any means, electronic or mechanical." Thank goodness.[4]

Hooper ended his nine-page introduction to this edition of *The Screwtape Letters* with a humble anecdote about finding C. S. Lewis up to his elbows in soap suds after dinner on 7 August 1963—when in fact Lewis was an invalid

---

[3]C. S. Lewis, *The Screwtape Letters* (West Chicago: Lord and King Associates, 1976) 22, 42.

[4] Incredible as it seems, becausee of an oversight *The Screwtape Letters* was not copyrighted In the United States for 35 years or more. If people had realized that, they could have brought out any number of editions as alternatives to the Macmillan edition. According to a 26 May 1989 letter from Hooper to a representative of the Portland C. S. Lewis Society, the Estate did not discover the oversight until 1977.

who had just got home from the hospital.[5] On 10 August Lewis was still too weak to write a letter or to receive guests. It is hard to imagine Lewis washing the dishes in such condition and laughing to Hooper, "If ever you tell what it is like in this house, you must say that not only are the servants soft underfoot but *invisible* as well."

Actually, Lewis had used the term "soft underfoot" in *The Screwtape Letters,* and it referred to the soft path that leads to destruction.[6] Would word master Lewis, loving people as he did, describe servants (invisible or not) as soft underfoot, like carpeting? And since he had a gardener, housekeeper, and live-in nurse at that time, the claim to no servants makes no sense. However, Hooper seems to charm most readers with this tale. Who wouldn't like to be part of the happy camaraderie that he describes?

Some recent editions of *The Screwtape Letters* have included Lewis's 1959 *Saturday Evening Post* essay "Screwtape Proposes a Toast," his only other writing about this literally infernal bureaucrat and the lowerarchy he is a part of. In its 1982 edition Macmillan added a censorious preface before the *Saturday Evening Post* essay, and an enigmatic note before that censorious preface. The note reads: "This criticism of American education was written in 1962 as a preface to a collection of which the 'Toast' was to be the title essay.[7] After Lewis died, his publisher gave the book a new form, one result of

---

[5] C. S. Lewis, *Letters to an American Lady* (Grand Rapids MI: Wm. B. Eerdmans Publishing Co., 1967) 120-22.

[6] Lewis's words at the end of Letter XII, on page 61 of the original Macmillan edition: "Indeed the safest road to Hell is the gradual one—the gentle slope, soft underfoot."

[7] In my opinion, Walter Hooper wrote this attack upon American schools. Douglas Gresham, who insists that there are no Lewis forgeries, has launched his own attack on American schools, and broadened it to all schools. "And all of the very best balanced, emotionally adjusted, best socially interactive, best educated children I have ever met have been home schooled.... Now as a psychotherapist [an unexplained designation] dealing with post-child-abuse trauma, I can tell you that one of the reasons they are so brilliant, these children, is that they get the one-on-one parent-child relationship which is so essential to the health and welfare of a child. The idea of putting your children in school...I don't care *what* the financial necessities are, that is the abuse of that child's potential and the abuse of that child's psychology. In the First World War the soldiers went to the battlefield and lived there for months, sometimes (if they survived) for years—in the blood-soaked mud, up to their necks sometimes, rats, mice, all those horrible things. And yet Jack regarded that as not the worst experience of his life; his school days, he thought, were even worse."(From Douglas

which was that Lewis's preface was lost. Now recovered, it is published here for the first time."

Readers gather that the preface was lost for twenty years. But according to records in the Bodleian Library, it seems that a typescript of this preface first appeared in the files of the intended publisher, the Geoffrey Bles company, in 1965 rather than 1962 (two years after Lewis's death rather than one year before) and stayed there, unused. According to Mary Clapinson of the Bodleian, Walter Hooper donated two typescripts of the "Toast" preface to the Bodleian in 1974.[8] (That is also the year when Hooper showed typescripts of *The Dark Tower* to several friends.) About six years later, circa 1980, Hooper deposited a more valuable handwritten copy of the "Toast" preface in the Bodleian (Dep. c. 764).[9] (That is also when Hooper deposited his valuable handwritten copy of *The Dark Tower* in the Bodleian.) By depositing the handwritten "Toast" preface rather than donating it, Hooper retained ownership, control, and exclusive access to that manuscript.

There are several impediments to assuming that the "Toast" preface is genuine. First, it seems unlike Lewis to belabor a three-year-old, nineteen-page satirical essay with a two-page preface explaining the satire. Second, the preface is inferior writing. Third, it is not like Lewis to insult his "duller" readers as he does here. Fourth, there is a resentful anti-American spirit in this preface far beyond Lewis at his prickliest. Fifth, in 1962 the antipathy for weak students would have hurt one of Lewis's stepsons, then a weak student.

In context the following phrases in the "Toast" preface don't sound like Lewis: (1) "without distinction of sex, colour, class, race or religion," (2) "a factitious egalitarianism," (3) "They [idlers and dunces] can punch [a dilligent student's] head and kick [his] stern," (4) "I had to face a tactical difficulty," (5) "I resorted to a further level of irony."

Furthermore, the writer's illogical handling of the word *democractic* in the "Toast" preface is the opposite of Lewis's handling of the word *democracy* in "Screwtape Proposes a Toast."[10]

Gresham's lecture "C S Lewis and Contemporary Culture" at the University of Tennessee, at Chattanooga, 16 April 1998).

[8]Dep. c. 775, fols. 298-309.

[9] Letter from Clapinson to Lindskoog, 29 March 1990.

[10] In "Screwtape Proposes a Toast," as first published in *The World's Last Night* in 1960, C. S. Lewis highlights the word *democracy* with quotation marks (later

If this muddle-headed preface (written to explain a clear essay) turns out to be a literary forgery, as I think it is, then the handwritten manuscript placed in the Bodleian, circa 1980, is a document forgery.

Walter Hooper's friend William Griffin published a continuation of *The Screwtape Letters* in 1989.[11] How is it, readers may wonder, that Griffin could publish a sequel to *The Screwtape Letters* for his own profit, when a nun was not allowed to publish a sequel to *The Last Battle* for charity?[12] (On 30 December 1950 Lewis wrote to an earlier nun, Sister Penelope, regarding sequels to *Screwtape* by other people. In his opinion a literary idea ought to belong to anyone who can use it, and literary property is a sort of simony. He thought his publisher might agree to such a project if proper acknowledgments were included.)

According to California screenwriter Randy Argue (and Walter Hooper), Lewis or his publisher sold the *Screwtape Letters* screen rights to 20th Century

---

publishers have used italics for the same purpose). Lewis explains that he is using the word there in its incantatory (catchword) sense rather than its true sense. In contrast, the author of the "Toast" preface uses *democratic* first in its true sense without quotation marks, and a second time with quotation marks followed by this explanation: "in the true sense." The latter is self-contradictory and also the opposite of Lewis's reasoning.

[11]"As tantalizing as *The Screwtape Letters*" is the cover promise on Griffin's *The Fleetwood Correspondence* (Doubleday, 1989, $15.95). This is a series of contemporary letters from a demon nephew who moved from London to New York to continue his work. Griffin notes in his preface, "The typescript reads as though it might have been written by Lewis himself...The two works *[Fleetwood* and *Screwtape]* have a remarkable resemblance." The book begins, "Most fetid Uncle, What the devil are you doing at Dimchurch? I just found your address in the *Directoire Internationale Diabolique,* in the red pages, no less!"

On page 140 a Christian advises his female friend, "First of all, if you want to sleep around, then do it, but not because some Harris Tweeded-dum or Harris Tweeded-dee pressures you to. Do it because you want to, and do it with someone you like. Second, don't do it even with him. There's this little commandment in Genesis..." (Griffin confuses Genesis with Exodus.) On page 148: "Desire streamed through their veins and arteries. They embraced, and the amatory adventure once begun would have continued if they hadn't heard a nervous cough." Needless to say, this prose is nothing like Lewis's.

[12] See the account of *The Centaur's Cavern* in Chapter 1. Richard Purtill has published a continuation of the Lewis fragment "After Ten Years" (located in *Of Other Worlds* and the *Dark Tower* collection titled *The Mirror of Helen* (New York: Daw Books, Inc., 1983).

Fox about fifty years ago, and Argue eventually obtained them. His fondest wish is to obtain actors of the stature of Anthony Hopkins for his imaginative adaptation of the story, but according to Walter Hooper, lawyers of the Lewis Estate hoped to invalidate the contract.

In 1994 the Lewis Estate allowed the Thomas Nelson company, in conjunction with Marvel Comics, to publish a new $9.99 adaptation of *The Screwtape Letters* that is "even more exciting to read." According to the promotion, "None of Lewis' poignant wisdom or wit is lost as his words are transformed into striking, detailed comic book drawings." In fact, however, this is a faithfully condensed and gaudily illustrated 96-page edition of Lewis's story, not a comic-strip adaptation.[13]

Introductions All Around

The Screwtape Letters is the ninth of twenty-seven books by C. S. Lewis with introductions by Walter Hooper at this counting.[14] Most of Hooper's introductions have a personal touch. Here is the tally at present, with brief excerpts.

1. *Poems*, 1964. Seven-page introduction. "When I was his secretary, he sometimes used to dictate poems. Even after he thought one was completed, he might suggest a change here. Then a change there."

2. *Of Other Worlds*, 1966. Six-page introduction. "At that moment I was pouring tea into a very large Cornish-ware cup..."

3. *Studies in Medieval and Renaissance Literature*, 1966. Four-page introduction. "'I have all seven volumes', I said. 'Have you?' he asked, his eyes twinkling. 'Yes,' I said, 'Would you like them?' There was a very long pause.

---

[13] The copyright information on this book does not mention the Lewis Estate or Macmillan, which gives the impression that the text was in the public domain.

[14] "Everything in the introductions is absolutely accurate and correct, and there is no controversy over here," Walter Hooper as quoted by journalist K. L. Billingsley in "The Highjacking of C. S. Lewis" in the October 1994 issue of *Heterodoxy*. "'Hooper's introductions have amused me for some time,' said Sheldon Vanauken, an old friend of Lewis's and author of *A Severe Mercy*. There couldn't possibly have been that many special moments between the two men.'"

'After what I have just said,' he fumbled, 'would you—*could* you part with them?'" [15]

4. *Christian Reflections,* 1967. Eight-page introduction. "I remember one very warm day when Lewis and I were reading in his study that I remarked, rather too loudly, 'Whew! It's hot as hell!'"

5. *Narrative Poems,* 1969. Eight-page introduction. "As far as I know, the only manuscript of *Dymer* to escape being burnt consists of eighty-six pages of rough draft...which were written in one of Lewis's notebooks now in my possession." [16]

6. *Selected Literary Essays,* 1969. Fourteen-page introduction. "I inherited from Lewis's library most of the texts he used while reading Greats and English."

7. *God in the Dock* 1970. Eleven-page introduction. "One day he and I were wondering what would happen if a group of friendly and inquisitive Martians suddenly appeared in the middle of Oxford...On the whole, we doubted whether the Martians would take back to their world much that is worth having."

8. *Fern-seed and Elephants,* 1975. Three-page introduction. "Professor Tolkien once teased me about C. S. Lewis...He had in his hands at that moment the seventh volume of Lewis's writings which I had edited."

9. *The Screwtape Letters,* 1976. Nine-page introduction. "When invited to write a preface for this special edition of *Screwtape* my mind was carried back to the inexpressibly happy period that I spent as C. S. Lewis's secretary."

10. *The Dark Tower,* 1977. Eleven-page introduction. "There were so many that it took all my strength and energy to carry them back to Keble College. That evening, while glancing through them, I came across a manuscript which excited me very much."

---

[15] Hooper says he enjoyed seeing his seven-volume *Vulgate Version of the Arthurian Romances* on Lewis's shelves. He does not say when he could have seen it there.

[16] Hooper ends his May 1969 Preface with this tribute: "It is a pleasure to name publicly my friends Dr and Mrs Farrer, Mr Roger Lancelyn Green, Mr Owen Barfield, Professor John Lawlor, and Mr Spuros Sitaridis, who, by their encouragement and wise advice, helped me in editing these poems." The first five are all recognized Lewis authorities. Is Mr Sitaridis the young Greek friend mentioned by Warren ("I've been thinking over the problem of your Greek friend...") on 13 December 1969, and by Pauline Baynes on 18 January 1970, in letters in the Chapel Hill collection?

11. *They Stand Together*, 1979. Thirty-seven-page introduction. "Meanwhile, Lewis and I became more intimate, and finally he asked me to become his companion-secretary and I moved into his house."

12. *The Weight of Glory*, 1980. Sixteen-page introduction. "'Informer!' roared Lewis. 'I have what no friend ever had before. I have a private traitor, my very own personal Benedict Arnold. Repent before it is too late!' I loved all the rough and tumble of this, and I fancy I pulled his leg about as often as he pulled mine."[17]

13. *Mere Christianity*, 1981. Twenty-eight-page introduction. "I learned of it when I became, near the end of his life, Lewis's private secretary."

14. *On Stories and Other Essays*, 1982. Thirteen-page introduction. "Best of all was the day when Mr. Fleming and I sat in the drawing room of the Athenæum Club in London [Owen Barfield's exclusive club, which Walter Hooper had joined], reading the original manuscript—which Lewis had given him."

15. *The Business of Heaven*, 1984. Seven-page introduction. "You will find that I hammer away pretty hard with passages about morality."

16. *Spirits in Bondage*, 1984. Twenty-eight-page introduction. "It was while I was his private secretary in the last months of his life that the curtain was lifted just a little."

17. *Boxen*, 1985. Fifteen-page introduction. "I first read the Boxen 'novels' during that part of 1963 when I was Jack's secretary and living in his home in Oxford. When he discovered how charmed I was..."

18. *First and Second Things*, 1985. Six-page introduction. "I think it was because Lewis thought I was planning to ask him the same question (I was) that he said to me, 'What would you do if you were shut up in a castle with a liberal theologian eager to explain away the Resurrection, the Incarnation, and the Virgin Birth?' 'I'm sure,' I replied, 'that I would go mad.'"

19. *Present Concerns*, 1987. Five-page introduction. "'Who is Elizabeth Taylor?' asked C. S. Lewis. He and I were talking about the difference between 'prettiness' and 'beauty', and I suggested that Miss Taylor was a great

---

[17] It is highly unlikely that Lewis somehow dipped into details of American history and used the name Benedict Arnold to signify a prototypical traitor; from the British point of view, Arnold was a patriot. Lewis would have referred instead to the notorious Second World War traitor Quisling. This troublesome transatlantic detail casts some doubt on the entire anecdote.

beauty. 'If you read the newspapers,' I said to Lewis, 'you would know who she is.'"

20. *Timeless at Heart*, 1987. Five-page introduction. "During the time I was a member of Lewis's household we discussed both the 'Critique' and the 'Rejoinder'. This led us to consider Our Lord's command..."

21. *Letters of C. S. Lewis*, 1988. Ten-page introduction. "I had been working on these letters for four months when I reached the inauspicious day of Friday, 13 November 1987. The realization of just how many changes I was having to make caused me to imagine Warnie looming behind me, much annoyed. I felt so uncomfortable about what I was doing that I wrote to George Sayer, asking for advice. What helped as much as anything was a conversation I had that evening with Father John Tolkien." (Before Hooper signs off with his name on page 19, he has referred to himself with personal pronouns one hundred and fourteen times on ten pages.)

22. *Christian Reunion*, 1990. Eight-page introduction. "I think the appeal must have been very strong, for this division is one of the few subjects Lewis never chose to write or talk about. Thus far I have found no one who remembers it, and I can't help but suppose that the essay is being published here for the first time."

23. *All My Road before Me*, 1991. Eleven-page introduction. "Another source is a notebook Warren Lewis gave me in 1964 and which contains, amongst other things, the original of Lewis's diary for the period 27 April 1926—2 March 1927."

24. *C. S. Lewis: Readings for Meditation and Reflection*, 1992. Nine-page introduction. "In 1956 Lewis married [Joy] in the Registry office to prevent her extradition."[18]

25. *The Collected Poems of C. S. Lewis*, 1994. Ten page-introduction. "My sincere thanks to Owen Barfield for all the help he has given me over these last thirty years."

26. *Una Gioia Insolita (A Rare Joy: Letters between a catholic piest and an anglican layman*, published in Italian by Jaca Books in Milan, 1995).[19]

---

[18] A puzzling and evidently erroneous claim. United States authorities were not seeking to arrest and prosecute Joy.

[19] This is an Italian edition of Lewis's letters to an Italian priest that were written in Latin. The English edition of these letters is *Letters, C. S. Lewis, Don Giovanni Calabria: A Study in Friendship* (Ann Arbor MI: Servant Books, 1988).

Four-page introduction. "If I had not known who the authors were, I could have believed that this was the correspondence between two of the Apostles."

27. *C. S. Lewis: Collected Letters, Volume I*, 2000. Five-page introduction. "When Lewis dictated letters to me, he always had me read them aloud afterwards."

Altogether, these twenty-seven C. S. Lewis books contain 308 pages by Walter Hooper, enough to fill a separate book. Surely C. S. Lewis would be amazed to see so much by another person between his own book covers, especially if Lewis never considered Hooper his permanent secretary after all.

In 1982 the production of Lewis books came to the point where Hooper saw fit to place his own dedication at the front of one, *On Stories and Other Essays:*

> To Priscilla Collins this collection of Lewis essays is dedicated by the Trustees of his Estate in token of their respect and admiration, and in gratitude for the unfailing support they have enjoyed from her in the endeavor to fulfill that trust in a manner worthy of its object.
>> Owen Barfield
>> Walter Hooper

Collins is a giant publishing conglomerate that bought the Geoffrey Bles company long ago, thus acquiring most of Lewis's books and making Priscilla Collins Lewis's primary publisher until her retirement. Collins is now HarperCollins, owned by Australian publishing baron Rupert Murdoch. But the rights to a few of Lewis's books are still elsewhere.

Strange Editing

U. S. rights to *The Pilgrim's Regress* are owned by the William B. Eerdmans Publishing Company, which sold reprint rights to Bantam Books. In 1981 Bantam published a mass paperback with explanatory notes by Dr. John C. Traupman.[20] Of all the hundreds of things that readers need to be

---

[20] John C. Traupman, Ph. D., ed., *The New College Latin and English Dictionary*, also by Bantam. Dr. Traupman was chair of the department of Classical Languages at Saint Joseph's University, Philadelphia.

told in order to get more out of *The Pilgrim's Regress* (because, as Lewis was quick to admit, he wrote it for a small circle of "highbrow" readers), Dr. Traupman chose thirty phrases to identify in his endnotes. Of those thirty, his explanation of nineteen of the phrases is "Source unknown."

For "The fool hath said...[in his heart there is no God]" Traupman's note is simply "Source unknown."[21] But for "The sin of Adam" he tried to be more helpful. He told the readers, "Source unknown. Lord Byron refers to an Ada."

Some of the harshest words Lewis ever wrote were about publishers. But ridiculous footnotes might not irritate him so much as changes or deletions in what he wrote. "The Humanitarian Theory of Punishment" was published in its entirety in the Australian publication *Twentieth Century*, but when Hooper included it in *God in the Dock* he cut off the final paragraph. There Lewis stated that in 1948 he couldn't get the essay published in England:

> One last word. You may ask why I send this to an Australian periodical. The reason is simple and perhaps worth recording: I can get *no hearing* [italics added] for it in England.

This bit of social history is particularly interesting now that Lewis's views on the topic are less politically incorrect than they were in 1948. But its deletion is a minor matter in comparison to other editorial liberties that Hooper has taken.

Counter to Lewis's wishes, for thirty-five years many of his letters have had *no hearing* because the estate routinely refuses to allow recipients, researchers, and writers to publish them.[22] Publishing privilege was being reserved for Walter Hooper, who said once that his future collection, *C. S. Lewis: Collected Letters*, might run to six volumes. Some eager readers optimistically envisioned six large volumes including all of Lewis's hitherto

---

[21] Psalm 53:1.

[22] The owner of a physical letter can do anything he wants with it (display it, describe it, sell it, destroy it), but he cannot publish it without permission so long as the writer or the writer's estate exercises copyright. If a petitioner is especially favored by Lewis Estate personnel, permission is granted. Thus in 1981 Richard Purtill was granted the use of fifteen previously unpublished letters in *C. S. Lewis's Case for the Christian Faith*.

unpublished letters that are known, and those in their entirety. Later, Hooper revealed that all the available letters would fill seven or eight volumes, but that C. S. Lewis Pte decided to publish only three. (This would be fewer than half the available letters.) The decisions about what to include and exclude are his.

Hooper has been restricting public access to the letters since 1967 or earlier.[23] This is regrettable, because in 1962 Lewis evidently thought that after his death readers might profit from publication of his pastoral letters to friends and strangers.[24] Withholding spiritual advice from an entire generation or two for commercial reasons could be considered simony.

One of the briefest Lewis letters to an inquirer that I've seen is this gem he sent to Corbin Scott Carnell in 1953: "Your letter finds me in the midst of exams and a complete reply is impossible now. If you are losing your faith in reason, why did you use all those reasons to tell me so?"

Fortunately, Sheldon Vanauken asked for and received Lewis's permission to use three of his letters in a booklet called "Encounter with Light," which was published by Intervarsity Press. That made Vanauken their copyright owner; but because he felt that it is wrong to own such a copyright and limit public access to Lewis's letters, he put the three into the public domain. (Read them in Appendix 12.)

It is not only spiritual advice that has been withheld. In 1978 I published a Christian education kit for young adults called *Voyage to Narnia,* and in the illustrated student response booklet I innocently included my first letter to Lewis[25] with a photocopy of his handwritten two-sentence reply. Because I

---

[23] See Roger Lancelyn Green's 13 April 1967 letter to Hooper in the Chapel Hill Collection.

[24] Walter Hooper, "Introduction," *Letters of C. S. Lewis* (London: Collins, 1988) 15.

[25] This is the letter I sent from Redlands, California, on 13 April 1956:
Dear Mr. Lewis,

I am a senior at the University of Redlands, a small college in Southern California. This year I have taken on some independent study in the field of English. For my subject I chose some of your books. My final paper is on your Narnian series and its theological significance. I can't tell you how much I have enjoyed this whole experience. I am hoping to continue the study of your writing when I eventually compose the thesis for my Master of Arts degree.

included his note, the copyright holders forced my publisher, the David C. Cook Company, to destroy 10,000 copies of the kit, each of which included an extremely handsome full-color poster; a large, beautiful full-color map of Narnia; and an eloquent tape recording of many memories of Lewis from his car-hire driver Clifford Morris.[26]

By the end of the century Hooper's six volumes of letters had been reduced to three, and in 2000 the first of the three was finally published. It consists of selections from 1905 to 1931, including some to Owen Barfield and other friends Lewis met at Oxford. Most of the letters, however, were written to Lewis's father, Albert; his brother, Warren Lewis; and his friend from boyhood, Arthur Greeves. Lewis's letters to Greeves already filled an entire book titled *They Stand Together*, and so their republication in this collection precludes first-time publication of many other letters that could have been chosen. Making as many Lewis letters available as possible is obviously not the highest priority of those in charge.

It will be interesting to see if Hooper includes any of Lewis's letters to Sheldon Vanauken in Volume Three of *C. S. Lewis: Collected Letters*. Vanauken was conspicuous by his absence in Hooper's mammoth *C. S. Lewis, Companion and Guide*, which included some people of far less importance to Lewis. Vanauken is unpopular with the Lewis Estate. In his session at Mattson's Summer Institute in 1998, Douglas Gresham referred to Vanauken as one of the people who came "out of the woodwork" after C. S. Lewis died and exaggerated their relationship with Lewis. When asked whether Hooper

---

I have recently prepared a brief introductory article about you and your writing for *HIS* Magazine, the Inter-Varsity Christian Fellowship publication. It is scheduled to appear next fall.

As you can tell, I am extremely interested in your work. I have just been granted a scholarship to a summer session at the University of London. In thinking about a visit to England, one of my first hopes was that I might meet you or hear you speak while I am there.

My course will last from July 9 to August 17. Will your summer plans enable me to see you then?

[26] Clifford Morris had originally presented his memories of Lewis on Oxford BBC Radio. He entrusted his only copy of that reel-to-reel recording to me on 27 December 1975, and on 29 October 1976 he sent me written permission to distribute cassette copies and to publish the transcribed text in *His* Magazine. I have now placed a copy of the cassette with John West for distribution with tapes from Seattle Pacific University's summer C.S. Lewis Institutes.

exaggerated his relationship with Lewis, Gresham said that he isn't sure that Hooper did exaggerate; perhaps it was just his publishers.

It will also be interesting to see if Hooper includes any of Lewis's seventeen letters to Clyde Kilby. But it will be especially interesting to see if he includes all of his own letters from Lewis, since they contradict some of his claims.

And it will be interesting to see if Hooper includes in Volume Three Lewis's complete December 1961 letter to Dom Bede Griffiths. As published in Warren's 1966 edition of Lewis's letters, the tender sentence is missing that proves that Lewis's marriage was consummated sexually.[27] When Hooper expanded and corrected the book in 1996, he had a chance to restore that crucially important detail; but he did not. Now he will have a second and final chance. (Hooper made the consummation of the marriage an issue by bringing it up decade after decade; see his essay "C. S. Lewis and C. S. Lewises".[28]

While postponing *C. S. Lewis: Collected Letters* Hooper revised Warren's 1966 book *Letters of C. S. Lewis*. Warren was upset because publisher Jocelyn Gibb ruthlessly shrank that book, and all the boyhood letters were cut out.[29] Fortunately, Warren could not foresee that in 2000 Hooper, his nemesis, would enjoy the privilege arrogantly denied to him, that of presenting Lewis's

---

[27] There is no way to tell if the crucial sentence was dropped by Warren himself or by the heavy-handed Jocelyn Gibb—or by Gibb in cooperation with Hooper.

[28] *G. K. Chesterton and C. S. Lewis: The Riddle of Joy.*

[29] In his 13 July 1967 letter to me, Warren said, "As regards the length of the book, don't blame me, but the publisher who for commercial reasons cut out all the material I had supplied for the first fifteen years of my brother's life—a mistake, I thought, for when I read a book of this sort it is the childhood and boyish years which always seem to me the most interesting."
There is no way to tell if Jocelyn Gibb was influenced by Walter Hooper when he made his draconian cuts in Warren's collected Lewis letters, but Hooper had established a friendly relationship with Gibb in the summer of 1963. Gibb organized and produced *Light on C. S. Lewis* in 1965, using Hooper as one of seven contributors. On the back of the American edition Hooper is identified as an American who met Lewis ten years earlier and lived with the two Lewis brothers as Lewis's secretary. In May 1969 Gibb assured the editor of the *Times* that these claims of Hooper's were true. Gibb also published the Green/Hooper biography of Lewis in 1974, including Hooper's false claims about his relationship to Lewis.

boyhood letters to the public. Worse yet, in his 1988 revision of Warren's Lewis letters collection Hooper would add a new introduction belittling Warren for alcoholism and editorial incompetence. And in a long footnote on pages 400-401, Hooper would condemn Warren's alcoholism again.[30] (The additional letters, explanatory notes, and index in Hooper's version are, of course, most welcome.)

Hooper regales readers with how Warren mishandled Lewis's letters, and he claims that he found and corrected several hundred inaccuracies in the first twelve pages. But readers who compare the two editions won't find anything like several hundred corrections on the first twelve pages. And sometimes the corrector needs correcting.

For example, Hooper repeats an error on page 439, in Lewis's helpful letter about prayer dated 31 July 1954. Lewis wrote the letter to a Presbyterian minister named F. Morgan Roberts on 30 July 1954; but it appeared in Warren's book with the date slightly wrong and the name changed to Mrs. Ursula Roberts. In 1980 Morgan Roberts sent photocopies of Lewis's letter and envelope to the *Canadian C. S. Lewis Journal* to set the record straight. Editor Schofield submitted them to Hooper, explaining the situation and expecting permission to publish them; but on 3 September 1980 Hooper refused. "The Trustees are bound to protect this property..." Then in his 1988 revision of Warren's book, he retained the name Ursula.

Hooper's introduction explains why he felt compelled to laboriously correct Warren's version of the book: "Both [Collins and the Lewis Estate] felt that it would be dishonest to advertise as Lewis's ...anything other than what he actually wrote..."[31] Some people approve the broadest standards of editorial privilege, Hooper says, but he observes strict, narrow standards.[32]

---

[30] Hooper's overly colorful passages about Warren's alcoholism puzzle readers who believe that Hooper is himself an alcoholic, as some North Carolina people believed his father was. (There is also a rumor that Warren's father Albert was an alcoholic.)

[31] *Letters of C. S. Lewis* (London: Collins, 1988) 11.

[32] Where does one draw the line between editing, reconstruction, and forgery? I propose the following limits on editorial license:

    1. Edited material must be 85% by the purported author or else labelled a reconstruction.

    2. Both edited and reconstructed material must be 100% faithful to the author's beliefs.

He says he does not even add explanatory footnotes or change simple spelling errors (like *tath* to *that*) without considering the conflicting philosophies of textual criticism.[33] In my opinion there is delicious irony in his claim to editorial scrupulosity, especially in the light of what he has done to Lewis's poetry.

In his Preface to *God in the Dock*, Hooper says:

> Those who compare the texts of the essays published here with their originals will discover, in a few instances, some minor changes. This is because I have Lewis's own published copies of some essays, and where he has made changes or corrections I have followed his emendations. I have also felt it my responsibility to correct obvious errors wherever I have found them.

(He does not specify the essays with changes in them. Furthermore, he does not explain Lewis's keeping published copies of those essays in light of the fact that elsewhere he insists that Lewis always threw published copies of his own writing into the wastepaper basket. Nor does he explain his acquisition of these unspecified publications and their current location.)

Lewis's sermon Hooper calls "Miserable Offenders" was first published 5 May 1946 in the booklet *Five Sermons By Laymen*.[34] None of the five sermons were titled.[35] Lewis said, "they do not feel that they can sincerely say

---

3. Neither edited nor reconstructed material may be presented in a simulated document unless that document is labelled a simulation.

[33] Walter Hooper, "Reflections of an Editor," *CSL* (August 1977): 1-6.

[34] These sermons were preached on Sunday nights in April and May, 1946, In St. Matthew's Church, Northampton. The booklet is extremely rare. Perry Bramlett located a copy in 2000 and compared the sentences in the booklet to those in *God in the Dock*. He found eight changes.

[35] Lewis's sermon, the first in the 32-page booklet, was preached on Passion Sunday, 7 April 1946. The second sermon in the series, the shortest, was preached by Lewis's ex-student John Betjeman. The future of Lewis's single most evangelistic essay, "All or Nothing," looks far bleaker. At the time of this writing it is not under copyright. But if anyone publishes it, the Lewis estate can copyright it when launching a lawsuit against that publisher. Because current copyright law is vaguely worded and biased in favor of literary estates, the Lewis estate can keep this essay out of the hands of readers for decades. I have a copy of the 1944 book, but all I can do it paraphrase

that they are 'miserable sinners,'" but Hooper changed that to "they do not feel that they can sincerely say that they are 'miserable offenders.'" In addition to omitting the italics that Lewis used to add emphasis to words in three different sentences, Hooper also changed the wording of four more sentences. He changed "this season of the year" to "the Lenten season." He changed "intolerable temper" to "miserable temper." He changed "When people begin to find the words of our service difficult, I do not mean difficult to understand but difficult to join in" to "when people begin to find the words of our service difficult to join in." And he changed "their character is day by day ceasing to be human and becoming more and more a subhuman chaos of impulses" to "their character is day by day ceasing to be human."

Poetic Justice or Injustice

Few people realize that when Lewis was twenty-seven years old he dreamed up a poetry hoax in hopes of tricking T. S. Eliot, who edited *The Criterion*. Lewis recruited three of his friends, and they started writing ridiculous "modern" poems for submission under the fictitious names of Rollo and Bridget Considine, a dowdy brother and sister who lived in Vienna. Lewis's motivation was to show that *The Criterion* was a poor judge of poetry, and his friends' motivation was mischievous fun. They had fun for a few days, and then evidently abandoned the project.[36]

Lewis was a passionate lover of traditional poetry and a lifelong writer of meticulously crafted poems. By the time he died in 1963 he had published about seventy-five poems in various places and had written more that he planned to include in a book. Unfortunately, Lewis did not finish preparing the book, and so Walter Hooper did the honors. He seems to have had no background in editing and no expertise in poetry, but in his preface to the 1964 collection he explains that he was Lewis's secretary and that Lewis used to dictate poems to him. In fact, he said, Lewis tended to go back and suggest a change here, then a change there. (Who could ask for a more appropriate editor than that?) But thirty-three years later, in 1997, Hooper deposited 113

Lewis's essay for my readers. (See my book *Surprised by C. S. Lewis, George MacDonald, and Dante.*)

[36] Lewis's account of the poetry spoof appears in *All My Road Before Me*, 410-14.

pages of poems in the Bodleian Library, all in what looks like Lewis's handwriting; not one of them is in Hooper's 1963 handwriting.

In the 1964 preface Hooper said he found some of Lewis's poems scribbled on scraps of paper, in the flyleaves of books, or in old notebooks. But in 1977 he revealed that in 1964 he had rescued from Warren's manuscript bonfire a blue folder with half of Lewis's poems in it.[37] "I was working in a small room, and my usual procedure was to lay out on a desk, my chair, my bed and wherever there was space the versions of a single poem, and with door bolted, try to establish an order of precedence."[38]

As a result of what went on behind that bolted door, forty-five of Lewis's previously published poems appeared in his posthumous books in revised versions, and twenty-six have been retitled.[39] (Hooper has never given out basic information about the poems that were unpublished in Lewis's lifetime; he doesn't tell how many of them exist in more than one version, or how many of them he himself has titled.)

In the August 1977 issue of *CSL*, the Bulletin of the New York C. S. Lewis Society, Hooper wrote, "Looking back over the years it makes me shudder to realize that the first task I undertook, the editing of Lewis's *Poems*, was the one which by almost every conceivable standard could have gone badly wrong. If you left a word or perhaps even a sentence out of a work or prose still stand a chance of making the meaning clear. But, as we all know, the omission of a comma can sometimes destroy the meaning of a poem. Why, I ask myself, did I begin so ambitiously?"

Most people never get to see the original published versions of the forty-five Lewis poems that are acknowledged to have been revised, except for three that appear in their original form in *The Pilgrim's Regress* and one that appears in *Letters to Malcolm*. The original published versions of all Lewis's

---

[37] In a taped question-and-answer session on 9 March 1979 in Portland, Oregon, Hooper stated "All the poems were going onto the bonfire."

[38] *CSL: Bulletin of the New York C. S. Lewis Society,* (August 1977): 2.

[39] "...I must say that I am surprised that any editor would present so many changed texts to the public without saying where he got them." That was Richard Wilbur's informal response to the news that under Walter Hooper's editorship more than half the poems published in Lewis's lifetime appear posthumously only in revised versions. Richard Wilbur is the second United States Poet Laureate, winner of two Pulitzer Prizes for poetry, and winner of both the National Book Award and the Bollingen Prize.

poems that I have seen are better than the posthumous versions, and in some of these poems over half the lines have been changed. The march for giants in "Narnian Suite" is extremely simple, and it is a good starting point for comparisons between the originals and their revisions.[40] (The original march for giants had much better wording and line breaks.) An inferior version of Lewis's "Under Sentence" appears in *Poems* as "The Condemned."[41] An inferior version of "Spartan Nactus" appears in *Poems* as "A Confession."[42] An inferior version of "The End of the Wine" appears in *Poems* as "The Last of the Wine."[43] And an inferior version of "The Day with a White Mark" appears under its own title.[44]

Lewis's poem "A Footnote to Pre-History" (published in *Punch*, 14 September 1949) is inappropriately changed to "The Adam Unparadised" in Hooper's *Poems*, but the text is not changed. Therefore Lewis's lines remain as written, and here is what two of them say: "Memory, not built on a fake from Piltdown, /Reaches us. We know more than bones can teach." In 1949 Lewis was ahead of the authorities in boldly calling the Piltdown a fake; the establishment did not admit that until they were forced to at the end of 1953. (Until then, new textbooks included the Piltdown Man with the Neanderthal and the Cro-Magnon.)

Lewis published a poem about trees in winter in *The Spectator* in 1939 under the title "Experiment," and then republished it in *Augury* in 1940 under the title "Metrical Experiment." In 1946 he sent a copy to master poet Ruth Pitter for her approval. But in Hooper's *Poems* four lines are changed and the title is changed to "Patterns." Since then, another version of the poem appeared in an autographed copy of the *Screwtape Letters*, in what looks like

---

[40] "Narnian Suite" first appeared in *Punch* magazine, 4 November 1953. To compare the fine original with its clumsy revision, see p. of *The Lewis Legacy*, (Autumn 1995):10.

[41] To compare the fine original with Hooper's clumsy revision, see *The Lewis Legacy*, (Autumn 1995): 12-13.

[42] To compare the fine original with Hooper's clumsy revision, see *The Lewis Legacy* 68, (Spring 1996): 16.

[43] To compare the fine original with Hooper's clumsy revision, see *The Lewis Legacy* 68, (Spring 1996): 16.

[44] To compare the fine original with Hooper's clumsy revision, see *The Lewis Legacy* 66, (Autumn 1995):11.

Lewis's handwriting. An American collector eagerly purchased it from a dealer.

The changes are more drastic in some of the more complex poems than in simpler ones. For example, Lewis's "Break, Sun, My Crusted Earth" was composed of three interlocking, tightly constructed stanzas of complex symbolism related to medieval cosmology.[45] In Hooper's collection the title "Break Sun, My Crusted Earth" is changed to "A Pageant Played in Vain," and the poem is twice as long. The first three stanzas in Hooper's version are trite and rambling, and the last three are Lewis's "Break Sun, My Crusted Earth" stanzas in the wrong order with key words changed. It is as if a mediocre writer who was mystified by Lewis's poem decided to expand it and clumsily destroyed it in the process.[46]

"Break Sun, My Crusted Earth" was published in 1940 on page 72 of the poetry collection *Fear No More*, along with Lewis's poems "Essence" (4), "The World Is Round" (85), and "Arise, My Body" (89). Lewis's authorship of those poems was not public knowledge, because only six copies of the book included the poets' identities. (One of those copies is in the Bodleian Library.) The title of the book comes from "Fear no more the heat of the sun," the first line of a song in Shakespeare's *Cymbeline*.

In *Poems* "The World Is Round" (the ideal title) was inexplicably changed to "A Poem for Psychoanalysts and/or Theologians," and twelve of the nineteen lines are altered, not for the better. "Arise My Body" is a sonnet about resurrection that has been changed to "After Prayers, Lie Cold," with minor changes in seven of the fourteen lines and omission of the stanza break. Ironically, of all Lewis's poems there were to choose from for the collection *Magdalen Poets*, published in 2000 by Magdalen College, Oxford, one of the three that editor Robert MacFarlane selected by Lewis is "After Prayers, Lie Cold."[47] (Another of the three is "Le Roi S'Amuse," first

---

[45] For an explanation of how this poem relates to *Till We Have Faces*, see "Ungit and Orual: Facts, Mysteries, and Epiphanies" in *Surprised by C. S. Lewis, George Macdonald, and Dante* by Kathryn Lindskoog (Mercer University Press, 2001).

[46] To compare the fine original with this clumsy revision, see *The Lewis Legacy* 76, (Spring 1998):7.

[47] In his introduction to the book, MacFarlane remarked "But 'Dawdlin' and 'Magdalen', as Ezra Pound pointed out, go well together, and others apart from Wilde have spent their time strolling the grounds, reflecting, and writing. C. S. Lewis

published in *Punch* on 1 October 1947. Among other things, the posthumous version inexplicably changes "making, remaking, exalting" to "ravaging, savaging, creating." It changes "strove" to "wove." And it changes "The blazing planets on an azure field" to "It was gay Behemoth on a sable field."[48])

Hooper's 1965 bibliography of Lewis's publications did not mention the existence of *Fear No More*, and so Hooper was apparently unaware of Lewis's part in that book until sometime between the 1965 and 1979 versions of his bibliography. He apparently got the three poems from Lewis's poetry folder, but it is hard to imagine Lewis setting aside the polished versions he provided to Cambridge University Press in favor of inferior versions. The easiest explanation is that radically injudicious editing altered the Fear No More versions in Lewis's poetry folder. And there is circumstantial evidence for this.

According to Walter Hooper, his guiding principle has always been to publish the versions of Lewis's poems that he judges to be the latest. But in his 1994 book *Collected Poems* he chose to publish "A Pageant Played in Vain," "A Poem for Psychoanalysts and/or Theologians," and "After Prayers, Lie Cold" instead of what he himself designates as Lewis's later versions ("Break Sun, My Crusted Earth," "The World Is Round," and "Arise, My Body").[49] It seems as if he prefers to publish his own versions of Lewis's poems rather than Lewis's no matter how he dates them. (A wag titled all these aberrant poems "the Waltered versions.")

There is another poetry revision (in this case a double revision) that Hooper has eschewed in favor of an earlier version. Lewis published his 10-line poem "Epitaph" in the July 1949 issue of *The Month*. It is about an anonymous deceased man, real or imaginary, and it ends "with hope that he/ Purged by aeonian poverty/ In lenten lands, hereafter can/ Reaume the robes he wore as man."

---

scribbled a poem about spring birdsong on Addison's Walk..." MacFarlane was no doubt referring to "What the Bird Said Early in the Year," a careless 12-line adaptation of "Chanson D'Adventure," a 14-line poem that Lewis published in 1938.

[48] It is slightly possible that the phrase "gay Behemoth" was (consciously or unconsciously) inserted because gay means homosexual and behemoth means something enormous in size or power.

[49] He makes this designation in the 1979, 1992 and 1996 editions of his Lewis bibliography.

In 1960 Joy Lewis was cremated, and by sometime in 1963 Lewis transformed "Epitaph"into an evocative eight-line poem to be inscribed on her marker in the local crematorium.[50]

Here the whole world (stars, water, air,
And field and forest, as they were
Reflected in a single mind)
Like cast off clothes was left behind
In ashes yet with hope that she,
Re-born from holy poverty,
In Lenten Lands, hereafter may
Resume them on her Easter Day.

In 1973 photographer Douglas Gilbert published a clear picture of this memorial stone in *C. S. Lewis: Images of His World*.[51] and Hooper was well aware of the book because his photo was taken for it; but he failed to mention the memorial poem in his 1965 and 1979 bibliographies. This suggests that he was unaware of the marker's existence for at least sixteen years after 1963, although he claims that he was Lewis's intimate friend that year and he is known to have frequented the general neighborhood of the crematorium ever since.

According to records of the library of the University of North Carolina at Chapel Hill, Walter Hooper's collected Lewis papers include a typed copy of Lewis's epitaph for his wife that—according to Hooper—was dictated and corrected by Lewis. (Except for some unspecified 1993 additions, the Hooper collection was placed there in 1980.) This raises an awkward question: how could Hooper possibly know that Lewis dictated the poem rather than writing it out for someone else to type? Where and when did Hooper belatedly find this piece of paper, since he was apparently unaware of the poem's existence until 1979 or 1980 at the earliest?

---

[50] This 1963 poem about resurrection is tied closely to a prose passage in Lewis's 1964 book *Letters to Malcolm*, and it also suggests the theme of Lewis's unpublished, undated poem "Your True Antiquities."

[51] Douglas Gilbert and Clyde Kilby, *C. S. Lewis: Images of His World* (Grand Rapids: Wm B. Eerdmans, 1973).

In 1988 Douglas Gresham published a photo of the poem as the frontispiece of his popular book *Lenten Lands*; which seemingly prompted Hooper to mention it in his 1992 Lewis bibliography.[52] There he revealed for the first time the existence of another version. "Lewis had written two versions of this epitaph, but without having his wife in mind, and one of these is found in *Poems*. Joy Davidman chose one for her own epitaph, and Lewis revised it extensively in 1963 before it was cut into the stone in this photograph."

On 5 October 1997, five years after telling the public about the second version, Hooper quietly placed in the Bodleian Library a small piece of writing paper watermarked Basildon Bond that had supposedly been in his possession since 1964. The first side, marked A, contains the epitaph Lewis published in 1949. The second side, marked B, contains a revision by either Lewis or Hooper and never published by either of them.

Why would Lewis have wasted time copying out both versions and labeling them A and B? (He obviously didn't label them A and B for his own instruction, but it's the kind of thing a forger might do for the benefit of his intended audience.) According to Version B, before Joy came on the scene Lewis had changed the deceased person in his original poem from an anonymous male to an anonymous female—not Joy. He had changed the male's abandoned possessions to an anonymous female's abandoned clothing—not Joy's. And he had written about an anonymous female's Easter Day—not Joy's.

The authenticity of Version B is questionable. Since Hooper was apparently unaware of the existence of Version C until the 1980s at the earliest, how could he know in 1992 that "Joy Davidman chose [Version B] for her own epitaph, and Lewis revised it extensively in 1963 before [Version C] was cut into the stone..."? To concoct a bogus Version B from the poem Lewis placed on Joy's marker in 1963, and to invent a story accounting for Version B, would be a ghoulish prank indeed.

As if the posthumous versions of the poems were not a big enough problem, in *The Collected Poems of C. S. Lewis* Hooper preceded them with a pugnaciously insulting "Introductory Letter" that Lewis allegedly wrote for his poetry in 1963. Unfortunately, this essay is even more hostile, sneering,

---

[52] Two years later, in 1994, he included it in *Collected Poems*.

arrogant, and malicious than the posthumous "Preface to 'Screwtape Proposes a Toast.'" One of its strange twists has Lewis warning future reviewers of his poetry: "no one whom I caught lying about me ever lied about me again." He even claims to have a reputation for spurring demons to prey upon people. Surely it is impossible to conceive of the real Lewis threatening future poetry reviewers with death or demonic afflictions, but this preface requires it. There is no wit or levity here, only bitter ire and a rancorous spirit.

Another peculiar thing about the history of this "Introductory Letter" is Hooper's astute evaluation of it seventeen years before he published it: "Some of you will possibly feel that I have betrayed the friend I intended to serve when I tell you that while Lewis was a long way from having completed such a volume of poems [a debatable contention], he had already written a short Preface to accompany it, which Preface I did not print in the [1964] book. The tone of it was so defensive, and in places so angry, that I believed—and still do believe—that it would have caused the poems to have been received very cooly."[53] In contrast, Hooper's wooly 275-word defense of the preface in his 1994 introduction is remarkably unpersuasive and offers no rationale for his change of position.[54]

Hooper began his own introduction to *The Collected Poems of C. S. Lewis* by promising, "This volume brings together for the first time all C. S. Lewis's short poems into a single volume." But in fact about twenty are left out. The strangest omission is probably the 34-line beginning of a 1932 narrative poem about Lewis's spiritual odyssey. Beginning with the lines "I will write down the portion that I understand/ Of twenty years wherein I went from land to land..." Lewis said he went half way round the world searching for a home. He was driven away from every land until he finally submitted to making his home in the one land he feared, where he finally found security.

---

[53] Hooper said this in his 13 August lecture "Reflections of an Editor" at the first annual retreat of the New York C. S. Lewis Society in 1977, and it was published in the August 1977 issue of *CSL*. His 1994 reversal suggests to skeptics the possibility that Bles, the publisher of the 1964 collection of Lewis's poems, rejected the preface; the 1994 publisher, Collins Fount, was far less scrupulous.

[54] This murky defense quotes Owen Barfield and amounts to no more than the claim that the preface is part of Lewis's life history. But that was just as true (or false) in 1964 as in 1994.

(This abandoned poem turned out to be an immediate precurser to *Pilgrim's Regress.*)

In 1974 Hooper included the first twelve lines on page 127 of C. S. *Lewis: A Life*; but the clear word *whose* was accidentally replaced with the word *whole*: "...oracles, whole [*whose*] airy sense/ I could not understand..." In 1992 Hooper stated in his Lewis bibliography that these are "the only surviving lines," but in fact they comprise only the first stanza of three.

The second stanza is a prayer to God to enable Lewis to complete this book for the sake of readers who might be helped. He likens God to a self-enkindled flame and himself to a fading candle. He describes God as unquivering light and warmth of the world, but says he feels too reverent to name him. In the third stanza, Lewis recalls that in childhood he heard the Christian story, but it didn't interest him. He was much more interested then in the joys of being alive in the world than in any news about his soul.

The first 34 lines of this untitled, unpublished poem in Lewis's own handwriting survive in the Marion E. Wade Center at Wheaton College in Illinois and in photocopy in the Bodleian Library, where they can be read in Lewis's letters to Owen Barfield. Unfortunately, no one can publish this poetry until Walter Hooper decides the time is ripe. In the new 1994 edition of *C. S. Lewis: A Life,* Hooper again includes only twelve lines, and the word *whose* is still rendered as *whole.*

Of all the oddities in the collected poems, however, the strangest is "Finchley Avenue," a seventy-six-line poem that Lewis allegedly wrote circa 1950 to describe life on an elegant residential street in London. Hooper claims to have rescued "Finchley Avenue" from Warren's bonfire—in the same notebook where he found the inept story "The Man Born Blind." "Finchley Avenue" has a few good lines, but as a whole it is a failure and amateurish.

> The avenue is full of life from nine till ten;
> The owners of these homes are hurrying then
> To catch their trains. They catch them, and when these are gone,
> By ones and twos the tradesmen in their vans come on...

But if one extricates lines 31-46 from this banal verse, one suddenly discovers a profoundly evocative poem that is Lewis at his best. It is not about life in London in 1950 after all; it is about Lewis's childhood home in Ireland, the history of the world, and the nature of cognition. Its obvious title is "Your

True Antiquities," from the first line. Its last two lines are memorable: "There first you felt the wonder of deep time, the joy/ And dread of Schliemann standing on the grave of Troy." It is as if someone who didn't understand Lewis's lovely poem about his turn-of-the century Belfast home saw fit to bury it in the middle of sixty lines of doggerel about mid-century London.

Lewis knew that he was not a great poet, but he knew that his craftsmanship was excellent. He no doubt felt like his mentor George MacDonald, who wrote "And I am jealous of my credit as a workman, that is, desirous that my readers should see the quality of the work I have done."[55] There is no question that Lewis cherished his poetry; but in 1964 and again in 1994 someone damaged much of his poetry and cheated readers of things he wrote.

Ironically, in 1997 a friend of Hooper's named Michael Ward launched a fundraising campaign in order to erect a £5,000 memorial stone in honor of Lewis at Addison's Walk in Magdalen College. The stone, unveiled in 1998, consists of "What the Bird Said Early in the Year," a clumsy 12-line adaptation of "Chanson D'Adventure," a 14-line poem that Lewis published in 1938.[56] On 27 May 1997 I sent Mr. Ward a cordial letter warning that Lewis's 1938 version was superior and would be more appropriate, but he answered that he was using Lewis's final version. When I asked him where the revised manuscript was located, he did not answer. As if in response, however, in October 1997 Walter Hooper placed in the Bodleian a copy of "What the Bird Said Early in the Year" (in what appears to be Lewis's handwriting)—with lines 13 and 14 crossed out. The timing suggests that this document was created to support Hooper's claim that his published version of the poem is authentic. The only bona fide poem by C. S. Lewis carved in stone so far is the one on Joy's marker in the crematorium.

In 1964 Lewis's poem "Prayer" was published posthumously in two different versions at once: the better one in Lewis's *Letters to Malcolm,* and the inferior one in Hooper's *Poems.* In *Poems* over half the lines are changed, and not for the better. Lewis sent his version to the publisher late in 1963, just before his death and it is hard to imagine him revising it as Hooper claims. In

---

[55] George MacDonald, *Sunday Magazine,* (1 December 1866).

[56] See my essay "Carved in Stone: What the Bird Did Not Say Early in the Year" in *Surprised by C. S. Lewis, George MacDonald, and Dante* (Macon GA: Mercer University Press, 2001).

Lewis's version God speaks through Lewis's "dumb lips"; in Hooper's version God speaks through Lewis's "dead lips." Ironically, one can't help wondering if perhaps it is Hooper himself who is speaking through Lewis's dead lips.

> The devil is the father of lies,
> but he neglected to patent the idea,
> and the business now suffers from competition.
> —*Josh Billings*

6

FORMS OF THINGS UNKNOWN

NOT WHAT LEWIS HAD IN MIND AFTER ALL?

In 1966, two years after manhandling *Poems*, Hooper published his second collection of posthumous Lewis pieces: *Of Other Worlds*. In spite of his much-vaunted scrupulosity, this was apparently an editorial escapade like his first one. In his introduction he mentions the existence of a fourth Ransom novel. He includes a confused, rambling posthumous essay by Lewis titled "On Criticism," with no explanation of where it came from or why Lewis would have written it. Perhaps, like some of the poems, it is a mixture of Lewis's work and someone else's.

Of Other Worlds includes three Lewis short stories: "The Shoddy Lands," "Ministering Angels," and "Forms of Things Unknown." The third one had never been published before, but it didn't attract much attention. Five years later, at the end of Chapter 7 in *C. S. Lewis: A Biography*, Hooper tried to correct that. He listed Lewis's three science-fiction short stories, but seemed oblivious to the qualities of the first two and spent only eleven lines on them together.[1] Then he spent thirty-seven lines promoting his favorite.

---

[1] In his preface to *The Dark Tower* (1977), Hooper inexplicably dismisses "The Shoddy Lands" as Lewis's playful pretence that he was writing a "stream of consciousness" story, although "Lewis was not fond of that chaotic genre of stories." Thus Hooper seems to misread "Shoddy Lands" as a superficial literary satire instead of a heartfelt moral and religious fable.

"The third story, 'Forms of Things Unknown,' is of much greater interest," he assures readers. "The description of the landing on the moon and of the scenery and physical conditions as Jenkin, the Selenaut, explores the area where previous space voyages have disappeared so mysteriously, is brilliantly imagined and described."

Hooper's high praise is curious, because this is an awkward, amateurish, rather mean-spirited story that doesn't sound like Lewis. Here are sample sentences:

"Gentlemen, I ask you to give three cheers for Lieutenant John Jenkin." (124)

The vermin [Jenkin's fellow astronauts] said, "He always was a chap who'd do anything to get himself in the limelight." (124)[2]

"Well," said Jenkin cheerily, "somebody's got to go." (127)

"Flesh-flies," he called them [the press]. (127)

He had wondered if the agoraphobia of that roofless and bottomless vacuity would overthrow his reason. (128)

The landing was not without terror, but there were so many gimmicks to look after, so much skill to be exercised, that it did not amount to very much. But his heart was beating a little more noticeably than usual as he put the finishing touches on his space-suit and climbed out. (128)[3]

---

[2] In his Screwtape parody "Hell and Immortality" Hooper twice referred to people as vermin.

[3] If Lewis were writing a story about an astronaut, it seems highly unlikely that he would have the man refer to features of his equipment as *gimmicks*, a mildly derogatory term derived at mid-century from American slang and usually indicating tricky devices or gadgets, especially those that attract attention or publicity. Lewis supposedly wrote "Forms of Things Unknown" at about the time when *gimmick* appeared in the 30 May 1953 issue of the *Economist* in the following sentence: "Some of Professor Triffin's colleagues were innately suspicious of what they called 'gimmick solutions' of this kind." See the 1972 *Supplement to the Oxford English Dictionary* (Oxford: Clarendon Press, 1972) 1231.

Hooper tried to promote "Forms of Things Unknown" again in 1977. He reprinted it in his *Dark Tower* collection and revealed for the first time that he had rescued it along with the Dark Tower fragment from Warren's January 1964 bonfire. He devoted a couple of paragraphs to showing how it relates to *Perelandra* and speculated about why Lewis didn't publish it. That September, in a long essay praising Hooper in *CSL*, Issue 95, Charles Brady followed Hooper's lead and claimed, "Of the four short stories [in the *Dark Tower* collection], "Forms of Things Unknown," which confronts moon-travelers with mythology's Medusa, is at once the most finished and the most arresting."[4]

Unfortunately for Hooper, no one paid much attention to "Forms of Things Unknown"—except Richard Hodgens. (Hodgens was the first person to join Henry Noel's New York C. S. Lewis Society when it began in 1969, and he attended until his premature death in 1989. He translated the first part of Ariosto's *Orlando Furioso* for Ballantine [1973], and sometimes published essays and reviews in *Film Quarterly* and *National Review*.)

On 14 April 1978 Hodgens carefully analyzed the *Dark Tower* collection for members of the New York C. S. Lewis Society, and his talk was taped. He praised "The Shoddy Lands," "Ministering Angels," and "After Ten Years," but detested "The Dark Tower" and obviously disliked "The Man Born Blind." He found "Forms of Things Unknown" a bad story, but an interesting puzzle:

> I think that "Forms of Things Unknown" is simply Lewis's attempt to write—not for publication, but simply for his own amusement—a sort of fictional illustration of a particular science fiction magazine cover. The surprise ending in 'Forms of Things Unknown' is when an astronaut encounters a Gorgon on the moon. In October 1958 on the cover of *Fantastic Universe* magazine, an American pulp, was a painting by Virgil Finlay, an original which did not illustrate any story in the magazine, and which showed an astronaut encountering

---

It is also unlikely that Lewis would have had an astronaut "put the finishing touches on his space-suit" before stepping out onto the moon, like entertainers who put the finishing touches on their costumes before stepping out onto a stage.

[4] Charles A. Brady, "Some Notes on C. S. Lewis's *The Dark Tower and Other Stories*," CSL (September 1977): 1-10.

a Gorgon. And this was about the time when Lewis was writing, presumably, these short science fiction stories. I suspect that that was the genesis of 'Forms of Things Unknown' and that he didn't mean to publish it any more than he meant to publish the title story 'The Dark Tower.'

The whole point of "Forms of Things Unknown" is its surprise ending, apparently taken from Virgil Finlay. Hodgens guessed that Lewis saw Finlay's idea on the front of the American pulp magazine in 1958. In 1958, however, Lewis was a fifty-nine year old academic at the height of his powers and also a newlywed whose wife was recovering from cancer. His professional and personal obligations were staggering. Why would he waste time turning Finlay's first-rate pictorial idea into a third-rate story?

On the other hand, when Finlay's idea appeared in 1958, Walter Hooper was a student at Virginia Episcopal Seminary; and in 1959 he became an English teacher of high school boys in North Carolina. A common English assignment in those days was for pupils to write stories about pictures on magazine covers provided by their teachers. It is entirely possible that Finlay's picture was used that way. And it would have been natural for Hooper to try his own hand at the story.

But reader Dale Nelson responded to the Hodgens news with news of his own. Nine months before Virgil Finlay's painting appeared on the cover of *Fantastic Universe*, William Sambrot's short story "Island of Fear" appeared in the 18 January 1958 issue of *The Saturday Evening Post*. In this story one Kyle Elliot comes across an island in the Aegean where he finds incredibly life-like human statues, like men turned to stone. In the final paragraph of the story, he remembers that the Gorgons were immortal. He hears a hissing sound behind him. "Though he knew he mustn't he turned slowly...and looked." "Forms of Things Unknown" (1966) strongly resembles Sambrodt's far superior story (1958).

The writer of "Forms of Things Unknown" prefaced it with an appropriate epigraph from *Perelandra*: "...that what was myth in one world might always be fact in some other." It is highly unlikely that Lewis would have prefaced any short story of his with an epigraph explaining the idea in the story, and it is particularly unlikely that he would have prefaced any short story with an epigraph from one of his own books. It would have been bad form.

There is a handwritten manuscript of this story in the Bodleian, either Lewis wrote the story or else both the story and the manuscript are forged. I am personally convinced that "Forms of Things Unknown" was itself a thing unknown—unknown to C. S. Lewis.

In his *Dark Tower* Preface Hooper stated enigmatically, "A book, once I have read and handled it, has always seemed to me an inevitable part of life—an open-and-shut case of fact, the origins of which grow dimmer as time passes." Perhaps in this disclaimer he was expressing hope that no one would ever question him about the origins of the three suspicious stories in that book: "The Dark Tower," "Forms of Things Unknown," and "The Man Born Blind."

In a page and a half of explanation, Hooper identifies "The Man Born Blind" with an unpublished story by Lewis that Owen Barfield read in the 1920s.[5] (Needless to say, the fact that Lewis wrote a story about a blind man before 1930 doesn't mean that Hooper's story is necessarily the one Lewis wrote.) Here again, Hooper rescued the story from Warren's bonfire. He found it in the same notebook with the poem "Finchley Avenue." Here again, part of the writing is so amateurish that it seems impossible that Lewis could have written it.[6] In spite of its potential, the story lacks both neuroscientific and psychological validity, and has neither allegorical nor fantastic coherence. The low quality of the dialog is especially appalling in light of Hooper's claim that Lewis added a few notes to the story years after he first wrote it.[7]

---

[5] Lewis's early story was about the problems that beset a blind man after successful eye surgery. Lewis was probably familiar with speculations about this subject in Locke's *Essay Concerning Human Understanding* or George Berkely's *A New Theory of Vision*. (See the fascinating 1995 Oliver Sacks essay "To See or Not To See" in his collection *An Anthropologist on Mars*).

[6] Charles Brady obligingly ranked "The Man Born Blind" second only to "Forms of Things Unknown" among Lewis's four short stories: "the haunting parable, 'The Man Born Blind,' which concerns itself, underneath, with the Johanine radiance that is the light of the world." He then dismissed Lewis's genuine "Ministering Angels" as infelicitous farce-humor, and said Lewis's genuine "Shoddy Lands" "does not quite achieve the objective correlative it needs."

[7] C. S. Lewis, *The Dark Tower and Other Stories,* ed. Walter Hooper (New York: Harcourt Brace Jovanovich, 1977) 11.

In the last sentence of the story, a man's body falls down into a quarry full of thick fog, and it makes a temporary rift in the fog before it hits bottom. It is doubtful that a keen nature-observer like Lewis would have imagined that a falling body makes a rift in fog. I think that Lewis would have seen this bit of description as a fiction writer's gaffe, and he would have chuckled over it.

As if that weren't enough, near the end of the story Lewis purportedly wrote this silly sentence: "'Do you see that?' shouted the violent stranger." "Did Lewis write that?" shouted this violent reader. I first challenged the authenticity of "The Man Born Blind" in 1988 in *The C. S. Lewis Hoax,* and in 1989 Walter Hooper made his manuscript of "The Man Born Blind" available to researchers in the Bodleian.[8]

It turns out that there was already another manuscript copy of the story in the United States. In 1987 Peter Joliffe, a document dealer in Eynsham, near Oxford, offered it to Dr. Edwin Brown, a collector of Lewisiana in Indianapolis. Joliffe did not say where it came from. In this version, the story is titled "Light" and Mary's name is changed to Anne. Although Brown didn't think the story was very good, he had faith in its authenticity because the handwriting looked like Lewis's, the paper looked old, and he trusted his dealer.[9] He kept it in a safe deposit box until 1997, when he sold his extensive collection of Lewis-related materials to a donor for presentation to Taylor University.

Perhaps the most surprising aspect of the saga of "The Man Born Blind" is the fact that in 1989 Nicolas Barker, Deputy Keeper of Britain's National Library, went to the Bodleian to look at two Lewis manuscripts there: *The Dark Tower* and "The Man Born Blind." He reported that "The Man Born Blind" is written in a light blue shade of ink that was not available until

---

[8] In "A Catalogue, Two Notebooks, and an Exercise Book" in the April 1994 issue of *Mythprint*, Joe R. Christopher describes Hooper's notebook marked "Lewis Ms. No. 31." He says that the pre-1930 story "The Man Born Blind" is written out there in blue ink, beginning on page 22, without a title. Expansions of the story are added in ink that looked black to Christopher. The rest of the notebook is filled with many random scraps, including the opening of *That Hideous Strength,* with Jane Studdock named Jane Ruddock. If genuine, that opening would have been written between 1940 and 1943.

[9] In a letter to the editor in *Christianity Today* (3 March 1989) Dr. Edwin Brown said, "I can attest that 'The Man Born Blind' was written by Lewis." He said his copy of the story is written on four pages of faded, lined foolscap and is titled 'Light.'"

1950. I corresponded with Barker about that, pointing out that if the manuscript is genuine, it was written before 1930. Although he is not sympathetic to my forgery charge, he insists that the manuscript ink did not exist before 1950.[10]

Scraps That Survived

Nicolas Barker found more of the post-1950 light blue ink on the back of page 2 of Hooper's 1938 Dark Tower manuscript in the Bodleian, in the twenty-one line beginning of a spiritual autobiography by C. S. Lewis. There are major problems in this autobiographical fragment in addition to the fact that the first word is *I*, and it does not seem to look like Lewis's usual *I*. First, the opening sentence says, "I was born on Nov 29th 1946 in a semi-detached house in the suburbs of Belfast, being the second child of a solicitor and a clergyman's daughter." The year 1898 has been written above the year 1946, which was crossed out. It seems unlikely that Lewis would have started an autobiography in 1946 on the second page of a manuscript he abandoned in 1938, using ink that did not exist until 1950.

By his own account, Walter Hooper owned this autobiographical fragment ever since January 1964. On pages 126-27 of his 1974 Lewis biography, Hooper describes Lewis's four early attempts at spiritual autobiography; but it seems that he never mentions this alleged 1938 (or 1946 or 1950) attempt anywhere.

A highly amusing scrap of Narnia exists on the back of page 1 of the Dark Tower manuscript. It is allegedly Lewis's abandoned beginning of *The Lion, The Witch, and the Wardrobe*:

This book is about four children whose names were Ann, Martin, Rose, and Peter. But it is most about Peter who was the youngest. They all had to go away from London suddenly because of the Air Raids, and because Father, who was in the army, had gone off to the War and Mother was doing some kind of war work. They were sent

---

[10] Unpublished letter to Kathryn Lindskoog from Nicolas Barker dated 6 August 1991.

to stay with a relation of Mother's who was a very old Professor who lived by himself in the country.[11]

It is obvious that Lewis could not have written this paragraph in 1938, because the war and the air raids and evacuation of children from London had not yet occurred! Are we supposed to think that in the 1940s Lewis opened his abandoned 1938 manuscript and wrote (with 1950s ink) the first paragraph of a children's story that he abandoned a few minutes later? (As Anthony Grafton points out in *Forgers and Critics: Creativity and Duplicity in Western Scholarship,* "The motives of the forger have varied as widely as those of any other kind of creative artist.")

In 1971 a hefty anthology appeared as a seventieth-birthday tribute to Clyde S. Kilby. It was *Imagination and the Spirit* (Eerdmans), edited by Charles Huttar of Hope College. The most surprising essay of the lot was one about C. S. Lewis by Walter Hooper. He revealed that Lewis and his brother had given him Narnian fragments hitherto unpublished; he not only quoted from them, but also supplied full-page photographs of two of the manuscript pages.

To the untrained eye, the samples look like Lewis's handwriting; but they do not sound like Lewis. For example, Lewis is supposed to have written a page of confused planning for *The Voyage of the Dawn Treader* that ends with the following: "Intervening history of Narnia told nominally by the Dwarf but really an abstract of his story wh. [sic] amounts to telling it in my own person." Can any professional author believe that Lewis bothered to

---

[11] Although Hooper mentioned it in his 1979 book *Past Watchful Dragons,* this bit of apocrypha was little-known until 2000, when HarperCollins launched a massive marketing campaign in preparation for a variety of Narnia products. One of the first steps was an elaborate Narnia site on the Internet that happened to include a misleading page about the origin of Narnia. "Clive Staples Lewis (or as he was always known to his friends, "Jack") was already an established writer of serious books on literature and religion, but, as a bachelor who didn't know many children, he had never thought of writing a book for young readers. Then, during the Second World War, when children from London were being evacuated to the country, four youngsters were billeted at Jack's home, the Kilns. Surprised to find how few imaginative stories his young guests seemed to know, the decided to write one for them and scribbled down the opening sentences of a story about four children—then named Ann, Martin, Rose and Peter—who were sent away from London because of the air raids, and went to stay with a very old professor who lived by himself in the country."

write such a stilted and useless note to himself? (Walter Hooper donated his outline to the Bodleian in a notebook that includes some of Lewis's 1926-1928 diary entries and other items.)

On 12 December 1978 Hooper expressed his appreciation to his friend Henry William Griffin, senior editor of Macmillan Publishing Company, for his work on Hooper's book *Past Watchful Dragons,* to be released in 1979. This book features about twenty-six pages of Lewis's writing about Narnia not included in Lewis's own books.

On pages 48-65 of *Past Watchful Dragons* Hooper includes the Lefay Fragment, allegedly written by Lewis in 1949 as part of *The Magician's Nephew.* The Lefay Fragment would merit a poor grade in any good accredited creative writing class. Lewis won the Carnegie Award for children's literature, and this story would win a booby prize. Yet one can see the first page in what appears to be Lewis's handwriting on page 305 of Hooper's section of *Imagination and the Spirit.* Ironically, Nancy Cole, a handwriting analyst engaged by Stanley Mattson in 1995 to vouch for the authenticity of *The Dark Tower,* was not aware that I challenged the authenticity of the Lefay Fragment. Therefore, she unguardedly reported that this handwriting on the LeFay Fragment differs from Lewis's usual style because of its larger size, elongation, decreased legibility, and resemblance to a careless scrawl.

Whether the bumbling LeFay fragment is a genuine Lewis scrap or a forgery, until now readers have been unaware that in mid-August 1963 Lewis specifically instructed Hooper to destroy his literary scraps. He sent Hooper and Douglas Gresham to Cambridge to clear out his rooms, and his brief but meticulous instructions, complete with diagrams, are available in Hooper's Chapel Hill collection. Lewis told Hooper that any typed or apparently complete manuscripts were to be brought home to him in his tin trunk. But he told Hooper that Douglas was to *thoroughly* tear up all scraps before they went into the waste paper basket so that none of them could ever get into circulation.[12] (Serious writers often feel that way about their scraps.

---

[12] On 6 August 1963 C. S. Lewis sent his resignation to Magdalene College, Cambridge, and on 8 August the Master of the College wrote to Walter Hooper about clearing Lewis's rooms. There was no rush, and late September would be soon enough. But if Hooper needed to do the job sooner, he was warned that there would be no hot water or other services after lunch on 17 August.

As editor Gregory McNamee lamented for Hemingway, "The publication of Hemingway's raw, unfinished, and even ghostwritten work only diminishes his hard-won reputation. It is a shameful betrayal.")

These written instructions from Lewis contradict what Hooper told John Dart in 1979 for the *Los Angeles Times:* "[Hooper] was told by Lewis he could keep any manuscripts he found at his Cambridge office where Lewis had finished teaching. Another unpublished piece, 'The Dark Tower,' was found stuck in a drawer, Hooper said."[13]

Feminism: A Matter for Concern

As if the 1946 autobiographical scrap in 1950s ink on the back of the 1938 Dark Tower manuscript didn't provide enough quandaries, another 1946 mystery has surfaced. In 1986 Hooper published the collection *Present Concerns,* which contains an essay called "Modern Man and his Categories of Thought." Lewis evidently wrote it for Bishop Stephen Neill of the National Council of Churches forty years earlier. Neill died in 1984, two years before the essay appeared, and therefore could not be asked about it.

Hooper doesn't say where the essay was from 1946 on, who owns the manuscript, or how and when it came into his hands. The essay begins, "Though we ought always to imitate the procedure of Christ and His saints, this pattern has to be adapted to the changing conditions of history." Stodgy or awkward sentences occur off and on for six pages; for example, "This education was formerly based throughout Europe on the ancients."

Hooper called Cambridge and agreed to empty the rooms on 14, 15, and 16 August. (If Douglas Gresham's account is correct, the two spent four more days in Cambridge while Hooper evidently continued his work off-campus.) Lewis drew Hooper a map of his small apartment, with concise notes saying exactly what was where and what to do with it. He wanted the oil portrait of his Grandfather Hamilton packed and sent to Church Hall in Belfast. Old exams were to be thrown away. Hooper was to help himself to copies of books by Lewis. Some books and furniture were to be sold. Many books, the important papers, a gilt clock, stationery, letters, and photos were to be brought home, along with honorary degrees, a gold medal, "and other such vanities." A tin trunk was there for use.

[13] John Dart, "Questions Raised on C. S. Lewis Lore," *Los Angeles Times* (24 March 1979) 1:30-31.

The author of this essay refers to Darwinism as Darwinianism, a relatively uncommon synonym that appears nowhere else in Lewis's published writing. Like most people, Lewis seemed satisfied with the word Darwinism, and the insertion of Darwinianism here could be a flourish by a pretentious forger. (All forgers are pretentious in that they are pretenders, and some are also pretentious by being a bit too showy.)

When Henry Noel read the essay with great care in 1994, he found ten features that struck him as uncharacteristic of Lewis.[14] I had found others. Here I will focus only upon the writer's attitude toward women: Men are "forced down" intellectually in today's "mixed society" because women do not grapple with "ultimate issues." "Hence, in our student population, a lowering of metaphysical energy." The emancipation of women thus "cuts us off from the eternal" because "the proper glory of the masculine mind, its disinterested concern with truth for truth's own sake...is being impaired."

I'm sure Lewis would have laughed at such patently ridiculous gender generalizations. He appreciated good female students and openly delighted in brilliant females like Dorothy Sayers; and he openly deplored the loutish or doltish males in academia. This is the man who wrote in 1955:

> I gladly admit that we number among us [cultured people] men and women whose modesty, courtesy, fair-mindedness, patience in disputation and readiness to see an antagonist's point of view, are wholly admirable. I am fortunate to have known them. But we must also admit that we show as high a percentage as any group whatever of bullies, paranoiacs, and poltroons, of backbiters, exhibitionists, mopes, milksops, and world-without-end bores. The loutishness that turns every argument into a quarrel is really no rarer among us than among the sub-literate; the restless inferiority-complex... which bleeds at a touch but scratches like a wildcat is almost as common among us as among schoolgirls.[15]

---

[14] Henry Noel founded the New York C. S. Lewis Society in 1969. In his opinion, even if some posthumous literature is questionable, it is better not to make accusations.

[15] C. S. Lewis, "Lilies That Fester," *They Asked for a Paper* (London: Geoffrey Bles, 1962) 109.

Hooper sometimes portrays himself as defending Lewis against unkind women. In *C. S. Lewis: A Biography* he defended Lewis against Oxford's Roman Catholic philosopher Elizabeth Anscombe, who bested C. S. Lewis in informal debate about a point in *Miracles* in 1948. Hooper claimed that Lewis told him that Anscombe did not really win her point after all, and Hooper attributed her apparent victory to unfair bullying. Given Lewis's reputation as a "butcher" even in friendly debate, and the fact that he altered the third chapter of *Miracles* because of Anscombe's input, his martyrdom at her hands is an odd proposal.

Five years after first writing about the 1948 Anscombe debate, Hooper returned to the subject and added 'A few years later [approximately twenty years later, it seems] when I met Miss Anscombe in the common room of Somerville College and asked what she remembered of the meeting, she removed the cigar from her mouth only long enough to say, 'I won.'"[16] When Stephen Schofield checked with Professor Anscombe about that account, she answered on 10 October 1979, "The story is not true."[17]

Hooper seems at times to caricature women. A year after his first volley against Anscombe he spoke to the New York C. S. Lewis Society and ventured that we seem to be already hearing cries of frustration and outrage from women who have tried to flout Lewis's view that women are more monogamous than men. He told about *The Dark Tower* (not yet published) and Lewis's prescient warning therein; in Hooper's words, "Ransom anticipates the bitter and frenzied feminists of today."[18]

On 9 December 1977 Hooper sent me his forty-first and most puzzling letter, in which he cordially expressed the hope that I had not changed and come to resemble "Miss G. E. M. Anscombe." He pictured me lighting a cigar, stirring a martini, and staring at proofs on my kitchen table while my husband and sons were forced to eat TV dinners; but he said he didn't think it was really true. Having corresponded with me for over ten years and having spent hours with me on two occasions in 1975, he had to know that I was the very opposite of what he described. Perhaps he was really intending for me to

---

[16] Walter Hooper, "Oxford's Bonny Fighter," in *C. S. Lewis at the Breakfast Table* (New York: Macmillan, 1979) 163.

[17] "Professor Anscombe Corrects Father Hooper," *The Canadian C. S. Lewis Journal*, (December 1979): 7.

[18] James Como, "An Evening with Walter Hooper," *CSL*, (July 1975): 6.

join him in disapproval of Professor Anscombe. Ironically, he was himself a heavy smoker and one who imbibes.

Three years later, on 25 January 1980 Hooper wrote to Barbara Reynolds that I, and one or two friends, tried to ban male pronouns in the Southern California C. S. Lewis Society's constitution and in its journal. This seemed so silly to everyone that it was rejected, he said, and so I quit the Society. A colorful account; but in the words of a certain Oxford philosopher, "The story is not true."

In August 1984 Hooper told interviewer Charles Glaize that in his opinion Lewis would carefully condemn women's liberation and would object to the following appeal from a "women's libber": "Do you believe women should have equal pay for equal hours?" According to Hooper, if one says yes to this, one is expected to like "abortion, divorce, and all those things."[19]

Five years later, Hooper was still excited about frenzied feminists. In an effort to "clear the decks" of falsehoods about C. S. Lewis, he offered the public a new essay titled "C. S. Lewis and C. S. Lewises" in the 1989 Eerdmans volume *G. K. Chesterton and C. S. Lewis: The Riddle of Joy.* In it he explains that there are three images of Lewis that he is trying to combat. First, is a sexist image concocted by feminists, whom he pities because they are not only comic but also unhappy and, in fact, furious people who eschew sunshiny books like the Narnian chronicles.[20] He calls such people "snappers" because of their obsession.[21] (It is hard to imagine whom these obsessed anti-Lewis feminists are because he never identifies them.)

---

[19] Hooper's concern for traditional female roles does not extend to the point of gallantry. After successfully courting J. R. R. Tolkien's daughter Priscilla and reportedly bringing her to North Carolina to meet his mother, then quietly deciding not to marry her after all, Hooper made public in his Chapel Hill of collection personal letters about the subject from John Lawlor (1969) and Pauline Baynes (1972), letters that must be painfully humiliating to Miss Tolkien.

[20] On page xvi of his 1980 introduction to *The Weight of Glory,* Hooper quotes Lewis's 1940 sentence "I begin to suspect that the world is divided not only into the happy and the unhappy, but into those who *like* happiness and those who, odd as it seems, don't." Hooper continues, "Without meaning any offence, I suspect that those who carry on about 'social justice' or whatever the current jargon is would not understand this. Still, that is the way it was." (Readers might wonder, what is the way it was?)

[21]"Snap! Snap!" "Snap! Snap! Snap!" Hooper writes when describing the feminist threat. Although he doesn't mention it, he is echoing Lewis's description of the source

Hooper makes the outlandish claim that one publisher (whom he fails to identify) wanted to revise Narnia and turn the four Pevensie children into "one...black, one Red Indian, one Chinese, and one white." Then the publisher wanted to reverse the parts of all the boys and girls, and to turn all the Narnians dark and the Calormenes white. Hooper assures his audience that he is on guard, defending Lewis against "witchhunters" who claim that Lewis was sexist and racist. Thus he simultaneously warns people that Lewis is under siege (putting Hooper under seige) and cheers them with the knowledge that he does all he can to defend Lewis.

According to Hooper, a feminist (unidentified) objected immediately to Lewis's essay "Modern Man and His Categories of Thought" when it surfaced. Hooper does not say where the essay came from, but he says that he "unearthed" it shortly before 3 February 1982. On that evening he gave it a "world premier" by reading it aloud to a small Oxford group—thus triggering an explosion from a feminist who was present. The fact "that anyone would attack Lewis" made Hooper "a little sore," and he had to be consoled by two pints of ale at the Bulldog pub across from Christ Church, Oxford.

Friendly Memories?

Where does Hooper tell about the feminist attack upon "Modern Man and His Categories of Thought"? In a peculiar publication, a twenty-page 1983 booklet with the peculiar title *A Cretaceous Perambulator (The Re-examination of)*, now attributed to Lewis in his official bibliography. Some readers find the booklet tasteless. Its main significance may be Hooper's surprising claim that Lewis was a talented forger.

Hooper explains that on 17 May 1983 at Browns Restaurant on 7 Woodstock Road he first showed the *Cretaceous Perambulator* document to friends. They decided to publish it on 22 November 1983, the twentieth anniversary of Lewis's death, "as a fitting memorial to the man [C. S. Lewis] who had been the cause of so much happiness." Fewer than 200 copies were printed, and all were numbered; they are collectors' items.

---

of his childhood phobia for insects, a detestable beetle with moveable pincers in an early picture book. Lewis described this "abomination" in the first chapter of *Surprised by Joy*, "Snip-snap—snip-snap."

Hooper claims that in April 1936 Lewis playfully forged forty-six sentences in his own boyhood handwriting (Hooper comments, "It is such a good forgery..."), and for good measure he also forged an illegible letter from Cosmo Gordon Lang, then archbishop of Canterbury. Both forgeries (or forgeries of forgeries—some find the archbishop's letter especially unconvincing) appear in *A Cretaceous Perambulator* as responses to a humorous exam that Barfield and Harwood concocted in 1936 to commemorate walking tours that Lewis took with friends six to nine years earlier.[22]

Some of Barfield's questions involve a mystic "caboodle" (men's lavatory painted heavenly blue) and "lovely quirinal"[23] (euphemism for "queer urinal"). One of the essay assignments for Lewis was "The Quirinal—its Uses and Abuses." The next one was "Milk-Float[24] versus πηνις [Greek letters used to form a nonexistent Greek word that would be pronounced *penis*]." According to Hooper, the reaction of his friends at Browns Restaurant to this slightly humorous booklet was "They were falling out of their chairs with laughter..." [25]

Another odd piece posthumously attributed to Lewis is the anonymous 1973 obituary for J. R. R. Tolkien that appeared in the London *Times*. Humphrey Carpenter told readers of *Tolkien, A Biography* that the obituary was by Lewis. Hooper included it in his official Lewis bibliography in 1979 and also in the 1992 edition. The Lewis Estate now copyrights the obituary.

---

[22] Although Hooper doesn't mention it, the exam seems to be a weak attempt to emulate *1066 and All That*, a humor classic by W.C. Sellar and R.J. Yeatman (New York: Dutton, 1931).

[23] Quirinal was one of the seven hills of ancient Rome and also means the Italian government. Quirinus was a Roman god of war.

[24] *Milk-float* was the British term for a milk truck.

[25] According to Hooper, in 1983 Barfield still recalled verbatim Harwood's spontaneous attempt at a limerick on 8 April 1930. Barfield and Harwood witnessed Lewis's friend Walter Field staying far too long in the toilet at Exeter Station. Because they needed to board the train for Oxford, Lewis, Barfield, and Harwood had to haul Field out of the toilet. But Lewis's account (on page 353 of *They Stand Together*) indicates that Barfield was not with Field and Lewis in the Exeter station that day. Barfield and Harwood motored north, Field and Lewis caught a train east to Bournemouth, and there seems to have been no comical event in the Exeter restroom after all.

In 1993 novelist Tim Powers happened to obtain a 1978 book titled *Eglerio! In Praise of Tolkien,* which includes the little-known obituary. Powers stated on page 1 of *The Lewis Legacy,* issue 57, why he thought the obituary couldn't be by Lewis.

In response, Stephen Schofield, editor of the *Canadian C. S. Lewis Journal,* obtained a copy of the obituary from the *Times* and asked Walter Hooper about it. Hooper answered, "I don't think Lewis wrote this piece." One bit of evidence he pointed out was that Lewis would not have called Inklings meetings "Bohemian." (I agree.) Hooper did not explain how or why the estate copyrighted the anonymous essay, and he did not say why he includes it in his Lewis bibliography.[26]

Changing Churches

Another of Lewis's strangest posthumous works began to surface in 1983 with Walter Hooper's claim that Lewis believed in Papal Infallibility. At least that seems to be Hooper's claim in his foreword to *Pleasures Forevermore.*[27] After lamenting over the Anglican "creation of priestesses," Hooper assures Catholic readers that—more than anyone else Hooper knows of—Lewis wanted the Church of England to unite with the Roman Catholic Church. Can one really suppose, Hooper asks rhetorically, that Lewis had no belief in the visible, holy, Catholic, and Apostolic Church? An odd question from an Anglican priest, if Anglicans believe that theirs is a visible, holy, Catholic, and apostolic church. (In 1984 Hooper had an audience with the Pope, and in 1988 he joined the Roman Catholic Church.)[28]

---

[26] The *Times* did not answer my inquiry about the authorship of the obituary. A likely scenario is that it began as an early tribute to Tolkien by Lewis and was expanded by anonymous journalists decades later.

[27] John Randolph Willis, *Pleasures Forevermore* (Loyola University Press, 1983).

[28] The rumor that Lewis embraced Roman Catholicism dates back to 1935. Lewis's *Pilgrim's Regress* was first published in 1933 by Dent, and then republished in 1935 by the Roman Catholic firm Sheed and Ward. Some readers have mistakenly assumed that Mother Kirk in the allegory is the Roman Catholic Church rather than the Christian church in general. On the flyleaf of the dust jacket Sheed said "...Mr. Lewis's wit would probably seem to Bunyan sinful. Certainly his theology would" and "The hero, brought up in Puritania (Mr. Lewis himself was brought up in Ulster), cannot abide the religion he finds there." The latter is an indictment of the Anglican

Sheldon Vanauken, himself a convert to Roman Catholicism, responded to the foreword: "Walter Hooper says he hasn't known anyone who so longed for reunion as Lewis did. If Lewis did, how would Hooper know?...I knew Lewis for twelve years, and often touched upon the 'question of Rome' in conversation and letters: but Jack would not talk about it. Others said that too."[29]

Hooper explains in his foreword that Lewis hid his Catholicism for the sake of evangelism, in order to make his appeal as broad as possible by avoiding controversy. Even so, he claims, Lewis received letters from people who thought he should be burned at the stake for mentioning the Virgin Birth. "It is not at all unreasonable that Father Willis should wish that Lewis had said more about the visible Church," Hooper observes. "I do too. But not if it wrecked the possibility of Lewis telling a mainly unbelieving world what Christianity is about." (Hooper does not explain why honesty about his beliefs worked for G. K. Chesterton but would not have worked for Lewis.)

Hooper tells a new story about Lewis. It seems that the Jesuit priests of Campion Hall in Oxford were so favorably impressed with *Mere Christianity* that they invited Lewis to come to speak to them about a reunion between their church and his. Hooper found a fragment of that talk written out on the back of a radio script, and he quotes two paragraphs from it in his foreword for Willis.

In 1990 Hooper published the entire essay (not a fragment), titled "Christian Reunion." It is the one new essay in the paperback *Christian Reunion and Other Essays.*[30] Hooper says in his introduction, "I have no idea who prompted him to write it, except that the invitation obviously came from Roman Catholics. I think the appeal must have been very strong, for this division is one of the few subjects Lewis almost never chose to write or talk about. Thus far I have found no one who remembers it, and I can't help but suppose that the essay is being published here for the first time. Even the manuscript has its own fascination; for it is written on the back of a few

---

Protestantism of Northern Ireland. Lewis marked those statements on the flyleaf of a copy in the Wade Center and wrote below, "The suggestions are put in by the unspeakable Sheed with no authority of mine & without my knowledge."

[29] Sheldon Vanauken in *The Lewis Legacy*, 49:3.

[30] C. S. Lewis, *Christian Reunion and Other Essays.* (London: Collins, 1990).

remaining leaves of the 'Mere Christianity' broadcasts given over the BBC in 1944. I expect this essay was written about the same time."[31]

In just seven years, the fragment on the back of a radio script had grown into a complete essay, and the 1944 audience of ecumenically-minded Jesuit priests at Campion Hall had disappeared off the face of the earth. (Whatever happened to the original radio script with only a fragment of the essay in Lewis's handwriting on the back? Where did the new one come from?)

There is a possible anachronism in the essay itself. The writer remarks that it would be difficult to get an agreed Faith versus Works formula today, especially in Germany. Thus Germany is referred to as an arena of theological debate at the time when it was a primarily an arena of terror, carnage and destruction near the end of World War II. Mentioning Germany without any reference to the war was unlike Lewis, whose mind was saturated with the war.

In this essay Lewis seems to say that he could accept all Catholic doctrines. But that can't be true. In the 24 October 1952 issue of *Church Times,* Lewis attacked canonization of saints as described in the *Catholic Encyclopaedia,* hotly opposing adoption of that practice in the Church of England.[32]

In 1956 Joseph Bayly, editor of InterVarsity Christian Fellowship's *HIS* magazine, checked with Lewis and reported, "I have recently had a reply from C. S. Lewis indicating that he has not become a Roman Catholic nor does he intend to take such an action."[33]

In the 1994 edition of *Jack,* Lewis's Roman Catholic friend George Sayer says that although most of Lewis's friends were Catholic, Lewis had no interest in joining them. He never attacked the Catholic Church or any other, according to Sayer; but he considered some Roman doctrines heretical, particularly the position of the Virgin Mary and papal infallibilty. Warren told Sayer that when he almost converted to Catholicism once, Lewis became very upset and rushed to Ireland to talk him out of it. [34]

---

[31] In 1989 Hooper showed this 1944 "Christian Reunion" manuscript to visiting American playwright Paul McCusker, and indeed the handwriting looked like that of C. S. Lewis.

[32] See *God in the Dock,* pages 337-338.

[33] Letter from Joseph Bayly to Kathryn Lindskoog, dated 7 May 1956. Published in *The Lewis Legacy,* 10: 4.

[34] George Sayer, *Jack* (Wheaton IL: Crossway Books, 1994) 421-22.

Nevertheless, the 18 November 1990 issue of the English newspaper *Catholic Pictorial* included the headline "Lewis would have died a Catholic." This was the year when "Christian Reunion" was published, encouraging that idea.[35] Reporter Frank Brookes interviewed Walter Hooper and concluded sincerely:

> But, says his biographer and Literary Advisor to the C. S. Lewis Estate, Walter Hooper, a former Anglican priest and now a Roman Catholic layman, "I feel sure that Lewis would have entered the Catholic Church had he lived. He would have made a terrific Catholic," said the one man in England who knew Lewis better than anyone else.

This rumor that Lewis was covertly Roman Catholic continues year after year alongside an erroneous assumption that Lewis was overtly Roman Catholic. Joe Adcock's offhand remark on 29 May 1992 in the *Seattle Post-Intelligence* is typical: "In 1952 Lewis was the quintessence of Roman Catholic, literary, intellectual bachelorhood." It might seem less than gracious for Protestants to protest.

Juvenilia Delinquency

In 1985 a thirty-year wait was over at last. In *Surprised by Joy* (1955) C. S. Lewis had described his childhood writing. In 1969 Lewis's early co-author, Warren, tried to get his cherished collection of Lewis juvenilia published; but Owen Barfield objected, and Lewis's publisher refused. (Warren would have been the perfect editor because he knew all about the pieces and their creation.) So it was that in 1985 Walter Hooper, evidently with Owen Barfield's blessing, had the privilege of editing the juvenilia and bringing it out in a handsome illustrated giftbook.

---

[35] "Your review of *Christian Reunion* is devastating and persuasive. The suggestion that Lewis was contemplating becoming a Roman Catholic is no more plausible than the idea that he was really an evangelical fundamentalist." Colin Brown, Associate Dean for Advanced Theological Studies, Fuller Theological Seminary, in *The Lewis Legacy* 49: 3.

Hooper's twenty-five pages of editorial comments are confused and contradictory, and the opening set of illustrations—attributed to seven-year-old Lewis, but probably done by a parent at his request—are definitely by an adult. The one illustration in the set that is really by a seven-year-old was intentionally excluded![36] But the worst problems in the book are "The History of Animal-Land" and "Encyclopedia Boxoniana." Both of these sections appear to be forgeries.

The seven-page "History" is so dull that its puzzling provenance is the most interesting thing about it. According to editor Hooper, in 1953 Lewis loaned his original manuscript to the eleven-year-old son of his friend Lord David Cecil. The boy inexplicably copied out the essay and gave his copy to Lewis; then Lewis supposedly gave the copy to Hooper a decade later. (The fate of the purported original is unknown.) Unfortunately for that illogical scenario, a 31 May 1968 letter to Hooper from Lord David Cecil in the Hooper collection at Chapel Hill seems to flatly contradict it.

In contrast, "Encyclopedia Boxoniana" is not juvenilia; according to Hooper, Lewis wrote it in 1927 and 1928 during two visits to the family home in Belfast By then he was an instructor at Magdalen College, had published *Dymer*, had started his first novel, and was starting his masterful *Allegory of Love*. There is no doubt about his continuing interest in the juvenilia and his intention to organize it better at that time, but the 15-page essay that Hooper presents in *Boxen* does not seem to be by Lewis. It is pompous, witless, long-winded, and insufferably "cute." Hooper says he rescued it from Warren's 1964 manuscript bonfire.

"Encyclopedia Boxoniana" includes some dreadful sentences, including "To draw out all that can be deduced from the texts, to attempt the solution of all problems and the removal of all contradictions in the light of general probability and skilful hypothesis, would have been to anticipate the future Boxonologist rather than to provide him with his tools." Hooper identifies himself elsewhere in the book as the "future Boxonologist" that Lewis had in mind, a fulfillment of a whimsical prophecy. By portraying Lewis as the

---

[36] That illustration was photographed by Douglas Gilbert and appears in *C. S. Lewis, Images of His World* by Douglas Gilbert and Clyde S. Kilby (Grand Rapids: Eerdmans, 1973).

source of such a term, an editor could thus point it toward himself in hopes
that it would catch on. But *Boxen* was so tedious that it did not catch on.

Exactly one decade after *Boxen* was published, a California handwriting
analyst named Nancy Cole was dispatched to the Bodleian by Hooper's friend
and defender Stanley Mattson, to vouch for the authenticity of Hooper's Dark
Tower manuscript. Unaware that I had challenged the authenticity of
"Encyclopedia Boxoniana" in *The C. S. Lewis Hoax* and *Light in the
Shadowlands*, she reported that Lewis's handwriting there was unusual; it was
less relaxed than elsewhere, less slanted, and more uniform.[37]

Nagging Doubts and Good News

Did Lewis really write "Introductory Letter," "A Pageant Played in
Vain," "Finchley Avenue," "The Dark Tower," the Preface to "Screwtape
Pro-poses a Toast," "On Criticism," "Forms of Things Unknown," "The
Man Born Blind," an autobiographical scrap on the back of the Dark Tower
manuscript, Hooper's Narnia scraps, "Modern Man and His Categories of
Thought," the J. R. R. Tolkien obituary, playful forgeries in *The Cretaceous
Perambulator*, "Christian Reunion," "The History of Animal-Land" and
"Encyclopedia Boxoniana"?[38]

Now that we have so many suspicious writings attributed to Lewis, an old
anecdote takes on new meaning. In 1965, Walter Hooper, Owen Barfield, and
seven others contributed to publisher Jock Gibb's collection of essays called
Light on C. S. Lewis. Hooper began his part by telling that C. S. Lewis threw
most of his own books and articles into the trash and forgot about them.
When Hooper became his secretary, he said, he showed Lewis a list of his

---

[37] See Appendix 10, The Nancy Cole Report.

[38] "Perhaps the worst of what Hooper has done is to make us understand Lewis
less than before, because now we 'know' things that aren't so. There's a similar
situation with a book by Henry Duksis, *The Forgotten Writings of Mark
Twain*... One scholar says the book should be taken out and burned: often when he's
trying to remember where he read something by Twain, he remembers it was in
Duksis, and therefore has no authority at all. Drat Hooper! Drat Duksis!" A letter in
The Lewis Legacy 52 from Thomas Tenney, editor of *The Mark Twain Journal*.

publications. "Did *I* write all these?" Lewis asked, and then accused Hooper of inventing most of them.[39]

So the first person to accuse Walter Hooper of inflating the Lewis corpus was C. S. Lewis himself, according to Hooper himself. Of course, the anecdote itself might be apocryphal. Whether that possibility spoils the irony or only increases the irony is a matter of opinion. But apocryphal anecdotes are of minor significance compared to apocryphal writings.

In light of all the suspicious, shoddy, unLewisian writings published under Lewis's name since his death, it is hard to believe that the excellent beginning of his fascinating first novel has been withheld from the public for over thirty years. For good news about that novel, read Chapter 7, "The Most Substantial People."

> It is bad enough to see one's own good things fathered on other people, but it is worse to have other people's rubbish fathered upon oneself.
> —*Samuel Butler*

---

[39] Walter Hooper, "A Bibliography of the Writings of C. S. Lewis" in *Light on C. S. Lewis*, ed. Jocelyn Gibb (New York: Harcourt, Brace & World 1965) 117. Gibb was Managing Director of the Geoffrey Bles publishing firm.

7

THE MOST SUBSTANTIAL PEOPLE

NOT FLIMSY FICTION AFTER ALL?

Incredible as it seems, there is an important unfinished novel by C. S. Lewis still waiting to be read. For almost thirty years this 5,333-word gem has been stored in the Wade Center with Warren Lewis's other gifts intended for everyone who cares about Lewis.[1] It combines Lewis's masterful style and readability with his usual focus on truth and goodness. Ironically, one Lewis expert after another has died without knowing it was there and without getting to read it.[2] Instead, they were misled into buying and trying to read *The Dark Tower*.

---

[1] When I asked long ago if the Wade Center or the Bodleian had the beginning of a Lewis novel about Dr. Easley, they didn't know they had it and said no. Because Lewis was eminently unqualified to write a novel about the practice of medicine, and thirty years after his death only three sentences of the alleged attempt were in evidence, I finally challenged the claim that two genuine Dr. Easley chapters existed. Michael Logsdon laid the suspicion to rest in the autumn 1993 issue of his Salinas Valley Lewis newsletter. He had learned from Walter Hooper that the fragment exists in Volume 9 (pages 291-300) of the eleven-volume Lewis Family Papers that the Marion E. Wade Center received from Warren Lewis in 1973.

Although the Lewis Family Papers are a treasury of Lewis lore, it seems that for almost thirty years no one (staff member, student worker, or volunteer) has prepared a simple table of contents for any of the eleven volumes, much less indexed them. (I have yearned to explore them for almost thirty years but lacked access.)

[2] The Wade Center allows people who can get there to copy passages by hand and advised me in 1994 that I could get the story and some 1922-1923 unpublished diary passages by sending someone to copy them. Clyde Kilby's friend Dean Picton

In 1973 Hooper had tantalized some readers by quoting three sentences from the opening of an early Lewis unfinished novel about a young English doctor.[3] But four years later, in his preface to *The Dark Tower*, Hooper treated the early fiction as if it didn't exist—assuring book buyers that with the addition of his new volume they would own "the complete fiction of C. S. Lewis."

"The Most Substantial People" exists in Volume 9 of the Lewis Family Papers in the Wade Center in Illinois, the Bodleian Library in Oxford, and the library of the University of North Carolina at Chapel Hill.[4] I believe there has been no summary or analysis of the story in print anywhere until now, and it seems that very few people are aware that it exists; yet Lewis valued it enough to save it permanently.

This neglected Lewis story is of particular interest for three reasons. First, now that Lewis's diary is available in *All My Road Before Me* (1989), readers can see how the story is based upon Lewis's extraordinary experiences in February and March of 1923 with two of Mrs. Moore's brothers, Dr. John Askins and Dr. Robert Askins. Second, Lewis the unbeliever, who seriously considered writing a thesis on the metaphysics of modern psychology, was in this novel considering a case of religious mania and the question of spiritual evil and hell.[5] Third, this fragment is proof that Lewis was already a talented fiction writer and master of dialog by 1927. This fragment refutes the claim that Lewis was an amateurish writer in the late 1920s, a claim used by defenders of the authenticity of "The Man Born Blind."

---

underwrote the cost of hiring a professional researcher to hand copy these materials. The task took her twenty-five hours, including several trips.

[3] Walter Hooper, "Preface" in *The Lion of Judah in Never Never Land* by Kathryn Lindskoog (Grand Rapids: Eerdmans, 1973) 8-9. Hooper quoted three sentences from Lewis's story, changing "the strictest uniforms of respectability" to "the uniforms of respectability."

[4] The Wade Center owns the eleven volumes of Lewis family papers typed by Warren and gave photocopies to the Bodleian. Without the permission of the Wade Center, Hooper gave or sold a microfilm copy of the Bodleian photocopies to his alma mater. These institutions do not make the material available in photocopies or through interlibrary loan.

[5] "The Most Substantial People" is somewhat reminiscent of the beginning of *Robinson Crusoe* in its references to a youthful life at sea, its cheerful style, and its use of descriptive detail. It has none of the sinister spirit of "The Dark Tower."

The Dark Tower and Other Stories includes six pieces of fiction: four short stories and two unfinished novels.[6] But it seems that only half are genuine: two of the four short stories are authentic and one of the two unfinished novels is genuine. All three of the genuine pieces were already published eleven years earlier, in the 1966 collection *Of Other Worlds*. It is easy to imagine why three pieces of ersatz Lewis fiction might have been added to the three that are genuine, but it is hard to imagine why such a valuable piece as "The Most Substantial People" was left out and ignored.

It is also hard to imagine why, in his only acknowledgement of the story, Walter Hooper misled readers about its content. As he explained it, Lewis's adolescent rejection of Christianity had caused him to become greedy for worldly success and hopefully, to write "an 'adult' novel."[7] According to Hooper, the fragment about Dr. Easley is "ample proof that [in about 1927] Lewis was still half-enamored with the bustling, enterprising, 'real' life" of Irish businessmen. Hooper says Lewis's story is "purely human" (completely secular and mundane), about "the only world in which he believed." An odd claim in light of Lewis's developing philosophical and metaphysical view of reality at that time as recorded in letters to Owen Barfield, allegorized in *The Pilgrim's Regress*, and described in *Surprised by Joy*.

Hooper gives the impression that the entire fragment is of one piece; he doesn't reveal the satirical nature of chapter 1 or the strange events that begin to unfold in the later section. In fact, he says flatly about Lewis's supposed admiration for Irish businessmen, "This is not satire."[8]

Saying that C. S. Lewis's 1927 work "The Most Substantial People" is not satire about businessmen is like saying that Sinclair Lewis's 1922 novel *Babbitt* is not satire about businessmen. Both Lewises were capable of skillful skewering. With Sinclair Lewis's prominence in the 1920s[9] and Lewis's

---

[6] The four short stories in *The Dark Tower* are "The Man Born Blind," "The Shoddy Lands," "Ministering Angels," and "Forms of Things Unknown." The two unfinished novels are "The Dark Tower" and "After Ten Years." Of these six, the three genuine works by Lewis are "The Shoddy Lands," "Ministering Angels," and probably "After Ten Years."

[7] What Hooper meant by an "adult" novel is not clear.

[8] Walter Hooper, "Introduction," *The Lion of Judah in Never-Never Land* by Kathryn Lindskoog (Grand Rapids: Eerdmans, 1973) 9.

[9] In 1930 Sinclair Lewis won the Nobel Prize for literature.

eclectic reading habits, it is quite possible that Lewis was familiar with *Babbitt* before he began "The Most Substantial People."[10]

In Lewis's first chapter a Belfast businessman, Hughie McClinnichan, says of a certain neighborhood, "Half the most substantial people in Belfast live up there." He goes on to mention that the Easley family is "very substantial." The rest of the story seems to revolve around the substantiality or insubstantiality of people, their claims, and their beliefs—some of which turn out to be chimeras. This is also the theme of *The Great Divorce* (1945), in which the unredeemed are ghostly, as in Dante's *Inferno,* and the redeemed are "solid people."[11]

There can be no doubt that "The Most Substantial People" is based upon two of Janie Askins Moore's brothers from Ireland, both medical doctors, and what happened in that unfortunate family early in 1923. Their tragedy traumatized Lewis, and he mentioned it briefly in his autobiography *Surprised by Joy.* But the full story has never been told until now.

After Dr. John Hawkins Askins served in World War I, something went wrong mentally and physically. He and his American wife Mary, whom Lewis detested, eventually moved to a suburb of Oxford to live within walking distance of his sister Janie Moore. According to a few 1922 diary entries, Lewis found him a stimulating and wide-ranging conversationalist.[12] On 11 November 1922 Lewis wrote in his diary that "the Doc" was in

---

[10] In *The Pilgrim's Regress* (written in 1932) Lewis playfully echoes a wide array of writings. In chapter 8 he seems to intentionally echo the beginning of chapter 3 of *Babbitt.* There Sinclair Lewis wrote, "To George F. Babbitt, as to most prosperous citizens of Zenith, his motor car was poetry and tragedy, love and heroism." In *The Pilgrim's Regress* C. S. Lewis invented an American named Gus who spoke reverently of his car: "She is a poem. She is the daughter of the spirit of the age. What was the speed of Atlanta to her speed? The beauty of Apollo to her beauty?"

[11] On 27 June 1922 C. S. Lewis wrote in his diary that he and Mrs. Moore agreed that his fellow student Leo Baker too easily accepted the barrier that tends to separate an intellectual from the "solid folk." Lewis's distaste for all kinds of elitism remained, but when he accepted Christianity the concept of solidity (substantiality) came to symbolize for him dependence upon God rather than cozy middle-class domesticity. He eventually taught that idolization of home and family life is a spiritual trap.

[12] *All My Road Before Me: The Diary of C. S. Lewis 1922-1927,* ed., Walter Hooper (San Diego: Harcourt Brace Jovanovich, 1991). In his usually helpful index, Hooper says that on page 41 of *All My Road Before Me* (in Lewis's diary entry for 26 May 1922) Dr Askins talks about perversion. To the contrary, on page 41 Dr. Askins

good form and while on an evening stroll the two discussed many things, then somehow fell to talking about physical death and all the horrors hanging over one. "The Doc said if you stopped to think, you couldn't endure this world for an hour. I left him and walked home. Flashes and bangs from Oxford where they were celebrating Armistice night..."[13]

The Doc was functioning well enough that on 17 December he was going to give his sister Mrs. Moore, his niece Maureen, C. S. Lewis, and their maid Dorothy vaccinations at home. That morning Lewis had an odd nightmare, like a premonition of evil to come. He dreamed that his friend Leo Baker (who had recuperated from illness at their home a few months earlier) was lying nude on the hearthrug for his vaccination. The Doc was using a peculiar wrench that snapped shut, and Lewis realized to his horror that the vaccination would also be a castration. Lewis started to flee and awakened from the nightmare. That afternoon the vaccinations went fine. Lewis didn't mention the Doc again in his diary until 13 January, when the Doc suffered hurt feelings so inappropriately that Lewis feared there was something drastically wrong with him. Lewis was right.

On 1 February Lewis recorded "a curious dream" that has been inexplicably left out of All My Road Before Me. An old lady took him in to see her sick son. One or two doctors were sound asleep by a bathtub filled with a neat pile of bedding and freezing cold water. Lewis lifted the bedding and found the body of a young man. "Ah yes, poor fellow," Lewis said; "He had a fit and so they had to drown him, of course." He turned to say something to the old lady just when Mrs. Moore came in and awakened him from the dream, to his great relief.[14] The dream corresponded uncannily to events that

---

and Mrs. S. talk about spiritualism, and Lewis asks why ghosts always speak as if they belong to the lower middle class. "We talked a little of psychoanalysis, condemning Freud..." Readers might suspect that something about perversion was omitted, but the Lewis Family Papers at the Wade Center reveal that all that was left out about Freud was "Mrs. S. said that he must have suffered from a sex complex himself." This raises two questions. In light of Lewis's similar assessment of Freud years later, why was Mrs. S.'s remark cut out? And why was this conversation described as a conversation about perversion?

[13] All My Road Before Me, 135.

[14] In Lewis's dream the old lady seems to represent Janie Moore (then about 51 years old). She had been like a mother to her little brother in childhood after their mother died, and she is the one who brought Lewis to him in middle age.

would unfold (largely in his own bedroom, where he had the dream) in the next two months; but those very events gave Lewis, who was always interested in dreams, a great aversion to anything uncanny. In his diary he did not mention the obvious correspondence between his dream and the events that followed.

On 5 February the Doc was more cheerful than he had been but looked wretched. He spoke to Lewis about the awful depths one sometimes sees underneath one's own mind. Lewis agreed that most of us can find "positive Satanic badness down there somewhere, the desire for evil not because it is pleasant but because it is evil." On 21 February the Doc was walking stiffly (a sign of paralytic disease) and talking about immortality and seemed on the verge of a breakdown. Lewis and Mrs. Moore agreed that ordinarily the Doc was "the most unoffending, the gentlest, the most unselfish man imaginable."

On 23 February the Doc was haunted by horrible, blasphemous, and obscene thoughts, and he was seized by violent screaming fits.[15] He was obsessed with the terror of going to hell, and at his most violent he had incredible strength. He couldn't be left at home with Mary, and so Mrs. Moore had them move into the Lewis household.[16] (Mary was a sullen, selfish woman who expected her hosts to wait upon her. Lewis said in his diary that he would have preferred a cheap army prostitute or an oily old gypsy woman living in his house.)

When he was lucid the Doc claimed that syphilis from his college days had doomed him to lunacy and death, but his brother, Dr. Robert Askins of Bristol, claimed it was all bunkum and nerves. He and another doctor chloroformed the patient, and then injected him with a narcotic that reduced

---

[15] In Lewis's dream on the morning of 1 February, the dead man had suffered a fit.

[16] Eight months earlier similar therapeutic hospitality had been successful. On Thursday, 22 June 1922, Lewis had discovered that fellow student Leo Baker was in the Acland Nursing Home with fever and mental confusion. At Mrs. Moore's suggestion, he invited Baker to transfer to their home. On Sunday, 24 June, Baker arrived by taxi in a bright blue dressing gown. On Wednesday, 28 June, Arthur Greeves arrived for an impromptu visit, and the two visitors got acquainted. Lewis's snoring disturbed Greeves that night. Greeves and Baker spent the morning discussing psychoanalysis, and Baker left at 3 P.M., much improved.

him to noisy rambling all night.[17] When Lewis finally had some tea with bread and butter the next morning, it made him sick. He expected the doctors to put the Doc into an asylum the next day, but instead they decided he had "mere hysteria" and should wait for admission to a hospital for veterans. They left the terrified man with his unhelpful wife Mary and Mrs. Moore, in Lewis's care.

On 25 February the "two charming guests" moved into Lewis's bedroom. More than two terrible weeks are recorded in Lewis's diary, but many of the details are left out of *All My Road Before Me*. In his lucid periods the Doc sometimes thanked Lewis so profusely and abjectly that Lewis could hardly bear it. Lewis disliked Mary dosing the Doc with excess drugs and losing her temper at him when he was in agonies of torment. Meanwhile, Lewis was getting behind in his graduate studies. A third doctor examined the Doc and agreed with the others that he was not insane and that his bouts of paralysis were emotional in nature. Robert came and again rushed away, then failed to return when Lewis desperately wrote for help. On 8 March Lewis wrote in his diary, "[Janie] was rather hurt when I described [Robert] as a cur..."

The Doc was evidently not a Christian believer, and neither were his sister Janie or his brother Robert. But their father had been a priest in the Church of Ireland. Furthermore, their brother William James Askins (1879-1955) was a priest in the Church of Ireland; at this time he was Rector of Kilmore. Yet there is no mention in Lewis's diary of any priest called in to minister to the Doc, although he imagined himself guilty of unforgivably heinous misdeeds and thought he was already in Hell.[18]

On 10 March Lewis recorded, "[The Doc] finally lay down on the sofa and I sat on the table and talked to him: all the old wearisome assurances that he

---

[17] The doctors obviously intended to drown the patient's panic in drugged sleep. The unconsciousness of the bedside doctors in Lewis's dream seemed to foretell the real-life doctors' obliviousness to the extremely serious nature of the Doc's affliction.

[18] In chapter 8 of his fantasy *The Great Divorce* the fictional Lewis falls into a fearful state of mind in which everything good looks like a sinister trick of malevolent gods. In this state of mind he recalls "poor Cowper," the devout but mentally ill Christian poet (1731-1800) who suffered from a relentless obsession about being damned to hell. William Cowper once dreamed that he was not damned after all, but when he awakened he believed that the dream was a beautiful illusion; then he felt worse than ever. His letters are considered among the most brilliant in English literature.

was quite alright, that it was nothing but nerves, that he was getting better, that there was no such place as Hell, that he was not dying, that he was not going mad...that he was not paralysed, that he could master himself. It is a sort of devil's litany that he must be as sick of hearing as I am of saying..."[19] At that point Robert arrived unannounced and explained why he had been unable to come sooner, and Lewis felt he had misjudged the man. (Lewis's change of heart toward Robert was left out of All My Road Before Me, and it is significant in two ways: it shows Lewis's readiness to think better of people, and it explains his later willingness to identify himself with Robert as the narrator of his first novel.)

Two days later, on 12 March, the tenderhearted Doc was forcibly carried off in tears to the hospital at Henley, convinced that he would never see his beloved family again. More concerned about his own survival than the Doc's at that point, Lewis wrote in his diary, "I could have gone down on my knees to thank any deity who cared to claim the credit for this release." On 17 March he noted in his diary that spiritualism, Yoga, and undigested psychoanalysis seemed to have contributed to the Doc's collapse. "I at any rate am scared off anything mystical and abnormal and hysterical for a long time to come."[20] On 6 April the Doc died, unconscious at the end. Over thirty years later Lewis told readers about the Doc's terrible suffering, without revealing his identity, in Surprised by Joy.

But Lewis didn't wait thirty years to incorporate the puzzling tragedy into his writing. In an undated letter that he wrote from Magdalen College to Owen Barfield at some point between 1923 and 1927, he tried to show Barfield the danger of occultism in a couple of pen sketches with explanations attached. A little man tied to the post of his own personality uses occult tools to chip away at the mirror before him that gives him a normal limited human view of reality. He doesn't notice the loving hands stretched out from clouds behind him. Once the mirror is all chipped away, an evil spirit comes

---

[19] All My Road Before Me, 217.

[20] Ibid., 221. Lewis had a philosophical interest in life's unexplained anomalies, and he also had an inborn nature that was highly intuitive and sometimes mystical. His father Albert Lewis seems to have suffered from more than normal anxiety and depression, as well as irritability. (In C. S. Lewis A. N. Wilson assumes that Albert's problem was alcoholism.) As a young man Lewis felt a strong need to protect his mental autonomy and to avoid nervous breakdowns.

through the empty frame and grabs him. Ahead are an ambulance, an asylum, and a cemetery, all clearly sketched.[21] Disagreement about occultism was central to "The Great War," an ongoing friendly debate between Lewis and Barfield.

Next, Lewis incorporated reflections of the Askins brothers into his novel "The Most Substantial People." There he combined the Doc's terror of hell with a vivid but good-natured satire of ordinary commercial greed. He was to fuse these two unlikely elements again almost twenty years later in a book that was especially dear to him, *The Great Divorce* (1945). One of the first characters in both stories was a materialistic businessman.[22]

Lewis began this story by remarking that maps don't show how far a town really extends.[23] London and Oxford may be said to exist only at their very centers; but Belfast extends all the way across the channel to Liverpool,

---

[21] These sketches and Lewis's commentary are reproduced in two books. Douglas Gilbert and Clyde S. Kilby, C. S. Lewis, *Images of His World* (Grand Rapids: Eerdmans, 1973) 44-45. John Warwick Montgomery, *Principalities and Powers: The World of the Occult* (Minneapolis: Bethany House, 1973) 171-74. Montgomery explains, "Sometime in the 1920s Lewis corresponded on the subject with Owen Barfield, who would later do irreparable harm to his talent by embracing Rudolph Steiner's occult Anthroposophy. One of Lewis's unpublished and undated letters of that period, written at Magdalen College, is headed 'The Real Issue between Us.' Lewis first describes his own approach by an analogy based upon Plato's myth of the cave: like every man, Lewis is bound to the post of finite personality so that he cannot turn around and observe reality directly; clouds behind him represent that ultimate reality or True Being. His understanding of the meaning of life comes by observing the mirror before him, which displays 'as much of the reality (and such disguise of it) as can be seen' from his position. He devotes himself to studying the mirror with his eyes ('explicit cognition') and also reaches backward with his hands 'so as to get some touch (implicit 'taste' or 'faith') of the real.' For Barfield the occultist, however, though his position vis-à-vis reality is necessarily the same as Lewis', his reaction to it is far different."

The businessman in "The Most Substantial People" wore a round bowler hat, and so did the similar businessman in *The Great Divorce*. Lewis ironically called the latter (in chapters 2 and 6) "the Intelligent Man," but some of the residents of Hell called him "Ikey," a derogatory nickname for Jews. Thus at the end of World War II Lewis was attacking anti-Semitism by attributing it to hateful people in Hell.

[23] Because this novel is going to be largely about the question of Hell and the possible incursion of Hell into a woman's mind here on earth, it is reasonable to assume that in his seemingly casual beginning about city boundaries Lewis had in mind the city of Dis in Dante's *Inferno*. Dis can extend to points on this earth, just as Belfast can extend across the channel to the port in Liverpool.

because as soon as one gets on the ferry in Liverpool, one is in Belfast. The food is Irish, the people are Irish, the dialect is Irish, and the manners are Irish. So it was that at 10 P.M. one February night the narrator of the story, Dr. Easley of Bristol, England, felt himself in Ireland for the first time as soon as he boarded the ferry in Liverpool.

The narrator's father, Geordie Easley, had moved from Ireland to England and died there, leaving a needy widow and little son. The boy had once met his aunt Mary Easley from Belfast, who held him on her unpleasant expanse of silken lap, called him "Laddie," and talked to his mother about a business slump. When poverty finally forced his mother to write to the Easleys for help, their answer arrived on the day after Christmas, the day of her funeral. Aunt Mary's oldest son, Scrabo, wrote what the narrator considered a singularly sincere, manly letter,[24] reciting a litany of financial troubles and telling of the pain he felt over being unable to help. He enclosed £5 and declared himself a uniquely unfortunate man.

Strangers helped the orphaned student complete his education, and he served as a penniless but carefree doctor on ships at sea for a few years. During that time all he received from the Easleys was an invitation to Scrabo's sister's wedding, and when she died a few months later they sent him her photograph. He had never met her.

About a year after Dr. Easley settled in Bristol and launched a thriving practice, Scrabo wrote in his usual frank, engaging tone to congratulate him. After that the Easleys wrote several times inviting him to visit. To his surprise, they mentioned their automobile, and he realized that they were much better off than before, although Scrabo still worried because he was not doing well.

Dr. Easley had to leave Bristol to serve in the trenches in France in World War I, and Scrabo complained bitterly in letters about the fact that he had to stay home to be with his mother. (He did not explain why.) The Irish were exempt from the draft, but Scrabo wrote about the possibility that the rotten English government might start drafting the Northern Irish and drain Ulster of the last of its manhood, thus inviting the Southern rebels to invade. It was the fear of Southern Ireland, he explained, that held many men in Ulster

---

[24] Lewis makes use of what is called dramatic irony, allowing readers to discern Scrabo's character before the narrator does.

when every nerve in their bodies was crying out to go to France. Not that he could go anyway, he added, because of his state of health. He wrote pages grousing about the British government. In a letter of Christmas greetings that Dr. Easley read in the midst of some unforgettable battlefield horror, Scrabo lamented that financial ruin was staring him in the face. If things got much worse, he declared, he would join the army and serve in France, but all is in God's will.

The next time that Dr. Easley heard from Scrabo was after returning to England, surprised to be alive and grieving for fallen comrades. Scrabo wrote that the family was desperately worried about his mother, and he begged his cousin to come to Belfast to help her. Later that evening, Dr. Easley found himself on the ferry to Belfast. On the ferry the same food was served for supper and for breakfast, of an overwhelmingly homely[25] and *substantial* type, eaten in large quantities. The boat was full of thickset men in snug blue serge suits, stiff collars, heavy, well-polished boots, and bowler hats. They conversed with liveliness rare in England and gave the impression that they were sound sleepers and hearty eaters. They spoke in a dialect similar to low Scotch, in a rude but genial style.

When he reached his two-berth stateroom Dr. Easley found that a fat man with a hard face the color of beefsteak was there. He was shaking rainwater off his hat onto the floor and had already taken the lower (more desirable) bunk. He said he was going to see if the bar was open and asked Dr. Easley if he was coming, then led the way, brushing people against the wall of the narrow passageway. Once they were in the smoking room his host (as Dr. Easley mistakenly thought him to be) began to make conversation. When Dr. Easley didn't understand the man's question about Bristol, he asked impatiently if Easley was not in business. No, I'm a doctor, Easley replied.

Hughie McClinnichan's probing questions annoyed Dr. Easley, but he attributed them to friendliness and answered that he was going to visit in the Wanhope Gardens section of Belfast.[26] Mr. McClinnichan surprised him by

---

[25] In England the word homely does not mean unattractive as it usually does in the United States; instead, it means simple or unpretentious.

[26] The Germanic word wanhope was in use in England as early as 1297, and it meant hopelessness and despair—especially despair of salvation. Thus the name of Scrabo's neighborhood foreshadows what Dr. Easley will encounter there. Lewis used this name again in the map of the world he designed for the endpapers of *The Pilgrim's*

enthusiastically describing various wealthy families that lived in that area, including the Easleys. He interrupted himself to suggest that one needed to ring the bell if one wanted to call a steward, and so Dr. Easley rang. McClinnichan went on talking, and when the steward arrived he happened to be bent down tying a bootlace while Dr. Easley ordered two whiskies.

McClinnichan lamented about the economy and taxes and government until the whiskies arrived, at which he expressed surprise and said how kind that was. Then he drank the whisky, sucked on his ragged grey moutache, and spoke about why he didn't consider letting his son go off selfishly to fight in the recent war. (He thought many young fellows went just to have fun and to get out of work. Decent people should stay home to look after Northern Ireland, and the strong young men idling on street corners with their hands in their pockets should join the army.) He wished he had never let his son go to school in England, but now the boy had settled down in the family business in Belfast and was getting good at it.

After more gossip about prominent Belfast families, McClinnichan finally learned Dr. Easley's identity and assured him that his cousin Scrabo was one of the richest men in Belfast. McClinnichan and Scrabo were friends. McClinnichan had often heard of the unfortunate Geordie Easley and his son the English doctor. ("Ach, we'll make an Irishman of you yet.") Easleys all know how to look after themselves, McClinnichan observed admiringly.

He asked if Dr. Easley was a friend of the Reverend Bonner's and was surprised that he hadn't heard of him. He explained that Bonner had been with the Easleys for a long time and had become a great friend of theirs. He was reportedly from a very wealthy family in England. McClinnichan noted that the Easleys never know anyone except nice people and that it would be a funny thing if Geordie Easley's son wasn't a friend of Hughie McClinnichan.

At that point Dr. Easley decided that the sort of heartiness in that red twinkling face and the stubby chins pressed over the high collar reminded him of some of Scrabo's letters. At tables all around there were self-important men like McClinnichan leaning forward, swapping stories, puffing at cigars, pounding empty glasses on tables flecked with the foam of bottled stout. The noise of their talk and the grinding and throbbing of the engine caused Dr.

Regress. In the northern sea, far from the Main Road, Lewis placed two islands: Mania and Wanhope. Wanhope itself is obviously akin to severe depression.

Easley to rise, excuse himself, and put on his coat and hat. At that point McClinnichan asked him if he would like another drink. When Easley paused to catch the words, McClinnichan quickly added that he didn't want another for himself, but perhaps Dr. Easley like one.[27] Easley thanked him, refused, and went out on deck.

A cold wind full of the sea smell whipped Dr. Easley's coat about his legs as he watched the waves of the ship's backwash racing by, then looked up an entire minute at the unmoving stars. He walked briskly back and forth on the deck, wishing that he were out at sea again, then wishing he were homeward bound. He wondered dismally if Scrabo would be like Hughie McClinnichan. Although he had known all kinds of Irishmen in his travels, people are different away at sea or in the war; there is no knowing what people will be like in their own homes. He felt a foreigner's timidity at the prospect of spending a few weeks in his cousin's house and felt squeamish about strangers assuming a kind of intimacy on the basis of some physiological accident in the 1800s. Yet what did he have to lose? At worst he would have wasted his vacation. Although family ties meant nothing to him, he felt his connection with these people tightening; it felt as if he was being fitted into a place prepared for him long ago in some complicated puzzle. He was going to become for the first time "poor Geordie's boy."

* * * ** * * * *

(At this point the story jumps ahead.)

The Reverend Bonner stood half-smiling, jerking his empty cigarette holder back and forth by moving his teeth. He looked intense, confident, and impersonal. Dr. Easley began by asking him to stop torturing Mrs. Easley and if possible to begin undoing what he had done to her. Bonner said he never talked to her on those subjects except at her request. Was he to refuse?

Easley responded impatiently that they both knew she was hovering on the edge of insanity and that it was only reasonable for him to ask Bonner to talk to her appropriately. But Bonner smiled a purely intellectual smile and said that being afraid of damnation is not madness.

---

[27] McClinnichan boasts about his business, but he slyly arranges for Dr. Easley to pay for their drinks. He does not offer to reciprocate until Dr. Easley is departing and it is too late.

Dr. Easley said "Good lord!" Look at her eyes and how she walks and talks! She never sleeps! Bonner replied that if Easley expected to be hanged in the morning, he too might be shaky and unable to sleep. Would that be reason for Bonner to try to convince him that he wouldn't be hanged? No, Bonner reasoned, her behavior was sane if her belief in hell was true. If Dr. Easley thought that anyone who believed in damnation was mad, he should pack off Bonner himself to an asylum.

Bonner agreed with Dr. Easley that it is sometimes right to hide the truth from an invalid in order to save her, but he explained that in this case a lie wouldn't save Mrs. Easley from what she feared. Instead, it would increase her danger.

Dr. Easley declared that if his aunt got "this infernal business" off her mind, he would endeavor to have her eating and sleeping properly and so happy in a few months that she might have years of healthy life ahead. Bonner replied that of course Mrs. Easley would be happier if she stopped thinking about her soul, just as Dr. Easley would be happier if he thought he was a great scientist. The danger to Mrs. Easley was not unhappiness and death, but damnation.

"Fire and brimstone?" Dr. Easley sneered. The question elicited from Bonner an excited discourse on the nature of reality. Our modern scientific worldview is only a ripple on the surface of human beliefs. A different world is always looming up behind and around our little scientific world, a world that no human can ever quite forget. If one were to describe what is known of the lives of the Easleys to anyone outside our culture, including Plato and Christ, and ask if it is likely to be well with them when the lid is on their coffins, what would their answer be? Bonner rushed on. If he was as certain as a man can be certain that an eternal, irremediable danger hangs over the Easleys, how could he stand by and let them walk into it?

Dr. Easley answered that Scrabo didn't fear hell, but realized that Scrabo, blind as a mole to spiritual reality, was a living, walking argument for hell-fire preaching, so he returned to the subject of Mrs. Easley's sanity. Even if he accepted Bonner's premises, he insisted, was driving her mad a way to save her? There is no religion that makes lunacy a passport to heaven.

Bonner replied that unless to believe in hell was madness, Mrs. Easley was not mad.[28] She was extremely frightened, and Scrabo was not frightened at all. In Bonner's view Scrabo was mad and Mrs. Easley was sane.

* * * * * * *

At this point the story breaks off, without a hint about what lay ahead for Dr. Easley, his patient, and the mysterious Reverend Bonner. But some of the things that Lewis had in mind are fairly clear.

First, it is clear that in the sense of being out of touch with reality, Scrabo was, like many people, ethically insane. Lewis considered materialism a delusion and self-satisfied greed self-destructive. They both cut people off from the reality of what is good and eternal. Hughie McClinnichan is Lewis's stereotypical extroverted but hard-hearted businessman, obsessed with money and worldly self-interest. Scrabo Easley is at least as hopeless as McClinnichan. (The name of his posh neighborhood is *Wanhope* Gardens.) In *The Great Divorce* the entrepreneurial businessman (the type who knows the price of everything and the value of nothing) inadvertantly reveals a glimpse of what drives him on: a secret fear too terrible to feel or to admit.[29] It is the fear of death—or, worse yet, terror of entities that will inflict hideous spiritual death. Bustling preoccupation with business can provide a greedy materialist with a false sense of security, a temporary feeling of safety.

Second, it seems clear that the mysterious Reverend Bonner, apparently devoid of human love and perhaps caught up in lust for spiritual authority, is himself in great spiritual danger. At this point Lewis said in his diary and letters that wrong kinds of interest in or contact with other levels of reality are dangerous. He warned Owen Barfield against occultism and similar shortcuts to hidden knowledge. Although Lewis was not yet a Christian believer, he believed in supernatural realities, and he believed in the conflict between good and evil. In his 1941 preface to *The Screwtape Letters* he warned "There are two equal and opposite errors into which our race can fall about the devils. One is to disbelieve in their existence. The other is to believe, and to feel an excessive and unhealthy interest in them. They themselves are equally pleased by both errors and hail a materialist or a magician [dabbler in the occult] with the same delight."

---

[28] Mrs. Easley was living in wanhope in Wanhope Gardens.
[29] C. S. Lewis, *The Great Divorce*, 13-14.

Finally, it is clear that as early as 1927 Lewis was concerned about the cure of souls, his own and others', although he did not yet believe in Heaven. He knew practically nothing about medicine, yet he cast himself as a fictitious doctor and perhaps intended to rescue fictitious Mary Easley from the same torture that had destroyed his real-life friend John Askins in 1923. He began the story about her fear of Hell with a playful idea about where the real borders of cities are. (The idea that Belfast extends to Liverpool had probably been in his mind since his many boyhood crossings.) His ideas about real borders and Hell and Heaven all came together in 1945 in *The Great Divorce:*

> Not only this valley but all this earthly past will have been Heaven to those who are saved. Not only the twilight in that town, but all their life on earth too, will then be seen by the damned to have been Hell. That is what mortals misunderstand. They say of some temporal suffering, "No future bliss can make up for it," not knowing that Heaven, once attained, will work backwards and turn even that agony into a glory. And of some sinful pleasure they say "Let me but have this and I'll take the consequences": little dreaming how damnation will spread back and back into their past and contaminate the pleasure of the sin. Both processes begin even before death. The good man's past begins to change so that his forgiven sins and remembered sorrows take on the quality of Heaven: the bad man's past already conforms to his badness and is filled only with dreariness. And that is why, at the end of all things, when the sun rises here and the twilight turns to blackness down there, the Blessed will say, "We have never lived anywhere except in Heaven, and the Lost, "We were always in Hell." And both will speak truly. [30]

It is especially hard to maintain this true perspective about bliss and suffering in the heat of life's emotions. In the very last essay Lewis ever wrote, "We Have No 'Right to Happiness'" for *The Saturday Evening Post,* he explains how it is that falling in love involves the almost irresistible conviction that fulfillment of this desire will mean lifelong heaven on earth.

---

[30] Ibid., 64.

"Hence *all* seems to be at stake. If we miss this chance we shall have lived in vain. At the very thought of such a doom we sink into fathomless depths of self-pity."[31] This is why ordinary people can be inordinately reckless and selfish in their pursuit of sexual happiness, Lewis explains. Strong erotic desire makes more towering promises about bliss and suffering than any other emotion, and those promises are often untrue even in the short term. I think Lewis knew this from personal experience with Janie Moore.

Lewis's thirty-year commitment to Janie Moore is an embarrassment to some people, and for over thirty years his brief marriage to Joy Davidman has embarrassed some people also. But in 1994 that unpopular marriage became an extremely popular source of romantic inspiration for the general public. What is the truth about C. S. Lewis's love life? Lewis's love life is the subject of chapter 7, "Will the Real Mrs. Lewis Stand Up."

I didn't invent the world I write about—it's all true.
—*Graham Greene*

---

[31] "We Have No 'Right To Happiness,'" *God in the Dock* (Grand Rapids MI: Eerdmans, 1970) 321.

8

WILL THE REAL MRS. LEWIS STAND UP?

NOT REALLY NOT REALLY
MARRIED AFTER ALL?

C. S. Lewis's love life was tragicomic. He was troubled at one time by a woman named Hooker who claimed to be his wife and was not. After his death, it was often claimed that when Lewis claimed to be his wife's husband, he was not. As Lewis told the story, he had a secret legal wedding without intent of any real marriage; later, he had an ecclesiastical wedding without hope of any real marriage; and later he had the surprise of a real marriage after all. But according to one biographer, he didn't mean it.

The lifelong confusion began when he was sixteen years old and bragged in a letter to his friend Arthur Greeves about "the great event." A pretty girl from Belgium had agreed to make love with him.[1] This letter was his last adolescent mention of the great event in surviving letters.

Lewis referred to the great event again when he was thirty-two and had borrowed the old letters from Greeves. According to Walter Hooper's transcription, Lewis referred ruefully to a number of adolescent letters about "my pretended assignation with the Belgian."[2] He said he would be mortified if

---

[1] C. S. Lewis, *They Stand Together* (New York: Macmillan, 1979) 65.

[2] Ibid., 424. This letter was dated 1 October 1931. I can't help wondering if Lewis wrote "intended" in place of "pretended." He would have been mortified, he said, by disclosure of these missing letters about an old repented and abandoned sin. I suspect

these letters about an old and abandoned sin became known, and so Arthur apparently destroyed them for him.

Ironically, seventy years after the great event or non-event with the Belgian girl, I felt C. S. Lewis would have been mortified to know that some people were offended by the idea that he had "the great event" with his wife; that others were offended by the idea that he didn't have "the great event" with his wife; and that more were offended that it ever became an issue. But perhaps C. S. Lewis would not be mortified now; perhaps he would smile ruefully at the joke fate played on him. His love life was largely one long story of hot desire, cold feet, bad taste, white lies, moral quandaries, and self-denial. He never really courted anyone. Yet he has emerged as a romantic figure in spite of himself.

It is clear that even before eighteen-year-old C. S. Lewis sailed away to the trenches of France in World War I, he was intensely involved with Mrs. Janie Moore, a handsome woman old enough to be his mother.[3] When he returned, they began living together.[4] His brother Warren used the word *infatuation*, and their father used the word *affair*. Lewis said little about the arrangement and kept it secret as long as possible. Mrs. Moore was an aggressive, highly opinionated Irish woman with few interests and a tempestuous temperament, but she was also expansive and affectionate. Her nickname for her husband, who was alive in Ireland, was "The Beast." Her own nickname was Minto, which allegedly referred to her habit of eating Mintoes candy.

C. S. Lewis's father felt that his son was an impetuous, kindhearted creature who let himself get caught by a needy woman who had "been through the mill." Worse yet, so long as Albert Lewis supported C. S. Lewis through extended university studies, he was also unwillingly giving to Mrs. Moore and her daughter. The widowed father longed for his son's affection and loyalty,

---

that the missing letters contained salacious descriptions of Lewis's real or imaginary experience with the Belgian girl.

[3] For a definitive study of Lewis's early relationship to Janie Moore, including evidence that she became his lover in 1917 (when he was eighteen years old), see Appendix 3, "The Mistress of C. S. Lewis" by John Bremer.

[4] In a 22 July 1971 letter to Roger Lancelyn Green, Jocelyn Gibb, Managing Director of Geoffrey Bles Publishers, complained that Green's handling of Mrs. Moore in the biography was too evasive for most readers. "…I know more than I ought to." In the Chapel Hill Collection.

and he bitterly resented the obvious fact that Minto came first. She was possessive and domineering.

In 1931 C. S. Lewis became a Christian believer, and Mrs. Moore remained an unbeliever. But like many people caught in an unsatisfactory marriage, he stayed with his acquired family.[5] She was one of the most uncongenial and inappropriate living partners the Lewis brothers could have found, but after his conversion Lewis evidently felt obligated to live as a celibate and take care of her until she died of old age.[6] (There is no basis for A. N. Wilson's outrageous suggestion that Lewis adopted Christianity primarily as an excuse to terminate his sexual relations with Mrs. Moore.[7])

In a negative sense Mrs. Moore was the first Mrs. C. S. Lewis—in cost and burden, if not in meaning and name. On 17 January 1951 Warren reflected bitterly in his diary about how Mrs. Moore had kept his brother from the advantages of both bachelorhood and marriage.[8]

About a year after Mrs. Moore's death, something happened that Lewis called "tragi-comical."[9] A hotelkeeper's wife from Ramsgate called him and asked when he was going to pay Mrs. Hooker's bill, which was overdue. Who was this Mrs. Hooker, he asked, and why should he be paying her bills?

"But she's your *wife!*"

---

[5] On 17 January 1932 letter Lewis told Warren how annoyed he was by a likeable neighbor who chuckled good-naturedly, "Ah you Irish! I love to listen to Mrs. Moore — wouldn't be happy without a grievance. It's really most remarkable."

On 21 January 1940 Lewis told Warren that she was relieved when his letter arrived "because of her usual inability to imagine any causes for silence except major disasters."

On 28 January 1940 Lewis told Warren, "I begin to suspect that the world is divided not only into the happy and the unhappy, but into those who like happiness and those who, odd as it may seem, really don't."

[6] According to the account by Joy Gresham's London friend John Christopher reproduced on page 16 of the Autumn 1991 issue of the *Canadian C. S. Lewis Journal,* Lewis allegedly told a friend of his that he was attracted to Joy but didn't now how to come to terms with physical desire after a quarter of a century of celibacy. The friend told Joy, and, with a smile, Joy told Christopher.

[7] A. N. Wilson, C. S. *Lewis* (New York: Norton, 1990) 128.

[8] Warren's comments are located on pages 236-69 of *Brothers and Friends* (San Francisco: Harper & Row, 1982). There are related comments on pages 224 and 265.

[9] Lewis's account in an unpublished letter to Dom Bede Griffiths, 17 May 1952.

It turned out that a woman named Mrs. Hooker had started running up bills and borrowing money on the strength of her claim that she was marrying C. S. Lewis. It worked for quite a while before someone finally contacted Lewis to collect.

The hotel keeper's wife called the police as soon as she finished talking to Lewis, and in early May he had to appear to testify against his supposed wife in Ramsgate police court. He had never been to a law court before, and it appalled him to see a fellow creature at bay, with no way of escape. If this is what a just trial is like, he exclaimed, what in the name of all devils must an unjust trial be like?

It was not that Lewis saw any innocence in his purported wife. She was a confidence artist with twenty-one previous convictions. She's a bad woman, he observed. He had no doubt that she should be exposed and brought to justice, but he pitied her. [10]

Lewis met some of the witnesses who had lost money to Mrs. Hooker, and their spirit impressed him. Not one of them said anything vindictive like "I hope she gets it in the neck." They all expressed sorrow, instead, that an educated woman like Mrs. Hooker chose to ruin her life with lies and thievery.

"Here, surely," Lewis reflected, "is an occasion of joy." He had to go to court twice, and it has been said that he also visited Mrs. Hooker in Holloway prison. Whether his compassion helped her any or not, it obviously did him good.

C. S. Lewis mentioned to me another dotty woman; one who assailed him with letters in gaudily decorated envelopes. She sent so many that he stopped opening any of them. This fact flatly contradicts A. N. Wilson's claim on page 235 of his Lewis biography that because of psychological maladjustment, Lewis was addicted to answering all the letters he received from people with problems—including one who signed herself "Jehovah." According to Wilson, a completely false kind of intimacy resulted.

Lewis demonstrated what Wilson calls an "astonishing" willingness to meet his readers. Wilson portrays "unseen ladies" who admired Lewis as

---

[10] "A hypocrite might (conceivably) repent and mend; or he might be unmasked and rendered innocuous." C. S. Lewis, "Lilies that Fester," *They Asked for a Paper* (London: Geoffrey Bles, 1962) 109.

faintly ludicrous at best, and he conveniently overlooks a prominent example: Ruth Pitter.

Ruth Pitter was the daughter of inner-city London teachers. She supported herself by gathering wildflowers and painting their delicate patterns on black tea trays. An artist with words as well as with paint, she often worked out poems in her mind while painting. She had an extremely keen eye and ear. After war shortages eventually closed down her successful tray business, she concentrated on poetry. She eventually became the first woman to win the Queen's Medal for Poetry, and she was installed as a Companion of Literature along with Arthur Koestler and Lord Clarke in 1974. She published several books of poetry and won many honors. But she did not win at love.

Along with hundreds of thousands of others, Ruth Pitter listened to C. S. Lewis's radio talks about Christianity during the Second World War. She listened simply because he was so entertaining; but before she knew it she was hooked and became a Christian. Eventually she found someone who could arrange for her to meet Lewis at the university. After he sampled her poetry for the first time, he said, "Why didn't someone tell me?" Although he had been working at poetry ever since he was a small child, she was a better poet than he was; and they both knew it.[11] He eagerly consulted her about his poems, and she gave him advice.

---

[11] I met Ruth Pitter when she was eighty-seven, and she told me she had been talking ever since she was three. "Don't get me started." She died at ninety-four in 1992. She had given me permission to reprint the poem "Swifts" from her 1975 collection *End of Drought,* published by Bartie & Jenkins of London, now superseded by Hutchinson & Co. Ltd.

Low over the warm roof of an old barn,
Down in a flash to the water, up and away with a cry
And a wild swoop and a sharp turn
And a fever of life under a thundery sky,
So they go over, so they go by.

And high and high and high in the diamond light,
Soaring and crying in sunshine when heaven is bare,
With the pride of life in their strong flight
And a rapture of love to lift them and carry them there,
High and high in the diamond air.

And away with the summer, away like the spirit of glee,
Flashing and calling, strong on the wing, and wild in their play,

Lewis's letters to Ruth Pitter fill an album an inch thick in the Bodleian Library. She could have asked a great price for them, but she treasured them so much that she couldn't sell them. Walter Hooper, who gathered documents for the Bodleian as a finder, persuaded her to donate her Lewis letters there.[12] (In contrast, Hooper sold his own Lewis letters to the University of North Carolina in 1980.) [13]

On 16 October 1950 Lewis inscribed a copy of *Dymer* for Ruth Pitter with the following verse: "Not for your reading, not because I dream/ To pay my debt for the still, ghostly beauty/ Of yours, but as the clown brings fruits and cream/ To a great lady, with his awkward duty." [14]

Ruth Pitter was so smitten by C. S. Lewis that at the end of 1953 she left London and bought a house in Long Crendon, about twelve miles from Oxford, in hopes of becoming Mrs. Lewis.[15] There she tactfully waited for him to respond to her presence, but he never came to visit her as often as she would have liked. The Lewis brothers and friends of theirs enjoyed her greatly, but Lewis didn't court her. The closest he came to it was to say to his friends Hugo Dyson and George Sayer, "I am not a man for marriage, but if I were I would ask Ruth Pitter." Alone and blind and apparently impoverished in her old age, she still smiled about that.

With a high cry to the high sea,
And a heart for the south, a heart for the diamond day,
So they go over, so go away.

[12] In the April 1971 issue of *CSL*, Walter Hooper stated, "A few years ago Pauline Baynes passed Lewis's map [of Narnia] on to me, and I donated it to the Bodleian's collection of Lewisiana." When I inquired of Miss Baynes, she told me she donated her map to the Bodleian at Hooper's request, and he delivered it for her.

[13] On 17 September 1980 Walter Hooper sold a collection of his papers to the University of North Carolina at Chapel Hill. Roger Lancelyn Green wrote one of the letters in the collection to Hooper on 13 April 1967; in it Green responds positively to Hooper's desire, in Green's words, "to prevent the drift of letters and MSS into Kilby's coffers." Green would no doubt have been dismayed to learn that this very letter, along with Hooper's correspondence from the Lewis brothers and well over a thousand other Lewisian letters, were going to "drift" into the University of North Carolina coffers.

[14] This copy of *Dymer* is in the Bodleian Library.

[15] Personal conversation with Ruth Pitter on 19 June 1984, in her home at 71 Chilton Road, Long Crendon.

Unfortunately for Miss Pitter, just when she moved to Long Crendon an extremely assertive woman moved to England. In 1952 Helen Joy Davidman Gresham arrived from the United States for a literary sojourn. Her talented husband William Lindsay Gresham had enjoyed great financial success with his novel *Nightmare Alley*, but he fell into alcoholism and debt. He joined AA, but by then the marriage was doomed. In September Joy invited Lewis to meet her for lunch at the Eastgate Hotel, and they enjoyed each other from the start. After six months in England, Joy went home in January 1953, eventually agreed to a divorce as Lewis had advised,[16] and returned to England in November with her two sons, who were eight and ten. According to author John Christopher, who was a London friend of Joy's, she had at least one brief affair at that time.[17]

It seems that Joy Gresham aimed at becoming Joy Lewis from the beginning. An article in the 20 September 1998 issue of *The Observer* said "Douglas Gresham. Lewis' stepson, is eager to redeem his mother's image. 'She was not above telling nosy friends that she was going to England to seduce C. S. Lewis.' he said, but added that there was nothing reprehensible about a woman falling in love with a man and setting out to attract his love to her."

On 24 January 1954 C. S. Lewis rather innocently invited Ruth Pitter and Joy Gresham to lunch with him at the Eastgate Hotel, so they could meet and become friends. In discussing that luncheon party years later, Ruth Pitter said, "It was not pleasant. It was not. I can tell you that much."[18] She wrote to Joy a few times between 1957 and 1960, but Joy never answered. She wrote out something about Joy and put it in a safe place, not to be opened for fifty years or more (presumably out of consideration for Joy's sons).

---

[16] According to Joy's sister-in-law Mary Ellen Gresham, the delay in the divorce proceedings was caused by Joy's unsuccessful attempt to get an annulment.

[17] In response to the 1986 television film *Shadowlands*, John Christopher published his memories of Joy in the April 1987 issue of *Encounter*. There he claimed that when Joy had no real hope of marrying Lewis, she had an affair she described as pleasant but unimportant with a likeable man who was good to her sons and who had a car (less common on those days) in which he took them places. Stephen Schofield published an excerpt from the article in issue of *The Canadian C. S. Lewis Journal*, (Autumn 1991): 16.

[18] Stephen Schofield, *In Search of C. S. Lewis* (South Plainfield, N. J.: Bridge, 1983) 114.

Like Ruth Pitter, Joy Gresham was a stimulating and witty intellectual who had been led to Christianity by Lewis's writing. (In my opinion, however, Douglas Gresham's claim that his mother and stepfather towered above all other 20th century intellectuals is insupportable.)[19] Like Mrs. Moore, Joy was an aggressive single mother, audacious and needing help. It was a powerful combination. Gradually Joy managed to make herself an important part of C. S. Lewis's life, although few of his friends liked her. [20]

It was not until Joy was denied further residence in England early in 1956 that Lewis decided to marry her in a civil ceremony.[21] It took place on 23 April 1956 and was kept secret. It made Joy and her two sons legal residents of England permanently, and that is all that Lewis intended—although it is agreed that Joy intended more.

C. S. Lewis's first letter to me was written on 24 April 1956, the morning after his civil marriage to Joy. He did not mention her existence then or when we met for tea in the Royal Oxford Hotel on 20 July. (I had studied his work independently for a year and a half for my honors project at the University of Redlands in California; upon winning an academic scholarship to summer school at the University of London, I wrote to him for the first time and asked if I could hear him lecture or meet him while I was in England.) [22]

---

[19] "Being isolated on a pinnacle of immense intellectual ability and intelligence, probably the greatest mind this 20th Century has seen, he was totally alone on this pinnacle.... And he discovered that there was someone else on the same pinnacle of intellectual ability. My mother..." (from Douglas Gresham's lecture "C S Lewis and Contemporary Culture" at the University of Tennessee, at Chattanooga, 16 April 1998).

[20] The story of Joy Davidman's life is told by Lyle Dorsett in *And God Came In* (New York: Macmillan, 1983).

[21] Joy's sister-in-law, Mary Ellen Gresham, suspects that Joy misled Lewis about the Home Office denying her further residence, allegedly because of past association with the Communist Party. She thinks Joy tricked Lewis. (Although McCarthyism and the "red scare" were rampant in the United States then, that was not the case in England. In 1956 I attended the Soviet film "Boris Godunov" and the Red Army Ensemble performance in London; both were mildly propagandistic but extremely popular anyway.) However, it is quite possible that Joy Gresham was denied further residence because she and her children had no clear means of support and she was a potential financial liability to the state.

[22] My student address in Redlands, California, probably reminded Lewis of Redlands, Bristol, England, the home of Mrs. Moore when he first got involved with her in 1917. (In 1956 I had never heard of Mrs. Moore or Redlands, England.)

As I entered the lobby of the Royal Oxford Hotel on 20 July, a portly man rose from a couch and said "Miss Stillwell?" I sat down next to him. The first thing Lewis did was to pull out his cigarettes and offer me one. This was the only time in my life that I regretted being a nonsmoker, because the first thing I had to say to him after hello was "No thank you, I don't smoke." But he congratulated me as he lit up, and urged me never to start; he said it's too hard to quit.

Next I ventured, "Dr. Kilby was surprised that you were willing to meet me, because people say that you dislike women." He boomed with laughter.[23] After that the visit was all fun. In reply to one of his remarks, I automatically responded with where it was located in one of his books. "That's the trouble with people reading your books," he said. "Your conversation is never new for them!" He told me that his original title for his new novel *Till We Have Faces* had been *Bareface*. But he didn't tell me anything about Joy Davidman, to whom it was dedicated. He told me that he liked *The Great Divorce* far better than *The Screwtape Letters* and considered it his neglected "Cinderella."

We chatted non-stop for an hour and a quarter.[24] We would have laughed if anyone had told us that almost thirty-five years later a fantasy version of

---

Coincidentally, thirty-two years after I contacted Lewis from Redlands, California, a newcomer to California and to Lewis affairs would launch the C. S. Lewis Foundation for Christian Higher Education in Redlands, California, and would take over the Kilns.

[23] Ruth Pitter wondered if Lewis didn't let off steam by portraying Mrs. Moore and her flaws in his *Screwtape Letters,* perhaps giving readers of that popular book the false impression that he hated women. In contrast, Pitter found Lewis an extremely perceptive *lover* of women.

[24] It happened that a couple of weeks after I met Lewis, I fell down the stairs at a London tube station for no discernable reason. Because I was petite and light-footed, this mystified me. About a week later I was struck with other bizarre symptoms. I didn't know it, but these were early signs of multiple sclerosis, which was slowly but inexorably starting to cripple me. Owen Barfield's adopted daughter Lucy, to whom Lewis dedicated *The Lion, the Witch and the Wardrobe,* was a young adult professional dancer when she was paralyzed by multiple sclerosis. Lewis had predicted in his dedication, "some day you will be old enough to start reading fairy tales again. You can then take it down from some upper shelf, dust it, and tell me what you think of it." That day never came, because of his premature death and her paralysis. I interviewed her in London's Royal Homeopathic Hospital on 28 December 1975; at

our meeting would be immortalized in a best-selling biography of Lewis.[25] Wilson said I was a penfriend of Lewis's (I wasn't) who wanted to marry him (I didn't). He said that I wrote to Lewis from a London hotel (I didn't) and that I was mystically married to Lewis in a library once (I wasn't). He even suggested that I considered 46 a magic number, and that after my own marriage I still hoped to marry Lewis. Being fictionalized by a famous novelist is a heady experience; but I wish he had made me into something exciting, like a communist spy, instead of a garden-variety nut case like the woman who signed herself "Jehovah."

All summer Joy was suffering leg pain. Doctors said it was rheumatism. In October a leg bone snapped because it was eaten through by cancer; and the cancer had spread. In November Lewis wrote to a correspondent in the United States, "I may be soon, in rapid succession, a bridegroom and a widower."[26]

In December he decided to make the secret April wedding into more than he had intended. Without giving any clarification, he announced in the *Times* on Christmas Eve, "A marriage has taken place between Professor C. S. Lewis of Magdalene College, Cambridge, and Mrs. Joy Gresham, now a patient in Churchill Hospital, Oxford." Readers assumed, of course, that it was a December wedding.

At last there was an official Mrs. C. S. Lewis. She was forty and he was fifty-seven. Both of them had stated in their writing that divorced Christians may not remarry when a previous spouse is still living; and Joy's first husband, Bill Gresham, was still very much alive, although Joy herself was almost dead.

Bill Gresham had been married once before he married Joy, and they were not Christians when they married. Lewis came to the conclusion that this invalidated Joy's first marriage in the eyes of the church, thus making it possible for him to marry her in a Christian ceremony. But Harry Carpenter,

---

that time she hadn't seen her Narnia books for several years because her personal possessions were packed away.

[25] See A. N. Wilson's, C. S. *Lewis,* 236-37.

[26] C. S. Lewis, *Letters to an American Lady* (Grand Rapids MI: Wm. B. Eerdmans Publishing Co., 1967) 61.

Bishop of Oxford, refused Lewis's request.[27] According to the Bishop's son, Humphrey Carpenter, his father was not opposed to the marriage; but he felt that if he approved it for such a famous man he would be besieged by similar requests.

Lewis heard that an ex-student of his, Father Peter Bide, was sometimes granted miraculous answers to his prayers for healing. The doctors gave Joy no hope at all, and the best that could be wished for was reduced suffering before death. So Lewis asked Peter Bide to come to Oxford to lay hands on Joy and pray for her healing. When Bide came, Lewis brought up the subject of Christian marriage. Bide thought that Lewis's reasoning about the matter was sound, and he believed that Joy's ardent desire to have her marriage solemnized by the church should be honored. He did not have the permission of the local bishop, but he married them anyway. On 21 March 1957, the Christian wedding took place at Joy's hospital bedside.

The amazing healing that took place in the following months is a much-told story. Warren Lewis wrote that it was obvious they not only loved, but were in love with each other. C. S. Lewis declared that he had in his sixties the joy that most men have in their twenties. Joy wrote to friends that he was a great lover. They took a belated honeymoon to Ireland. Lewis later referred to Joy as his daughter and mother, pupil and teacher, subject and sovereign, comrade, friend, shipmate, fellow soldier, and mistress. She referred to herself triumphantly as Mrs. C. S. Lewis.

There is no question about the fact that Lewis's marriage was a great disappointment to his old friend J. R. R. Tolkien, a staunch Roman Catholic who disliked Joy in the first place and could not approve of a marriage to a divorced American in any case. Lewis had compounded the damage by not informing Tolkien of the marriage, letting him find out as the news spread. Tolkien's resentment of Joy Lewis faintly echoed Albert Lewis's resentment of Mrs. Moore; both felt that Lewis let himself get taken in by the wrong people.

Although Lewis didn't insist that it was a miracle, Joy's remission seemed miraculous. She improved wonderfully in 1957. They enjoyed well over a year of cancer-free marriage. During that happy period I asked him about his

---

[27] Humphrey Carpenter, "Of more than academic interest," *The Sunday Times* (27 February 1994): 2.

family, and he answered that he lived with his wife, his two stepsons, and his unmarried brother.

Joy's cancer returned late in 1959. To fulfill a dream of hers, they flew to Greece on 3 April 1960 with Roger Lancelyn Green and his wife June. They returned late on 14 April. On 16 April Lewis sent me his seventh brief letter. He explained that he couldn't answer sooner because he had been away from home and returned to an appalling pile of correspondence. "[I] have already spent 14 hours driving the pen across the paper!" Indeed, all his other letters had been postmarked near midday; this one was postmarked 7:15 P.M.

I had such a horror of burdening him that I ceased writing entirely. I had no idea that his wife was ill.

On 14 July 1960 composers Donald Swann and David Marsh visited Lewis to talk about the music they were writing for *Perelandra*. Swann tells the story in his autobiography *Swann's Way: A Life in Song*: "It was a quiet morning and we went to Lewis's home in Oxford for breakfast. We strolled around his lovely garden with him, talking about the opera. After about an hour he said, 'I hope you will excuse me. I must go now because my wife died last night.' He left us. I was very moved. Quite overcome. It is just another story of this very gracious gentleman who always looked after his guests. I mean, at a time like that! What did we matter?"

On 20 December 1961 C. S. Lewis wrote to his ex-student and old friend Dom Bede Griffiths, a Benedictine monk in India, that something interesting had happened. When Joy died, Lewis had prayed that God would take away the lifelong burden of his sexual nature. Then he became free of all sexual desire. And now he could recall fully and gratefully the act of love in his marriage without any more desire or arousal.[28]

Lewis's friend George Sayer knew and liked Ruth Pitter; at the end of the 1994 edition of *Jack*, his biography of Lewis, he speculates that if Lewis had been in good health as a widower he might very well have married his friend Ruth Pitter at last. According to Sayer, Lewis turned to Ruth and confided in her after Joy's death.[29]

---

[28] This letter is in the Wade Center. Most of it is published in both editions of Lewis's *Letters*, but this brief passage near the beginning was left out.

[29] There is a rumor that Lewis told Pitter about shocking information he had discovered in Joy's personal papers, information that will be revealed in the future. According to this rumor, George Sayer and Walter Hooper know Joy's secret. This

When Lewis died in 1963, I sent his wife a sympathy letter. I didn't know that she had died. Most Lewis readers here didn't even know that he had been married.

Due to the fact that the 1974 biography *C. S. Lewis* had two authors, it has two opposing views of the marriage. Green wrote a convincing chapter attesting to its vitality and completeness.[30] But Hooper claimed, without offering a source or explanation, that in 1930 Lewis identified himself as one who cannot ever marry.[31] According to Hooper, the 1917 promise to Paddy Moore enforced bachelorhood upon Lewis, and Lewis preferred living with Mrs. Moore to marriage anyway. Moreover, in 1963 Lewis confided to Hooper that he had always been a bachelor at heart. (Not, perhaps, the most gallant remark for a widower to make.)

In August 1974 I wrote to Walter Hooper, "Do you know if Lewis changed his mind about a divorced Christian remarrying? I would like to know his conviction on that point because that decision has to be made by so many acquaintances today. People ask me for his opinion on it sometimes, and it is a mystery to me."

On 5 September he answered that the Anglican position is that divorced people may not re-marry, and he was sure that Lewis did not consider himself married to Joy in the strict and most complete sense. "Do you get my meaning?" Two people living in the same house does not constitute marriage. Roger Lancelyn Green had written the marriage section in their biography, and Hooper wanted to re-write it with the facts some day. (He issued a new edition of the biography about twenty years later, but it was not rewritten after all.)

I was confused, so I asked again. Hooper answered on 16 September that there was no physical union, but he didn't want to be quoted on that for fear

---

would seem to tie together Warren's diary entry for 10 March 1969 (see the last part of Chapter 10) and Ruth Pitter's letter to Hooper dated 25 July 1974, in the Chapel Hill collection. There she refers to material Hooper withheld from the Lewis biography, cards she and Hooper prepared that can be played when the time is ripe, and the possibility of confiding in George Sayer. Pitter's correspondence with Hooper makes it clear that she was misled about his relationship to the Lewis brothers. In 1984 she indicated to me that she had not heard from him for a long time.

[30] "Surprised by Joy," Chapter 11 in C. S. *Lewis*.

[31] Green and Hooper, 107.

of displeasing Joy's sons. There are many who are angry because Lewis married Joy, he said, and there are many others who will dislike Lewis for not making it a complete marriage. I was puzzled by his claim about anger and dislike, but I inquired no more.

In 1976 Chad Walsh, a friend of Lewis and a close friend of Joy, published an essay affirming the completeness of the Lewis marriage. Walsh describes Joy: "She was not a beautiful woman except for her eyes, which were large, dark, lustrous, and bright with probing intelligence."[32]

Once in 1979 Hooper claimed that Lewis's civil marriage to Joy was the result of her apparently fatal disease. "...when it seemed to be that she was dying, Lewis went to the Registrar of Marriage to prevent her being sent out of the country. And the Registrar's marriage was only to prevent her from having to die in the nursing home."[33] (A peculiar claim, because Joy was not yet sick at the time of the marriage in the Registrar's office.)

That year Hooper devoted several pages in *They Stand Together* to delicately explaining Joy's "marriage" to Lewis. Hooper dismisses the idea that Joy's non-Christian marriage to her already-divorced first husband didn't count: "Lewis himself was wary of such casuistry..." Then why did Lewis lead people to believe that he was really married to Joy? "Lewis could not, without embarrassment both to the lady and himself, reveal the precise nature of their 'marriage.'"[34] If Hooper expected this kind of equivocation to have much impact, he was disappointed.

In 1982 he finally issued a bold public statement: "For religious as well as physical reasons, Lewis's marriage was not consummated."[35] (Strange as it seems, in the same book he included a 25 June 1957 letter from Lewis to Dorothy Sayers in which Lewis explained away Joy's marriage to Bill Gresham and celebrated his own joyful marriage to her.)[36]

In 1987 Hooper finally pulled out all the stops in a masterfully delivered speech in Seattle where he received a standing ovation. The speech, titled "C. S. Lewis and C. S. Lewises," is published in a 1989 collection titled C. S. *Lewis and the Riddle of Joy*. In the first section, Hooper repeats his familiar account

---

[32] Chad Walsh, "Afterword," *A Grief Observed* (New York: Bantam, 1976) 137.

[33] A taped question-and-answer session in Portland, Oregon, on 9 March 1979.

[34] *They Stand Together*, 536.

[35] Walter Hooper, *Through Joy and Beyond* (New York: Macmillan, 1982), 151.

[36] Ibid., 143-45.

of his whereabouts in 1963: "Not long after I met him, Lewis had me move into his house, the Kilns, as his private secretary. It was during those months [sic] when I was privileged to be part of his household..."[37]

Hooper devotes the final six pages of this 18-page essay to showing that the public has misunderstood Lewis's book *A Grief Observed*. First he reveals that Lewis once asked him his opinion of something Joy said about the States. Hooper blurted out that she was wrong about *everything*. Later, according to Hooper, Lewis's friend Dr. Havard assured him "Besides the fact that [Lewis] wanted to know what you think, he had never believed everything Joy said about the States."[38] This anecdote suggests that Lewis preferred Hooper's opinions to Joy's.

The following facts are important background for the rest of Hooper's 1987 speech. Letters in the university library at Chapel Hill show that in February 1962 Hooper notified Lewis that he was starting to write a volume about him for the Twayne series. Lewis demurred and advised, "Far better to write about the unanswering dead!"

On 14 December 1962 Lewis received Hooper's Lewis bibliography in the mail; on 15 December Lewis complimented Hooper for his thoroughness and told him about a new essay to add to the list. (Hooper eventually lost the contract, and Joe R. Christopher ended up writing the book.) Hooper planned to come to Oxford in June 1963, and Lewis agreed to check his chapters for accuracy then. Lewis planned to be in Ireland in August; but as it turned out, in July he almost died, and in August he was an invalid. Hooper was on hand to be of service. According to the report on Hooper's London reminiscences in March 1977, "Lewis needed such constant reminding [about his own works] that the casual observer would be likely to take Walter Hooper for the instructor, and Lewis for the instructee."[39]

According to Hooper's 1987 speech "C. S. Lewis and C. S. Lewises," once he got to Oxford he forgot about the chapters he had brought for Lewis to check. One evening when he was an invalid Lewis mentioned that he was the real author of *A Grief Observed*, published under the pen name N. W. Clerk

---

[37] Walter Hooper, "C.S. Lewis and C. S. Lewises," in *The Riddle of Joy* (Grand Rapids MI: Eerdmans, 1989) 35.

[38] Ibid., 45

[39] "An Lewis Evening in London" by Mary Kirkpatrick in *CSL* (April 1977): 1.

in 1961. (Is it possible that a meticulous scholar and helpful tutor like Lewis
would have overlooked this major gap in Hooper's bibliography for eight
months and then revealed it so casually?)

According to Hooper, he read the book straight through while Lewis
smoked his pipe and watched; then Lewis explained that this book was not
really an autobiographical account by a bereaved husband. It was pure
fiction. Lewis had pretended it was a true story so people would be helped by
it, but he had also pretended he was N. W. Clerk so people wouldn't think it
was his own true story.

Hooper says that for months after this 1963 incident (he doesn't say which
months they were) he saw Lewis receive gift copies of A Grief Observed from
people who thought it would help him cope with the 1960 loss of his wife.
Lewis also received many letters from people who said they thought that N.
W. Clerk was Lewis. "I don't recall anything which seemed to irritate him so
much," Hooper recalls. If Hooper is correct, the idea that Lewis was shattered
by Joy's death bothered Lewis more than her death itself. Hooper explains this
by pointing out that Lewis found it annoying when people didn't understand
"an author's ability to 'invent.'"[40]

Hooper's account becomes even more confusing when he tells how Lewis
gave him evidence that A Grief Observed is only fiction. In A Grief Observed
Lewis said he was writing his thoughts down as they come to him, in four
manuscript books. He said the fourth manuscript book was an old one with
some arithmetic at the back. Hooper says he asked Lewis if the fourth
manuscript book was real or not. In answer, Lewis took a manuscript book
from his shelf and gave it to Hooper; there was nothing of A Grief Observed
inside—only some 1910 arithmetic along with childhood stories about Boxen.
In contrast, Hooper now owns a fifty-one-page manuscript of Grief Observed
in what appears to be Lewis's handwriting (not written in four notebooks),
which he keeps in the Bodleian. He has also placed a typed copy of that
manuscript in the Bodleian.

A graduate student named John West was present in Hooper's enthusiastic
July 1987 audience. In October 1988 he wrote a letter to Hooper asking about
an apparent discrepancy he had discovered. The 1974 biography co-authored
by Green and Hooper says, "The whole experience [of Lewis's grief after Joy's

---

[40] Ibid., 46.

death] is told with almost unbearable poignancy in *A Grief Observed*, a collection of almost daily thoughts and attempts at self-analysis jotted down during the first few months after her death, and published under the pseudonym of N. W. Clerk in 1961. The possibility of its publication was mentioned under pledge of secrecy to Green, who stayed at the Kilns for several days at the beginning of September 1960..."[41]

Hooper replied at length on 30 October 1988. He explained that the passage in question was written by Green, who knew it was not true. Hooper had objected to treating *A Grief Observed* as if it were straight autobiography, but Green prevailed and the biography was published with that pretence in it.

If *A Grief Observed* were an autobiography, it would then indicate that Lewis's marriage was consummated. There was a great debate raging about the issue, Hooper explained, with most Roman Catholics maintaining that the marriage shouldn't have been consummated and most American evangelicals maintaining that it was consummated. Hooper said he had received numerous letters from both factions. He knew that it was not consummated, however, because Warren had once told him so. (There is no record of Hooper revealing this while Warren was alive.)

According to Hooper, as soon as the Green/Hooper biography was published in 1974, A. C. Harwood, Owen Barfield's co-trustee, objected to the idea that *A Grief Observed* was factual. He told Green and Hooper that Lewis had told him the marriage "had never been completed." There is no record of Hooper revealing this while Harwood was alive. Furthermore, in a letter that Harwood wrote to Hooper on 5 February 1965 he said he preferred not to issue *A Grief Observed* in paperback so soon because it was "such an intimate and personal thing."[42]

Hooper adds that a letter from Lewis to someone whose identity may not be revealed "showed up" in 1974 substantiating what Hooper heard Warren and Harwood say that they had heard Lewis say. The mystery letter may be made public in 1998, he said; but that did not happen.

Hooper says that in the face of these complaints, Green told him that if they were ever given a chance to revise the book they should change it and tell the truth. (There is no record of Hooper revealing this while Green was alive.)

---

[41] Green and Hooper, 277.

[42] In the Chapel Hill Collection.

I discussed the biography with Roger Lancelyn Green at his home on 1 January 1976, and he did not express the slightest desire to alter his account of the Lewis marriage. To the contrary, he seemed pleased with it.

When Hooper wrote to John West in 1988, Green had recently died and could not be questioned. (This brings to mind Lewis's 1962 advice to Hooper, "Far better to write about the unanswering dead!") But Sheldon Vanauken was still very much alive. In 1994 he said:

> Lewis told me in 1961 that he had published *A Grief Observed* under the pseudonym N W Clerk because it was so personal. I instantly sent to Blackwell's for it, and therefore have the first edition. Lewis had had long accounts of my own grief. In '57 at Cambridge we had talked about the love of a spouse. Subsequently he told me of Joy's healing, and then of the cancer's return, and then of her death. With all that in the background, he knew I would read *Grief* as precisely the way it was with him. Moreover, in the '70s when I was publishing *A Severe Mercy*, I had a letter from Barfield, who liked it but thought I had displayed grief too nakedly—like Jack. He had always wished Jack had not done so. In other words, Barfield wrote as though he accepted *Grief* as authentically Jack's experience.[43]

Why would Lewis and Barfield have misled Vanauken about the truth of *A Grief Observed*? Why would Warren have misled people by claiming that *A Grief Observed* described his brother's marriage exactly? He called it Lewis's most personal book. More puzzling yet, why would Walter Hooper suddenly reverse himself in 1996 after more than twenty years of insistence that C. S. Lewis told him *A Grief Observed* was pure fiction? In his volume *C. S. Lewis: A Companion and Guide*[44], Hooper placed *A Grief Observed* in the autobiography section and devoted six pages (196-202) to summarizing the book as "raw emotions," "blatant honesty," and "a cry from the heart." He made no

---

[43] Sheldon Vanauken in a letter to Kathryn Lindskoog dated 30 March 1994.

[44] *C. S. Lewis: A Companion and Guide* (New York: HarperSanFrancisco, 1996).

mention of his previous claims, much less the reason for his turnaround.[45] But the entertainment industry probably played a part in it.

Joy Davidman had no luck in the entertainment industry. She won a chance at Hollywood scriptwriting in 1939 and spent a few months in California writing for MGM; but her scripts were not accepted, so she gave up and returned to New York. Little could she have guessed that she was destined to success as the subject of a film script rather than the writer of a film script. Forty-five years after her stint as an American scriptwriter, an English scriptwriter named William Nicholson has made a fortune writing three different scripts about her.

In 1985 two paperback books about the Lewis marriage were published: William Petersen's *C. S. Lewis Had a Wife* and Brian Sibley's *Shadowlands*. Although Nicholson's 1985 BBC film used Sibley's title, the book and the film are not alike. The film was the vision of one man: director Norman Stone, a Christian who had to struggle for funding for the project. It won "best single television drama" and "best television actress" awards from the British Academy of Film and Television in 1985. It appeared on American television in 1986, and it can now be purchased as a videocassette. It is reportedly BBC's best-selling program.

In this heartrending drama, Nicholson condenses seven years into three. The Oxford settings are superb. Lewis (Joss Ackland) is no longer red-faced and full of gusto; instead, he is soft, blue-eyed, and grandfatherly. Joy (Claire Bloom) is no longer a brassy New Yorker with rather dowdy looks; instead she is a luminously beautiful woman of refinement and sensitivity. She leaves Lewis with two adorable little boys rather than a couple of teenagers. The Kilns is a clean house set on a hill, and those who live there are no longer chain smokers.[46] The film is not a serious documentary, but it communi-

---

[45] In his review of *C. S. Lewis: A Companion and Guide* (see the *CSL Bulletin*, September-October 1996) James Como reveals that he previewed parts of the book in manuscript, and the published entry on *A Grief Observed* "bears virtually no serious resemblance" to the original, "surely owing to the influence of Douglas Gresham." Further, Como charges that Gresham "dictated" cutting of some other sections by Hooper. Because he is a close friend of Hooper's, Como seemed to be expressing complaints he got from Hooper.

[46] Professor A.L. Rowse, an acquaintance of Lewis's since 1926 and an academic adversary, remembers him with respect but comments tartly in the following unpublished letter dated 13 December 1993:

cates quickly and simply the truth of the Lewises' love and the tragedy of their parting.

In 1989 Nicholson followed his first success with a brand new Tony Award-winning version of *Shadowlands*, this time for the stage. In London, on Broadway, and in venues from there to Australia, audiences were thrilled by it. It has remained popular and is sometimes translated into other languages; for example, its first performance in Estonian occurred on 31 March 2000 at the Rakvere Theatre. (In the stage version there is only one stepson, and there is a glimpse of Narnia beyond an open wardrobe.)

In 1993 Savoy Pictures produced the major motion picture version of *Shadowlands* by Nicholson. This time it was directed by Richard Attenborough and starred Anthony Hopkins as Lewis and Debra Winger as Joy. According to London's *Sunday Times*, those three stars alone cost the studio $6 million, and total cost was $22 million. As soon as the film came out, public interest in Lewis soared. In July 1994 the popular film became available on videotape.

Nicholson, Attenborough, and Hopkins are self-avowed religious agnostics. They were drawn to the idea of a stuffy scholar out of touch with real life, whose defenses were overwhelmed by an unusual woman and whose heart was broken when she died. Theirs is the universal story of an awakening of the human spirit. Hopkins, who describes himself as a naturally shy and inhibited man, says that *Shadowlands* is "about life, our mortality, seizing the day."

"I am glad that I remained always on good terms with CSL, though we were at opposite poles intellectually..."

"I couldn't have borne Lewis' vulgar beer-drinking, smoking, pub-crawling, the scruffy way he lived. He was no aesthete, as I was. And he was very queer in his relations with those two awful women—I wouldn't have wanted to meet them, much less know them. Perhaps a masochistic streak in Lewis."

"However, he was a good man, which I do not claim to be. Also more gregarious, more of a 'good fellow' than this solitary misanthrope."

Thirty years earlier, on 22 October 1963, Lewis made light of being forced to retire early from his beloved professorship: "I am finding retirement full of compensation. It is lovely to reflect that I am under no obligation to read Rowse on [Shakespeare's] Sonnets."

Content to illuminate the glib, hesitant, and sheltered character created by Nicholson, Hopkins says he read nothing by or about Lewis. Winger, on the other hand, wanted to understand the real Lewises and their marriage. She not only read and understood a great deal of Lewis's writing; she journeyed to the Marion E. Wade Center and spent a night in Wheaton poring over the collection of Joy's letters there. Douglas Gresham praises her acting but says his mother was actually much more caustic than Nicholson's Joy. Everyone seems to agree, however, that Edward Hardwicke's portrayal of Warren is wonderfully accurate.

A very silly romance novel based on the film was promptly published by Signet (a division of Penguin) for the United States, England, Australia, Canada, and New Zealand. Author Leonore Fleischer gushingly portrays Lewis as a smug, wealthy celebrity "with almost all of his own hair" and a "poor little dried-up heart." (She reports that Lewis taught there are three rather than four kinds of love. She leaves out friendship.)

As Humphrey Carpenter has noted, the true story was far more elaborate and far more dramatic than the story in the film. Nicholson, Gresham, and others point out that this is a fictional drama based upon a real event. Dramatic liberties concerning time, place, purpose, and personality fill the film. For example, Lewis was neither shy nor inhibited, and he never successfully drove a car; but in the film he is shy and inhibited and does drive a car. The memorable scene of Lewis and Douglas embracing after Joy's death did not take place in the Kilns attic, which was only a crawl space. Lewis was not left with one little ten-year-old stepson; he was left with two stepsons, fourteen and sixteen. In light of all this, the message at the beginning of the film is surprising: "This is a true story."

Long before she took part in the first *Shadowlands* film, Claire Bloom had taken part in another C. S. Lewis project. She read Lewis's book *Prince Caspian* for Caedmon Records in 1979, and her photo and career credits appear on the back of the album along with an essay by Walter Hooper.

There, by the face later known to television viewers as that of Mrs. C. S. Lewis, Walter Hooper states, "I was Lewis's secretary at the end of his life, and after his death in 1963 I inherited his papers." How could the American Walter Hooper, who had only met C. S. Lewis on a summer visit to England in 1963, have inherited his papers? That is the subject of chapter 9, "Forging a Friendship."

> Statements which I know to be untrue all but convince me,
> at any rate for the moment,
> if only the man says them unflinchingly.
> —*C.S. Lewis*

9

FORGING A FRIENDSHIP

NOT A GENUINELY COPIED
SIGNATURE AFTER ALL?

"Like Father, Like Son" is the perfect title for H. N. Kelley's happy two-page article about C. S. Lewis and Walter Hooper that appeared in the Christmas issue of *The Anglican Digest* in 1982. Lewis once remarked in print that perhaps there is nothing more astonishing than the discovery that there are people very, very like oneself. Walter Hooper is so much like his mentor C. S. Lewis, Kelley exclaims, that as you sit in his living room chatting with him you keep forgetting that he is not Lewis.

Hooper used to live with C. S. Lewis, Kelley continues. Most books by or about C. S. Lewis since his death have been edited, written, or annotated by Hooper. Kelley thinks the writings of the two merge seamlessly.[1] In Kelley's mind Hooper resembles the bronze bust of C. S. Lewis on a pedestal in his living room, and his voice sounds like Lewis's recorded voice.

Hooper starts most days by dipping a nib pen into an inkwell, Kelley adds, as Lewis did it. Lewis's furnishings must have been similar to Hooper's. Hooper's books resemble Lewis's books. Lewis would have liked Hooper's flowers. A day spent visiting Hooper has the texture of a day straight out of a Lewis biography, Kelley continues.

---

[1] In *The Weight of Glory* (New York: Macmillan, 1980) xi, Hooper claimed to have been both Lewis's live-in secretary and his literary assistant.

Kelley believes that Lewis referred to Hooper as "the son I should have had," and that when Lewis died on 22 November 1963, Hooper found that he had been designated Lewis's literary executor. Kelley was obviously enchanted with Walter Hooper.[2] Many people are.

One similarity that Kelley missed was that Hooper allegedly smokes cigarettes in the special way that C. S. Lewis did. In the printed text of a speech Hooper gave in California once, he said, "Lewis didn't use an ash tray, but took his cigarette and flicked it like this. Did you see that? I've been doing it all day."[3]

A member of his audience later wrote in a report published in the bulletin *Mythprint*, "the gentle, almost murmuring voice of Father Walter Hooper, relating another anecdote of our Chosen Rabbi C. S. Lewis, perhaps accompanied by that marvelous S-shaped gesture guaranteed to seed the carpet with ashes from the August Cigarettes of Professor Lewis (or his own)...."[4]

When one recalls that Walter Hooper's 1979 seminars across the United States were called "A Visit with C. S. Lewis," it seems fitting. The only trouble with Lewis's "marvelous S-shaped gesture" is that people who knew him say they never saw him smoke that way.

Once Hooper had become the famous son of his home town, the *Reidsville Review* in North Carolina printed his reflections about some of his formative experiences.[5] One was his teaching post with the English department at the University of Kentucky, where he says he taught the 1960-1962 terms. During his first month in Lexington he served as night watchman in the Henry Clay house, sleeping in Henry Clay's own bed. When he found better lodging, he says, he was spared the embarrassment of waking up to find a child pointing at him and asking if he were Henry Clay—or Henry Clay's ghost.

---

[2] H. N. Kelley, "Like Father, Like Son," *The Anglican Digest* (December 1982): 8-9.

[3] Walter Hooper, "Reminiscences," *Mythlore*, (June 1976): 6-7. This is the text of the speech given 16 August 1975 but it has been heavily edited by Hooper, with the bonfire cut out.

[4] Judith Brown, notes in *Mythprint: The Monthly Bulletin of the Mythopoeic Society*, (November 1975): 9.

[5] Barbara Terry, "From Reidsville to Oxford, England: A Fan Letter to Lewis Started It All," *Reidsville Review* (26 May 1975).

Hooper says he took over C. S. Lewis's own bedroom in 1963 when Lewis was too ill to go upstairs. Lewis informed Hooper that Hooper was now sleeping under the very blanket that nine-year-old C. S. Lewis had slept under at boarding school in 1908 after his mother died. Hooper says he treasures that blanket from C. S. Lewis's childhood to this day.[6] (Hooper also says that he handled the blankets on Lewis's sickbed: "He slept under something like twelve blankets—at least! I remember lifting those oh so many blankets so he could get out of bed…quite a job it was.")[7]

"I begin with an apology," Hooper said in a formal address about Lewis in 1975. Although in print he calls himself the world's foremost authority on Lewis, in person he is remarkably humble. Hooper has been thought of by some as a man of overweening modesty.

> I am reminded of the funeral arranged for Abraham Lincoln in Springfield, Illinois. Because the great man could not himself be there to speak, and because a great many of his friends had died as well, his old dog Fido was brought, so to speak, out of mothballs.[8] *He* was alive. Now I think you must receive me as something of a 'Fido'… For that is all I claim to be.[9]

Victor Searcher's three-hundred-page volume *The Farewell to Lincoln*, which includes every verified detail of the funeral services in the capital, the twelve-day journey to Springfield, and the burial there, makes no mention of an old dog named Fido attending the funeral. The closest animal one can find is Lincoln's old horse Robin following the hearse in Springfield.

That's all right. It seems that Hooper wasn't teaching English at the University of Kentucky and sleeping in Henry Clay's bed in 1960 anyway. He was teaching in a boys' boarding school in North Carolina.[10] But Hooper

---

[6] Walter Hooper, "Introduction," in C. S. Lewis, *They Stand Together* (London: Collins, 1979) 9.

[7] Walter Hooper, in a recorded interview by Charles Glaize in August 1984.

[8] In *Boxen* (San Diego: Harcourt Brace Jovanovich, 1985) 18, Hooper refers to Lewis as his old friend.

[9] Hooper, "Reminiscences," 5.

[10] "Upon leaving the Virginia Episcopal Seminary, Hooper was offered a teaching post at Christ School in Arden, N.C., a post which he held for two years." (Terry,

really did stay briefly in the Henry Clay house later and teach in Kentucky. In fact, he was still an entry-level instructor there in the spring and fall semesters of 1963. He was thirty-two years old. 1963 is the year when, according to his entries in reference books, he was serving as C. S. Lewis's private secretary in Oxford.[11]

One of Hooper's fond anecdotes about C. S. Lewis took place when Lewis and Hooper attended church together "one Easter."[12] But in 1963 Easter fell on 14 April, and Hooper did not go to England until June. Hooper spent the summer in England and returned to Kentucky for the fall semester. Lewis died in November. It appears impossible that Lewis and Hooper could ever have attended church together on Easter.

When I aired this and other discrepancies in Hooper's claims about his education, career, and relationship to C. S. Lewis in "Some Questions about C. S. Lewis Scholarship" in the summer 1978 issue of *Christianity & Literature,* his co-trustee Owen Barfield protested "such offensive and probably libelous insinuations as, that he has deliberately misled the public regarding his academic and clerical qualifications and that he invented a

---

"From Reidsville to Oxford.") Christ School was a boarding school for boys thirteen to eighteen years old.

[11] In 1990 the University of North Carolina Press at Chapel Hill (Hooper's *alma mater*) published *Telling Lies in Modern American Autobiography,* in which Timothy Dow Adams presents a justification of misrepresentation in autobiographical accounts, based upon the kind of relativism that Lewis pilloried in *That Hideous Strength.* Adams's preface begins with this statement: "All autobiographers are unreliable narrators, all humans are liars, and yet, as I will be arguing throughout this book, to be a successful liar in one's own life story is especially difficult, because what we choose to misrepresent is as telling as what really happened, because the shape of our lives often distorts who we really are, and because as Roy Pascal reminds us, 'consistent misrepresentation of oneself is not easy'...I believe autobiography is the story of an attempt to reconcile one's life with one's self and is not, therefore, meant to be taken as historically accurate but as metaphorically authentic."

[12] James Como, "An Evening with Walter Hooper," *CSL: The Bulletin of the New York C. S. Lewis Society,* (July 1975): 6. Como introduced guest speaker Walter Hooper at the 11 July 1975 meeting by reminding those present of the Lewis books that Hooper has edited, his position as Executor of the estate, and the fact that Father Hooper is "the Society's best friend."

fictitious bonfire to account for the disappearance of certain MSS!"[13] (Indeed, the Barfield law firm later sent me a letter threatening to sue.)[14]

Eugene McGovern, then editor of *C.S.L.*, bulletin of the New York C. S. Lewis Society, exclaimed in high dudgeon, "She seems prepared to suggest the possibility that in the absence of documentary evidence to the contrary, we should consider the possibility that less than a year before Lewis died an unknown young American appeared on the scene, wheedled his way into Lewis's affection, and then after Lewis's death grabbed all that he could lay his hands on..." "...when she notes that his recollections differ from those of others, she comes very, very close to simply calling Walter Hooper a liar." McGovern concluded with a tribute to Hooper's "selfless dedication" and "unobtrusive scholarship."[15] On 20 November 1979 Hooper responded to the questions by saying "I have determined not to answer any of these questions, as I don't suppose for a moment tht they really want answers."

At the library of the University of North Carolina at Chapel Hill, where Hooper has placed his papers, his biographical note says that in 1963 he was a graduate student at the University of Kentucky. But Kentucky records show that he was never a graduate student there. In the spring of 1963 Hooper sat in on lectures by Dr. Robert O. Evans about contemporary British novels. Hooper talked with Dr. Evans about the possibility of writing a doctoral

---

[13] "Dialogue," *Christianity & Literature* 28 (Fall 1978): 9-10. A few years later a couple of friends of mine happened to transport Barfield to and from a lecture engagement. One of them asked him casually when the bonfire occurred, and to her surprise he answered with irritation that there was no bonfire.

[14] Royds Barfield, London attorney for the C. S. Lewis estate, sent me a signed letter dated 12 November 1980. The firm had advised its clients that there was very little doubt that certain allegations and implications I had made concerning the conduct of Walter Hooper (and Owen Barfield, by implication, as joint Trustee) were plainly defamatory. The two had so far declined to take legal action against me, but I was to understand that their patience was not inexhaustible.

This warning referred to my questioning the bonfire story and the length of Hooper's tenure as Lewis's companion-secretary. I first questioned the authenticity of *The Dark Tower* in my book *C. S. Lewis: Mere Christian* (third edition, 1987), pages 195-96 and 242—and no legal threats arrived. In 1989 Multnomah Press received a letter from Royds Barfield requesting that *The C. S. Lewis Hoax* be withdrawn from the market, but Multnomah declined and heard no more.

[15] "Dialogue," *Christianity & Literature* 28 (Fall 1978): 10-11.

dissertation on Lewis after he passed qualifying examinations for the doctoral program.

In the summer of 1963 Evans was in Oxford teaching Shakespeare to a group of student tourists when Hooper was attending a different summer course for visiting students there.[16] The two saw each other a few times before Dr. Evans left Oxford in early August, unable to meet Lewis for himself because of Lewis's severe illness. He had enjoyed Hooper's enthusiasm about the great man which came to happy fruition, and he recalled it all in 1979 when he happened to read an article about Hooper in the *Los Angeles Times*.

During Hooper's 1979 tour of twenty cities, John Dart, religion editor of the *Times*, attended Hooper's seminar at the Pasadena Civic Auditorium and interviewed him at the Times-Mirror Building.[17] Dart identified Hooper as "the U. S.-born [not English] bachelor Anglican priest who is well established as a gatekeeper for much of the Lewis lore and literature" and reported that Hooper declined to respond to the questions in *Christianity & Literature*. Hooper told Dart "There are 58 questions…and I am simply too busy to answer." Hooper deplored the motives of questioners: "I can't understand why anyone would want to poison the wells and sharpen the knives and somehow separate those who admire Lewis."

For balance, Dart contacted Hooper's friends William Griffin, senior editor at Macmillan, and Paul Ford, author of *Companion to Narnia*. Griffin said, "The Lewis Estate is lucky to have as careful and dedicated a person as Hooper," and Ford said that questioning Hooper "detracts from the

---

[16]In 1963 the "British University Summer Schools" program was held at Stratford-upon-Avon, Edinburgh, and Oxford. The course at Oxford was made up of 120 students studying "History, Literature and the Arts of Seventeenth Century England" at Exeter College from 1 July to 9 August.

It is possible that the "grant" Hooper has referred to which allowed him to go to England was the Gl Bill of Rights or assistance from the Church of the Good Shepherd in Lexington, Kentucky. A few scholarships were available for the course, and the deadline for scholarship applications was 1 March 1963. The inclusive charge for room, board and tuition for the six-week course was only £90 (approximately $254).

[17] John Dart, "Questions Raised on C. S. Lewis Lore," *Los Angeles Times*, (24 March 1979): 30-31. This article was prompted by Hooper's 12 March presentation at the Pasadena Civic Auditorium.

marvelous scholarship that Walter has done, from Lewis himself, and from the work of Kay. There is a suspicion of Walter that is unwarranted."

Upon reading the article, Dr. Evans wrote first to the *Los Angeles Times* and later to the Director of the Southern California C. S. Lewis Society to vouch for Hooper.[18] In doing so, Evans revealed the crucial fact that Hooper lived at a summer school program in Oxford in 1963. Hooper was at Exeter College attending a busy live-in course that lasted from 1 July to 9 August, including lectures, tutorials, and excursions. All of Hooper's accounts of his activities that fateful summer omit the program at Exeter College. (In the Chapel Hill collection there is a note that Austin Farrer wrote on 23 July 1963 to Hooper's Exeter College address.)

In November, book dealer Nigel Sustins of Surrey sprang to Hooper's defense in the *Canadian C. S. Lewis Journal*:

> Walter Hooper does not need to verify his "credentials." The length of time spent with Lewis before his death is immaterial. It is for work done since Lewis's death that we owe Walter Hooper such an immense debt; for painstaking scholarship, and for years spent helping countless individuals all over the world wishing to know more of Lewis.[19]

---

[18] Robert O. Evans, letter to William Geiger of Whittier College on 21 September 1979:

"To begin, I knew Walter Hooper when he was at UK....

"In the summer of 1963 I was in residence at Lincoln College in Oxford, lecturing on Shakespeare, in conjunction with the Stratford theatre, to a group of foreign students, mostly Scandinavians. I knew Hooper was in England, and my wife and I took the trouble to meet with him more than once. He was at that time very enthusiastic about his meetings with Lewis though he was living in another Oxford college near Lincoln taking a different summer course."

After his retirement a few years later, Dr. Evans expanded on those memories: "I am virtually certain Hooper was living at the college then and paying occasional visits to CSL at the house. Certainly he was not CSL's private secretary in late July and early August when the program was undertaken."

In a 4 April 1987 letter to me, Dr. Evans reminisced about Walter Hooper and noted that he had "a rather chameleon quality," but that he never seemed at all mendacious. 'A Boswell-like quality," Dr. Evans observed, "is strong in some students." Hooper never gave Evans the impression that he was planning to move in with C. S. Lewis nor that he was going to become Lewis's secretary.

[19] *Canadian C. S. Lewis Journal*, (November 1979): 5.

It is true that Hooper has endeared himself to thousands who wish to know more about Lewis, but the length of time that he really spent with Lewis is hardly immaterial. Furthermore, I suspect that Hooper's painstaking scholarship reflects a phenomenon described by theologian James M. Robinson: "The sociology of scholarship has been such as to reward those who get exclusive rights and then climb up the academic ladder with the status of those publishing important materials. In reality, they are not publishing it but blocking its publication."[20]

Trivial as historical details may seem to many, including Nigel Sustins, the accuracy of Hooper's claims are important. For example, Lewis did not refer to Hooper as "the son I should have had." The story about that remark is located on page 303 in C. S. *Lewis: A Biography,* where Hooper claims that Lewis said it to his housekeeper Mrs. Miller. But apparently Lewis's remark about the son he should have had was just a remark he should have made. After the biography came out, Mr. and Mrs. Miller vehemently denied that Lewis ever said anything like it.[21]

In 1979 alone Hooper went on record twice about the intimacy of his friendship with Lewis: "Meanwhile, Lewis and I became more intimate, and finally he asked me to become his companion-secretary and I moved into his house" and "I don't think I've ever known anyone quite so intimately as C. S. Lewis."[22] But in a telephone interview fifteen years later Hooper told journalist K. L. Billingsley that he is not responsible for claims about his intimacy with Lewis on the jackets of books.

Hooper also told Billingsley that no one of any note has been interested in the "alleged inaccuracies" of his account of his relationship with Lewis.[23] But Billingsley also interviewed Sheldon Vanauken. "Vanauken believes Hooper

---

[20] Quoted by John Dart in "Fragments from an Earthen Jar: James Robinson and the Nag Hammadi Library," *The Christian Century,* (1 March 1978): 214.

[21] A tape-recorded personal interview with Leonard and Molly Miller at their home in Eynsham on 27 December 1975.

[22] In the introduction of *They Stand Together* and in a tape-recorded question-and-answer session in Portland, Oregon.

[23] Quoted in "The Highjacking of C. S. Lewis," a 4000-word article in the October 1994 issue of *Heterodoxy* by journalist K. L. Billingsley.

has 'obviously blown up' his friendship with Lewis in England, which Vanauken says could not have lasted more than one month."[24]

Although many claims about the affinity between C. S. Lewis and Walter Hooper do not hold up, there is no doubt that Hooper was enamored with C. S. Lewis and things British long before he visited England in 1963.[25] He actually writes with a nib pen like Lewis's, and his ordinary penmanship for the past thirty years resembles Lewis's. (Although Hooper types, he claims to write so much by hand that he uses two quarts of ink a year. He says he writes 1,500 to 2,000 letters annually to people who want to learn more about Lewis.) In addition to his musical, dramatic, and rhetorical talent, Hooper is gifted with unusually neat, controlled penmanship.

On 28 July 1975 Walter Hooper made one of the most stunning revelations possible about his handwriting and his relationship to Lewis. He and his Oxford living partner and co-author Anthony (Tony) Marchington were speaking about Lewis, Tolkien, and British schools at Rockingham Community College in Hooper's home town—Reidsville, North Carolina.[26] The entire talk was clearly tape-recorded for the college library. Hooper (44, in clerical garb) introduced Marchington (about 20, in rowing-team garb) as a well-known Oxford athlete and second-year chemistry student at Brasenose

---

[24] Vanauken is conspicuous by his absence in Hooper's survey of Lewis's friends and associates in his massive 1996 reference book *C. S. Lewis: A Companion and Guide.*

[25] In a review of *The C. S. Lewis Hoax,* in *Mythprint* (February 1989): 7-9, editor David Bratman cited a possible coincidental parallel between the careers of Bertrand Russell (1872-1970) and C. S. Lewis: "In 1960, Russell was visited by Ralph Schoenman, an American graduate student of obscure background, who quickly became an important figure in his life as indispensable secretary and spokesman. Undeniably dedicated and eloquent, he nevertheless aroused in many people a suspicion that he was manipulating Russell's image to enhance his own importance. Several years later, Russell disavowed Schoenman."

[26] Reidsville was a tobacco and textile town of about 11,000. Walter McGehee Hooper (known as Coot in childhood and young adulthood) was born on 27 March 1931, the third of five children of Arch Boyd Hooper, a successful self-employed plumber, and Madge Kemp Hooper, a traditional housewife. Arch Hooper was described in the *Greensboro Daily News* as "a man with a cherubic face and a streak of merry mischief." The writer spoke of "a puckish glint in Walter's makeup." Walter and two of his three brothers graduated from the University of North Carolina at Chapel Hill. He has been described by a Reidsville friend as upwardly mobile and a bit of a rebel in that he did things his way instead of conforming to the rules.

College. (On page 22 of *The Dark Tower* the author had C. S. Lewis ask his friend Orfieu "hang it all, who's going to win the boatrace [the Oxford-Cambridge boatrace] this year?" Such a question is glaringly inappropriate in the mouth of Lewis in a story attributed to Lewis, because he cared nothing at all about athletic games or Oxford-Cambridge sports rivalry.)

In his talk at Rockingham Community College Hooper did not mention the yet-unrevealed Lewis bonfire, which he would describe for the first time in California a couple of weeks later. But he told his audience that C. S. Lewis never had any secretarial help until he himself volunteered. (He didn't mention Lewis's usual secretary, Warren.) Lewis's letters "*had* to be in handwriting" Hooper said, without explaining why. (There was a typewriter in the Kilns, and when Warren drafted letters for Lewis he always typed them.)

"I learned to actually imitate his own handwriting and forge his signature, which *(chuckle)* he enjoyed very much."

This claim that he can imitate Lewis's handwriting and forge his signature is Walter Hooper's own tape-recorded statement in his own voice, just as clear as the day he made it in in 1975.

Four years later, on 27 June 1979, Hooper told his story about forging Lewis's signature again a little differently. This time he claimed in a handwritten letter to Stephen Schofield that his handwriting and Lewis's were alike to start with, and it was C. S. Lewis himself who first noticed the similarity. At first Lewis would dictate letters to Hooper and sign them. But eventually he had Hooper sign the letters for him.[27]

In all the decades when Warren Lewis was his brother's secretary, he was not given the responsibility of signing any letters with his brother's signature. (A 21 July 1967 letter from Warren to Schofield makes that clear.)[28] Such

---

[27] Walter Hooper made this statement in a letter dated 27 June 1979, written in his "Lewisian script." The claim and relevant penmanship samples (contradicting the claim) were published on pages 8-9 of the April 1980 issue of the *Canadian C. S. Lewis Journal*.

[28] "Yes, his capacity for writing sympathetically to all kinds of people with so many kinds of problems was astonishing—and the care with which he turned from his own heavy work to deal with each. I acted as his secretary for many years, and looking back, I am surprised at the small number of letters he let me draft for his signature—hardly ever any except those dealing with trivialities."

abandon with a brand new friend is puzzling. If any questionable 1963 C. S. Lewis letters should ever turn up and be checked for authenticity, their being written and signed by Hooper instead of Lewis would simply illustrate his claim that Lewis had instructed him to do the signing. It is a troublesome situation.

For the literary executor of an important estate to own a private cache of papers from the great writer and also to be able to forge that writer's penmanship is a dangerous opportunity for fraud. Such an executor might be tempted to supplement his collection of genuine Lewis documents with new ones of his own creation.

Two letters that Walter Hooper wrote for C. S. Lewis in 1963 are available for examination. The originals are in the Marion E. Wade Center, and they were published in Lewis's *Letters to an American Lady*. The first one was dated 27 July and began, "Jack asked me to tell you that letter writing is physically impossible, his fingers jerk and twitch so. His physical crisis has greatly disordered his intelligence and he is vividly aware of living in a world of hallucinations." Hooper accidentally switched at that point to Lewis's exact words to the lady, signed the letter Jack, and posted it that way.

On 10 August Hooper wrote to the American lady again for Lewis, beginning, "I am Professor C. S. Lewis's secretary writing to tell you some facts concerning Professor Lewis's present state of health. I felt you were entitled to this history. I trust that you will not mind it coming from my hand, but so it must." He signed it Walter Hooper.[29]

The lady, Mrs. Mary Shelburne, received one more letter from Lewis before he died, dated 30 September. It was in his own handwriting, and he told her that because his brother Warren was away, he had no help with correspondence and could not write much. (That is strange in light of the fact that Walter Hooper says he was Lewis's companion-secretary until late September. But it correlates perfectly with the fact that on 18 August 1963 Oxford resident Kay Farrer wrote to Lewis that she hoped to see Walter *to say goodbye*. She knew he was leaving very soon.)

Walter Hooper's two letters to the American lady definitely do not look as if they were written by Lewis. At that point Walter Hooper's script was larger

---

[29] C. S. Lewis, *Letters to an American Lady* (Grand Rapids MI: Wm. B. Eerdmans Publishing Co., 1967) 120-21.

and more open than that of C. S. Lewis, very much the standard American handwriting taught in United States schools. Such script is the ideal for American teachers, and indeed Hooper's B.A. and M.A. were both in education; he tried his hand as a sixth-grade teacher at an elementary school in Chapel Hill, North Carolina, in 1956-1957, and then taught in a boys' boarding school in Arden for two years in 1959-1961. His penmanship was just right.

The 1963 handwriting in letters to Mrs. Shelburne was not a fluke; Hooper's 1979 claim that his handwriting was like Lewis's in 1963 is manifestly untrue. Between 1965 and 1975 Hooper's known handwriting style changed radically and came to resemble the handwriting of C. S. Lewis. (According to Nicolas Barker of Britain's National Library, "Among the Lewis papers at the Bodleian and in Library's own correspondence files, there is a representative collection of letters in Hooper's hand which show that his hand has been modified in size and ductus so that it resembles Lewis's, whether consciously or unconsciously."[30]) Is it possible that in addition to changing his normal handwriting, in private Hooper also developed the ability to actually forge the handwriting of C. S. Lewis? It is fair to ask, because in 1975 Hooper claimed he had intentionally accomplished that feat.

In *The C. S. Lewis Hoax* I mentioned that in Hooper's film *Through Joy and Beyond* one can see Hooper's hand writing out words of young Lewis in appropriate script for 1913. But in answer to my suggestion that this was evidence that he can produce skillful facsimiles of Lewis documents, Hooper replied in the *Canadian C. S. Lewis Journal* that no one tried to duplicate Lewis's handwriting in the film. According to Hooper, the reenactment filmed on 4 August 1978 used Lewis's very own steel-nibbed pen and Lewis's own words, but the penmanship was not meant to resemble Lewis's.[31]

In fact, according to Hooper, the hand in the film belonged to someone who had probably never seen Lewis's handwriting; so it is a coincidence if the penmanship seems to resemble young Lewis's. (He didn't say why the man who allegedly did the writing remains anonymous.) Hooper doubts that a forger could forge words that fast anyway, and he claims that his own hand

---

[30] Nicolas Barker, "C.S. Lewis, Darkly," *Essays in Criticism*, no. 4 (October 1990) 60: 364.

[31] *The Canadian C. S. Lewis Journal 77* (Winter 1992): 17-18.

was too bony and hairy to appear in the scene. In fact, it took thirty seconds for the hand to copy out only seventeen letters, a slow rate; and in my 1975 snapshot showing Hooper's hands they look neither bony nor hairy.[32] When the videocassette version of *Through Joy and Beyond* came out, the handwriting scene had been removed. Like variations in the accounts of how and when Hooper's handwriting came to resemble Lewis's, there are variations in the accounts of how Hooper became an Anglican priest. David Barrett's 1987 book C. S. *Lewis and His World* (Wm. B. Eerdmans and Marshall Pickering) has several errors, including the claim that Hooper was an American priest when he met C. S. Lewis in 1963.[33]

According to articles about Hooper in his home area newspaper the *Greensboro Daily News,* he left his teaching post at the University of Kentucky to become Lewis's secretary in 1963; and after Lewis's death he decided to study theology in England and become a priest. In the *Episcopal Clerical Directory* he did not list his theological training, but according to his entries in *Contemporary Authors* and *Crockford's Clerical Directory,* he got his seminary training at St. Stephen's House, Oxford.[34] According to a 1 February 1978 letter from The Reverend Canon Dudley Barksdale of the Diocese of Lexington, "Fr. Hooper did some seminary work in the United

---

[32] Sharon Cregier reported in *The Lewis Legacy,* Issue 52, "When we saw the film 'Through Joy and Beyond' in 1984 at the C. S. Lewis conference at St Deiniols [Wales], with Walter Hooper, it seemed to me that it was a foregone conclusion that the hand was Hooper's. I have photos of Hooper's hands from St Deiniols. His hand does not seem to be excessively hairy."

[33] On 30 July 1965 Walter Hooper stated in a personal letter to me, "Yes, I am an Anglican priest and it was my great pleasure to serve as honorary curate for a year in the parish church of which Lewis was a member."

In fact, C. S. Lewis died November 22, 1963, and not until September 27, 1964, was Hooper ordained a deacon in the Diocese of Lexington, Kentucky (with the Bishop of Oxford acting for the Bishop of Lexington). Although Hooper's letter seemed to indicate that he had been an assistant priest for one year in the church in Headington Quarry where C. S. Lewis was worshipping before his death, in actuality he was a deacon at that church between 27 September 1964, and 27 June 1965, when *Warren* Lewis was worshipping there.

[34] Coincidentally, Hooper is not the only Lewis biographer who has attended St. Stephen's. A. N. Wilson spent a year there once, and his comments about it were aired in an article titled "The Busy, Busy Wasp" by James Atlas in the 18 October 1992 issue of *The New York Times.* "It was a madhouse, a homosexual world of a particularly high-camp—a girls' names and feather dusters kind of world...it was beyond belief."

States, then taught at the University prior to going to England. He studied at several places in England and was certified to the then Bishop of Lexington, the Rt. Rev. William Moody..."

In fact, Hooper attended Virginia Theological Seminary for two years (1957-1959) and was admitted as a candidate for holy orders in the Diocese of North Carolina on 16 March 1959. But he was dropped as a candidate on 8 September 1959, and later removed his name from Virginia Theological Seminary's alumni roster. He explains that difficult period in an illustrated interview titled "A Dead Man's Secretary" in the Summer 1987 issue of *Carolina Alumni Review,* a magazine with circulation of 44,000. Hooper's presiding bishop in North Carolina required all candidates for the priesthood to be examined by a psychiatrist, Hooper says, and the psychiatrist's great question was "What would you do if you were locked in a room with a naked woman and a bed?"

According to Hooper, the psychiatrist told the bishop that under Hooper's gentle surface he was boiling with rage. Worse yet, the seminary decided that he needed twice-weekly visits with a psychiatrist. The seminary was determined to "monkey about with one's psyche," so he left theology in exasperation and returned to literature.

Hooper was an entertaining teacher, popular with the boys who lived at Christ's School in Arden, North Carolina; but rumor has it that he left under a cloud. In the summer of 1961 he moved to Lexington to teach at the University of Kentucky and possibly earn a doctorate. There he was welcomed into the family of his recent student Charles Davis. Charles's father, John Davis, was an attorney, active in the Church of the Good Shepherd, where T. Clark Bloomfield was rector. Bloomfield is said to have helped Hooper with money from the church's discretionary fund; and after Hooper moved to Oxford in January 1964, Bloomfield sent him a monthly stipend to help him obtain a degree in literature.

Indeed, on 27 October 1963 Lewis's new friend Austin Farrer was confident that he could get Hooper into the University, and sent him application forms and advice. But on 9 December Farrer notified Hooper that he had been rejected. (Farrer suggested that Hooper might do research in Oxford while preparing for a doctorate in the United States.) Perhaps in the midst of his disappointments at the end of 1963, Hooper did not break that news to Father Bloomfield.

In April 1964 Bishop William R. Moody of Lexington accepted Hooper as
a long-distance postulant. (On page ix of Hooper's 1964 preface to C. S.
Lewis's *Poems* he thanked a patron named Charles Böhmer for his support,
but didn't mention the continuing support from Lexington's Church of the
Good Shepherd.) In June 1965 the Bishop of Oxford, acting for Lexington's
Bishop Moody, ordained Hooper a priest.[35] According to an informed source,
at this point Bloomfield realized that Hooper was not a graduate student in
literature after all, cut off the academic stipend, and declined Hooper's appeal
for further aid.[36]

There are evidently no records of how and why the transatlantic ordination was arranged. Hooper failed to transfer canonically out of Kentucky
until 21 October 1977—almost fourteen years after he had moved to England
and started pretending at times that he was English. According to the 1980
biographical note attached to his personal papers at Chapel Hill, Hooper "has
served as chaplain of several of the Oxford Colleges, including Jesus and
Wadham." But that is an exaggeration. His only chaplaincy was at Wadham
from 1965 to 1967; and according to Oxford rumor he left that post under a
cloud. He was an assistant chaplain (not chaplain, as sometimes listed) at
Jesus College from 1967 to 1971. He celebrated the mass as an assistant rector
of the Anglo-Catholic Church of St. Mary Magdalen in central Oxford for

---

[35]"I was ordained after I met him..." Hooper told members of the Portland C. S.
Lewis Society in their question-and-answer session. In fact, Hooper was ordained a
year and a half after Lewis died, and two years after Hooper met him.

[36] When Robert O. Evans of Lexington, Kentucky, read these surprising facts in
The Lewis Legacy, Issue 45, he volunteered more information:

I knew Bishop Moody of course and also Clark Bloomfield, although I did not
attend that church. Bloomfield was much beloved by his parishioners and stayed a very
long time. The Church of the Good Shepherd also housed the Bishop's offices and the
seminary Bishop Moody founded for mostly older candidates, which is no longer
functioning.

In those days there was no Cathedral in the Diocese. Bishop Moody built instead a
Cathedral Domain, a sort of summer camp with church up in the mountains. Later he
founded another church which was only nominally an Episcopalian venture. It was in
the hunt country and devoted to the rich, horsey bunch. Of course it attracted a fair
share of arch conservatives.

Moody was against women priests, against the Book of Common Prayer revision
(rightly, I thought, as the revision is dreadful), and I am sure he would have been much
shaken to learn more about Walter Hooper. I am glad he died in his innocence.

many years beginning in 1971. His 1973 application for a chaplaincy at Exeter was unsuccessful.

Hooper's twenty-three year career as an Anglican priest ended in 1988, when he joined the Roman Catholic Church. (One of his surprised readers murmured upon hearing the news, "Oh well, Rome's loss is Canterbury's gain...") He adopted the belief that his Anglican orders—deacon and priest—had been invalid, and so he stopped wearing clerical garb and calling himself "Father." He understands, however, why people who still believe in the Anglican priesthood would still consider him a priest although he does not. He says that certain Roman Catholics are urging him to become ordained.[37]

Some people agree with Hooper that he was never an authentic priest although he thought he was; some believe he is still an authentic priest although he thinks he is not; and others don't know what to think. Whether or not Hooper was ever in any sense C. S. Lewis's personal literary assistant who helped him with his writing is another important question. This was Hooper's new claim in 1980.[38] As well as the extent of Hooper's friendship with Lewis, which has always been unclear.

Virginia author Sheldon Vanauken (author of *A Severe Mercy*), answered a set of questions about his own friendship with C. S. Lewis in a 1979 interview that was never published until 1988, when it appeared in *The C. S. Lewis Hoax*. Pages 2 through 4 survive, and Vanauken provides them for the light they shed on some of Lewis's personal relationships.[39]

Interview with Sheldon Vanauken

Q: That's very interesting. You did know Mr. Lewis rather well then, didn't you?

---

[37] *The Newsletter of the Salinas Valley C. S. Lewis Society*, 1/1 (Winter 1992): 9.

[38] Walter Hooper, "Introduction," in C. S. Lewis, *The Weight of Glory*, rev. ed. (New York: Macmillan, 1980) xi.

[39] Sheldon Vanauken sent me a copy of these pages in 1980 or thereabouts, and I filed them. When I was working on *The C. S. Lewis Hoax* I remembered them and asked if I could use them. Vanauken replied on 22 February 1987: "The interview was never published, and it's safe to conclude it never will be now. I just got it out and re-read it (it's all I have now, that fragment). I shall withhold the name of the interviewer; but yes, you may use it."

A: Not as well of course as some of the Inklings and his old friends.
But it's all in my book. On those visits to Cambridge I told you
about, I felt we were very close indeed.

Q: Was there any special reason for that?

A. Yes. A combination of things. All the correspondence about my
wife's death and about grief. And now Lewis being married and
facing *his* wife's death. Bound to make us closer.

Q: You said in your book that he said he was in love with her when
you met in Oxford that year. Did he say more about it at
Cambridge?

A: I don't recall a specific statement, but it was sort of an understood
thing behind all our talk. Everything I said was based on the idea
that he felt about Joy as I felt about Davy; and everything *he* said
implied that, too. I don't doubt it at all.

Q: In Carpenter's book, *The Inklings,* there is a slight suggestion that
Lewis's marriage was never consummated. What is your
opinion of that?

A: I don't believe it. Not for a minute! What Carpenter said was that
there wasn't any evidence that it had been consummated. That's
rather silly. How many marriages can you think of where there
is evidence? In fact, what evidence can there be? Even children
don't really *prove* anything, do they? Unless they have the
Romanov nose or something. Even in the old days when the
groom used to hang a blood-stained sheet out of the window, he
could have pricked his finger or cut the throat of a mouse,
couldn't he? Anyhow, look at those later letters in my book, when
Joy was up and shooting pigeons. They sound like a
consummated marriage to me. And, even more so, *A Grief
Observed.*

Q: About that there's been a suggestion that *A Grief Observed* is
fiction, as proved by his using a pseudonym.

A: Come on! That's nonsense! He has a frightful grief, so he writes of
some other grief! Nonsense! He didn't publish any of his other
fiction under a pseudonym. He wrote as N. W. Clerk because it
was unbearably personal. Besides, the real proof is, he told me
about it as his own grief in a letter I've lost; and I ordered it

straight away from England, first printing. Anyway, no fiction was ever like that. Certainly not!

Q: Okay. Very convincing. Now, Mr. Vanauken, in *A Severe Mercy* you refer to some letters from Lewis that for one reason or another were not included, and you just now mentioned a lost letter. Can you tell me anything about the lost letters?

A: A little perhaps. There was a second letter on the question of homosexuality, as he had said he'd write after talking with others. I lent it to a homosexual student who wanted to copy it, and he lost it, unfortunately. As well as I remember, he came to the same conclusions. Then there was a letter, very agonized, about Joy's death. I decided it ought not to be saved and tore it up.

Q: How many letters would you say were lost or not retained by you?

A: Perhaps half a dozen or a bit more. All but that homosexual letter were late ones, after the "Severe Mercy" one. There was one I'd love to find again. It was about his heroine Orual in *Till We Have Faces* before it was published or even named perhaps. I used to put letters from him in his books, and I remember shifting this one into *Till We Have Faces* when I got it. I don't know what happened to it, unless I lent the book to someone and they stole it, blast them!

Q: The last letter in *A Severe Mercy* was dated June 1962. Was that the last letter from him?

A: Oh, no. Certainly not. There was at least one more in '62. I tried to space letters out so as not to burden him, you know. And there was one in early '63, the year of his death. By early I mean the first three or four months of the year. I had told him that I expected to be in England in the late summer and autumn, and he said he would be looking forward to seeing me. He talked a bit about how he was thinking of Joy, now that more time had gone.

Q: That was the very last one?

A: I think so, except for a note in November, the month he died, inviting me to tea at the Kilns.

Q: He was still able to write then?

A: Oh, yes. I didn't know of course that he'd been so ill in the summer, in hospital and all that. He may have said in the note that he'd been unwell, or perhaps that was when I was out there.

Q: He told you all about the illness that afternoon?

A: I don't know if it was "all" but it was a good deal. He told me he'd been out of his head and that they thought he was going to die. And some more about his present condition: why they couldn't operate. I could see he wasn't very well. He warned me he would doze off for a few seconds while we talked, and he did. It was frightening. I didn't think he was going to die in a matter of days—in fact, we arranged a second meeting in a fortnight—but I thought I would never come to England to see him again. But we got the tea together—we were alone in the house—and he was cheerful and even brisk at moments. But when that other meeting came due, he was dead.

Q: What did you and Lewis talk about?

A: Everything. It was actually a rather wonderful last meeting. It was blowing and raining outside and all snug within. We talked about Joy and Davy and meeting them again. He spoke of his recent article, "We Have No Right to Happiness." And about my booklet "Encounter with Light," which he had seen long before. It was written in 1961, and he had let me use three of his letters to me in it, which is why they weren't copyrighted.

Q: Anyone may use them?

A: That's right. I even excluded them from the copyright of *A Severe Mercy*, thinking Jack would have liked that. Anyway, he liked the booklet.

Q: Had Mr. Lewis ever mentioned Walter Hooper in his letters?

A: No. No reason why he should have done. When I had that last letter in '63, Walter Hooper hadn't come over yet, had he?

Q: But of course he told you that afternoon, when he was talking about the hospital, about Father Hooper's help and being his secretary afterwards?

A: No.

Q: Not at all? It says in the *Biography* that Lewis regarded him as the
son he never had and all that. And Hooper was a fellow
American, too.

A: Practically a neighbor: North Carolina, you know. But Jack didn't
mention him.

Q: Why didn't he, do you think?

A: No idea. Jack may not have thought of Virginia and North
Carolina being so close. Also, by then Walter had gone back to
the States. Jack did talk about his brother, the Major, what a help
he was with letters and all that.

Q: But no mention of Walter Hooper?

A: No.

Strange as it is that C. S. Lewis never mentioned his new companion-
secretary to Sheldon Vanauken, it is even stranger that Lewis never
mentioned him in his 1963 letters to old friends such as Arthur Greeves.

One assumes that Walter Hooper would not consciously exaggerate his
closeness to C. S. Lewis, in light of the derision such behavior is apt to cause.
(Wilfred Sheed's acerbic comment, "Claiming close friendship with the recent
dead is a knavish trick" comes to mind.)[40] But the relationship has been
misrepresented repeatedly for well over thirty-five years.

On the back of the 1966 book *Light on C. S. Lewis*[41] Hooper is identified
thus: "An American scholar when he first met Lewis some ten years ago on a
grant that enabled him to study Lewis's work, Hooper eventually became
Lewis's secretary, and lived with him and his brother."[42]

In early May of 1969 Jean Wakeman, a friend of the Lewises, wrote to the
London *Times* on Warren's behalf protesting that Walter Hooper had not
been Lewis's secretary as long as the paper claimed. The editor replied to her

---

[40] Wilfred Sheed, *The Good Word* (New York: Dutton, 1978) 3.

[41] Jocelyn Gibb, *Light on C. S. Lewis* (New York: Harcourt, Brace & World,
1966).

[42] This account moved Hooper's trip to England back seven years to 1956 and
added a prestigious-sounding grant.

that Hooper was reducing his claim to one year, during which he lived at the Kilns with the Lewis brothers.[43]

Warren, who had never even met Walter Hooper until Hooper returned to England after Lewis's death, was exasperated.[44] On 12 May 1969 he wrote to Hooper in protest:

Dear Walter,

I am getting very tired of the business arising out of that unfortunate press statement that you had been Jack's "amanuensis in the last years of his life."

The latest development is that someone who knew Jack well, and who wrote to the paper pointing out the inaccuracy, received a reply from The Editor, *Times Diary*.

I have seen this, and here is the relevant portion:

"...Not only does the publisher, Mr. Jocelyn Gibb, stand by what he has told us; we have now spoken to Mr. Hooper himself. He says that he was Lewis's amanuensis for the last year of his life, though he concedes that he was in the USA when Lewis died. He says that he 'lived in' with C. S. Lewis and W. H. Lewis while working as C. S. Lewis's secretary..."

What information Gibb had and where he got it from I do not know, and on this point it would be idle to speculate. But as for your part in the business, if you are correctly reported, this simply makes confusion worse confounded.

---

[43] Ten years later, in his film *Jack Remembered*, Hooper remarked to Owen Barfield: "As you know, I went on living with Warnie after Jack died...."

[44] Twenty years later, the 15 January 1989 issue of *The Sunday Telegraph* reported, "John Wain, Oxford Professor of Poetry, describes the relationship between Hooper and Lewis as being like ivy growing over a house." Wain was a fond ex-pupil of C. S. Lewis and a good-natured but canny observer of the Oxford scene.

(1) ...In point of fact, so far from being here for a year, I am told on good authority that you were here for approximately the whole month of August, after which you returned to the States.

(2) At no time did Jack, you, and I live together in this house. On the only occasion when you stayed here, namely during August 1963, I was in the hospital in Ireland. And in fact we never met until after Jack's death.

This cloud of misapprehension which has risen before I have even seen Chapter I [of the Green/Hooper biography] causes me some forebodings. True, as I am to see the work chapter by chapter to check for errors, I am pretty well safeguarded. But if this business is a sample of what I am to expect, my search for inaccuracies is going to be no sinecure!

Yours,

Warnie

Copy to J. Gibb. Esq. [45]

The two men were on a collision course, and Warren was in no position to prevail. What would eventually come of his protests? That is the subject of the next chapter, "They Fall Together."

> Laziness, credulity, and a preference for avoiding complicated and unpopular controversies often contribute as much to successful cover-ups as all the theories of conspiracy put together.
> —*John Fraser*

---

[45] This letter is preserved in Walter Hooper's collection at Chapel Hill.

10

THEY FALL TOGETHER

NOT A STOLEN MANUSCRIPT AFTER ALL?

The two "C. S. Lewis secretaries," Major Warren Lewis and Walter Hooper, were supposedly good friends after C. S. Lewis's death. They were both polite, friendly bachelors who lived on in Oxford; both book-loving men; both devout Christians; and both passionately devoted to the memory of C. S. Lewis. But their friendship was doomed to disaster before it began. In fact, it allegedly began before it began, and that was the beginning of the problem.

As Hooper told the story at the end of the Green/Hooper biography, on 14 July 1963 Lewis asked Hooper live in the Kilns as his private secretary from then on.[1] In 1991 Hooper improved on the story: "...although we didn't know it at the time, he was to retire from Cambridge a few months after I met him [sic]. Lewis and I believed that we had begun a partnership which would last for years, and we settled into a way of life which each found restful....Now, at the risk of infuriating some overly-intense Lewis enthusiasts in this country, I will confess that to my very considerable astonishment Lewis never

---

[1] Hooper claims that he lived at the Kilns while Lewis was hospitalized and he was helping Lewis in the hospital. But research shows that he received his mail at his Exeter College address during Lewis's hospitalization. Even more significantly, it would make no sense for Hooper to commute all the way from the empty Kilns (in Headington Quarry) to the Oxford hospital when his room in Exeter College was only a ten-minute walk from the hospital.

caused me to feel that I was out of my depths."[2] (An odd claim in light of the fact that on 1 August 1963 Hooper wrote to Roger Lancelyn Green, "Major Lewis is expected home in a fortnight. Until that time I have been handling Jack's correspondence.")[3]

Perhaps Hooper has exaggerated his role during Lewis's 15 July–6 August hospitalization. According to his account on page 302 of *C. S. Lewis: A Biography*, he and Austin Farrer were together much of 16 July, when they rushed to the hospital together to visit the awakened Lewis; then they had Communion with him the next day. But in the Chapel Hill collection there is a 17 July letter from Farrer to Hooper informing him that Lewis was awake and lively, and inviting Hooper to 11 A.M. Communion. (In 1963 in England many people still wrote letters rather than making telephone calls. In major cities there were two or three mail deliveries and pickups a day, and prompt, accurate delivery was taken for granted.)

So far, there are only two available letters that Hooper wrote for Lewis, both to American Mary Shelburne and published in *Letters to an American Lady*. Both are confused. The first one has a strange shift in voice from third person to first person. In the second one, Hooper tells Shelburne that Lewis had his heart attack "during the last hours of the night" and that his coma lasted "nearly 24 hours" until 3 P.M. the next day. But if Lewis's attack occurred in the last hours of the night and the coma ended at 3 P.M, the coma did not last "nearly 24 hours." And according to William Griffin the heart attack actually took place at 5 P.M.

In September 1963 Walter Hooper saw a tide in his affairs which taken at the flood might lead to fortune. His fall semester at the University of Kentucky had begun on 5 September and would end on 21 December, and then his semester break would last until February 1964. Warren was still away in Ireland when Hooper made his momentous offer to C. S. Lewis: he

---

[2] Walter Hooper, "C. S. Lewis: The Man and His Thought," featured in Cynthia Marshall's 1991 collection *Essays on C. S. Lewis and George MacDonald* (Mellen Press, 1991). The subtitle of this 116-page, $59.95 book is *Truth, Fiction, and the Power of Imagination*. Ironically, two of Hooper's sentences are "Unfortunately, Dr. Beversluis is not the only one to twist the facts of Lewis's life out of recognition" and "...Lewis said to me 'Can't people understand *invention*?'"

[3] This letter is preserved in Walter Hooper's collection at Chapel Hill.

would return to the Kilns for the entire month of January 1964 to be Lewis's paid secretary.

In the generally excellent 1994 edition of *Jack*, George Sayer still reports trustingly "Late in September [the month was August], Walter Hooper had to go to the United States to wind up his affairs there and to teach for one more term before coming back to act as Jack's permanent secretary."[4] However, the longest letters that C. S. Lewis ever wrote to Hooper were dated 20 September and 11 October 1963, urging him not to make a return visit to the Kilns until June 1964 (summer vacation), or April (spring break) at the very earliest.[5] Lewis spelled out reasons for Hooper to delay his proposed visit and also warned that he could not pay Hooper more than £5 per week for his help. He added that Hooper's idea of studying at one of the Oxford colleges during his visit would not be practical. (Hooper applied anyway.) Lewis apologized for the limits of his hospitality and assured Hooper that he was welcome.

On 24 September Molly Miller wrote to Hooper at Lewis's behest, advising him not to return until the winter was past. She chatted on happily; informing him that some ashtrays he gave her were so pretty she hung them on her wall. Witnesses agree that Hooper had charmed Lewis and Lewis's worried friends and associates that summer while Lewis was mortally ill and Warren was away. (One of these friends was Kay Farrer. Her impression of him on 16 June 1963 was "...that specially American warmth and sincerity...")[6]

Warren had returned to the Kilns by the end of September and was back at his post as Lewis's secretary, but Hooper's powers of persuasion somehow prevailed. Lewis reversed himself in a brief note on 23 October, agreeing to Hooper's arrival for a long visit on the third or fourth of January. On 18 November Molly Miller cheerfully notified Hooper that they had a card table

---

[4] George Sayer, *Jack* (Wheaton, Illinois: Crossway Books, 1994) 407. If Sayer had read Richard Ladborough's 16 December 1963 letter to Walter Hooper in the Chapel Hill collection, he would have seen that Lewis expected only a visit from Hooper in 1964.

[5] The claim that Hooper had ten years of letters from Lewis has often been repeated. There are in fact eight letters from Lewis to Hooper, spanning nine years: four of the eight span September-October 1963. The dates on the letters are 30 November 1954, 2 December 1957, 2 July 1962, 15 December 1962, 3 September 1963, 20 September 1963, 11 October 1963, and 23 October 1963. Their length varies from 26 words to 333 words.

[6] See the Chapel Hill collection.

where he could work. The house was warm and cozy. Lewis had asked her to advise Hooper that he wasn't giving or receiving Christmas gifts.

Five days later, on 23 November, Molly wrote again in despair: "I'm very grieved to have to tell you Mr. Jack passed away 5:45 last evening." She described it all. She was in the house and heard him fall to the floor: "such a heavy thud..." "His funeral is 10 A.M. Holy Trinity Church Tuesday morning, if there is no hitch..." "We shall recover but at the moment can't see how."

Twenty years later, when interviewer Charles Glaize asked Hooper about Lewis's death, he said, "Well, I was not in England on that day. I had come back for business to the United States...I believe the first thing I started doing—without analyzing it—was to pray to C. S. Lewis. What I felt very much on my mind as I prayed to him was, 'Now that you see all, can you still call me a friend? Do I still amount to anything? I hope so.'"[7]

Hooper elaborated, "Major Lewis had been away all the time that I knew C. S. Lewis." Glaize answered, "Lewis' brother?" Hooper replied, "Yes. He returned after his brother's death."[8]

Neither Warren nor Hooper attended the small funeral for C. S. Lewis in his old churchyard on 26 November 1963; and neither one was eager to admit that fact afterwards. Warren did not attend because he was trying to drown his sorrow in alcohol, and Hooper did not attend because he was living and teaching in Kentucky.[9] George Sayer has described the funeral in his book *Jack:* "I remember Barfield, Harwood, Tolkien, Colin Hardie, Lawlor, Peter Bayley, Maureen and Leonard Blake, Douglas, David, the Millers, and Paxford."[10]

After the funeral, Barfield invited a few people into the Kilns to hear the reading of the will. The executors and trustees—Barfield and Harwood—were

---

[7] Lewis correspondent Vera Gebbert asked Warren for Lewis mementos after his death in 1963, and Warren sent her Lewis's pipes, which she donated to the Wade Center. Yet in 1997 Hooper gave Charles Colson a pipe, alleging that it was Lewis's.

[8] In a tape-recorded, unpublished interview that took place in August 1984.

[9] William Griffin, on page xxv of his book *Clive Staples Lewis: A Dramatic Life,* said that he was at the funeral "albeit figuratively." In that unusual sense both Warren Lewis and Walter Hooper were there also, no doubt, with thousands of others.

[10] According to William Griffin's research, David was absent and a few others were present.

to hold Lewis's assets in trust, first for the education of David and Douglas, and second for Warren's support. After Warren's death, all that was left would go to David and Douglas. Sayer was dismayed that Lewis left Fred Paxford, who had worked for Lewis for over thirty years, only £100.

"Well, it won't take me far, will it?" Paxford said. "Mr. Jack, 'e never 'ad no idea of money. 'Is mind was always set on ' 'igher things."[11]

There is no public account of how either Warren or Hooper got through the sad Christmas season after Lewis's death, but Hooper had something new to look forward to. He told friends in Lexington that he was returning to Oxford to handle C. S. Lewis's literary remains; they had the impression that he arranged this with Owen Barfield. He flew back to Oxford in January as planned. At the end of January he began a leave of absence from the University of Kentucky,[12] moved into a room in Wycliffe Hall, and moved into the center of Lewis affairs. The events that followed led to an angry climax that seems hard to believe.

Len and Molly Miller, the household helpers, said it was not frugality that caused Warren to move out of the Kilns on 19 May 1964 so much as it was his nerves. In the Kilns he was beset by impressions of his brother at every turn, and so he asked the Millers to locate him a house near theirs, which they did. They found him one on Ringwood Road, Headington. It is a fact that for months he slept there at night and spent most of his days at the Kilns, using two houses instead of one. He was extremely distraught.

That June I received a letter that turned out to be the ultimate in irony. On 11 June 1964, Clyde Kilby sent me good news: "In the same mail with your letter was one from Chad Walsh informing me that Walter Cooper [sic] of Oxford is in process of editing CSL's unpublished manuscripts. So there is a good deal of Lewis to come, I am glad to say."

My sister took a snapshot of the Kilns for me in the summer of 1964 and happened to meet Molly Miller in the yard. The two walked to Mrs. Miller's

---

[11] *Jack*, 411.

[12] Lewis W. Cochran, Vice-President of Academic Affairs at the University of Kentucky, says that Walter Hooper was employed as a full-time instructor in the then department of English, speech, and dramatic arts, and resigned effective 31 January 1964. According to notes in the University archives, Hooper seems to have been on leave of absence from 1964 to 1966.

house, where she invited my sister in to talk. There she poured out her serious concern about Warren's alcoholism.

"I again went to live with Major Lewis," is how Hooper states his September 1964 move to 51 Ringwood Road (the word "again" is unexplained).[13] Why was this experiment undertaken? Hooper was preparing for ordination and launching himself as Lewis's editor. He needed a room, and so Warren obligingly offered him the extra room in his house on Ringwood Road. Unfortunately, having the same address does not guarantee friendly companionship. That month Warren recorded in his diary his inability to get information about his financial situation (from Owen Barfield) and his lack of anyone to chat with. He was deeply depressed and lonely, and it is safe to assume that he was medicating himself with alcohol.

By the end of the year Hooper was emerging from total anonymity to prominence through Lewis's book *Poems* (1964). It was in his introduction to *Poems* that Hooper introduced himself to readers as Lewis's companion-secretary. Lewis specialists were surprised to learn of the personal secretary's existence and eager to learn about Lewis from him.

As soon as *Poems* was published I read it and saw that, in my opinion, the most significant poem of all was "Reason and Imagination," which Hooper had evidently misunderstood, because he mistitled it "Reason." Over eleven years later Hooper graciously arranged for me to have tea at the Atheneum Club on 2 January 1976 with Owen Barfield. I was eager to hear what Barfield would say about "Reason and Imagination," because I thought he had a special interest in Samuel Taylor Coleridge's views on the same subject. To my dismay, he had never heard of the poem (which I described to him in detail), much less read it; and he didn't express any particular interest in Lewis's posthumous literature.

One reason Lewis and Barfield enjoyed their friendship was because of the intellectual stimulation of disagreement and debate. Lewis said of Barfield, "He has read all the right books but has got the wrong thing out of every one. It is as if he spoke your language but mispronounced it." It occurs to me that

---

[13] "Reflections of an Editor," 3.

perhaps a busy fellow writer with little sympathy for one's point of view is not the wisest choice for a literary executor.[14]

Evidently, Barfield accepted Hooper's editorial work from the beginning without reading it. A full decade would pass after that disconcerting 1976 discovery before I got the idea that part of the posthumous Lewis literature was forged.

As Hooper explained to the New York C. S. Lewis Society on 13 August 1977, his career began when he saved the poetry of C. S. Lewis from annihilation and then decided to publish it.[15] Immediately after C. S. Lewis's death, according to Hooper, Warren wanted to move into a smaller house in order to save money, and so he made the great three-day bonfire that Hooper called "the desecration."[16] One of the things Warren tossed out for burning was Lewis's most ardently prized possession, the blue folder into which he had collected his poetry that he hoped to bring out in a book. Fortunately, Walter Hooper felt led to go to the Kilns and arrived on the scene in time to rescue the poetry folder from the flames.[17] It was the same blue folder that Hooper had brought home to Lewis from Cambridge five months earlier.

In mid-August 1963 Lewis had sent Hooper and Douglas Gresham to Cambridge to clean out his rooms, and it took a week; Douglas entertained himself elsewhere while Hooper went through Lewis's papers. In Lewis's written instructions to Hooper he emphasized that from his desk drawer he wanted two containers, "one orange, one some other colour," containing loose sheets—some typed, some handwritten. "These are all my poems." (These instructions are preserved in Hooper's Chapel Hill collection.)

Perhaps Hooper has combined the two Cambridge containers ("one orange, one some other colour") into one blue folder to improve the story. But he failed to mention any orange container or blue folder in his 1964 preface to *Poems*. There he mentioned finding Lewis's poems on scraps of paper, on

---

[14] In a classic case, Edgar Allan Poe had the posthumous misfortune of getting Rufus Griswald for his literary executor.

[15] Walter Hooper, "Reflections of an Editor," *CSL: The Bulletm of the New York C. S. Lewis Society*, (August 1977): 2.

[16] Hooper used the term *desecration* on page 42 of his "Introduction" for *They Stand Together* (London: Collins, 1979).

[17] See Chapter 3 for the bonfire story.

the flyleaves of books, and in notebooks.[18] The blue folder first emerged on 13 August 1977, when Hooper first regaled the New York C. S. Lewis Society with his bonfire story.

Hooper has magnanimously assured readers that he did not think Warren's intended annihilation of the blue folder showed any lack of love toward his brother; it was just Warren's way of cleaning house.[19] Needless to say, if Warren didn't have a manuscript bonfire after all, saying he did and forgiving him for it is not so magnanimous. Furthermore, the confusion and contradiction about how Hooper obtained Lewis's poems does not increase confidence in the integrity of the poems themselves. According to an American friend of Hooper's, he once claimed to have altered a poem by Lewis; and now it seems evident that he altered many of them.

In 1964 Warren didn't realize that Hooper was moving into his affairs as well as his house, and functioning as an unofficial member of the Lewis Estate. It seems that co-trustees Owen Barfield and Cecil Harwood were only too glad to have an eager young helper relieve them of some of their responsibilities. They were both Anthroposophists, a religion that Lewis considered occult, and Harwood kept very busy in London as head of the Anthroposophical Society in Great Britain.

On 12 January 1965 Molly Miller wrote a note to Warren's attorney. (I suppose that might have been Owen Barfield.) She said, "Dear Sir, Major Lewis requests you to prepare soon as possible the necessary documents to include in his will that he wishes to leave to his housekeeper Mrs. Maud Emily Miller...£5,000."

The letter ended up in Hooper's possession. He notified Harwood about it. Harwood responded on 5 February, "Is the Mrs. Miller to whom you refer Jack's charwoman-housekeeper? Has she—if she it be—really attained a

---

[18] Thirty-three years after claiming that he had found Lewis's poems here and there, on 5 October 1997 Hooper deposited a random assortment of poems on scraps of paper in the Bodleian. He finally did this just four months after I asked his friend Michael Ward of the Oxford C. S. Lewis Society about the location of the scraps.

[19] In August 1965 I wrote to Hooper and asked if the copy of my thesis that I sent Lewis in 1957 might be tucked away somewhere in the Kilns. Instead of answering that Warren had burned all Lewis's papers in a three-day bonfire, Hooper replied that he didn't remember seeing my thesis among Lewis's effects, but that Major Lewis might have it.

position to influence Warnie in this way? I cannot sufficiently admire and praise the way you have shouldered this burden."[20] Lewis's stepsons were well provided for and Warren had no relatives except a few far-away cousins, so his desire to leave a gift for Mrs. Miller is apt to strike readers today as reasonable; at that point she had been his friendly housekeeper for over a dozen years. But Barfield, Hooper, and Harwood disapproved.

On 22 February Warren noted that one aspect of old age he had not foreseen is boredom.[21] Hooper's residence with Warren lasted about eight months, and it was a painful period for everyone. There is no question that Warren was drinking heavily; and according to the Millers, Hooper sometimes kept Warren awake at night with visits from noisy young men. At the end, Hooper suddenly moved out with no warning.

"I had to leave my old home in Headington Quarry and move into Oxford,"[22] Hooper wrote, accounting for his departure. By "my old home" Hooper apparently meant the Ringwood Road house in Headington (adjacent to Headington Quarry), where he had lived since September 1964. On 28 June Molly Miller wrote to Hooper about picking up the clothes he left behind, which indicates that he was not looking in on Warren.

By this time Warren had suffered a minor stroke that left his right hand and his speech temporarily impaired. He ended 1965 in Warneford Hospital, which he detested so much that he sometimes called it the Hellhole. On 1 January he wrote in his diary, "So begins a new year, and it is hard to imagine that it can be more miserable than 1965."[23] Fortunately, Warren Lewis did not have any more years as miserable as 1965. Tracing the rest of his life with the aid of his published diary reveals a story at times poignant, at times inspiring, at times delightful, and at times shocking.

The Major's diary is a series of large blank books that he filled with his neat notes and essays and occasional illustrations of various kinds, such as clippings. His topics varied from his personal spiritual life and daily events to observations about his constant reading, news of interesting people, and nature descriptions. He enjoyed browsing in his past volumes, and he noticed

---

[20] In the Chapel Hill collection.

[21] *Brothers and Friends: The Diaries of Major Warren Hamilton Lewis*, ed. Clyde S. Kilby and Marjorie Lamp Mead (San Francisco: Harper and Row, 1982) 254.

[22] Hooper, "Reflections," 4.

[23] *Brothers and Friends*, 255.

there the prominence of his three greatest pleasures in life: the company of C. S. Lewis, books, and scenery—in that order.

In his diary Warren described his typical day in 1966. From rising at 7:00 A.M. to retiring at 11:00 P.M. after a cup of Ovaltine, his days were methodical. They included prayers and Bible reading, breakfast, a morning walk, morning coffee with Mrs. Miller, lunch at 1:00 P.M. with the Millers, a drive with them or a nap after lunch, tea at 4:00, supper at 6:00, and television at the Miller home from 7:00 to 9:00. All the periods between these events were filled with Warren's main occupation, reading books.[24]

Fortunately, 1966 turned out much better than 1965. In April Warren was both glad and sorry about the advance copy of his own eighth book, *Letters of C. S. Lewis,* when it arrived from his publisher.[25] Other people had radically changed the book, and he had not been given proofs to check before publication. Even his dedication had been cut out. His own version of the book had been titled *C. S. Lewis: A Biography* (the title used by Green and Hooper in 1974 and by A. N. Wilson in 1990), and it portrayed Lewis's life through selected passages from his letters, with transitions by Warren. Changing his book into a traditional collection of letters made it far less appealing, in Warren's opinion. But he was pleased anyway.

On 16 June 1966 Warren turned seventy-one. His birthdays were always important to him. This time Len and Molly Miller took him to Whipsnade Zoo, his first visit there since two trips with his brother in 1931. The zoo delighted him. A week and a half later, on 26 June, Clyde S. Kilby appeared at the Kilns to meet Warren, all the way from Wheaton, Illinois. Warren took a liking to him. A week later, the Millers and Warren Lewis took Dr. Kilby to see the Whipsnade Zoo, and Warren enjoyed the outing immensely.[26]

On 19 August the Millers and Warren took Dr. Kilby on another happy jaunt. Warren observed in his diary that the more one saw of Kilby, the more one realized the charming modesty and naivete at the root of his character. He noted that since Wheaton College was making a definitive collection of C.

---

[24] Ibid., 257.
[25] Ibid., 256-57.
[26] Ibid., 260-62.

S. Lewis materials, he was adding a codicil to his will leaving all the Boxen materials from Lewis's childhood to Wheaton College.[27]

Less than two weeks later, Arthur Greeves died in his sleep in Ireland. Warren Lewis was deeply moved by the death of this lifelong acquaintance who had been a close friend of his brother's.

A few weeks after the death of Arthur Greeves, a Greeves relative mailed Warren a package that Greeves had addressed to him in advance. Inside were 225 letters from C. S. Lewis to Greeves, spanning Lewis's life from 1914 to 1963. Warren decided to donate them to the collection at Wheaton College.

Christmas morning 1966 was perfect: bright, windless, with frost on all the puddles. But to Warren, and—he supposed—to most people his age, it was a sad day. He thought of the many Christmas mornings in all kinds of weather when he and C. S. Lewis had trudged off from the Kilns for the 8:00 A.M. communion service. Before the day was over, however, he had finished re-reading *All Hallow's Eve* by their old friend Charles Williams, and he found himself wondering aloud if God had inspired Williams when he wrote it. "Anyway, golly what a book!"[28]

Two days later Warren recorded an event that shows his benevolent alertness and good humor at the end of 1966. So far as he knew, the Blue Tit is the only bird addicted to cream. One in his neighborhood had discovered the milk bottles often left at Warren's door in the morning. On this morning the bird had not punched a hole in the foil cap with his beak, but had clipped all around the cap as neatly as a human could have done with scissors, "then made a hearty cream breakfast— which I did not grudge him."

Although every day of Warren's life after C. S. Lewis's death was dominated by the bereavement, he found happiness where he could. On 3 March 1967 Len Miller drove him to Malvern, where he enjoyed a weekend visit with George and Moira Sayer. On 11 March he began reading most of Shakespeare's plays, a spare-time project that he worked at for ten months. On 17 April he finally moved back into the Kilns, this time with Len and Molly Miller agreeing to live there with him as family. In exchange for this kindness, they would receive a cheerful new house in Eynsham after he was gone, to be theirs until they both died.

---

[27] Ibid., 265-66.
[28] Ibid., 267.

(In 1975 I visited the Millers in their sunny house in Eynsham. They spoke of the Major with immense fondness and claimed that his drinking problem was partly seasonal. On the anniversaries of a couple of tragic battles of World War I, Warren would become morose and sink into a period of heavy drinking; but he was a gentleman through and through, they insisted. He battled his alcoholism year after year, with some successes and some failures. Their account of his character tallies exactly with the character of his diary entries and what C. S. Lewis told Hooper about him: "He is the politest of men."[29])

In 1969 Warren felt beset by insoluble problems. He was seventy-three years old and no doubt growing weary. On 8 February 1969 he recorded in his diary the lunch he had with Glenn Sadler, a graduate of Wheaton College and friend of Clyde Kilby:

...disclosure of yet another of Walter's Jesuitical maneuvers. It appears he has now written to Clyde saying that Jack's letters to Arthur are merely on loan to Wheaton, being the property of the Bodleian's where they must sooner or later be returned—which is untrue. Apparently there must have been a demur from Clyde met by Walter with the suggestion that Lily Ewart of all people should be called in to decide whether Bodleian or Wheaton is the owner of the letters! Lily, who has almost as much right in them as has Jan, our house cat! And all this about letters which were beyond dispute my property and given by me to Wheaton. In his tireless, unscrupulous busybodyness Walter is the perfect Jesuit.

When I first read this in the Marion E. Wade Center, I wondered if Glenn Sadler or Warren Lewis could have been mistaken about the matter, and so I checked later with Dr. Kilby. He said it was all true.

On Ash Wednesday Warren wrote to George Sayer that he had heard that Walter Hooper might be appointed an executor of the Lewis Estate. He didn't dislike Hooper, he said, but he was so upset about his "quite astonishing talent for *infiltration*" that he feared that Hooper would try to take over his

---

[29] C. S. Lewis letter to Walter Hooper on 11 October 1963, Chapel Hill collection.

affairs.[30] Furthermore, he worried that if Hooper started to come visiting as often as a couple of times a week (Hooper claims that he did so),[31] the Millers would dislike it and might move out. He feared that he would have to consider leaving Oxford.

On 10 March 1969 Warren recorded more bad news in his diary:

> George [Sayer] came up in time for supper last night and stopped until this morning as a preliminary to making one of a claret tasting committee at Balliol, and an enjoyable visit it has been. It would have been even more so if we had not had to waste so much time discussing the blocking of a nightmare proposal from Owen Barfield that Walter Hooper should be appointed heir apparent to an Executor's position. Apparently he has had the impudence to tell Owen that such a suggestion is approved by me! George, I'm glad to say, is as emphatically opposed to the idea as I am myself, and we roughed out letters of protest which we were to send to Owen, I posting mine via George this morning.

On 21 March 1969 Warren sent a courteous letter to Hooper to say that there was a disturbing rumor in the United States that Hooper had become literary executor of the Lewis Estate. A correspondent had asked Warren, "How did Hooper become the executor? Some one had to appoint him? What are his duties?" Warren's message to Hooper was "Now so far as I know there is no such person unless it is myself as inheritor of Jack's MSS."[32]

Warren's protests to Barfield and Hooper did no good; and according to *Contemporary Authors*, Hooper was officially appointed in 1970.[33]

On 12 May 1969 Warren lamented again in his diary:

---

[30] In March 1979 Hooper told John Dart of the *Los Angeles Times*, "Major Lewis and I were the closest of friends." ("Questions Raised on Lewis Lore," 24 March 1979.)

[31] "I was to see Major Lewis very frequently—usually once or twice a week— for the rest of his life." Hooper stated this on page 4 of "Reflections of an Editor." On 26 October 1977, Leonard Miller responded to that in a letter, "Walter certainly didn't visit him as often as he says." Warren's letters to Hooper in the Chapel Hill collection bear out Miller's claim.

[32] This letter is in Hooper's Chapel Hill collection.

[33] Walter Hooper's current title as an employee of the C. S. Lewis Pte is Literary Advisor of the estate. His past titles have included Executor, Trustee, and Manager.

I'm in further trouble about Walter. Jean wrote to the Times protesting against their statement that he had been Jack's secretary for "some years" before J's death and has now had a reply from the Editor to say that Jock Gibb "sticks to his guns" and that they have been in touch with Walter himself, whose claim has now abated to "a year." But he then made the astonishingly impudent assertion that he had "lived in" with J. and me here whilst so doing. This is simply untrue. I never met him until after J's death, and Molly, whose memory is to be trusted in such matters assures me, as does Len, that the period for which he forced himself on poor J. was the month of August 1963! I'm afraid there is no way of blinking the fact that in his frantic endeavor to put himself over as one of J's oldest and most intimate friends he has now been guilty of a couple of what are called in Parliament "terminological inexactitudes."[34] I've written to him of course, but he has a front of brass and will no doubt continue to present his false image to the public—and what can I do? I dread the statements he may make after my death in the book, which he will have the skill to make with seeming authority. I wish J. had never met him.

Warren was right; his 1969 letter to Hooper asking him to stop the pretence did no good at all. In 1970 the American dust jacket of *God in the Dock* (Lewis essays edited by Hooper) stated "Walter Hooper, a long time friend and for some years personal secretary of C. S. Lewis." "Some years" was the term used on the British edition also.

On 25 August 1970 Hooper first visited the fledgling New York C. S. Lewis Society, which met at the home of James Como; and he told "many intriguing anecdotes of Lewis's life and friends." This is how Hooper was identified in the society's eleventh bulletin:

Mr. Hooper became Lewis's secretary in 1963 and attended him during his final illness. At the time of Lewis's death, both he and his

---

[34] This term used by Warren Lewis was made famous by Winston Churchill in a speech to the House of Commons on 22 February 1906.

brother, Major W. H. Lewis, asked Mr. Hooper to accept the tremendous responsibility of taking charge of the Lewis papers and manuscripts, publishing them at his own discretion. Mr. Hooper has carried forward this enormous—but fascinating and prestigious— task with distinction.

In 1971 Hooper published the following sentence in *Imagination and the Spirit* (a collection of essays edited by Charles Huttar in honor of Clyde S. Kilby and published by Wm. B. Eerdmans): "When I was living at the Kilns (his house in Oxford), Lewis was affectionately termed 'The Boss' by everyone there: his brother, secretary (myself), housekeeper, and gardener."[35]

Shortly after Warren's death in 1973, Cecil Harwood, co-trustee of the Lewis Estate, wrote to Hooper: "It was a wonderful stroke of destiny—nearer to what the East calls Karma—which brought you into Jack's life when it did. No one could have done for him what you did in the last few years of his life and after his death. Everyone who knew Jack must be eternally grateful to you."

As recently as 1987 *C. S. Lewis and His World* featured Walter Hooper in its largest portrait aside from one full-page portrait of C. S. Lewis. The bold-print caption identified Hooper thus: "Father Walter Hooper, who became Lewis's secretary in his last years."[36] The portrait occurred almost twenty years after Warren and his friends tried in vain to stop the tale and eight years after the matter was aired in the *Los Angeles Times*. The fabrication by Hooper that Warren detested has an uncanny survival record.

In the Kilns to this day there is a guest book placed there under the auspices of the C. S. Lewis Foundation and signed by Walter Hooper. After living in the Kilns for two weeks in August 1963 and then living in a variety of other places for almost two decades, until he moved into Vine Cottage, he signed the Kilns book this way: "March 28th 1988—Walter Hooper—Vine

---

[35] Walter Hooper, "Past Watchful Dragons: The Fairy Tales of C. S. Lewis" in *Imagination and the Spirit: Essays in Literature and the Christian Faith Presented to Clyde S. Kilby*, ed. Charles A. Huttar (Grand Rapids MI: Wm. B. Eerdmans Publishing Co., 1971) 286.

[36] David Barrett, *C. S. Lewis and His World* (Grand Rapids MI: Wm. B. Eerdmans Publishing Co., 1987) 43.

Cottage, 30 St. Bernard's Road, Oxford. And before I lived in Vine Cottage, I lived HERE."

Another big worry of Warren's in 1969 was that Hooper was appointed to co-author the official biography of C. S. Lewis along with Lewis's chosen biographer Roger Lancelyn Green.[37] On 25 July Jock Gibb, the publisher, met Warren for lunch at Oxford's Randolph Hotel. Warren recorded in his diary:

> Len drove me to the Randolph to keep a lunch engagement with Jock Gibb. We had allowed time for a traffic block so of course there wasn't one, and I sat for ten minutes in the sun outside the Ashmolean [museum] watching the passing traffic. Mobs of tourists about, some on foot, some in coaches, but all obviously having one emotion in common—boredom. Odd that so many people have not got enough imagination to envisage the type of holiday there is a chance that they will enjoy. Jock turned up on time and it was pleasant to meet him again. This pub, like so many I go into these days, has altered out of all recognition. A good plain lunch in a room where all the waiters were Spaniards, and much good talk over coffee afterwards. I was amused at how perfectly he has taken the measure of Walter's foot whilst giving his merits full credit. I was very much relieved to learn that J's life was not as I had supposed to be the joint work of Walter and Roger; Roger will be the sole author and Walter's share in the work is strictly limited to the collection and arranging of materials.

Jock Gibb's assurance did not turn out to be true, as Warren no doubt realized later. Publication of the Green/Hooper biography, however, was inexplicably delayed by Hooper (according to Roger Lancelyn Green) until after Warren's death; so he never saw what it said.[38] It was just what he feared.

---

[37] Roger Lancelyn Green's deferential letter to Hooper on 13 April 1967 seems to indicate that the estate would decide who should write Lewis's biography—Hooper alone, or Hooper with Green. More than two years later, Warren was still being intentionally misled about that arrangement.

[38] On 29 December 1970 Walter Hooper wrote to me that he expected to finish the Lewis biography in the summer of 1971. On 7 October 1971, he wrote to me that he

It seems likely that Warren Lewis (not to mention C. S. Lewis) would have snorted with irritation at Hooper's interpolations of himself throughout the biography beginning with the year 1930. Before Hooper finally comes on the scene by visiting England (298), he has already appeared twenty-five times in the story in such insertions as "when Walter Hooper asked," "as Walter Hooper observed," "when Walter Hooper suggested," "as he told Walter Hooper," and even "When Walter Hooper met the Archbishop of Canterbury."[39]

The last chapter of the Green/Hooper biography indicates that Hooper arrived in England in time to be a companion to C. S. Lewis throughout his last spring term at Cambridge. This is an error. The claim that Hooper lived "as part of the household for several months later that year" is an error. And

---

was still at work on the biography. On 8 November 1972 he wrote to me that he still had three chapters of the biography left to write. Finally, on 3 February 1973, he wrote that the biography was finished and in the hands of the publisher. It was then released in 1974.

When I interviewed Roger Lancelyn Green at his ancestral home, Poulton Hall at Poulton-Lancelyn near Cheshire on 1 January 1976, I asked him what had caused the delay between 1971 and 1973. He told me the long delay was still a mystery to him and had been quite a frustrating experience. Green said he had to go ahead and write most of the book himself while waiting for Hooper to join him on the project. Green wrote chapters 1, 2, 3, 6, 7, and 10, plus material that had to be cut out because of the book's excess length; after Hooper received Green's chapters, he filled in later with chapters 4, 5, 8, and 9—plus an account in chapter 10 of his own role in Lewis's life. It took Hooper four years to produce those four chapters, Green observed, and Hooper never explained the delay to Green.

Because I wanted to be sure that there was no possibility of my misunderstanding Green or remembering wrong, I wrote and asked him to repeat what he had told me about coauthoring the biography. His answer was delayed by illness that interfered with his handwriting; the illness was later diagnosed as Parkinson's disease, which forced him to depend upon his son Richard Lancelyn Green to be his scribe near the end of his life. In a neat but laboriously written letter to me dated 1 March 1978, Green repeated his outline of the composition of the biography, including the fact that it took Hooper four years to produce his four chapters.

[39] To me it seems obvious that these insertions are in the style of Walter Hooper, not the style of Roger Lancelyn Green, and that many of them are things Green would not have known about.

of course the indication that Hooper left C. S. Lewis in late September, after Warren returned from Ireland, is an error.[40] He left in August.

There is a curious passage by and about Hooper on page 303 of the biography. Hooper tells how once when he was out of the room, a visitor asked C. S. Lewis if he was not uncomfortable about having Hooper live in his house and intrude upon his private life. "But Walter is part of my private life!" Lewis shot back. Hooper continues his account as if he were someone else:

> "Looking back, I find it hard to understand why Jack was so very kind to me," writes Hooper. "He was so vastly superior to me in every way that this fact—being known to *both* of us—may have made it easy to see me as a friend, perhaps, as he once said to Mrs. Miller, 'the son I should have had.'"

In those few lines, Hooper attributes to Lewis two statements about his own importance to Lewis—both said when Hooper was not in Lewis's presence and supposedly could not hear. When the biography was published, the person who heard the first statement was dead and could not be questioned. But Mrs. Miller was alive and denied that Lewis ever made the second statement.[41]

As a result of these embellishments in the biography, most readers have the impression that Walter Hooper was central in the life of C. S. Lewis. As *C. S. Lewis: A Biography* is summarized in *Masterplots 1974 Annual*[42], it is the biography of a famous twentieth century scholar written by two close associates. The summary begins this way:

---

[40] Green wrote to me on 1 March 1978 that the material about Hooper in the last chapter was by Hooper. He indicated on a tape-recording in the Wade Center that he would like to correct the last chapter.

[41] Personal interview with Leonard and Molly Miller in Eynsham on 27 December 1975. Mrs. Miller hotly denied the Lewis quotation wrongly arribured to her. Leonard Miller reaffirmed her denial in a letter to me later. (Mrs. Miller died in 1976, and Mr. Miller died a few years later, long before Douglas Gresham started to portray them as despicable villains in his book *Lenten Lands*.)

[42] *Masterplots 1974 Annual*, ed. Frank Magill. (Englewood Cliffs NJ: Salem Press, 1975).

Principal personages:
C. S. Lewis, famous writer and scholar
Joy Davidman Lewis, his wife
Roger Lancelyn Green, writer and friend of Lewis
The Reverend Walter Hooper, scholar and associate of Lewis

Only four "personages" are mentioned. Warren Lewis is left out. And the writer of the summary can scarcely be faulted for the mistake.

It is painful to read the record of Warren's helpless worrying about Walter Hooper. Apparently Warren's age, distaste for confrontation, sense of propriety, alcoholism, and heart trouble all conspired to make him impotent in Lewis affairs. But he was not totally impotent. He had an idea. He reviewed his diaries, excised one page, and willed the set to Wheaton College. When he died at the Kilns on 9 April 1973, his whole story went to America, where he meant it to be read.[43] Dr. Kilby withheld it for a few years in hopes that Hooper would decide to set the record straight. He prayed daily for Hooper. Whether that helped Hooper or not, it probably helped Kilby.

In 1974, one year after the Major's death, Hooper published an ostensibly fond tribute to him in *CSL*. "I was on intimate terms with him during the last ten years of his life," he stated. Ironically, he went on to indicate twice in this tribute that he had lived with both brothers at the Kilns—the very claim that exasperated Warren beyond words, as he well knew.

With an odd kind of gallantry, Hooper avoided naming the Major's alcoholism as such ("I...feel that I should not write about [that] here"), but told the entertaining story that has, he said, passed into legend in Drogheda, Ireland. Once Mother Mary of the local hospital, in her late seventies, found Warren missing and drove her car to the White Horse pub; to the astonishment of everyone there, she walked into the bar, collected the heavy man, and carried him away.[44] In 1974 I didn't know yet that Hooper hadn't lived with both brothers in the Kilns, but I thought I sensed malice lurking

---

[43] Warren enjoyed reading published diaries, and he had a strong conviction that diaries should be preserved and read.

[44] Walter Hooper, "Warren Hamilton Lewis: An Appreciation," *CSL* (April 1974): 5-8.

behind the supposedly comic White Horse "legend". A year later I stumbled onto the reason.

In the summer of 1975 Barbara Griffin, a library assistant at Wheaton College, took it upon herself to show me some of Warren's diary entries before she retired and moved away. "It's probably one of the best things I ever did," she reflected later. When the first shock of Warren's charges against Hooper (as recorded in this chapter) wore off, I started gathering facts; and in 1978 I raised questions about Hooper's contradictory accounts in my *Christianity & Literature* article, "Some Questions about C. S. Lewis Scholarship." Not one answer was forthcoming.

Then the storm that had been brewing for a decade broke in 1979, when Hooper published *They Stand Together: The Letters of C. S. Lewis to Arthur Greeves (1914-1963)*. This book has some bizarre features.

Hooper has claimed that it took him ten years to edit Lewis's 296 letters to Greeves for publication. Since the letters were clearly written and in good order in the first place, and Hooper's competent footnotes are modest in number, the idea of a decade of editing seems outlandish.[45] One year of part-time work would be generous. But timing is the least outlandish of the strange features in this book.

The thirty-seven-page introduction by Walter Hooper culminates with an amazing attack upon Warren Lewis. Hooper begins by claiming that Warren's dislike of Mrs. Moore didn't exist until 1964, when he projected upon her the misery caused by his alcoholism. This flies in the face of Warren's diary entries decades earlier and C. S. Lewis's own words on the subject. On 18 April 1951 Lewis wrote to a Mrs. van Densen that he had lived most of his private life in a house full of senseless wranglings, lying, backbiting, follies, and *scares*. He had hardly ever gone home without terror about what might have happened next. Only now (after Mrs. Moore's recent death) did he begin to realize how bad it had been.[46]

Hooper tells how he and Owen Barfield wisely pressured Warren to remove his scathing criticism of Mrs. Moore from his introduction to Lewis's

---

[45] In "A Minor Problem in *They Stand Together*" *The Lamp-Post* (June 1990): 16. Joe Christopher cites a few trivial errors or lapses in Hooper's editing of the book.

[46] Lewis's exact words are quoted by Warren Lewis in *Brothers and Friends*, 265.

Letters;[47] yet this very introduction by Hooper soon becomes a scathing attack upon Warren. Hooper explains that when he met C. S. Lewis "early in 1963" (it was June), Warren had already gone off on one of his binges.[48] At this point the story heats up.

C. S. Lewis had tried to be as generous as possible with Warren, Hooper says, by making him the sole beneficiary of the literary estate; but he had to appoint a couple of friends as executors of that estate to prevent Warren from "ending up in a ditch." This account leaves out the fact that the estate fully supported both step sons until they were twenty-one or completed school, and that they received full control of the estate after Warren's death. Furthermore, it seems to imply that Warren was not deserving of his share of support from the estate and that a worthier brother would not have warranted appointment of executors—preposterous suggestions. Hooper fails to mention that Owen Barfield's legal firm handled Lewis's business and legal affairs all along; and when Lewis died, Barfield became literary executor, delegating responsibilities as he saw fit.

According to Hooper, C. S. Lewis used to lament about Warren, *"Who* is there to look after him when I'm gone?" (Hooper may be the only one who heard this.) After C. S. Lewis's death, it occurred to Hooper that he should be the answer to that lament.[49] As he tells it, he visited Warren every day in early 1964, and they usually had a pint or two of beer at the local pub. But Warren took his annual summer vacation in Ireland because the pubs rarely close there and also because the Oxford hospitals would no longer accept him as an alcoholism patient.

In Ireland Warren "roosted" in a hospital at night and drank all day. Hooper joined Warren on 21 July 1964 and spent seven days pub-crawling with him. Warren breakfasted on three triple gin-and-tonics and then taxied

---

[47] *They Stand Together,* 23.

[48] Ibid., 30.

[49] Hooper has also quoted similar helpless lamenting by Warren Lewis after C. S. Lewis's death: "'What, oh what,' he groaned, 'would Jack think if he saw me being carried off to the work-house?'" This was published in Hooper's article "Warren Hamilton Lewis: An Appreciation." In a letter dated 29 November 1977, Leonard Miller responded doubtfully, "I don't think the Major would have said that about the workhouse...As for the mental state of the Major, he certainly was an alcoholic. But this did nothing to make him a lunatic as some people are trying to make out. Have you read any of the Major's books?"

from one pub to another all day, drinking a triple-whiskey at each. Hooper does not make it clear if he drank also, but he says he was trying to care for the Major. All in all, Hooper spent four such vacations in Ireland with Warren, and he tells how they would get out of the taxi to see something and fall down into a hollow together. The story gets progressively worse.

On one trip the two were invited to a lovely inn for dinner, and the place was "full of high-ranking clerics and American tycoons." Warren had a few drinks and went to the restroom. Suddenly he bellowed, "Walter! Walter, come here!" Walter rushed in after him and found that Warren could not open his trousers because a well-meaning nun had put them on him backwards that morning. So Hooper saved the drunken Major from disaster in the restroom. Warren's behavior was so draining that the Drogheda hospital told him not to return.

Back in Oxford, Warren would sit in his study chair for as long as two weeks at a time without getting up for anything, eating nothing, drinking as much as six bottles of whiskey a day (Hooper's exact claim on page 34).

Warren could not tell day from night, so he called for Hooper's services at any time. As a result, Hooper spent more than a year without one night of uninterrupted sleep. (This long year was evidently squeezed into the eight months when the two men lived together.) Not even then, he remarked, could he bear Warren any bad will. Hooper suffered so much that he had to recognize how selfish Warren was, but he loved him anyway.

Hooper has never mentioned in print that in spite of Warren's alleged selfishness, he gave the needy American free lodging for eight months.[50] Nor that Warren gave him half the royalties from Lewis's collected poems.[51] Nor that Warren gave him half the royalties from Lewis's taped lectures.[52] Nor that Warren gave him Christmas gifts.[53] Nor that Warren was the one who paid for Hooper's annual "Friends of Jack Lewis" parties.[54] In fact, Hooper spoke of those parties as if they were his gift to Warren: "Warnie loved the

---

[50] Ten years later, Hooper sometimes pointed out to new acqaintances, as if from habit, that his collar was frayed and his shoes had holes in them.

[51] See Warren's 9 May 1964 letter to Hooper in the Chapel Hill collection.

[52] See Warren's 22 May 1971 letter to Hooper.

[53] See Warren's December 1967 and 1968 letters to Hooper.

[54] See Warren's Whitsunday 1972 letter to Hooper.

annual 'Friends of Jack Lewis Party' which I organized to keep the Inklings and their friends in touch..."[55]

After Warren moved back into the Kilns with the Millers in 1967 he was sober more often, Hooper says. All that he had gone through with Warren seemed worth it when he spent some of the most pleasant days in his memory at the Kilns then. The Millers, the Major, and Hooper made a "family" of four who had many happy times together before Warren died in 1973.

But long before those happy latter days, a scandalous event had occurred, which Hooper recounts for us in his Editor's Note following his Introduction. On a dank morning in November 1966, Hooper arrived on his daily visit to the Major at Ringwood Road to tend to his needs. (This was the month before the Blue Tit got into the cream by the front door, and in his diary the Major seems lucid and competent.) There was a good fire in the grate. On this day a registered parcel and letter arrived from Belfast, and Hooper had to help Warren open them. The parcel contained the 225 C. S. Lewis letters to Greeves. Lily Ewart, a sister of Greeves, had sent along a letter asking Warren to deliver these letters to the Bodleian for Arthur. (Arthur had no particular interest in the Bodleian Library, and so his alleged decision not to give the letters to Warren seems questionable.)

Hooper read Lily's letter aloud to the inattentive Warren so many times that he was able to memorize part of it and, fortunately, happened to write it down in his diary that day. It sounds almost too fortunate to be true, and it also sounds unnecessary. Arthur was dead, but Lily was alive; she was perfectly capable of repeating her message and making sure that Arthur's intentions had been carried out. But apparently neither Warren nor Hooper considered that fact at the time or later. That very morning, Warren destroyed the letter and seized the Greeves collection that had been entrusted to him. He pretended that Arthur had given the letters to him (Lily Ewart could have contested that if she had heard about it), and sent the bundle off to Wheaton College. Naturally, trustees Hooper and Barfield notified both the Bodleian and Wheaton that the 225 Lewis letters had been confiscated by

---

[55] *They Stand Together*, 35.

Warren. (According to Dennis Porter, Keeper of Western Manuscripts at the Bodleian, Hooper did not inform the Bodleian about the theft at that time.)[56]

Hooper's story is detailed and dramatic, but it leaves out some crucial facts. Hooper received a 30 March 1967 letter from Warren notifying him that Clyde Kilby had asked Warren to bequeath the Greeves letters to Wheaton College. Warren asked Hooper to return the Greeves letters after he finished looking them over. On 7 August 1967 Warren wrote again to Hooper about the Greeves letters because Kilby had not heard from Hooper as expected. Warren asked Hooper if he was still working on them and when he could send them to Kilby. On 9 August Hooper replied with a plan for sending them over with Owen Barfield, who would be going fairly soon.[57]

How could Warren have stolen the Greeves letters in November 1966 and dishonestly posted them to Wheaton, then entrusted them to Hooper and Barfield for much of 1967? Why would Barfield transport stolen documents out of England? Why didn't the Bodleian requisition the stolen letters from Wheaton? Why did Hooper and Barfield keep the theft secret from 1966 to 1979? Why didn't Hooper tell about it in 1974 in the Green/Hooper biography?

Hooper cites Lily Ewart as his one witness that Arthur had intended for Warren to place the set of letters in the Bodleian Library, and he cites his own diary entry as proof. But Lily Ewart was alive for ten years after she purportedly wrote her letter to Warren Lewis and he purportedly destroyed it. Unfortunately, Lily Ewart died in 1976, and Hooper did not tell about her alleged letter to Warren until 1979; so no one could contact Lily Ewart about her alleged claims that allegedly survive now in Walter Hooper's 1966 diary.

Actually, because of a letter-exchange agreement, photocopies of all the Greeves letters were in the Bodleian Library anyway. (When fifty more letters from Lewis to Arthur Greeves were donated to the Bodleian Library by way of Walter Hooper, they were kept "under seal" and the Bodleian was not allowed to send copies to Wheaton until after *They Stand Together* was

---

[56] An unpublished 28 March 1979 letter from Dennis Porter to Alice Gregg, Librarian at Loma Linda University in California.

[57] See Warren's 30 March, 7 August, and 10 August 1967 letters to Hooper.

published. The unexplained delay raises a slight question about the authenticity of some of those letters.[58])

There is a major difference between some of the original letters to Greeves and the photocopies. Certain passages in the letters were blotted out in later years because they were about embarrassing sexual topics that the two letter writers did not want others to know about. But modern technology can retrieve such censored passages.

In Hooper's opinion, it is one of life's most pleasant comedies to see elderly people embarrassed by things from their younger years. (He does not explain his concept of pleasant comedy.) It was charming of Arthur Greeves, idling before his death, to try to make Lewis's letters more "respectable." Therefore Hooper decided to publish the deleted passages, contrary to the intentions of Lewis and Greeves.[59]

Bob O'Donnell and David Elders of Lord and King Associates (the Illinois producer of *Through Joy and Beyond*) went to Wheaton College for Walter Hooper and photographed the deleted passages with infra-red and ultra-violet fluorescence photography.

The deleted passages, which refer to Arthur Greeves's attraction to boys (he never married) and C. S. Lewis's attraction to sado-masochism, are set off in the text of the book by < pointed brackets > so they are easy to locate. Those who consider this tasteless are apt to stand accused of sharing Arthur Greeves's misguided sense of propriety. (In the new volume of Lewis letters spanning 1905 to 1931, published in 2000, Hooper reproduces the retrieved passages and highlights them with pointed brackets again; and he also points out this feature in his introduction.)

But at one point Walter Hooper himself displays a surprising sense of delicacy. When giving C. S. Lewis's reasons for disliking Malvern College, on page 10 of this very introduction, Hooper daintily omits what Lewis saw as pervasive preoccupation with homosexual relationships among his fellow

---

[58] Hooper pointed out the delay in his introduction to *They Stand Together* and stated enigmatically, "We didn't want to act precipitately."

[59] The content of some of the restored passages was discussed by Joe R. Christopher in his article "What Was Arthur Greeves' Sexual Orientation?" in *The Lamp-Post* 14/1-2 (June 1990): 17-20. Christopher concludes that although George Sayer disagrees in *Jack*, the evidence in the restored passages (rechecked at the Wade Center at Christopher's instigation) shows that Greeves was homosexual.

students there. Lewis wrote of this frankly, openly, and very negatively in his autobiography; but Hooper skips it. Conservative readers might wish Hooper had skipped the allure of pederasty and sado-masochism instead.

The extraordinary introduction ends with Hooper's usual thanks and acknowledgments that are almost courtly in their grace. For example, he links Owen Barfield to his title: "Lewis's finest legacy to me—my friend Owen Barfield has *stood by me* [italics added] all the way."

Barfield responded with a laudatory review of the book, praising Hooper's introduction and censuring my recent article in *Christianity & Literature:*

> [T]he Introduction, besides giving the reader an alarming picture of the mountain of work which a one-man encyclopedia necessarily involved, contains a brief history of the editor's [Hooper's] personal association with C. S. Lewis, and with his brother after his death. This is a long way from the first product of that scholarly aptitude for research and that self-dedication, first to the two brothers themselves and then to the whole Lewis legacy, which all who are deeply interested in Lewis and his utterance for their own sakes have come to associate with Fr Hooper—and which incidentally has not failed to evoke from the odd corner here or there the sort of baseless detraction 'that patient merit of the unworthy takes.' It is surely the finest up to date."[60]

Hooper thanks Anthony Marchington along with Owen Barfield. "I am fortunate beyond all covenant," Hooper vows, "in living in the same house and being helped so much by Anthony Marchington who is, as Lewis said of one of his contemporaries, 'the sole Horatio known to me in this age of Hamlets.'"

This all sounds very serious; but Anthony Marchington was the author of the Lewis Bonfire hoax-letter, and things are not always as serious as they seem. The original edition of this book was a Collins hardback with a burnt-orange dust jacket. The inside back flap of the jacket presented the following information about Walter Hooper:

---

[60] *Seven* (March 1980) 1:129.

Hooper discovered the works of C. S. Lewis just on the point of entering the army in 1954, and so totally smitten was he by Lewis that he went through basic training with a rifle in one hand and a copy of Lewis's *Miracles* in the other. He began corresponding with C. S. Lewis in 1954. After leaving the army he read theology and soon took up a post at the University of Kentucky lecturing on Medieval and Renaissance English literature. After some years there he received an invitation from Lewis to visit him in Oxford, and he took a leave of absence for the simple but to him, very significant pleasure of spending an afternoon with Lewis. What was expected to be a simple tea party has lasted fifteen years. A week after they met in the spring of 1963 Lewis asked Hooper to remain in Oxford as his companion secretary, which position Hooper was more than delighted to accept. Their friendship grew to the point that Lewis called him "the son I should have had."

"Some years" as a lecturer on Medieval and Renaissance literature, Lewis's specialty, seems impossible on two counts. Hooper was at the University of Kentucky only five semesters; and he was an entry-level instructor, not a professor. He had not qualified yet for graduate studies. (According to Dr. Robert O. Evans, the primary medievalist at that time was Dr. Arthur K. Moore, followed by Dr. Steve Manning.[61]) It is possible, of course, that as an entry-level instructor Hooper was allowed to teach a sophomore survey of British literature along with freshman composition, and the first half of the survey would include a section on Medieval and Renaissance literature. But teaching such a brief introduction is far different from being entrusted with upper division and graduate courses as the claim "lecturing on Medieval and Renaissance English literature" implies. Furthermore, in Britain, where this book was published, the term *lecturer* indicates advanced academic status that Hooper certainly did not attain.[62]

---

[61] In a letter dated 3 November 1987, Dr. Evans stated, "I can say this much: Hooper was never a professor at UK...He certainly did not teach medieval lit."

[62] In his article "Why Isn't There a Volume of Dorothy L. Sayers' Letters?" in the fall 1990 issue of *The Mystery Fancier* Joe R. Christopher tells what he found in the papers of her agent David Higham at the University of Texas at Austin. On 12 April 1965 Hooper wrote to Higham offering to edit Sayers' correspondence. A total of 11

According to Lewis's letters, Hooper requested a meeting and Lewis simply agreed. Hooper went to England for summer school, not for an afternoon tea party. He didn't take a leave of absence from Kentucky until two months after Lewis's death. It was during Lewis's mental derangement in mid-July, not on June 14, that Lewis asked Hooper to help with correspondence. Hooper did not remain in England as Lewis's secretary, and no one heard Lewis call him "the son I should have had."

Aside from these matters, the introduction can stand.

Of course, book jackets are not noted for accuracy. They often include inaccuracy or exaggeration. The inside front flap of *They Stand Together* indulges in outright hyperbole: "This work, which was ten years in preparation, is clearly the finest piece of scholarship ever done on the writings of C. S. Lewis...the wit, the Christian apologetics, and, in some letters hitherto under seal, the heart-break of seeing an older brother slither into tragic alcoholism...With this volume Walter Hooper has taken a laurel which few will share." The contrast between Walter Hooper winning a laurel and Warren Lewis "slithering" into alcoholism, as well as "roosting" in a hotel, is remarkable. One can imagine how C. S. Lewis would feel. (Warren's alcoholism caused both brothers much pain, and C. S. Lewis sometimes complained bitterly in private. But he would have been horrified at a public attack upon Warren.)

Certain alert readers of the original Collins edition of *They Stand Together* were apt to notice something odd before they ever opened the book.[63] The front cover features handsome photos of the young Lewis and the young Greeves, both set in ovals. They are flanking a sketch of Oxford's Magdalen Tower, which thrusts up between them. The tower seems to be an illogical symbol of the friendship, since the tower was a key landmark in

---

letters about that possibility are in Higham's file, some of them asking about Hooper's qualifications. On 29 June 1965 Hooper said that he had held a post at the University of Kentucky lecturing on Medieval and Renaissance Literature.

[63] The 1988 cover design of the original Collins edition of Hooper's *Letters of C. S. Lewis* also employs a visual trick that will be noticed immediately by some observant people. The subject is a large dull-red writing pen; ink behind the pen turns into a bright lake and sunrise. But on each side the artist has placed the profile of a male face, chins almost touching the pen; once noticed, the two faces are obvious. This kind of trick design is explained and illustrated in *Gestalt Therapy* by Frederick Perls, Ralph Hefferline and Paul Goodman (New York: Dell Publishing Co., 1951) 25-26.

Lewis's academic life but had nothing at all to do with Greeves, who lived indolently in Ireland and never even attended a university. (He attended Slade School of Art briefly.) The common passion of the two men for rural Irish scenery could have provided a more appropriate symbol, and one that did not happen to strongly resemble a design often used in the homosexual subculture in various guises. [64]

An even more disconcerting part of the cover is the title. *They Stand Together* happens to be a little-known homosexual euphemism on both sides of the Atlantic. [65]

Another playful euphemism arrived in my mailbox just a few months before *They Stand Together* arrived. In a letter dated 9 December 1977, Walter Hooper gave a clear and reasonable answer to my question about Lewis's attitude toward practising homosexuals. But Hooper spelled the word *homosequals*. He has clear handwriting and is ordinarily a superb speller. I have forty-one letters from Hooper, and this is the only time he substituted one letter for another. He wrote *homosequality* twice, *homosequals* once, and *homosequal* five times. He also wrote *heterosequal* once. But in the same letter he wrote *extremely* once and *expect* twice, and he spelled them correctly. I found this puzzling, to say the least.

It is certainly possible that no one intended the title *They Stand Together* as a little inside joke. But instead of passing off the double meaning as an insignificant coincidence after I pointed it out in *The C. S. Lewis Hoax,* Hooper's defenders huffily insisted that there is no such homosexual euphemism. (How would they know?) [66]

---

[64] In 1979, the year after the homosexual motif appeared on the dust jacket of *They Stand Together,* Collins published a gift book edition of *The Screwtape Letters* illustrated in cartoon style by Papas. Whether Papas intended a comic homosexual implication at the beginning of Letter 31 on page 131 or not, the suggestion is there for readers disposed to notice it. (A description of the cartoon would be indelicate.)

[65] I have been informed of this underground use of the term by one English person and one American who don't know each other, without my asking for the information. Since then an American affirmed that use of the term when asked. However, because of the embarrassing nature of the topic none of the three were willing to be cited on the topic in a footnote.

[66] I made no assumptions about who chose the title *They Stand Together.* In the January 1989 issue of *CSL,* William Griffin (then religious books editor for *Publishers Weekly*) revealed that Walter Hooper chose the title and that Griffin was his Macmillan editor at the time.

Lewis used the phrase "they stand together" when writing about friendship in *The Four Loves*, but editors of *They Stand Together* didn't tell their readers about that connection in the first printing. Although it would have been simple enough to insert the passage from *The Four Loves* in a later printing to explain the title, they dropped the title instead. In spite of a few years of entries in reference books and bibliographies, *They Stand Together* suddenly became *The Letters of C. S. Lewis to Arthur Greeves (1914-1963)*. After I pointed out the telltale title change in 1994, they changed it back again.

Somewhere, Screwtape or someone else must still be laughing about the title change and the original British cover design. But C. S. Lewis and Warren Lewis would not appreciate the joke.

Another rather sad joke on Warren Lewis in 1969 was the rejection of *Boxen*. Warren expected Jock Gibb (of the Geoffrey Bles company) to publish his beloved collection of childhood writing and drawing. In February he agreed with Jock Gibb's plan for Hooper to pick up the juvenilia at the Kilns and deliver it to Gibb in London. In high spirits, Warren warned Gibb: "Mind, if you lose any of these books, I will return from the grave to make your life a torment!"

But at their lunch at the Randolph Hotel on 25 July 1969, when Gibb assured Warren that Hooper would not co-author Green's biography, he broke the news that they were putting the Boxonian Saga "on ice." The stated reason was that it might accidentally be regarded by the public as the origin of Narnia. Warren could see that this objection did not make any sense and that there must be a different, unspoken reason for the rejection.

Four months later Warren enjoyed a noon visit from Roger Lancelyn Green, who asked to borrow the eleven-volume Lewis Family Papers as resource material for the biography. Warren agreed, but his reluctance to entrust them to such a dependable friend shows how protective he felt about his treasured family documents.[67]

---

[67] Warren agreed to let Green borrow the Lewis family papers, and this is what he noted that in his diary entry for 26 November 1969:

"Roger Green turned up soon after twelve thirty as per agreement and left for London at 2:15. It was an enjoyable break for me, and we had some good crack. Rather against my better judgment I consented to let him borrow the complete Lewis Papers when he is ready to make use of them for the life; it would have been churlish to refuse

Green told Warren that Barfield opposed publication of *Boxen* because the stories are dull and lack literary merit, and Green was no doubt sincere. But dullness and lack of literary merit did not mitigate against lavish publication and promotion of *Boxen* a few years after Warren's hopes were dashed. The privilege of publishing *Boxen* went to Walter Hooper. It seems a bit sad that people who were profiting from Lewis's estate did not see fit to add some warmth to Warren's last three years by humoring him with a small printing of *Boxen*. He would have produced an accurate, authoritative, and insightful volume, written with good humor and good sense. Instead, Walter Hooper and editors at Harcourt Brace Jovanovich produced a pompous volume full of mistakes and intentional misrepresentation.[68]

On 22 May 1971 Warren wrote an exasperated letter to Hooper for turning Warren's half of the income from some Lewis cassettes over to Barfield. (Apparently, Warren gave Hooper half the royalties from the *Four Loves* tapes marketed by the Episcopal Radio-TV Foundation.)[69]

> It was neither the time nor the place to express my horror on hearing that you had sent the Cassette cheque to Barfields. Why? The arrangement we had come to was that you should pay the sum received into your own bank and, having deducted your share, should send the balance to me in the form of a cheque drawn on your account.
>
> Do you realize what you have done? Barfields will undoubtedly deal with this as if it was a Curtis Brown Royalty—and under a rash arrangement made with Owen Barfield after Jack's death 50% of all Royalties is handed over to Barfields out of which to pay my Income tax and provide an emergency fund to meet 'a rainy day'; but they not me are the judges of what constitutes a wet day, and ever since the scheme started the sky has in their view remained cloudless.

---

him, yet I shrink from letting such a treasured and irreplaceable collection out of my own keeping...I look forward to his coming down for the night to discuss the book with me some time next year."

[68] For the story of *Boxen*, read Appendix 4, "Stealing the King's Ring."

[69] This letter is in Hooper's Chapel Hill collection.

By steady and regular importunity it may be just possible that towards the end of the summer we may be in a position to benefit to half the extent we would have done if you had stuck to the arrangement made between us! But it would be wiser to write the money off as faerie gold.

Barfield's handling of his finances had frustrated Warren ever since Lewis's death, although he seemed to go along quietly. On 26 August 1968 he had been deeply saddened when Barfield notified him that Lewis's charity fund for needy people was nearly empty and closing down. Evidently, it didn't occur to Warren to ask why Barfield had not set the fund up in a way to allow it to continue.

Near the end, Warren asked Len Miller to take over his checkbook. Looking into things, Len discovered that Warren had accumulated quite a bit of money in the fund that he knew nothing about, money that was his to use. Warren was as happy as a child when he found out. Rightly or wrongly, the Millers felt that Barfield had done a sloppy job all along as Lewis's attorney in his life and was far less than solicitous about Warren after Lewis's death.[70]

In January 1972 Warren had a pacemaker installed. On 22 February he wrote Hooper a cordial letter in which he thanked him for sending an autographed copy of *God in the Dock* to an American correspondent named Vera Gebbert[71] and charging it to Warren at Blackwell's. He included a seemingly innocent remark: "How did they know that you weren't a con man?"

In March he wrote to Hooper again: "You might tell Roger [Lancelyn Green] next time you see him that I'd be glad of the return of any volumes of the Lewis papers from which he has extracted the honey; the matter is not

---

[70] Leonard Miller described this period and what he saw as chronic mismanagement of the business affairs of the Lewis brothers in a tape recording made at the Miller home in Eynsham, England, on 27 December 1975.

[71] Vera Gebbert recalls Hooper: "...we corresponded for years. I knit him mufflers for every Christmas of our letter-writing but, unknown to me, he had lusted for my letters from CSL, but never said a word about it. And when he learned that I have willed all the articles (to Wheaton), books, pipes, tea mug, etc., from CSL, he stopped writing altogether and has never, to this day, replied to a single one of my letters." Published in *The Lewis Legacy*, 18:1.

urgent—at least I hope it isn't—but it would be troublesome if I died with all or a proportion of them in Roger's hands."

In June Warren enjoyed a visit from a professional photographer from the United States, Douglas R. Gilbert. Gilbert came to the Kilns to take pictures of the Major's memorabilia, some of which would appear in *C. S. Lewis: Images of His World*.

In July Warren wrote to Hooper, "I am constantly tired now, in addition to giddy fits—in fact I'm nearing the end of the road." In August he went to Ireland. There his health worsened, and he had to stay all winter. The Millers took care of the Kilns and his business, and Leonard flew to Ireland to visit him for several days every month.

In April 1973, Warren finally returned home to Oxford and died in the Kilns on 9 April. The Millers instantly notified a courier appointed in advance by Clyde Kilby to pick up Warren's irreplaceable diary and other family papers from his bedroom on the day of his death. Thus, a year after Douglas Gilbert went to the Kilns to photograph samples of Warren Lewis's personal collection, the collection was sent to the Wade Center in Illinois. Gilbert could have stayed home and photographed it there.

It seemed when he died that Warren had been defeated by Hooper on almost every issue except sending his papers to Wheaton. But Warren, "the politest of men," had tucked a little dynamite into those papers. From the grave he is now accusing his accuser.

For over a decade and a half, Hooper has accused Warren of burning mountains of Lewis papers in January 1964 and stealing a batch of Lewis letters in 1966. In both cases, all the evidence thus far is against Hooper's charges. Is it possible that Hooper himself is the one who burned or stole important Lewis documents? Warren thought so. In his diary he recorded hearing about it from a good friend who said he heard about it from Hooper:

> He told me of a theft made by Walter during my absence that is of such a nature that it is better not to record it even here. According to Walter's own account, he "found" documents in Joy's handwriting in the spare bedroom here (then occupied by David, incidentally) throwing a curious light on her relations with J. and, still according to Walter, burnt them. Leaving aside the amazing impudence of this theft I'm certain (a) wherever he found the papers it was not in the

spare room and (b) that in view of their contents he so far from destroying them, has hidden them away to be published as soon as it is safe to do so. Which cannot be in my lifetime thank God! I begin to be very tired of Walter's pranks. He has a brazen impudence exceeding that of Ponsonby Staples...What can ordinary civil people do with such a man?[72]

In 1977 Hooper explained his sudden ascendancy to control of the Lewis estate by saying, "It was partly my ownership of certain Lewis papers which turned me into an editor and has determined the course I have followed, as best I could, for the last fourteen years."[73] What if the Lewis papers that contributed most to his career were those mysterious missing papers of Joy's? He spoke about them publicly in 1987, as if to forestall suspicions:

Although Mr. Nicholson has the Joy Gresham of the film write some very interesting letters to Lewis, it is a pity that none of her actual letters have survived. Indeed, it seems that perhaps all of the writings she left at the Kilns have vanished. Major Lewis, writing to an American friend in 1967, mentions there being some of her "papers" still in his possession. I have no idea what happened to them. However, very soon after Lewis's death, I read the diary Joy kept from 1952 to 1955. That, too, has disappeared.[74]

By the time Hooper was willing to talk about Joy's diary, Dr. Kilby had followed Warren to the grave, defeated in his hope that Hooper would voluntarily correct his historical fantasies. Kilby had tried to hint at the problem in 1982 in *Brothers and Friends,* a collection of Warren's diary

---

[72] See Warren's diary, 10 March 1969. According to an account given by Chad and Eva Walsh's daughter Damaris Walsh McGuire, Hooper also confided in her parents about this matter or something similar. See "Memories and a Mystery," a typescript of her account in the Wade Center.

[73] *CSL*, (August 1977): 1.

[74] Walter Hooper, "C.S. Lewis and C. S. Lewises" in *The Riddle of Joy*, 49. Hooper does not say how he gained access to Joy's 1952-1955 diary or what it said. Anyone inclined to put the worst possible interpretation on Hooper's account might conjecture that he confiscated Joy's diary and has used it to gain concessions from Douglas Gresham.

excerpts. But at the last minute Harper & Row ruled that out. An editorial note on p. xxviii explains, "It should also be noted that certain passages in this manuscript were deleted at the request of and as a courtesy to the C. S. Lewis Estate." Fifty-one-year-old Walter Hooper and eighty-four-year-old Owen Barfield had won again. They had no legal control over Warren's diary, but they wielded great influence; their desire for deletions prevailed.

Long before Warren's diary was censored, my 1978 article "Some Questions in C. S. Lewis Scholarship" had sunk unanswered, with barely a ripple, taking most of my career as a Lewis scholar down with it. From then on I was shunned by many influential people in Lewis affairs, some of whom I had considered good friends. Invitations dwindled, manuscripts were rejected, letters went unacknowledged,[75] and my name gradually disappeared from various publications and bibliographies. Kilby had warned me that would happen. After it did, one of the editors at Harper & Row explained to a mutual friend of ours, "Lindskoog doesn't know how to play this C. S. Lewis Game."

How has the C. S. Lewis Game been played since then? That is the subject of Chapter 11, "The Business of Heaven."

> Few people read literary scholarship except scholars, but as a pastime, it's about as refined as ice hockey. More than that, it is still, to a remarkable extent, a white man's game.
> —*Carolyn See*

---

[75]Among more than two-dozen people prominent in Lewis studies who have failed to acknowledge my letters are Owen Barfield, James Como, Colin Duriez, Donald Glover, William Griffin, Margaret Hannay, Terry Mathis, Stanley Mattson, Eugene McGovern, Richard Purtill, Jerry Root, Brian Sibley, G. B. Tennyson, Andrew Walker, and A. N. Wilson.

11

THE BUSINESS OF HEAVEN

NOT UNWORLDLY WISDOM AFTER ALL?

"Yes," is the last word C. S. Lewis ever put on paper. On 22 November 1963 Warren was answering a letter that had come for Lewis. He needed to make sure he answered it correctly, but Lewis had trouble staying awake and was probably dozing just then. So Warren jotted a note on the letter asking Lewis, "Shall I tell him that your commercial acumen is a minus quantity?"[1] When Lewis read that question later, he wrote "Yes" beside it for Warren. Then at about 5 P.M. he died, leaving behind this world of shadows and commerce.[2]

So it was that Lewis's very last enduring statement wasn't about his faith or his dearest loves or his hopes for his books. Instead, it was about a subject

---

[1] On Wednesday, 20 November 1963, a man who had visited Lewis one week earlier asked his advice on a business matter. The letter was handwritten on stationery from the Horsa Holdings company, and the company seal in the upper left corner depicts a small boat with two fish under it and the Latin phrase "Parvus sed bellator" (small but spirited). The return address was 119 Gt. Ancoats St., Manchester 4.

[2] Below Lewis's "Yes," Warren wrote "Answered 22/11/63 W." On 22 February 1965 Warren taped the letter into his diary and wrote across the top of the letter, "The last job I did as SPB's [Lewis's] Secy. On the day of his death."

Warren apparently tore off and discarded all but the top four inches of the letter. The fragment says: "Dear Dr. Lewis, I apologise for the delay in writing to thank you for your kindness to my wife and I when we called to see you last Wednesday. What a wonderful recollection Judith has been left with!"

that didn't interest him at all: business.[3] And in light of what has happened since then, it was a highly appropriate subject for his last written word. When Lewis breathed his last, there were plenty of people with commercial acumen waiting in the wings.

It wasn't that Lewis disliked money; he was always glad to get it. But he considered business matters an intolerable bore.[4] When he finally hired a literary agent, the stingy publisher[5] who had steadfastly refused to increase his royalties suddenly found that he could increase them after all. Lewis decided that agents more than pay for themselves by negotiating better contracts, and he wished he had hired one sooner.

Lewis wanted to receive fair royalties for his writing, and then he wanted to give away enough of his income to make a difference. In fact, for his specifically Christian writing he felt that he should give all his profit from royalties to the needy, and his Christian speaking was free from the start. He expressed his contempt for commercial greed attached to spiritual gifts in *The Great Divorce*[6] and in *The Magician's Nephew*. In the latter Uncle Andrew

---

[3] Lewis's earliest surviving attempt at a novel, which I call "The Most Substantial People," begins as a satirical observation of certain Belfast businessmen and their commercial acumen. See Chapter 7.

[4] Chad Walsh said of Lewis "He was an incredibly unworldly person about such things as money." Chad Walsh, "Afterword," C. S. Lewis, *A Grief Observed* (New York: Bantam, 1976) 143.

[5] On 20 July 1956 Lewis told me jovially that *Till We Have Faces* would be his last book with his longtime publisher the Geoffrey Bles company because of a difficult man there who took advantage of his good nature. He said the break would be difficult, but that he was determined. A look at his bibliography, however, shows that aside from *The Magician's Nephew* (London: The Bodley Head, 1955) and *The Last Battle* (London: The Bodley Head, 1956) he failed to break with the Bles company after all. (When Lewis completed *The Last Battle* early in 1953 he wrote to owner Geoffrey Bles and told him so, evidently intending to stay with him. I assume that the difficult man who temporarily drove Lewis away might have been Jocelyn Gibb, who took over the company in 1954 and later caused Warren much unhappiness.)

[6] In chapter 2 of *The Great Divorce* the Intelligent Man is taking a bus trip from hell to heaven. He doesn't think heaven would suit him ("I'm not going this trip for my health"), but he sees it as the possible source of valuable commodities. "I'd start a little business. I'd have something to sell...I'd make a nice little profit and be a public benefactor as well." Chapter 6 shows this insubstantial ghost suffering agonies of frustration and pain in his attempt to sneak a solid, heavy golden apple back to the bus for importation to hell. An angel warned him "There is not room for it in Hell," and urged him to stay in heaven: "Stay here and learn to eat such apples." But to no avail.

exclaimed, "The commercial possibilities of this country [Narnia] are unbounded. Bring a few old bits of scrap iron here, bury 'em, and up they come as brand new railway engines, battleships, anything you please. They'll cost nothing, and I can sell 'em at full prices in England. I shall be a millionaire...The first thing to do is to get that brute [Aslan] shot." Uncle Andrew saw divine Narnia as a money-maker and didn't know the real value of anything.

Lewis enjoyed the fact that his small circle of good friends included Robert E. Havard, his physician, and Owen Barfield, his attorney. He gladly left his physical and business affairs in their hands because those subjects didn't interest him. Unfortunately for Lewis and everyone who wishes he had lived longer, Dr. Havard's personal warmth was not matched by professional dilligence. Neglect of Lewis's enlarged prostate gland led to neglected kidney trouble, which in turn severely damaged his heart. Although Lewis believed he was following a low-protein diet near the end, he still ate certain high-protein foods. His catheter was unsanitary and in shocking condition when he had his heart attack in July 1963. That Lewis kept dozing off in November was a danger sign that his kidneys were poisoning him, but no one at the Kilns realized they needed to take him to the hospital to save his life.[7]

There is some evidence that Owen Barfield, who preferred arts and philosophy to law, was sometimes less than diligent in managing Lewis's business affairs. Spotty management may have contributed to the fact that in spite of Lewis's strong commitment to charity, charity was not included in

---

The Intelligent Man could not conceive of dwelling in spiritual reality; to him heaven was only a source of products that could make him financially successful in hell and give him an illusion of safety from the terrors of spiritual darkness.

[7] Dr. Havard, who wrote an afterword for *The Problem of Pain*, no doubt meant well. On 21 August 1979 he wrote to Robert Baylis that he was sorry to hear that Bob O'Donnell had eliminated Havard's interview from the film "Through Joy and Beyond" because his family might have enjoyed seeing it some day. He assured Baylis that although Walter Hooper may exaggerate sometimes, he is a truthful man whose facts can be trusted, if not all his judgments. "I saw a lot of him during C. S. L.'s last days and subsequently." Because Havard could not possibly have seen Hooper in September, October, or November 1963, it seems either that Havard saw a lot of Lewis during those months and later imagined that Hooper had been present, or else that Havard did *not* see a lot of Lewis during those final months and later imagined that he had done so.

his will.[8] In the decade after Lewis's death, Warren continued to contribute to their church and also sent checks to a few of his brother's needy correspondents. If Barfield had given Warren more money from the trust he would probably have given away more.[9] Warren's will provided generously for Leonard and Molly Miller (whom Douglas Gresham has described as villains),[10] but the small remnant of Lewis's personal charities died with Warren in 1973.

---

[8] If Lewis had left one-third of his literary estate to each of his stepsons and one-third to a designated charity, that charity would have been able to do good since 1973 with its share. An especially appropriate use of one-third of his royalties would have been a foundation to subsidize translations of his books into other languages and to donate copies of his books to libraries everywhere.

It is hard to imagine Joy Lewis or her sons objecting to a three-way division of the royalties, although she was reportedly ambitious for her sons. "Once, when Joy was telling Lewis that in the event of her death she wanted her sons to be amply endowed, she emphasized the point with a hard wallop of her walking stick across the top of the kitchen table." Stephen Schofield, *In Search of C. S. Lewis* (South Plainfield NJ: Bridge Publishing, Inc., 1983) 220. See http://www.discovery.org/lewis/cslewis.html to view Lewis's will.

[9] In an undated letter to C. S. Lewis, circa 1929, Bede Griffiths revealed his idea for offering a free stipend to Owen Barfield: "I have a proposition to make which I should like to know if you think feasible. If Barfield should not be able to get anything from an American university, do you think it would be possible for us to make an arrangement about it. We (that is, I and two friends) have an income of about £800 a year between us, which it is impossible (at least morally) to spend all on ourselves. Do you think Barfield might be let to accept a sort of Closed Fellowship for the purpose of bringing out an edition of Coleridge, or anything else he likes to do? We don't know exactly how much we shall have over, but we could certainly provide £100 a year for two or three years. Would that be enough to tide him over? If you think that it would be of any use & that we could arrange it, you might suggest it to him. I don't think he ought to have any difficulty about accepting it, as the money is ours —or rather exclusively my two friends —only by legal right, and *morally, since he is serving a good purpose, he has as much right as any of us.*" (Italics added.) Griffiths obviously felt that Lewis would have some sympathy with his opinion that charity is a moral obligation.

[10] At the end of Douglas Gresham's *Lenten Lands* (New York: Macmillan, 1988) he announced that when Warren died in the Kilns on 9 April 1973 someone caught Leonard Miller treacherously stealing gold cufflinks off the warm body. According to another anonymous witness of Gresham's, after Fred Paxford's death Miller tried to burglarize Paxford's little home in broad daylight and turned pale with anger when he found it empty. Gresham was in Australia during both alleged crimes and could not have witnessed them. Miller was a devout Christian, retired from a good job, and well

It was long assumed that David and Douglas Gresham owned and controlled the lucrative Lewis literary estate since inheriting it after Warren's death in 1973;[11] but when he became prominent in the early 1990s, Douglas Gresham revealed that the pair had sold their halves of the estate to a holding company soon after obtaining it.[12] All along, most people have innocently assumed that whoever now owns and controls C. S. Lewis's literature must share Lewis's beliefs and purposes; but those concerned about the holding company's behavior were convinced that this is not the case. When asked about the company, Gresham answered that he knew nothing

---

provided for in Warren's will. He was remarkably friendly and generous to various Lewis enthusiasts who sought him out after Warren's death (Clyde Kilby, Faith Annette Sand, Terri Williams, Carol Green, myself, and probably others). At the time of Paxford's death Miller lived in a new middle-class house in Eynsham crowded with attractive furnishings; he would have had no use for poor old Paxford's humble leavings in Oxford. When questioned about his allegations of thefts by the Millers, Gresham has usually declined to elaborate; but in answer to my challenge in *The Salinas Lewisian* Gresham eventually explained that no one literally stole cufflinks off Warren's corpse. Furthermore, when confronted with some of the documentary proof that Maureen Moore inherited and sold the Kilns furnishings, he explained that his description of the theft was meant symbolically.

[11] In "War of words on bonfire books" in the 29 January 1989 issue of London's *Sunday Times,* Geordie Greig assured readers, "The only beneficiaries from the Lewis legacy are Lewis's two stepsons, so there is no suggestion that Hooper or Marchington made any money on the books."

[12] Although his mother and maternal grandparents were not practicing Jews, David Gresham adopted the Jewish faith as a boy and has reportedly lived at times as an Orthodox Jew. He has lived in England, France, and the exclusive Los Angeles suburb of San Marino, and was rumored to be a professional gambler. In 1994 he was reportedly married to a Buddhist and living in India. By all accounts, he wants nothing to do with Lewis affairs aside from his financial arrangement with the estate.

In contrast to David, Douglas Gresham is a public figure. "When I was twenty-one I left the college, and the country, and emigrated to Australia, where I became first a farmer, using the small capital my grandmother had left me, and then a broadcaster. This second career lasted ten years; and I was fortunate to be very successful at it. I was also fortunate with a series of real estate transactions; and thus when the time came for me to benefit from Jack's estate, which was in the late seventies, I was already fairly comfortable. Even now I don't think I could claim to be very wealthy." A letter from Douglas Gresham in *The Canadian C. S. Lewis Journal 70* (Spring 1990): 19. Since then he moved from Tasmania to Ireland and became gatekeeper for the Lewis estate. He has a large country estate, travels the world, and accepts many speaking engagements.

about it. (As writer Jeffrey Frank once observed, "When people shrug off the question of who owns what, they are shrugging off the question of who controls what.")

One determined Lewis reader investigated public records until he learned that the Lewis literary estate, now called the C. S. Lewis Pte Ltd. is an offshore (tax-sheltered) holding company named UITGEVERSMAATSCHAPPIJ EKSTER B.V and owned by anonymous investors. The company was previously based somewhere in the Channel Islands, and its board is officially in Singapore, although it seems to have no active office there. (A Lewis reader in Prince Edward Isle located the holding company address in a Singapore business directory on the Internet, but when a Singapore emissary visited that address she found the office occupied by two ordinary commercial businesses that had nothing to do with literature. Thinking the office might serve as a maildrop, I sent an inquiry in an envelope marked "Please forward if necessary or return to sender." I received no answer and no returned envelope.) [13]

Next, a Pinkerton investigator (hired by another frustrated researcher, not by me) traced the company's finances to Liechtenstein, the country favored by many of the world's most wealthy because of complete inaccessibility of financial records there to outside authorities. Some people who deposit their assets in Liechtenstein might do so without breaking the tax laws of their own countries, but others do so in illegal ways. (For results of this research, See Appendix II.)

The president of the C. S. Lewis Pte Ltd. is a lawyer named Rudolph Sieber, a resident of Switzerland (which borders on Liechtenstein). At last report, the directorship of the C. S. Lewis Pte, Ltd. is based in Ireland, and marketing director is Melvin Adams, a resident of Greystones, a seaside resort in County Wicklow that is a popular Dublin commuter town about fifty

---

[13] C S Lewis Pte
2 Handy Road
#07-02 Cathay Building
Singapore

Dear Sirs:
I have been advised that this is your correct business address, and I am just checking to make sure that it is correct. Please advise me.
Sincerely,
John Lindskoog

miles from Gresham's estate. (Ireland is a tax haven for people connected to the arts and entertainment business.)

Walter Hooper's current title as an Oxford employee of the C. S. Lewis Pte is Literary Advisor of the estate. (His past titles have included Executor, Trustee, and Manager.) By the end of 1999 London's Curtis Brown Literary Agency lost its C. S. Lewis Pte account, and C. S. Lewis Pte set up an agency called the C S Lewis Company Ltd (with spokesman Simon Adley) to handle these lucrative matters. It was located first in Lymingtin and then in Bristol. The C. S. Lewis Pte is hardly averse to secrecy or to change.

According to Douglas Gresham, he and David sold their halves of the Lewis estate to a holding company (now known as C. S. Lewis Pte Ltd) shortly after inheriting them in 1973. He announced in 1994 that he is an employee of that holding company "For some years now poor Walter Hooper [sic] has not been the person who decides what material under copyright control, owned by, or controlled by, the C. S. Lewis Estate, is to be published and what is not. I am employed by that estate to recommend on quality control and copyright infringement.... You may not like some of the decisions which I have made. However, I have not yet made one which I regret." [14]

During a session at the 1998 Oxbridge conference, Gresham was asked who owns C. S. Lewis Pte Ltd. He said that although the firm employs him, he doesn't know who owns it. Moreover, as long as the company pays him well, he doesn't care who owns it. He made it clear that he is now the appointed gatekeeper for the company, pointing out that C. S. Lewis Pte Ltd has followed all of his suggestions up to now. (One of those was threatening to sue the creative California couple that produced the excellent suite of lyric-less *Dawn Treader* compositions that they were ready to distribute at cost.)

In 2000 a potential thunderbolt was released in a "leak" from an insider: the sole shareholders in C. S. Lewis Pte Ltd are said to be David and Douglas Gresham. If true, that explains David's statement that his only interest in Lewis is in the income he receives from Lewis's estate. (Why would he receive money from the estate if he sold it as soon as he inherited it?) And it explains Douglas's fierce loyalty to the financial interests of the estate, although he considers himself the protector of the Lewis legacy. It also casts new light on

---

[14] Douglas Gresham in the summer 1994 issue of *Newsletter of the Salinas C. S. Lewis Society.*

Douglas's staunch defense of Walter Hooper's editorial decisions; if he is Hooper's employer, Hooper's decisions are essentially Douglas's. (He can contradict them when he pleases, as he did in 1998 when he circumvented the issue of 1950s ink on the 1938 Dark Tower manuscript by claiming that Lewis wrote it circa 1958.) And it would mean that Douglas wears two hats; his public hat as an employee of the estate, and his private hat as co-owner of the estate. (Thus he is his own employer, and that employer remains anonymous.) [15]

In 1990 Nicolas Barker, Deputy Keeper of the British Library, responded to *The C. S. Lewis Hoax* in the Oxford journal *Essays in Criticism,* pointing out that executors of a literary estate are obligated to maximize the estate's earnings as well as to respect the memory and reputation of the deceased author. When the executors are also trustees, financial profit may legally take priority over the author's reputation. Within bounds, executors may alter or adapt the author's writings for financial gain. [16]

The decisions of literary executors do not, however, give British publishers the freedom to mislead purchasers, as Lewis publisher Collins learned in court in 1991. Collins was fined £10,401 that year for selling low-quality thriller novels that looked as if they were by the popular novelist Alistair MacLean. Jonathan Lloyd, director of HarperCollins trade division, said, "It was never our intention to mislead the public."[17] But on 19 December 1991 the *London*

---

[15] This is much like Hooper's use of two hats when he was permissions gatekeeper for the Lewis literary estate. He would very reluctantly inform people that the Trustees had decided against requests, never revealing that he made the decison alone or in consultation with Owen Barfield.

[16] Nicolas Barker, "C. S. Lewis, Darkly," *Essays in Criticism,* 60/4 (October 1990): 361. "... the special position of literary executors of a 'live' estate (that is, one still earning royalties under current copyright legislation) has to be acknowledged. They have a double duty: to respect the memory and reputation of the author, and to maximize the estate's earnings (the latter may legally take priority over the former if the executors are also trustees). For a variety of reasons, then, executors may legitimately withhold publication of material that will in their judgment depreciate the estate in literary or monetary value. They may, although their judgment is more open to question here, alter or adapt an existing text if, in their view, it will add to the appreciation [financial value] of the estate."

[17] Alistair MacLean earned £20 million in thirty years, with eighteen titles that sold over a million copies each. After he died in 1987, Collins started issuing novels by young Alastair MacNeill based on plots that MacLean had left behind. Although

Review of Books observed, "There are rich pickings still to be had in the jungle of literature, where dead authors half-buried in brambles continue to yield abundant fruit...In a class of their own come the surrogate writers who are authorized to enrich the leftovers of a dead storyteller."

The true story of the Lewis literary estate has turned out to be a cross between a business primer and a detective novel. In contrast, the twisting tale of the Kilns has turned out to be like a Gilbert and Sullivan comic opera. According to an agreement Lewis made with Mrs. Moore in 1930, upon Warren's death the Kilns went to her daughter Maureen Moore (Mrs. Leonard Blake). Due to an extremely unusual family inheritance, Maureen had become Lady Dunbar of Hempriggs, owner of a castle and property in Scotland. George Sayer reports that Joy once tried to get Maureen to relinquish her future right to the Kilns in favor of Joy's sons, but she refused. In 1968 Maureen sold off the Kilns property, and part of it was subdivided into a confused clutter of houses backing up into the Kilns front yard.

After I learned of Warren's death I wrote to Walter Hooper on 22 July 1973: "It must seem to many Lewis lovers that the Kilns should be set aside as a literary shrine. Is there no possibility of the estate purchasing it for that purpose and renting it to people who could appreciate it? I wonder who allowed the new house to be built on the front lawn and if it could ever be moved." On 7 August he answered that inheritance tax might consume all the royalties for a year or two[18] and he didn't think the beneficiaries (David and Douglas Gresham) would be interested in my idea anyway. However, Lady Dunbar would be glad to sell the house to anyone who wanted to buy it for a museum. She was asking only £25,000 (approximately $60,000).

Unfortunately, in 1973 neither Wheaton College nor anyone else felt able to purchase the Kilns for a Lewis landmark. As a result, Mr. and Mrs. J. W.

Collins included MacNeill's name on the books, MacLean's name was far more prominent. In 27 September 1991 magistrates at Stratford-upon-Avon found HarperCollins guilty of misleading readers by selling 355,000 copies of "greatly inferior" *Night Watch* and *Death Train* as if they were by MacLean. Even at his worst, a literary expert testified, MacLean was superior to MacNeill.

At the end of chapter 2 of *Nightwatch* (MacNeill's imitation MacLean novel about an imitation Rembrandt painting) a museum director named Stanholme stared at the fake Rembrandt. "I still can't believe it. A forgery. Isn't anything sacred any more?"

[18] Rumor has it that because of the way the will was written, estate taxes had to be paid twice: once after Lewis's death, and again after Warren's death.

Thirsk, a university librarian and a university instructor, bought the Kilns, improved it, and reared their children there, appreciating the literary and historic significance of the site. After ten years they were planning to move to Japan temporarily, and so they offered the Kilns for about $120,000, then its market value.

In 1983 a middle-aged Wheaton College alumnus and Southern California entrepreneur named Robert Cording met Douglas Gresham at a dinner in his honor at the home of Lyle Dorsett, then Curator of the Marion E. Wade Center.[19] Gresham mentioned the idea of the Wade Center buying the Kilns; and because that was not an option, Cording launched the idea of a Kilns Limited Partnership. He decided to offer investors (at $5,000 per share) a way to help preserve the Kilns along with the privilege of free short-term lodging there when they visited England. Investors could expect their shares to appreciate in value if real estate values continued to increase.

Meanwhile, J. Stanley Mattson moved from New England to Southern California in 1983 to become the new fundraiser at the University of Redlands.[20] According to his résumé his specialties included marketing, solicitation, development, administration, persuasive public speaking, and public relations. In three years fate was going to land Mattson right in the middle of the Kilns project, which would catapult him into a battle for *The Dark Tower*.

Stephen Schofield and I happened to visit the Kilns on 19 June 1984, Mrs. Thirsk's birthday, and happily discussed the impending purchase with the Thirsks. The house looked immaculate. (I had seen its disheveled exterior in 1975 when repairs were in process.)

Cording was evidently an energetic visionary and promoter rather than an actual investor in his own project.[21] During the early days of the Kilns

----

[19] Robert Cording's father was a Wheaton College music professor. His mother, Ruth Cording, was a volunteer at the Wade Center.

[20] According to his résumé, the longest term in Mattson's career was in Canaan, New York, where he spent seven years developing and managing truckstops for Georgeport, Inc. He says that starting with a $2500 loan, he raised $1,235,000 in equity capital and $1,750,000 in bank financing, then transformed a bankrupt operation into a $5,500,000 business with a staff of ninety employees and 790 acres of land.

[21] Aside from being a general partner of the Kilns, Inc., Robert Cording was Treasurer, Founder and Chairman of the Board of Omega Entertainment, a Christian

Project he was helped by donated money, time, and expertise from various people. He and his Southern California supporter Paul Ford[22] distributed a handsome prospectus to Lewis enthusiasts.

Lyle Dorsett and his assistant Marjorie Lamp Mead were volunteers from the start, and Dorsett served as Cording's Kilns curator; but that activity was separate from their employment at the Wade Center. In lieu of a salary, in February 1985 Cording made Dorsett a limited partner and gave him two $5,000 shares in the Kilns. A couple of months later he gave a share to Mead and a share to the Wade Center itself, hoping the two organizations would be closely related. But Dorsett and Mead realized that the Kilns needed more attention than they could possibly provide, and on 7 June 1985 they resigned from the project, returning all four gift shares to Cording.

A few months later, Cording's shareholders were informed that financial reversals had rendered the partnership inoperable and that it was being dissolved. As one shareholder analyzed the debacle, too much capital was used for purposes other than the down payment, and choosing a flexible interest rate for the mortgage instead of a fixed rate proved disastrous. In 1986 the investors were asked to consider themselves donors, but to whom they had donated has never been clear.

A new seven-page prospectus suddenly appeared, soliciting support for a new venture called the Kilns Association, with addresses in both California and Oxford. The Oxford address was simply that of the Kilns, and the California address was that of the President of the Board of Directors, Paul Ford, who was then a theology instructor at Loyola Marymount University in Los Angeles. (The other board members were Robert Cording; Vic Bogard, a successful California contractor; William Abraham, a Texas banker; and Thomas Schmidt, a professor at Westmont College in Santa Barbara, California.)

---

film and video distribution company. He later became President of Questar Pictures, Inc., his motion picture production company. The similarity of the names Questar Pictures, Inc., and Questar Publishers, Inc. (the original 1994 publisher of *Light in the Shadowlands*) is entirely coincidental.

[22] Paul Ford has been a staunch supporter of Walter Hooper since 1975. In 1979 he stated in the *Los Angeles Times* that my questions about Hooper's accounts detracted from Hooper's scholarship, from Lewis himself, and from my own work. He said my suspicion was unwarranted.

In the new 1986 prospectus no background was offered on the defunct partnership except that "a more specific long-range vision developed." "It was agreed" that a simple Lewis museum and private hostel would seem "contrary to Lewis's style." Public use of the home of "a private and humble man" might be contrary to his wishes. Therefore the Kilns would instead become a free residence hall for three to six selected liberal arts graduate students, presumably bachelors, at Oxford.

According to the new 1986 plan, Kilns improvements such as fresh paint and installation of new household appliances would be largely completed in the summer of 1987. A full-time spiritual and administrative director would be installed in 1988, and a $50,000 on-site resource center with computers and microfiche facilities would be installed in 1989. In 1990 the acquisition of neighboring houses would begin (estimated cost $250,000 each) for the director's residence and future conferences. (Paint and appliances were supplied in time for the 1998 centennial, but the other goals remain unfulfilled into the 21st century. Year after year, the target dates were quietly changed as new donors were recruited.)

Three classes of membership were originally available to potential donors, all of whom were to apply by letter when sending their initial contributions. Charter membership, the second tier, offered donors a personalized, framed and numbered certificate; a color photograph of the Kilns; a newsletter; and the donor's name inscribed on a commemorative plaque in the drawing room of the Kilns. Lifetime membership offered all that and the possibility of free lodging at the Kilns, for a minimum contribution of $2,500. (The three-tiered plan was abandoned at some point.)

It happened that in 1986, just when Ford and Cording started their optimistic venture, Stanley Mattson completed his terms as vice-president of the Redlands Chamber of Commerce and director of corporate and foundation relations at the University of Redlands. He then began taking steps to fulfill an old dream of his, founding a Christian college. Mattson admittedly didn't know much about C. S. Lewis, but he knew that Lewis's name would suit his purpose well. (He sometimes refers to a Mere Christian College.) He issued a proposal beginning: "The C. S. Lewis College Foundation has been established to explore the feasibility of developing a Christian undergraduate liberal arts college/institute on, or immediately adjacent to, a major secular university campus."[23] Meanwhile, he worked part-time for a public agency in Redlands directing improvement of commercial facades.

In 1987 things moved quickly for him. He started calling his C. S. Lewis College Foundation the C. S. Lewis Foundation for Christian Higher Education and began planning a C. S. Lewis Summer Institute called Oxford '88, featuring an array of distinguished guest speakers including the Bishop of London, Richard John Neuhaus, Carl F. H. Henry, Thomas Howard, Peter Kreeft, George Sayer, Owen Barfield, and Walter Hooper.[24]

According to a newspaper interview with Mattson, the purpose of his Summer Institute was to explore the relationship between Christian faith and the arts; but eleven years later, in his 1999 fundraising letter, he indicated that the basic purpose of his Institutes was financial. There he reported that the net financial surplus from Oxbridge '98 was only $8.80 per person. Over 800 attended, so the total surplus from tuition ($7,040) had taken time away from other fundraising activities. (He does not say how much profit he expected, except that it should be commensurate with what he would have cleared if he had invested the time in other fundraising.) In 1999 he had already "initiated preparations" for Oxbridge 2001, "Time and Eternity: the Cosmic Odyssey," in order to increase attendance. (Until now some Mattson-watchers have assumed that the primary purpose of those conferences was publicity, prestige, access to affluent donors, and data for grant applications; that makes more sense than the idea of realizing significant profits from tuition.)

It isn't clear when Mattson first made contact with Hooper, but Paul Ford had been a friend of Hooper's since 1975. As an alumnus of the University of North Carolina at Chapel Hill, Mattson might have read two glowing articles about alumnus Walter Hooper in the *Alumni Review:* "It all started with a cup of tea," in the March 1980 issue and "A dead man's secretary" in the

---

[23] Stanley Mattson's university background included earning a B.S. in elementary and early secondary education in 1959 at the State University of New York in Oswego; an M.S. in American and European history in 1964 at the University of Wisconsin in Madison; and a Ph.D. in a combination of American history, European history, and American literature in 1970 at the University of North Carolina at Chapel Hill.

[24] According to Mattson, the 1988 Institute cost $50,000 more than it brought in, but a couple of donors made up the deficit.

Summer 1987 issue. In 1987-1988 Mattson, Ford, Cording, and Hooper were drawn together by their common interests and overlapping agendas. It seems that Mattson needed an immediate focus for his fledgling foundation; Ford and Cording needed better promotion; and Walter Hooper needed someone to squelch the forthcoming *C. S. Lewis Hoax.*

On 26 March 1988 the Kilns Association and the C. S. Lewis College Foundation quietly but officially merged, with Stanley Mattson as president, Paul Ford as vice-president, and Tom Schmidt as director of restoration. Mattson officially assumed full responsibility for care and preservation of the Kilns. During Oxford '88, Mattson stayed at the Kilns; afterwards he traveled to Wordsworth's Dove Cottage in the Lake District for ideas. He concluded that the Kilns should become a living museum, to serve also as a Christian study and retreat center with decor and fixtures from the late 1930s and early 1940s. Each room should be named after one of the past Kilns residents to personalize it.

In the 18 November issue of *Christianity Today* Paul Ford lamented the publication of *The C. S. Lewis Hoax.* He revealed that he had advised publishers to reject the manuscript He said he saw the book as my struggle to show that I was more important to Lewis than Hooper was. He dismissed my questions by pointing out that they were several years old (giving the false impression that they had been answered). He remained convinced there was a bonfire and that Lewis wrote *The Dark Tower.* In the same article Hooper said, "It's a curious way to celebrate the twenty-fifth anniversary of Lewis's death. I've been looking forward to celebrating his great legacy. Our attention should be on him, not me."[25]

On Sunday afternoon, 20 November, Stanley Mattson held a reception in Redlands to introduce his new C. S. Lewis Foundation office. The reception was the first I had heard of Mattson or his foundation, and so I called to inquire. To my surprise, he was eager to come to Orange to meet me, although I assured him I could not contribute financially. I was glad to have him come.

---

[25] "Book Charges Fraud over C. S. Lewis," *Christianity Today,* (18 November 1988): 56. Six months later, in his 26 May 1989 letter to a correspondent in Oregon, Hooper responded to *Hoax* by using the words depressed, havoc, cruelly shattered, false, and distressed. He thought she would be glad to know that some admirers of C. S. Lewis were trying to answer the many charges in my book.

On Tuesday morning, 13 December, Mattson and the friend he has called in print his "resident psychiatrist," Dr. John Benson of Redlands' Charter Hospital, came to meet me and spent an hour or more in casual chitchat, talking mostly about vocal music and Mattson's future college. (In the following decade the possible locations would be narrowed down to Princeton, Duke, Claremont, and Amherst.) I gave him a copy of *The C. S. Lewis Hoax* as he left and was puzzled by his reaction; he seemed flustered and said he hadn't heard of it. The statement was obviously not true, although I was not yet aware of his close association with Ford and Hooper.

My disease worsened in December and January. On the fateful morning of 25 January 1989 Mattson called to say that he and Dr. Benson wanted to come at 9:30 the next morning so he could ask me questions about my book's documentation. I greatly preferred an afternoon visit because my paralysis was more severe in the morning and I would be home alone, but he was insistent and settled on 10 A.M. I didn't know he had just been to England and back because of *Hoax*. Later that day I learned that he had asked in confidence for a pastor from my church to meet him at my house at 10 to comfort me about having to withdraw my new book. It was obvious that I would prefer to receive shocking news when my husband came home from teaching school in the afternoon, and so Mattson's secret plan struck me as an ambush of some kind. Intensely upset, I had a friend call Mattson to cancel the visit, and I sent him a friendly note offering to answer his questions by mail. (He has never asked me one question about my documentation.)[26]

The next morning at 9 A.M. I received a bizarre call from London. Writer Geordie Greig of Rupert Murdoch's *Sunday Times* taunted me about *Hoax* being proved wrong by a panel of four experts at the Bodleian. Knowing this claim had to be as phony[27] as Marchington's soot analysis, I didn't argue; I

---

[26] "I'll be happy to answer any questions you have, but I think it is efficient if we discuss *Hoax* in letters first to lay the groundwork for personal discussion. That would enhance precision and clarity and provide a record for us both—with exact quotations in case they are ever wanted. I have no agenda in this except friendship and openness. I am at your service." This was handwritten on mythopoeic stationery decorated with symbols of C. S. Lewis, J. R. R. Tolkien, and Charles Williams literature. Because I wrote the note after midnight, I dated it 26 January 1989. It was posted before 9 A.M.

[27] See Appendix 2.

was amused and curious. In contrast, Mr. Greig repeated himself more and more excitedly, as if exasperated that he couldn't upset me about his forthcoming article. (I'm sure he was just trying to enhance his article by bluffing me into sobbing or blurting out something foolish that he could quote.) At about 9:30 he seemed to give up and said good-bye politely in a normal voice. Five or ten minutes after we hung up it suddenly dawned on me: I was supposed to go into shock and receive the comfort of a pastor and a psychiatrist at 10 A.M.

That very day Mattson wrote me a single-spaced letter more than three pages long, referring to himself as a professional scholar of American literature (an inappropriate identification, so far as I can tell). As a newcomer to the world of Lewisian scholarship, he said, he was at a loss to understand why no one had subjected my ten-year-old claims [about the bonfire] to the closest scrutiny. He said he found this collective silence on the part of my colleagues most extraordinary given the seriousness of my charges.

"In the name of all that is consistent with the most fundamental standards of ethics and scholarship," he exclaimed, why did I not subject the manuscripts in question [Hooper's private property] to the rigorous examination of an impartial jury of experts long ago? In order to correct Lewisian scholarship, Mattson said, he had appointed Dr. Francis Warner to assemble "the most authoritative experts in the field of handwriting analysis," in order to examine the manuscripts for authenticity.[28]

Mattson said he had instructed Warner to write a report and send it directly to *Christianity Today* and other publications, which Warner did. Mattson did not offer me the report. He couldn't tell me how much it grieved him to find me in the present circumstance, he said as he broke the news. Insofar as the experts did render a unanimous opinion on all the charges that

---

[28] Being familiar with the nature of forgeries and the science of document authentication, I knew that it is humanly impossible for a panel of handwriting experts to prove a document authentic. What I suspected was that there was no panel of handwriting experts anyway, and that proved true. I got the distinct impression from the amorphous quality of Mattson's letter that he had not read and digested *Hoax* and didn't know which manuscripts were included in the Warner Report. I still think that was true. In my opinion, Hooper engaged Mattson in the capacity of a public relations agent in order to derail *Hoax*. Hooper, who was on the scene and acquainted with the alleged panel members, as Mattson was not, orchestrated the Warner Report.

related to the particular issues of forgery, he earnestly counseled me to accept the findings with charity—and issue a public apology to Walter Hooper in major publications. Mattson closed his counsel with the following bene-diction: "It is my prayer that God might somehow be glorified, and the memory of C. S. Lewis honored, by the example of a caring and principled community of Christian scholars wrestling with difficult issues..."[29]

Sure enough, Greig's article appeared in the 29 January *Sunday Times*.[30] (He included Hooper's statement, "I have been terribly hurt by these awful allegations. At times I have wanted to go to sleep and not wake up.") I sent the letters editor a letter correcting Greig's errors, but she rejected it; she insisted that Warner had led a respectable panel of independent document examiners. Her response was not surprising in light of her paper's history of naiveté concerning document authentication. In 1968 the *Sunday Times* paid a healthy six-figure sum for the bogus secret diaries of Benito Mussolini—which had in fact been written by an Italian mother and daughter forgery team. In April 1983 the *Sunday Times* paid $400,000 for rights to publish passages from Hitler's sixty-two volume handwritten diaries. In both cases, facile assurances of authenticity carried more weight than earnest warnings about forgery.

Dennis Porter, one of the two Bodleian librarians who reportedly served on Mattson's panel of four, assured me he had not done so.[31] The department

---

[29] Some readers of Dickens' *Martin Chuzzlewit* or viewers of the accurate Masterpiece Theater production see an uncanny resemblance between the rhetoric and behavior of Stanley Mattson and those of Dickens' memorable Mr. Pecksniff. (This was first brought to my attention by a reader who referred to "the Pecksniffian Stanley Mattson.")

[30] Greig mistakenly reported, "Last week a panel of Oxford dons, asked to set up an inquiry by the C. S. Lewis Foundation for Christian Higher Education in Redlands, California, decided *The Dark Tower* and *Boxen* were genuine. Four academics, headed by Professor Francis Warner, Oxford's pro-proctor elect, spent two days examining the manuscripts. 'It is terrible that such accusations were made,' said Dr. Judith Priestman, a panelist." The article was riddled with errors. To begin with, there was no "panel of Oxford dons," no one spent two days examining manuscripts, and *Boxen* was not in question. Among other things, Greig said that Hooper was a priest in 1964 when he saved Lewis's manuscripts from the bonfire and that I am from Redlands.

[31] On 7 February 1989 Dennis Porter wrote "I know nothing about a 'committee' and so have not served on one...In a purely private capacity (and not, of course, in

chair of the other librarian assured me that she had not spoken on behalf of the library and that the *Sunday Times* had misquoted her.[32] That left only Hooper's friend Francis Warner and Warner's friend R. E. Alton; the two had no background in contemporary document authentication and refused to reveal when they looked at Hooper's manuscripts, much less what they looked for. The three-page double-spaced Warner Report told how the manuscripts were packaged and coded in the Bodleian Library and (to the millimeter) the exact size of every piece of paper, the number of lines on each page, the colors of the lines and paper, and even the colors of the manuscript folder and the notebook spines. Warner also gave the date and return address of a letter Hooper sent him in 1983, although he said nothing more about the letter.[33] Hooper had his attorney, Royds Barfield, send the Warner Report to my publisher with a cover letter.[34]

Mattson's next project was to convene a twelve-member academic jury and six observers for a closed one-day trial of my *C. S. Lewis Hoax* in Redlands on 21 April 1989. First he read aloud from the civil courtroom's

---

any sense speaking for the Bodleian) I said that I thought [the Dark Tower manuscript] was in Lewis's hand. Perhaps the press has somehow transformed that into a membership of a committee carrying out chemical tests etc. (as a complete non-scientist I would be quite useless on such a committee)."

[32] On 31 March 1989, Mary Clapinson, Keeper of Western Manuscripts, wrote to me that although Judith Priestman considered the Dark Tower manuscript genuine, she did not speak for the Library. *"The Sunday Times* was, as alas newspapers often are, incorrect in reporting in quotes a comment on your challenge to the authenticity of the manuscript. Neither Dr. Priestman nor I would regard it as 'terrible that such accusations' could be made."

[33] The Warner Report reminds me of a passage in my decorative book of Gilbert and Sullivan lyrics that Mattson and Benson had glanced at appreciatively in my living room on 13 December. In *The Mikado*, Pooh-Bah told the king details about an event that had not taken place, then got caught by his lie. He excused his embroidery with this phrase: "Merely corroborative detail, intended to give artistic verisimilitude to an otherwise bald and unconvincing narrative."

[34] The actual Warner Report was so meaningless that it was ignored, but in the 8 November 1995 *Wall Street Journal* a letter writer named James Davidson made an amazing claim about Alton: "His opinion made the difference between the documents [of C. S. Lewis, Donne, Shelley, and Wilde] being worth a million dollars or nothing." According to Davidson, Alton could tell that the Vince Foster suicide note was a forgery. (Davidson's claim to fame is the $35 videotape "Unanswered—The Death of Vincent Foster," which was severely criticized by *60 Minutes* in October 1995.)

Book of Approved Jury Instruction (he served as combination jury foreman and judge), and then the jury discussed (for an average of under ten minutes each) a list of forty complex points provided by my publisher. Most of the jurists seemed to have barely skimmed *Hoax* if they had read it at all. Some made the remarks "She's using homophobia in order to sell books to evangelicals," "Paxford wouldn't have denied the bonfire," and "She must have used George Sayer's blurb without permission." No evidence was admitted, and no witnesses or cross-examinations were allowed. In fact, there was no defense. I was not allowed to observe, much less to testify. The ballots were counted after the jurists departed, and one of them later complained that because of his votes they could not have been entirely unanimous as reported.

The Mattson jury included two theology professors, Paul Ford and Tom Schmidt; two English professors, David Downing and George Musacchio; one professor of Italian, Barbara Reynolds of Cambridge; and a philosophy professor, Richard Purtill. Most of the jurors were friends of Hooper. There was also a rare-books dealer from San Francisco named Jennifer Larson, an elementary education professor from San Bernardino, and four others including Mattson.[35]

Mattson said he would give out transcripts and an official report on the trial within days, but neither one ever materialized.[36] (A jury observer said the transcript would have been mortifying and that Barbara Reynolds prohibited it.) Three jury members told me independently later that they regretted taking part.

I was appalled by Mattson's devious behavior, and in an effort to follow Biblical injunctions about estrangement and conflict (Matthew 5:23-24, 1

---

[35] In his 26 May 1989 letter to Oregon, Walter Hooper told the Portland C. S. Lewis Society that Mattson visited him a few days earlier with the report about the meeting, but that he didn't know who the twelve members of the "panel of inquiry" were. He said he hadn't had time to read the report, but he enclosed a "Summary Statement."

[36] Mattson and Hooper have always told inquirers that they have on hand an excellent report on the jury proceedings, and they have sometimes given out a quotation or a brief excerpt from the alleged report, but the report itself has never been seen. (This secrecy seems to contradict the definition of the word *report*.) According to witnesses, the events described in Hooper's very brief excerpt didn't take place, which suggests that the excerpt was written in advance and that the planned scenario was not followed.

Corinthians 6), I wrote to his pastor, Larry Poland of Redlands, on 19 May 1989, asking him to attempt a reconciliation between Mattson and myself. Although he was an evangelical who often quoted the Bible (I got on the mailing list of his own parachurch fundraising organization, "MasterMedia International"[37]) he responded by telephone, saying that both he and Mattson give priority to their professional pursuits such as Christian education, and could spare no time for reconciliation.[38]

Mattson publicity impressed *Christianity Today* enough to warrant an entire page in its 16 June 1989 issue. The article "A 'Hoax' Observed" quoted trustingly from the foundation's statement (not the promised detailed jury report): "panel members 'unanimously concluded that the major allegations leveled against [Hooper]...are wholly unsubstantiated.'" Mattson explained to his interviewer that *Hoax* should not have been published because "accusing a literary executor of forgery and illegal procurement of documents is analogous to accusing a banker of embezzlement." He told *Christianity Today* of an alleged Oxford University expert in document forgery who, with a small team, authenticated the questioned documents in the Bodleian earlier in 1989. "Mattson acknowledged, however, that the tests performed by the team were not exhaustive." (An odd thing to acknowledge, because there were no tests.)

Mattson was also quoted in *The Christian News* on 3 July 1989. He said his jury found *Hoax* "an acute failure" in dealing responsibly with the complex issues of forgery analysis. To the amazement of many, his jury suggested that I should have used carbon dating on the Dark Tower manuscript. Mattson and his jury were apparently unaware that carbon dating is used on items several centuries or several millennia old, not on items twenty to fifty years old.

---

[37] Ironically, in his September 1990 fund-raising letter, Poland capitalized on his interview with ex-witch Hezekiah ben Aaron and promised to produce a set of interviews with him on videotape. Ben Aaron was exposed as a fraud that was running a scam, but Poland clung to the idea that he was genuine and that the man's sensational tales about leading the Church of Satan were valid.

[38] In his 26 May 1989 letter to Oregon, Hooper expressed two fears: that Mrs. Lindskoog and her friends would become even more embittered and fight all the harder against those who reject her teaching, and that Mrs. Lindskoog might go on and on declaring manuscripts of Lewis to be forgeries, causing an unending series of forensic examinations to be necessary.

On Friday, 7 July 1989 Chris Eliot, a young reporter for the *Los Angeles Times*, interviewed Stanley Mattson and was told that Multiple Sclerosis has made me mentally deranged. Mr. Eliot interviewed me at my home that very afternoon and repeated to me what Mattson had told him. (He chuckled about it.)

In late summer Mattson's trial filled the first two pages of Westmont College's handsome alumni quarterly *La Paz*.[39] Jurists Tom Schmidt and David Downing claimed that *Hoax* is devoid of serious scholarship, that the posthumous Lewis literature is genuine, and that Hooper has not abused his executorship. Schmidt explained that vindicating Hooper is a high priority of the C. S. Lewis Foundation, and he accused me of ignoring Hooper's efforts to set the record straight about "his early friendship with Lewis."[40] Downing added that Hooper's biographical exaggerations were not serious in the first place and that Hooper corrected them in 1980. In fact, however, Hooper had not corrected them and was publishing them afresh that very year.[41]

In addition to running his ambitious 1989 campaign to exonerate Hooper of editorial malfeasance, Mattson announced a million-dollar fundraising campaign aimed primarily at major donors. One of his fundraising letters said, "By the grace of God, we have assumed full responsibility for the care and preservation of 'the Kilns'...Please respond generously..." He didn't mention that in the five years since the Thirsks sold the Kilns in good condition for $120,000, it became a ramshackle rental dormitory and the mortgage skyrocketed from $50,000 to $150,000. This happened under the care of three of his own trustees. In early 1995 Mattson announced that the mortgage was now up to $250,000.

One of Mattson's fundraising ideas was placing bronze plaques in the Kilns to commemorate specific donors. Lewis's study and bedroom plaques would cost $100,000; living area rooms would cost $50,000 each; Mrs. Moore's and Joy Lewis's bedrooms would cost $40,000 each; and the bedrooms

---

[39] "Is There Really a C. S. Lewis Hoax?" *La Paz* (June 1989): 1-2. At this time Mattson's son was a student at Westmont.

[40] See Appendix 8, "Letter to *La Paz*."

[41] On page 36 in *The Riddle of Joy* (1989) Hooper states, "Not long after I met him, Lewis had me move into his house, the Kilns, as his private secretary. It was during those months when I was privileged to be part of his household that Lewis sent me to Cambridge to handle some business for him. When I got home..."

of the stepsons and Warren, along with the kitchen, would cost $30,000 each. The British branch of Mattson's foundation is a registered charity called the Kilns (Oxford) Limited. Walter Hooper serves as one of its three directors.

In his impressive fundraising brochure, Mattson listed Lady Dunbar of Hempriggs and Douglas Gresham as Honorary Vice Chairmen of the Kilns Restoration Committee of Endorsement.[42] The two Lewis heirs were lending their names to Mattson's appeal for sacrificial giving for the Kilns, so Stephen Schofield questioned the amount of Gresham's contribution to the cause. Gresham answered hotly that Lewis himself didn't value the Kilns, and like Lewis he prefers to give directly to humanitarian causes.[43]

On 28 June 1990 Mattson and Hooper announced at Seattle Pacific University's Lewis Institute that England's leading paper chemist, Julius Grant, had just examined the *Dark Tower* manuscript and pronounced it genuine. Mattson assured inquirers that he would provide the Grant Report immediately. But thirteen months later Julius Grant died at age eighty-nine, and Mattson had no report he was willing to give out after all. Nevertheless, the phantom Julius Grant Report was reported as fact in the 9 January 1992 issue of *Oxford Journal,* and that erroneous article was reprinted in *The Canadian C. S. Lewis Journal.* (For facts about the Grant report, see Appendix 9.)

---

[42] On 26 May 1969 Hooper told a correspondent that Dr. Mattson had recently gone to Oxford to discuss the restoration of the Kilns with Douglas Gresham and at that time reported to Hooper about his April "panel of inquiry."

[43] "As to whether or not I or my brother decide to contribute to the restoration of the Kilns, firstly let me remind you that Jack and Warnie themselves cared so little for the house that had it not been for my mother, the building would probably have fallen down around us. I, like Jack, feel that people are more important than houses, however much nostalgia they may have attached to them; and thus, also like Jack, I prefer to apply my giving to charitable concerns which have a direct bearing on the welfare of people in need, particularly disadvantaged children. Secondly, if everyone is interested in my 'gratitude or ingratitude for my personal fortune', let me tell you at once that I am not in the least grateful for money no matter where it comes from. If gratitude exists at all outside the minds of optimists, it is owed for the home Jack gave me, (and I do not refer to the house), the love and care he extended to my mother and myself, and the lessons he taught me, and not for the results of the work of publishers, editors and agents since he died.

"Finally on this topic let me point out to you that what I decide to do with my money whether earned, unearned, or even stolen, is none of your business and none of your readers' business either."

The 1989 Warner report and the 1990 Grant report failed to turn the tide for Walter Hooper. Late in 1990 Mattson sent a letter to California handwriting analyst Nancy Cole, and she would eventually play a role in the C. S. Lewis Foundation's campaign to vindicate Walter Hooper.[44] In 1991 Mattson announced a million-dollar fundraising campaign all over again, as well as his second Lewis Institute in Oxford. He issued a new version of his publicity folder with the list of Fellows of the Kilns Restoration Committee of Endorsement expanded from thirty to forty-six. An array of respected Christian leaders, scholars, and artists allegedly endorsed Mattson's call for "major gifts." But when a few of them eventually learned that their names were being used in fundraising appeals without their permission, they asked to have their names removed. George Sayer, named there as Honorary Chairman of the Committee, had resigned two years earlier and knew nothing about the names added in 1991. If Mattson's foundation were a qualified member charity of the Evangelical Council for Financial Accountability, he would be held to stricter accuracy.[45]

(Lewis himself urged his radio listeners and readers of *Mere Christianity* to be well-informed rather than naive donors to charities: "He wants us to be simple, single-minded, affectionate, and teachable, as good children are; but He also wants every bit of intelligence we have to be alert at its job, and in first-class fighting trim. The fact that you are giving money to charity does not mean that you need not try to find out whether that charity is a fraud or not."[46])

---

[44] To read how the Cole plan backfired, see Appendix 10.

[45] In Jane Bryant Quinn's column "Lighting the Amen Corner" in the 28 December 1992 issue of *Newsweek*, she advises, "For information on conservative Christian charities, try the 13-year-old Evangelical Council for Financial Accountability (ECFA), which requires member groups to meet reasonable standards of ethics, governance and disclosure...For a free list of its 715 members, write to ECFA at P.O. Box 17456, Washington, D.C. 20041 (or call 800-323-9473).

She concludes, "Before giving to a charity, ask for a copy of its IRS 990 form—not to analyze the data (who can understand it?) but to see if the group will send it out...I do believe that the majority of religious charities function in good conscience. But conscience gets a boost from that still, small voice that warns us someone just might check." In fact, Mattson has failed to respond to requests for copies of his charity's IRS 990 form. His charity is known to the IRS as C S Lewis College Foundation, and its employer identification number is 33-0247175.

[46] C. S. Lewis, "The Cardinal Virtues," Book III, *Mere Christianity*.

A major breakthrough for Mattson was getting his foundation mentioned in the credits at the end of the film *Shadowlands:* "C.S. Lewis Foundation of Redlands, California." This resulted in scores of calls, visits, and letters. A decade of concentration on public relations and fundraising gradually enabled him to increase his staff in order to expand his public relations and fundraising, which enables him to invest more in public relations and fundraising. Mattson has traveled widely for teas, desserts, seminars, roundtables, radio and television interviews, church and university presentations, and personal contacts. His mailings have gone out to thousands, and for wealthy potential donors he provides a luxurious prospectus that includes a videotape. He frequently urges Christians to pledge monthly donations, and he also welcomes gifts of cash, stocks, bonds, legacies, trusts, valuables, office equipment, used cars, and various kinds of goods and services. He has sold art prints, and he developed a mail-order catalog to sell "THInklings" books (including *The Dark Tower*) and assorted merchandise. (In 1999 he called for some individual to donate $5,000 to update the catalog.)

The 1998 Lewis Centennial was a boon for Mattson's fundraising. For one thing, about then Tom Phillips, former president of Raytheon and the man who introduced Charles Colson to *Mere Christianity*, donated $25,000 to the foundation.

According to a November 1998 article by John Ezard in the *Daily Telegraph*, titled "Lewis's house of books and cobwebs," "the Kilns, in a cul-de-sac at Risinghurst, near Headington, has been almost restored to its 1920s and 1930s ambience by his American and British devotees, at a cost estimated at close to £1 million. Although it is still a private house, occupied by tenants, visitors are occasionally shown over it, according to its owners, the C. S. Lewis Foundation...When fully restored, it will be used as a C. S. Lewis study centre for visiting professors." Perhaps the £1 million estimate includes operating costs of the C. S. Lewis Foundation; the Kilns improvements themselves are ludicrously modest and simple in the light of such exaggeration. But the Lewis Foundation uses such figures routinely without ever explaining them.

We must raise $1.2 million this fiscal year to bring these plans to full fruition. So, if you are able, I'm asking you today to prayerfully consider making an extremely generous, tax-deductable donation or pledge of $10,000. It will enbolden Christian professors from different professions to risk asking the tough questions of colleagues and students in open dialogue—questions about the larger meaning and purpose of life, and its implications in the 21st century.... If you can make a tax-deductable pledge of $85/month or more, or send a gift of $1000 or more, I will be pleased to send you an EXTRA FREE GIFT of our carefully crafted and logo'd Lewis Centennial Pen and Pencil set.

Among other appeals, Mattson sends out a brochure called "How to give a Living Legacy Gift," with a photo of C. S. Lewis on the cover. Apparently Lewis has just glanced up from some papers he is holding on his desk. He looks expectantly and almost beseechingly into the potential donor's eyes, as if to say "Do this for me." Inside is the invitation to memorialize someone or celebrate something with a donation to the Foundation. In one appeal, Mattson writes:

> Since 1986, the C. S. Lewis Foundation has been advancing the renewal of Christian thought and academic freedom within the mainstream of contemp-orary colleges and universities.
>
> When you choose to give a Living Legacy gift you'll have the assurance that you're enhancing the works of the Foundation and helping the next generation recover our rich Christian intellectual and artistic heritage.
>
> You may choose to instruct the funeral director to insert the following in the Obituary Notice: The family suggests contributions be made to C. S. Lewis Foundation, P.O. Box 8008, Redlands, CA 92375.
>
> To acknowledge Bereavement, Wedding, Christmas, Anniversary, Moth-er's Day, Birthday, Father's Day....

Whatever Mattson means about his advancing the renewal of Christian thought and academic freedom, perhaps a donation to acknowledge April Fool's day would be appropriate.

Ever since 1988, Mattson has been selling a vague but grandiose vision of the Kilns as a pivotal gathering place for Christian scholars and artists from around the world, "helping scholars of faith find their voice." He asks donors to endow "competitive study grants, conferred annually by an internationally distinguished awards committee." He says he needs at least one more house near the Kilns to accomodate six to twelve resident scholars, a Head Resident or Warden, a Director who is "a senior Christian scholar," and forty to fifty participating scholars a year. Who these people will be, how they are to be selected, and what they are actually going to do at the Kilns has never been spelled out.

By early 1993 Mattson started advertising for dozens of American volunteers to bring themselves to Oxford to refurbish the Kilns between 5 July and 8 August. England has an abundance of people who could do such work without the cost of transatlantic flights and board and room, but the 1993 American pilgrimage to Oxford to rescue the Kilns did more than repair some of the damage caused by neglect. It also served as a dramatic public relations coup and launched a five-year fundraising event. As a human interest story, this spread the news on both sides of the Atlantic that Mattson's foundation was working valiantly to save the Lewis legacy. What the ongoing stories and photos didn't show was that until 1997 the Kilns remained a neighborhood eyesore, and it was newly graced with a Christian cross in the roof tiles on its northeast corner, facing the road. Whoever tiled the cross into the Kilns roof no doubt had good intentions, but as either exterior design or Christian advertisement it seems an unfortunate experiment. Fortunately, it became less distinct as years passed.

In conjunction with the summer work project, Mattson engaged Douglas Gresham to record a fundraising appeal that was relayed by telephone to targeted donors across the United States. The fundraising calls were successful enough that Gresham—who is an excellent speaker and says he was once known in Australia as 'The Voice"—became an active spokesman for Mattson's Foundation.[47] He flew from his home in Ireland to Southern California to take part in Mattson's special Orange County premier showing of *Shadowlands* on 6 January 1994 and addressed an audience of three hundred. As a celebrity guest on radio shows since then, Gresham sometimes describes aspects of his life in the Lewis household. Radio hosts quote from the Foundation's promotional material. Gresham speaks of Stanley Mattson's sacrificial struggle to bring Christianity back into education, and he includes a moving inspirational appeal for donations.[48]

At Oxbridge '98 he said he was not a Christian when he wrote *Lenten Lands* in the late 1980s. He dates his conversion to about 1990. When asked whether he is still an Anglican, he said no, that he is not a member of any church. If someone had to describe him as something, they could call him a "mere Christian." One reason he doesn't want to be affiliated with any church is that it allows him to preach to any sect or denomination or even any "cult." (He worships at home, and has not told about his preaching engagements.)

Gresham is an employee (and perhaps co-owner) of the C. S. Lewis Pte; his current title there is Quality Control and Copyright Infringement Consultant. (*People* magazine identified him as executor of the estate.) His double

---

[47] Douglas Gresham is an entertaining, highly persuasive public speaker. "I made my living for some years as a professional radio and television personality...And my broadcasting career was extremely successful. In fact, the highlight of it was—and still remembered to this day, in the city of Perth in western Australia—that I'm the man who sold 2,000 tons of chicken manure in six weeks to an urban population. And what really comes out of that, you know, is that people who give up believing in God fall for anything." (from Douglas Gresham's lecture "C S Lewis and Contemporary Culture" at the University of Tennessee at Chattanooga, 16 April 1998).

[48] On 1 March 1993, on "The Bible Answer Man" broadcast from Christian Research Institute in San Juan Capistrano, California, Gresham said, "The goal of the C. S. Lewis Foundation is basically to found a college—on one of the great secular campuses—which is devoted to reintroducing Christianity into American education. That is the one hope your nation has of coming back to life. It's the one hope you have to drag you back from the pit of hell to which you are careening at present. And when I say *you*, I don't mean just you. Europe is doing it too, and many of the other countries of the world. It is the one hope to get Christianity back into your families, back into your schools, back into your universities. It is the only way there is any hope for your nation."

role in Lewis affairs—officially serving both the C. S. Lewis Pte and Mattson's C. S. Lewis Foundation—parallels Hooper's double role.

As the Kilns myth grew, writers have sometimes referred to the house as a "fairy-tale cottage" set in a "magic wood." In 1994 reporter Reg Little of the *Oxford Times* visited and gave a realistic assessment: "The house at the bottom of Lewis Close hardly looked a magical place. Dating from the 1920s, only its scruffiness and the sparcity of flowers...made it stand out from far more desirable properties in the cul-de-sac." He warned that visiting the Kilns while it was a rental dormitory could be a shocking experience.[49]

What no one guessed in 1994 was that in spite of annual solicitations based on the promise of imminent opening of the Kilns as a study center, it would continue as a rental dormitory clear into the next century. By 1998 it had been renovated and improved, and washbasins had been installed in all the bedrooms (there is only one bathtub and one toilet). But there was still no sign of the highly publicized study center. Instead, the Kilns was still doing double duty for the C. S. Lewis Foundation as a magnet for charitable contributions and a source of about £1,800 monthly rental income. Here is a timeline of the published plans that have kept donations flowing for more than a decade:

1989: C. S. Lewis College was scheduled to open in 1995.

1993: Kilns Study Centre was scheduled to open in 1995, and C. S. Lewis College rescheduled to open in 1997.

1996: Kilns Study Centre was rescheduled to open in 1996, and C. S. Lewis College in 2001.

1997: Kilns Study Centre rescheduled to open in 1998, Lewis's Centennial year.

1998: Kilns Study Centre rescheduled to open in 1999.

1999: Kilns Study Centre rescheduled to open in 2000.

2000: Kilns Study Centre rescheduled to open in 2001.

---

[49] Although the cul-de-sac offers very little parking space, Mattson converted the Kilns garage into an extra room. The cul-de-sac lacks enough space for buses, and in 1994 Kilns neighbors complained to their city councilor about parking problems.

In fact, in 1999 a Kilns ad appeared in newspapers, and a handsome sign with the Kilns in the background appeared in Thornton's, a secondhand book shop on Broad Street in Oxford. The sign said:

> Rooms to Let
>
> C.S. Lewis' Former Home
> The Kilns, Headington
> Telephone Oxford: 741865 or 767689
> E-Mail: kilnsemail@aol.com
> Share this six bedroom fully furnished home with five
> others. Monthly rent from £250–350
> Tenancy Period: 1 August, 1999-30 June, 2000

After the ad was posted, Mattson announced great progress in his July 1999 fundraising letter. He had recently received two foundation grants (one for $50,000) and several very generous gifts from individuals; to enhance his foundation's financial health, he added eleven new members to his board. Member Ken Williams, the recently retired vice president of McDonell Douglas (who personally donated $25,000) was chairing the first Annual Fund Campaign with a goal of $650,000.

In 1994 Reg Little wrote, "Even in its present poor state there is enough to suggest that the Kilns has the potential to become one of Oxford's busiest tourist attractions. It might lack the beauty of Dove Cottage in Grasmere or the atmosphere of the Parsonage at Hayworth but then Wordsworth and Brontë industries don't have *Shadowlands*. The film catapulted the Lewisiana industry through the stratosphere..."[50]

What came of the down-to-earth forgery charge that has proved so

---

[50] Reg Little, "Pottering about the Kilns," *Oxford Times* (5 August 1994).

irritating to people allied with the stratospheric Lewisiana industry? That is the subject of the next chapter, "Battle for the Dark Tower."

> It is difficult to get a man to understand something when his salary depends upon his not understanding it.
> —*Upton Sinclair*

12

BATTLE FOR THE DARK TOWER:

NOT A CONTEST AFTER ALL?

The battle for *The Dark Tower* is like a medieval fantasy taking place today. An unfinished dark tower suddenly appeared in Lewisiana in 1977, casting a sinister shadow across that lovely land. The grand viziers announced with trumpet fanfare that they had restored this abandoned tower to its proper place for the pleasure of the populace. But after a quick thrill of curiosity, most of the populace backed off with a bewildered shrug or hurried by with a respectful little shudder. It was odorous, some said. It was not clean. For eleven years the mysterious tower loomed darkly in their sweet sunny land. It was designed so badly that not one builder could think of a way to finish it. Then at dawn one day in 1988 a notice was nailed to the tower door: This Tower Is a Hoax.

People started murmuring: If the ugly tower was not a genuine landmark, it must be the work of an outside trickster or an inside traitor. Some scrutinized it for the first time. Many called for an inspection by stonemasons and alchemists. A few dared to jeer at the tower and urged the viziers of the inner rings of Lewisiana to remove it from their sight. These scattered few occasionally pelted the locked door of the dark tower with protests and petitions.

Year after year, the nameless landlords of the tower remained invisible, and viziers Hooper and Barfield remained behind its stone walls, refusing to answer questions. [1] Stanley Mattson, their freelance champion, threw himself into routing the rebels with a cannonade; but most of his allies evidently decided to watch discretely until the outcome was certain. Nevertheless, one by one various true Knights of the Tower and occasional mercenaries have girded themselves and sallied forth from various places, flags waving, engaging in sorties to defend the lords of the Lewis domain—and their visible retinue—from blasphemous accusations. [2]

William Griffin is such a fighter. At the end of October 1988 *The C. S. Lewis Hoax* was sent out to reviewers. On 4 November I heard that Griffin, past editor at Harcourt and Macmillan and then religion editor for *Publishers Weekly*, took the book personally, and was extremely upset about

---

[1] Soon after *The Dark Tower* was published, Hooper was portrayed in *CSL* as a noble young warrior. "Walter Hooper is surely the Childe Roland among this century's literary executors. In his admirably edited *The Dark Tower and Other Stories*, which assembles all of C. S. Lewis's shorter fiction so that the fictional tally is now complete, Father Hooper once again sets the 'slughorn' to his lips and, 'dauntless,' awakens echoes of interlocking themes in the mind's ear of Lewis's readers. " Charles A Brady, "Some Notes on C. S. Lewis's *The Dark Tower and Other Stories*," *CSL*, 95: 1.

[2] Responses to the real-life religious-academic hoax in Lewis affairs seem to echo responses to the fictitious religious-academic hoax in Angus Wilson's 1956 novel *Anglo-Saxon Attitudes*. (Angus Wilson has no connection to contemporary novelist A. N. Wilson.) In that story, historian Lionel Stokesay and a crew of antiquarian excavators discovered in 1912 the lost A.D. 695 tomb of Bishop Eorpwald. In the stone coffin they found a rare Saxon wooden fertility symbol, meaning that early British Christianity was actually semi-pagan.

In Wilson's story, after forty years a scholar named Gerald Middleton realized that Stokesay's son had planted the pagan figure in the coffin to discredit his father, accidentally discrediting the early church instead. When Middleton confided in Kay, his grown daughter, she urged him to seek proofs and to speak up. "It's a question of academic honesty." (Our sharing the same nickname and values is a coincidence.)

In response, one offended scholar said, "I hope no one thinks, for one minute, that I am taking any notice of all this ridiculous nonsense." Others defended the status quo because they wanted Middleton to protect Stokesay's reputation and the "rosy glow" of his historic discovery. "Surely you don't want to poison my memories..." "Does it matter now?" "You make a lot of your conscience."

"It's not *my* conscience," Gerald cried, "it's the good faith of a humane study in a world rapidly losing its humanity."

In the end, one scholar sighed, "We'll have to use every resource to play [the truth] down. The whole thing's so sadly un-English." "Nonsense," said another. "There are fools and scoundrels in every country."

it. I found this bewildering because I had only mentioned him in passing as author of *Clive Staples Lewis, A Dramatic Life.* I immediately wrote to introduce myself and to clarify the matter.[3] He did not respond.

On 21 December I wrote again to Griffin, assuring him of my concern and asking him to advise me of any errors or oversights in *Hoax.* His only answer was a statement in *Publishers Weekly* on 13 January 1989: "Lindskoog's book may have its points. It is also riddled with error." (In Oxford eleven days later a couple of men signed the strange three-page statement that would be falsely publicized in the press as an authoritative study.[4])

In the January 1989 issue of *CSL* Griffin assailed me for suggesting that Hooper had indulged in what he called "rascality, roguery, and forgery." He and Hooper were responsible for the title *They Stand Together,*[5] he explained, and because I suggested that they had played what he called "a homosexual prank of international scope on the reading public," "a morally loathsome trick" in the religious publishing world,[6] I should either hand in my ticket as

---

[3] "I was rather shocked that you found anything in my book reflecting in a negative way upon your character as an editor. In the first place, I assumed that a Collins editor was responsible for *They Stand Together* and that it did not receive any substantive editing other than Hooper's..."

"More to the point, it never occurred to me that anyone involved in the production of *They Stand Together* would feel blamed by me for the latently homosexual title. I made it clear that few people know about that *double entendre.* My personal assumption was that some editor was finally responsible for ending the joke, not starting it. Isn't that the case?...I feel sure that my readers will think of you as I do, as an innocent bystander."

[4] False publicity for the Warner Report is the kind of journalistic disinformation that Lewis pilloried in his novel *That Hideous Strength.*

[5] I was surprised at Griffin's revelation; I had no assumptions about who chose the title *They Stand Together* or who served as Hooper's editor.

[6] Griffin's disapproval of my charge about a *double entendre* does not indicate any disapproval of *double entendres* themselves; they often proliferate in his own writing and that of his favorite writer, William Shakespeare. See for example his chapter in *Carnage at Christhaven: A Serial Mystery Novel,* ed. William Griffin (San Francisco: Harper & Row, 1989) 1-9. Griffin indroduces Felicity French, "whose virgin wool sweater clung rather too willingly to her athletic frame." A male character bumped into her and asked, "Are these for real?" Soon Felicity was tugging at her sweater. "It had a tendency to rise; the panting hart of the Psalms, which decorated the sweater front, strained upward for liquid nourishment." "Your fire I'll light after dinner," Felicity promises. "...Father, we thank you for bringing us together..."

a C. S. Lewis scholar or else hand in my ticket as a Christian. "I write figuratively, of course, Christianity being just the right religion for people who sin and come to their senses afterward."

He went on to say that I had packed innuendoes like Styrofoam scallops around Hooper's frail porcelain-vase character, sealed it in a box, kicked it around until my leg fell off, and then opened the box and showed that the tender vase is intact. [sic] "I think one can concede at this point that there has been a hoax in the C. S. Lewis world, but if Mrs. Lindskoog ever hopes to find it, she would do well to look within."

On 8 November 1989 Griffin went to the Bodleian during a storm to see the Dark Tower manuscript for himself. On pages 5 and 6 of *CSL*, Issue 240, he drew a "duckological" conclusion: if it looks like a duck and walks like a duck, it must be a duck. If it looks like a Lewis manuscript, it must be a Lewis manuscript. "As for the charge that *The Dark Tower* has been forged, all references to it from now on, it seems to me, should refer only to the manuscript, and the bearers of that charge should give proof that he/she has actually seen it."[7]

Both *Carnage at Christhaven* and *The Dark Tower* begin with several pages of chit-chat between a few professionals who have been summoned without explanation to a mysterious private gathering that will last for days. Griffin is a character in *Carnage at Christhaven,* just as Lewis is a character in *The Dark Tower.* Griffin calls his fictional self "S.J." Smith in reference to his past real-life membership in the Society of Jesus (he was a Jesuit). When S.J. finds Felicity's bed and leaves pralines under her pillow, Griffin sounds more like a devotee of comic writer S.J. Perelman than a devotee of Jesus, which is (in my opinion) part of this literary joke.

[7] My response to Griffin published in *CSL,* Issue 242, included the following: "Mr. Griffin says of the Dark Tower manuscript, 'the writing looked like Lewis's.' Indeed it did. But that hardly has any bearing upon the question of forgery. The writing (in some cases printing) looked authentic to respected experts in the cases of Konrad Kujau's forged Hitler diaries (1981-1983), Thomas Chatterton's forged Rowley documents (1764 - c.1850), Mark Hofmann's forged Mormon documents (1980-1985), Thomas J. Wise's forged Romantic pamphlets (1890-1934), John Jenkins's forged Texas documents (1972-1989), William Henry Ireland's forged Shakespeare documents (1793-1794), Clifford Irving's forged Howard Hughs documents (1968-1972), James MacPherson's forged Gaelic documents (1776 - c.1800), and Sir Edmund Backhouse's forged Chinese documents (1913-1973). Ironically, Samuel Johnson was attacked as long as he lived for accusing James MacPherson of forgery; and Sir Edmund Backhouse, now known to be a thief and a criminal sociopath, is honored on a marble

Next Michael Piret, an Oxford friend of Hooper's, exclaimed in the 14 May 1989 issue of *The Living Church:*

> The book, it's true, is almost laughable at points. But not often. It is too filled with hatred and resentment to be very funny, too disturbing a reminder of how malignant the imagination can be when it puts the worst possible construction on the life and motives of another...The book is beyond a joke...[Lindskoog] may still have the opportunity to salvage some semblance of scholarly integrity by issuing a profound public apology to Walter Hooper for having made this monstrous charge of forgery. But as long as she lacks the wisdom to do even that, I cannot imagine that her other accusations deserve such prestige as an answer would afford.

(Since 1978 the claim that questions about Lewis affairs don't deserve an answer has been the usual answer.) Piret promised to eat all sixty-two pages if the *Dark Tower* manuscript proves to be a forgery, not realizing, evidently, that famous forgeries become valuable documents in their own right.

The next pro-Tower offensive was "The Kathryn Lindskoog Hoax: Screwtape Redux" by Tolkien expert John D. Rateliff in *Mythlore 58.* He began:

---

tablet at the Bodleian as one of its greatest benefactors. 'The wheels of God grind slowly...'

"I make two pleas to people concerned about the integrity of the Lewis corpus, which is being damaged either by false documents or by my charges about false documents. First, everyone on either side of the question can profit from reading Robert Lindsey's excellent account of the Utah forgeries and the science of document authentication in *A Gathering of Saints* (Simon and Schuster, 1988). Second, those on either side with some knowledge of computers can check the study by Carla Faust Jones described in her article 'The Literary Detective Computer Analysis of Stylistic Differences Between "The Dark Tower" and C. S. Lewis' Deep Space Trilogy' on pages 11-15 of *Mythlore 57,* Spring 1989. The originator of the Literary Detective program has affirmed Jones's results, and no one has yet criticized her study in any way. Her work was the basis of my charge that *The Dark Tower* is a literary forgery, and therefore the continuing silence about her 'genetic fingerprinting' of *The Dark Tower* seems increasingly strange."

This is an appalling book. That it should ever have been published at all is distressing; that it should be issued by a Christian publisher festooned with a broadside of apparently laudatory comments from old friends of Lewis (Dom Bede Griffiths, George Sayer), Lewis scholars (Joe R. Christopher, Nancy-Lou Patterson), and professional Christian writers (Sheldon Vanauken, Frederick Buechner, Walter Wangerin) is nothing short of amazing...Screwtape would be delighted.

Rateliffe continued to be appalled for four pages.

In the fall 1989 issue of *Reflections*, a Roman Catholic quarterly review of books, G. K. Chesterton expert George Marlin called *Hoax* "specious," and "utter nonsense," grasping at any straw and probably a product of envy. He announced that in 1988 Dr. Stanley Mattson "formally requested Oxford's Bodleian Library for a professional judgment on whether or not the manuscript purporting to be by C. S. Lewis called *The Dark Tower* is a fraudulent document. The papers were examined by noted scholars and handwriting experts." The resultant Bodleian report, according to Marlin, settles the matter: *The Dark Tower* is unquestionably in Lewis's handwriting. Marlin pays tribute to Hooper for devoting his life to the protection of Lewis's spiritual and intellectual legacy and for fighting the enemies who seek to misuse Lewis.

In the fall 1989 issue of *National Honors Report*, Dabney Hart of Georgia State University in Atlanta warned against "Kathleen [sic] Lindskoog's book *The C. S. Lewis Hoax.* "Honors students must develop the habit of reserving judgment until they have weighed as much evidence as they can find...I do not suggest, however, that they should read Lindskoog's book and judge her evidence for themselves." Without explaining why, Hart concluded, "There is no reason even to raise the question about the genuine Lewis legacy." On "The Talk of the Nation" on National Public Radio on 30 November 1998 she said, "I resent the fact that the title suggests that C. S. Lewis perpetrated some sort of hoax, which of course is not the case at all. I don't know enough about Walter Hooper and the way he has exercised his literary executorship to be able to say whether the points made in that book are accurate or not. But I think the whole approach of the book, it seems to me, is misguided." (By then

Hoax was eleven years old; she didn't mention *Light in the Shadowlands*, which was then five years old.)

In the course of 1989 I had asked Harcourt, Macmillan, Collins, and Elizabeth Stevens (Lewis Estate Agent of the Curtis Brown literary agency) for their positions on their posthumous Lewis materials. Harcourt and Macmillan failed to answer. Editor Leslie Walmsley of Collins and Elizabeth Stevens of Curtis Brown both answered that they had no reason to doubt the authenticity of those works.

In March 1990 the most famous and important of all *Dark Tower* defenders joined the fray at the behest of Walter Hooper and Collins, publisher of *The Dark Tower*. A. N. Wilson says he wrote *C. S. Lewis: A Biography* for the two of them. Ignoring the letter I had sent him on 13 January,[8] he said on pages xiv-xv of his preface that since the central thesis of *Hoax* has been disproved, he doesn't think it will be published in Great Britain "though it was bought by a British publisher at the Frankfurt Book Fair in 1988." (The purchase in Frankfurt is a fabrication that improves his story.)

Wilson's main point about *Hoax* is that the Dark Tower manuscript is in the Bodleian Library, and "experts have made it clear beyond doubt that it is

---

[8] Dear Mr. Wilson:

I read your article in the 24 December *New York Times* and noticed that according to a note on page 27 this essay will appear in your forthcoming book C. S. *Lewis, A Biography*. In case that is true, I must ask for a correction.

Counter to your information, no part of my 1988 book has been proved false by anyone.

Although journalist Geordi Greig reported in the *Sunday Times* in January 1989 that a committee of experts had proved Walter Hooper's "Dark Tower" manuscript genuine, the report proved false. No committee of experts had examined the manuscript, much less tested it. Greig told me that one of the committee members was Dennis Porter of the Bodleian. I wrote to Porter and have a signed letter from him stating that he did not serve on such a committee, would not qualify for such a committee, and was not aware of such a committee. The fact is that two well-meaning defenders of Walter Hooper, completely innocent of the science of document analysis, were mistakenly identified as an impartial committee of experts. Their uninformed friendly conjecture is a far cry from document authentication, as Jennifer Larson of the Antiquarian Booksellers Association of America testified publicly on 21 April 1989.

written in Lewis's hand." Wilson also claims that I wrongly mistook Hooper's title *They Stand Together* for pederastic argot (*pederasty* often means pedophilia, and so I intentionally used the term *homosexuality*) and that *Hoax* is a diatribe, one of the most vitriolic personal attacks on a fellow scholar he ever read. Readers acquainted with Wilson's journalistic impishness are apt to recognize playful self-mockery in that charge, but those who don't know about his personality and who haven't read *Hoax* are apt to take him seriously.[9]

In the summer 1991 *Canadian C. S. Lewis Journal*, Evan Gibson suggested "Perhaps Wilson's book should be titled *C. S. Lewis: A Novel*." By then Wilson had formally announced his atheism. In an interview with Peter Mullen for the 1 February 1991 *Church Times*, Wilson took a parting shot at Lewis: "Writing that biography of C. S. Lewis was one of the things that made me renounce my Christian faith....A blessing of my present state of mind is that I feel very close to the bishops: none of us believes in God."[10] In the summer of 1994 Jonathan Brewer of Cornwall, England, made a study of Wilson's Lewis biography and listed several hundred specific errors or flaws in it. (For my own 1990 list of some of the falsehoods, fallacies, and fantasies in Wilson's biography of Lewis, see Appendix 5.)[11]

---

[9] Wilson's claim about authentication of the *Dark Tower* manuscript in the Bodleian Library was repeated without question on pages 618-619 of the winter 1990 issue of *Modern Fiction Studies*.

[10] Cynical journalists note that the prodigiously prolific Wilson, a successful novelist, biographer, essayist, children's author, television critic, television personality, comic, tabloid gossip, religious pundit, and professional doubter, says his motive for it all is "cash." He supposedly markets himself for an annual income of between £50,000 and £100,000. His conversion to atheism was analyzed as a clever media career move on page 10 of the 19 July 1991 issue of England's *Private Eye*.

[11] Reviewers who are offended by Wilson's glib Freudian debunking of Lewis's beliefs find a worse example of the same thing in David Holbrook's *The Skeleton in the Closet: C. S. Lewis' Fantasies: A Phenomenological Study* (Lewisburg: Bucknell University Press, 1991). He says Lewis's fiction is dangerous and perverse, hardening the soul rather than refreshing it. According to Holbrook, the name of Miss Prizzle, a teacher in *Prince Caspian*, refers to a "bull's pizzle." On page 139 he says "Taking into account Lewis's secret inclinations towards woman as revealed in the Greaves [sic] letters, we may suspect behind the name 'Prizzle' a fantasy of whipping a woman with a dried bull's penis—the excitement of which, to one like Lewis, would be obvious."

The May 1990 edition of *30 Days,* an international Roman Catholic magazine, attacked both *Hoax* and Wilson's book in an article that had one devil writing to another:

> I must say that Kathryn Lindskoog's book did not do as much damage as we had hoped. The accusation that the literary advisor of Lewis' estate had forged posthumously published Lewis material was disposed of by a handwriting expert called in by the official investigation, and Walter Hooper's name was cleared. Also, I noticed you were not able to persuade Hooper to descend to Lindskoog's level: and this sort of heroic silence from an injured party does our cause no good at all.[12]

In 1990 Professor Don Cregier and Dr. Sharon Cregier of Prince Edward Island twice offered to cosponsor with J. Stanley Mattson and his C. S. Lewis Foundation an unbiased professional scientific analysis of the *Dark Tower* manuscript.[13] The answer was silence.

On 25 June 1990 philosophy professor Richard Purtill gave the most imaginative *Dark Tower* defense of all. At a public lecture at Seattle Pacific University guest speaker Purtill read aloud from his projected conclusion to *The Dark Tower,* a series of recent letters from the novel's fictional hero Scudamour to Purtill himself. Scudamour begins his letters to Purtill by affirming the novel's Lewis authorship, dismissing my forgery charges, and sympathizing with "poor Hooper":

> I've never heard of the literary controversy you mentioned, but it seems to me, as it does to you, that it's quite irresponsible to accuse someone of literary forgery on such a slender basis.

---

[12] Leonie Caldecott, "A Nether View," *30 Days* (May 1990): 74. As part of his "heroic silence," Hooper has refused to answer questions or argue. Instead, he refutes witnesses against him by pointing out their mental incompetencies: Warren Lewis was drunk, Molly Miller's mind was affected, Roger Lancelyn Green lied, Fred Paxford was senile, and Kathryn Lindskoog's disease has destroyed her mind.

[13] The Cregiers made their formal written offers in letters to J. Stanley Mattson and the C. S. Lewis Foundation on 20 May 1990 and 27 August 1990.

You may certainly write to me again now you know the situation, but I'm not sure what use I can be to you in scotching the effect on poor Hooper, who, by the way, is mentioned with affection in one of Lewis's last letters.

I'm not quite sure I'm glad you wrote, but I'll be glad to do anything I can to help. How Lewis would have hated all this innuendo and accusation.

Yours very truly,
Michael Scudamour.[14]

Purtill went on after his playful continuation of *The Dark Tower* to tell his audience that attacks on the story are unfounded, irresponsible innuendoes and non-arguments. "Is the allegation being made that Hooper *lied*?" He added that I am jealous, possessive, overboard, and out on a limb. Once *The Dark Tower* is proved genuine, he warned, people who have been turned against it might turn against Lewis. *Hoax* is "a terrible, rotten book."

Next, Andrew Walker struck a glancing blow for *The Dark Tower* in *A Christian for All Christians: Essays in Honour of C. S. Lewis*[15]. One of the essays in that collection, Joe Christopher's "Biographies and Bibliographies," mentioned in passing that there are questions about the authenticity of some of Lewis's minor posthumous works such as "The Dark Tower." At that point Walker added "Editor's note: Speaking for ourselves, we are quite convinced that 'The Dark Tower' is a genuine Lewis story (though badly written)."[16]

---

[14] When I received a recording of Purtill's speech, I decided to write to Scudamour myself:

Dear Michael Scudamour,

I understand why you resent my book. After all the dangers you went through in *The Dark Tower*, it must be traumatic to face the possibility that you are the brainchild of Walter Hooper instead of the brainchild of C. S. Lewis. However, if protagonists in novels are to develop well-rounded characters, they usually have to go through trials and disappointments.

Sincerely,

Kathryn Lindskoog

[15] *The Dark Tower* in *A Christian for All Christians: Essays in Honour of C. S. Lewis* (Sevenoaks, Kent, England: Hodder & Stoughton, 1990).

[16] When I respectfully asked Walker what convinced him that *The Dark Tower* is genuine, he replied on 21 August 1990 that he was not willing to engage in "correspondence or written conversations" concerning Hooper or the *Dark Tower*,

Walter Hooper happened to be a member on the board of Walker's C. S. Lewis Centre in London, a Registered Charity "dedicated to tackling the problems of the modern world." Furthermore, Andrew Walker happens to be a member of Stanley Mattson's Committee of Endorsement.

In October 1990 the prestigious Oxford-based quarterly journal *Essays in Criticism* published "C. S. Lewis Darkly" by Nicolas Barker. He included several completely erroneous assumptions or rumors in it: that Lindskoog developed animosity toward Hooper, probably in 1964; that she was tricked by Marchington's 1978 bonfire letter, which enflamed her hostility toward Hooper; that Lindskoog says the entire plot of *The Dark Tower* resembles that in *A Wrinkle in Time*; that Lindskoog thinks Gervase Mathew commented wrongly about *The Dark Tower*; that Lindskoog thinks one of Lewis's students or correspondents might have written *The Dark Tower*; that Lindskoog thinks part of the Lewis juvenilia was forged; that Lindskoog has no evidence at all that *The Dark Tower* is forged; and that Marchington probably wrote his 1978 hoax letter because Hooper had been hounded by bonfire questions since 1964. Barker concluded that the writing in *The Dark Tower* is poor, but that explains why Lewis didn't finish it. "Hooper may possess such gifts ['knowledge and skill in *pastiche*'], may further possess stocks of paper of the sorts used by Lewis and a supply of appropriately coloured inks, but there is no sign that he has put any of them to criminal purpose."

That is when I formally offered to debate any individual or combination of *Dark Tower* defenders (including Lewis's giant publishers with or without their lawyers) orally or in writing, in the format and forum of their choice.[17]

---

and "evidence for and against this and that." He said he has far more important things to do in attempting to continue Lewis's work than to enter into disputes about it. When I suggested that he had already entered into the dispute by publicly defending *Dark Tower*, he warned that if I write to him again he won't reply.

[17] To Walter Hooper, Owen Barfield, and Stanley Mattson from Kathryn Lindskoog:

It has been twelve years since I first raised puzzling questions about C. S. Lewis affairs, and it has been two years since I published even more bewildering questions in *The C. S. Lewis Hoax*. Since then I have revealed many more problems in *The Lewis Legacy*. Strange as it seems, in spite of your combined power, prestige, financial resources, and rhetorical skills, you have not yet felt ready to discuss the facts or address the issues.

I now formally challenge you to extensive written (and possibly oral) public debate. I am willing and eager to debate all three of you at once and any combination

Their answer was silence. (I suppose the magazine *30 Days* might call this "heroic silence" like Hooper's.) It occurred to me that *Tower* defenders seemed to follow Screwtape's advice, "Jargon, not argument, is your best ally."[18]

Finally, in 1991 Don Cregier of the University of Prince Edward Island decided to underwrite an unbiased analysis of *The Dark Tower* by Scotland's famous forensic expert in ascertaining authorship, the Reverend A. Q. Morton.[19] (Morton's book *Literary Detection: How To Prove Authorship and*

---

of your allies. (You are welcome to recruit aides such as William Griffin, Michael Piret, Paul Ford, Tom Schmidt, Barbara Reynolds, Richard L. Purtill, A. N. Wilson, and editors from Collins, Macmillan, Harcourt, and Norton.) I offer the pages of *The Lewis Legacy*; and if you select a more prominent periodical for the debate, so much the better.

I hope to receive your initial written response to my challenge by 20 October 1990; and I will publish that news in the November issue of *The Lewis Legacy*.

[18] From the first paragraph of Screwtape's first letter to Wormwood in *The Screwtape Letters*.

[19] A.Q. Morton, M.A.B.Sc., B.D., F.R.S.E., is a classical scholar, an ordained minister of the Church of Scotland, and the author of eight books and over twenty-three major papers.

His ascertainment of authorship was explained and demonstrated by Jillian Farringdon (who has worked for more than twenty years with Dr. Michael Farringdon of the University College, Swansea, Wales, in the field of literary-computing) her book *Analyzing for Authorship* (University of Wales Press, 1996) and her article "'The Back Road' and the Linguistic Voice of D.H. Lawrence" in *D.H. Lawrence Review* 24:1, 57-64. She began the latter:

The unique physical identity of human beings has long been provable by forensic means: the fingerprint, and, more recently, the D.N.A. genetic code. Now statistical examination of language has established that each human being also has a demonstrably consistent use of language. Different pieces of recorded utterance (spoken or written) produced by one person over a wide period of time, and irrespective of the vagaries of a life-story, including all manner of illness and other trauma, can be shown to be homogeneous: your language-use remains identifiably *yours* throughout your lifetime.

The method, developed by A. Q. Morton, Fellow of the Royal Society of Edinburgh (currently attached as Research Fellow of Glasgow University) is based on adapting a statistical method of averaging samples by cumulative sums (hence its name, the "cusum" technique). This method can plot a person's language-use so as to produce a graph showing deviation from the average of sentence length, and of an identifying feature within the sentence. It has demonstrated that each person's language habits remain consistent, whatever the form (or genre) of utterance....

Fraud in Literature and Documents was favorably reviewed in *Scientific American* in 1979, but he came to Cregier's attention through recent articles about him in the *Times Literary Supplement*[20] and the London *Times*.[21])

Morton used two samples over twenty sentences long from *Out of the Silent Planet*, the same from *Perelandra*, and three such samples from *The Dark Tower*. His sixty-two-page report dated 20 February 1991 reveals that the first twenty-three sentences of chapter 1 of *The Dark Tower* and the first twenty-four sentences of chapter 4 of *The Dark Tower* (in which the stinging man vilely penetrates his first victim) are not by the author of *Out of the Silent Planet* and *Perelandra*. But the first twenty-five sentences of chapter 7, which is the last chapter of *The Dark Tower* (the part that Richard Hodgens considered the beginning of a new book worthy of Lewis), match the author of *Out of the Silent Planet* and *Perelandra*.[22] Chapter 7 contains nothing obscene. Morton calls *The Dark Tower* "a composite work" by more than one author. In private he calls its statistical pattern "a dog's breakfast."

Next, Morton compared "Christian Reunion" to its preface by Hooper and announced his results on ABC Radio in Australia on 7 May 1991. (Hooper was invited to take part in the program but declined.) Morton had found that slightly over forty percent of "Christian Reunion" does not match the writing pattern of C. S. Lewis—but it matches exactly the writing pattern

---

As a forensic test of language-use, accepted since 1991 in the highest Court of Law in England, the Appeal Court, and also in the "Old Bailey" (the Central Criminal Court), as well as in the Central Criminal Court in Dublin, Morton's cusum technique has long passed the stage of experimentation. Over the past four years, it has been successfully tested in the literary field on over 2,000 authors—including blind tests—and in different languages ancient and modern.

It will no doubt become a valuable test of verification in the attribution of literary authorship, both for anonymous texts and doubtful texts. The cusum analysis of *New Essays by Henry Fielding* (University of Virginia Press, 1989)—6 essays found and attributed by Professor Martin Battestin, published with a statistical analysis by Michael Farringdon—is a project planned for undertaking at Virginia next year.

[20] "Authorship: the nature of the habit" (17-23 February 1989): 164, 174.

[21] "Discovering the truth in a word" (16 August 1990): Science and Technology section.

[22] Morton had never heard of Hodgens or his opinions and had no personal interest in the outcome of the test. He says of his testing method, "The only person unlikely to welcome it is the scholar whose convictions it fails to confirm."

of Walter Hooper. The apparent editorial interpolation consists of paragraphs 3, 4, 5, and 6 in the ten-paragraph essay (the section that indicates that the writer does not disagree with any Roman Catholic doctrine).[23]

(Four years later, I would publish this news in *Light in the Shadowlands*. As if in response, in five months Walter Hooper deposited a "Christian Reunion" document in the Bodleian library. Although the handwriting looks like Lewis's, according to one analyst it has more rightward slope and is taller, and the pronoun I is not like Lewis's. The same was also true of the *I* on the back of the Dark Tower manuscript, and there is irony in the idea that a talented forger's hand might equivocate about his identity in this way.)

I sent news of Morton's two tests to several important American periodicals with an interest in Lewis, but to my surprise they were not at all interested. One of the editors responded, "I see little way for us to make use of the information. The allegations are serious ones, and, as you know, they affect rather an extensive network of scholars and self-appointed Lewis representatives."[24]

I decided to turn to less prominent periodicals. In the September 1989 issue of a conservative journal of our culture called *Chronicles*, Gregory McNamee had observed, "Commercial publishers can exist, of course, only to the extent that they profit from their work, and there is no end of recent cases in which greed has triumphed over literary integrity." So a friend of mine sent in the news of A.Q. Morton's tests. Editor Katherine Dalton replied that while there are good questions about whether Mr. Hooper forged *The Dark Tower*, there is simply not enough evidence to convince an outsider. She didn't say how much evidence would be enough to warrant a passing mention in *Chronicles*.

The C. S. Lewis aficionado who heard the forgery charge earliest and fought it hardest, my dear personal friend Stephen Schofield, was exasperated

---

[23] See Morton's article "Ascertaining Authorship Today: The Disunion of Christian Reunion," which includes explanatory graphs, in *The Lamp-Post*, (March 1993): 4-7. Morton concludes, "The fact that a large section of this essay is not by C. S. Lewis and is by someone who cannot be distinguished from Hooper suggests that some explanation of how this came about would be helpful."

[24] On 8 October 1991, A. M. Rosenthall made the following observation in the *New York Times:* "Silence has a loud voice. It shouts, 'Nothing important is happening—don't worry.' So, when something important IS going on, silence is a lie."

by Morton's results and assumed he was a charlatan. In 1986 Clyde Kilby had sent Schofield, editor of the *Canadian C. S. Lewis Journal,* the news that I believed *The Dark Tower* and "Man Born Blind" were forgeries, and Schofield didn't object. In fact, he was enthusiastic about *Hoax* in 1988. But in January 1989 he was visited by Stanley Mattson and invited to an exclusive viewing of Hooper's Dark Tower manuscript in the Bodleian: "I walked into the Bodleian to examine the manuscript and I didn't have to think twice. I know his writing better than my mother's."[25] He confidently instructed me to send the following apology to Hooper, with copies to the press:

Dear Walter Hooper,

In my book, *The C. S. Lewis Hoax,* (I really should not have used the word hoax, and very much regret using it) in Chapter Two some of my conjecture is wrong. I apologize abjectly.

Sincerely,
Kathryn Lindskoog

This instruction struck me as suspiciously similar to the one I had received from Schofield's new acquaintance Stanley Mattson. A few days later author Salman Rushdie received the Ayatollah's demands for a similar apology—along with death threats. I don't suppose Rushdie guessed then how long he was going to be hounded; I know I didn't.

No matter how much I assured Schofield that I am sincere in my conviction that *The Dark Tower* is a forgery, he did not believe that I was sincere. Week after week, month after month, year after year, he wrote dozens and dozens of letters urging me to recant. (Meanwhile, our frequent exchange of letters about other subjects and occasional gifts continued to the end.) He got permission to publish a photocopy of the first page of the Dark Tower manu-

---

[25] Erlend Clouston, "Computer says Lewis novelette is fake," *The Guardian* (7 September 1991): 1. Simultaneously, an article by A.Q. Morton about ascertaining authorship appeared in the September 1991 issue of the *Journal of the Law Society of Scotland.*

script in his *Canadian C. S. Lewis Journal*. My repeated explanations about forgery and famous contemporary forgers struck him as subterfuge because he was sure that if handwriting in the majestic Bodleian Library looks like Lewis's, it must be genuine.

In response to A. Q. Morton's 1991 computer analysis of *The Dark Tower*, Schofield promptly spent well over $1000 (£668) on a couple of "handwriting experts" who added their reports to the Warner Report, agreeing with everyone (including me) that the Dark Tower handwriting looks like Lewis's.[26] Schofield was sorely disappointed that I did not surrender.

After three years, he was more determined than ever to make me confess my error, and as sure as ever that he would know a forgery if he saw one. At the time I was immersed in the subject of forgery while writing my book *Fakes, Frauds & Other Malarkey*, and I impulsively tried my hand at it.[27] I dashed off a good-natured burlesque for Schofield from Utah's notorious forger and murderer Mark Hofmann: "My name is known to literary curators and attorneys from coast to coast," he supposedly boasted. The counterfeit Hofmann concluded, "How could [Lindskoog] recognize Hitler's handwriting if she saw it, since he wrote in German? I enclose a sample to prove my point." I included a photocopy of some forged Hitler handwriting from the newspaper. To my dismay, Schofield printed the letter, the supposedly genuine Hitler handwriting and all, in his spring journal under the heading "American Authority."[28]

---

[26] I studied photocopies of the full reports in detail, looking for meaningful content in vain, and sent inquiries to the authors, R. Morrison, a private detective in Cheshire, and Jacqueline Sawyer, a professional handwriting analyst in Bristol. Neither could tell me of any forgeries they had ever uncovered or how they might identify a good forgery as such if they ever examined one. It turned out that Mrs. Sawyer was getting her information about the *Dark Tower* affair directly from Hooper (perhaps he got her the job), and Mr. Morrison was so uninformed about forgeries that he didn't know the Hitler Diaries were forged. (When I can't believe this, I go back and read my files.)

[27] *Fakes, Frauds and Other Malarkey* (Grand Rapids: Zondervan, 1993).

[28] The real Mark Hofmann has claimed, "As far back as I can remember I have liked to impress people through my deceptions. In fact, some of my earliest memories are of doing magic and card tricks. Fooling people gave me a sense of power and superiority. I believe this is what led to my forging activities." The only trouble with this account is that Hofmann is a chronic liar.

Next, I tried to get him to notice the convoluted satire by sending him a preposterous flurry of silly April Fool's forgeries, a total of fourteen letters and bogus articles in three weeks. Among others, he received a second letter from Hofmann, one from the famous Hitler forger Konrad Kujau, and one from the famous forger Clifford Irving. (I had told Schofield about all these famous forgers.) Not one of the fourteen letters and articles agreed with me. One was a 30 March *Los Angeles Times* article by Ralph Nader defending *The Dark Tower* and quoting Schofield himself. His favorite item of the fourteen was the following, allegedly from the letters column of the 4 April 1992 *Los Angeles Times:*

> I agree with Stephen Schofield that *The Dark Tower* is not a forgery, but it was not written by C. S. Lewis. Part of it was written in my own dining room in about 1950 by my husband the late Cecil R. Jacobsen.
>
> Cecil and four friends from MGM were dreaming up a science fiction plot and used C. S. Lewis's Deep Space trilogy for a starter. One of them, Edward (Streath?), had been a student of Lewis's and was still on very good terms with him. The men took turns, then sent their first six chapters to Lewis, who agreed to add a bit of his own and to copy the whole thing out for Edward. (He had sent Lewis many food parcels after the war.)
>
> At some point the men went their separate ways and the project was abandoned. (David published two minor science-fiction novels a few years later.) I still remember that Cecil began the first page by saying there were four men present, then listing five.
>
> FLORENCE JACOBSEN
> Glendora

Schofield was so happy to be proved right about Lewis's handwriting that he sent me a letter joyfully admitting that *The Dark Tower* story was "baloney," so bad it couldn't possibly be by Lewis. In his enthusiasm, he convinced *The Guardian* to publish Florence Jacobsen's news. I warned *The Guardian* that there was no Florence Jacobsen, and Schofield was shocked to learn that he had been fooled. I sent him a sincere apology and a list of the fourteen forgeries, but he still thought some of them were genuine. He couldn't believe it was all an innocent April Fool's spoof. He reported my deed as if it was a criminal scheme, and it is sometimes repeated that way to this day.[29] I regretted accidentally tricking my friend so badly and never mentioned his brief admission that *The Dark Tower* was too bad to be by Lewis. Stephen Schofield left these Shadowlands in 1993, and I miss him.[30]

When *Guardian* reporter Erlend Clouston was preparing his Schofield-generated article "Computer says Lewis novelette is fake," he interviewed Hooper on the telephone, and Hooper denied having added anything to any work by Lewis. He said, "The Dark Tower manuscript is in the Bodleian Library. The man who exposed the Hitler Diaries has confirmed it is genuine.[31] Almost everything of Lewis's I have published in the past three years has been dismissed by some people as a forgery. Some of the views expressed they don't like, and they find it easier to say they are forgeries than to change their views of Lewis."[32] A spokesman for HarperCollins told

---

[29]The C. S. Lewis entry in the 1993 edition of the *Encyclopedia of Science Fiction* immortalizes my prank that went awry in a way that misrepresents it, based on an inaccurate report in a science fiction newspaper: "It has been strongly suggested by Kathryn Lindskoog (1934-) in *The C. S. Lewis Hoax* (1988) that the Reverend Hooper—CSL's secretary for only one month—forged various items of posthumously published CSL material included in *The Dark Tower*, a charge which has been rebutted. Lindskoog has offered a vigorous counter-rebuttal in 'The Dark Scandal: Science Fiction Forgery' (1992 *Quantum* #42) but in that year it was revealed that she herself had been forging evidence (letters)—indeed, she admitted as much. What there can be no doubt of is that the works assembled by Hooper have affected readers as being both sexually poisonous and egregiously amateur." "C.S. Lewis," *Encyclopedia of Science Fiction*, ed. Peter Nicholls and John Clute (St. Martin's Press, 1993) 716-17.

[30] When Steve died, I said to my husband that I was imagining Steve's surprise when C. S. Lewis welcomed him to Heaven with the words, "I *did not* write *The Dark Tower*." "You will be just as surprised," John replied, "if when you die C. S. Lewis welcomes you to Hell with the words, "I *did* write *The Dark Tower*."

[31] Hooper was evidently referring to the fact that on 26 June 1990 eighty-eight year old fiber chemist Julius Grant (one of the men who exposed the Hitler Diaries) went to the Bodleian Library at Stanley Mattson's behest to look at the handwriting on the Dark Tower manuscript. He did not test the paper (his field of expertise). He said the handwriting looked like Lewis's (not his field of expertise). He did not confirm that the Dark Tower manuscript was genuine.

[32] As editor of *God in the Dock* (Grand Rapids: Eerdmans, 1970), Hooper is familiar with Lewis's essay "Bulverism" (pages 271-277) in which Lewis denounces the ploy of assuming that an opponent's position is wrong and attributing it to wrong motives. Lewis says, "you must show *that* a man is wrong before you start explaining

Clouston that they have no reason to believe that *The Dark Tower* is not genuine and that they had sold five hundred copies of *Dark Tower* in the past two months.

I had sent news of A. Q. Morton's findings to the Wade Center, and in September 1991 I sent the steering committee what I considered an exciting and impartial suggestion, with a request for a response.[33] The answer was silence. I also sent Morton's results to all twelve Mattson jurists, requesting a brief response of any kind. Only Jennifer Larson responded, and that was to express her lack of interest.

The overwhelming silence in Lewis circles was balanced by keen interest from a few distinguished outsiders. H. Boone Porter, Senior Editor of *The Living Church*, wrote, "As you have made us aware, there is a great deal of falsification in the literature of the religious world, and A. Q. Morton's test may establish a new standard of integrity." Richard Wilbur wrote, "The Rev. Morton's method of detecting false attribution by the analysis of stylistic habits impresses me, insofar as I can understand it..." Michael Aeschliman wrote, "Your material from Morton seems to me to spread authoritative new light on the issues." Russell Kirk wrote, "Your thesis about the authorship of The Dark Tower certainly seems thoroughly substantiated."

The year of Morton's tests was also the year when Jared C. Lobdell and Peter Schakel sprang to the defense of *The Dark Tower*. The 1991 collection *Word and Story in C. S. Lewis*, edited by Peter J. Schakel and Charles A. Huttar, included Lobdell's "C. S. Lewis's Ransom Stories and Their Eighteenth-Century Ancestry." In the book's preface, Schakel claims that Lobdell's

---

why he is wrong." Lewis used the following hypothetical illustration. Someone suspects that Lewis's belief he has a large bank balance is the result of wishful thinking. That person can't prove his idea by examining Lewis's psyche; instead, he must check the figures. "If you find my arithmetic correct, then no amount of vapouring about my psychological condition can be anything but a waste of time."

[33] "It seems that the forgery charges are not going to go away, and right now the Wade Center has a wonderful opportunity to contribute in an even-handed way to establishment of a genuine Lewis canon. I propose that the Wade Center should invite the Reverend A. Q. Morton of Scotland, the world's leading stylometrist, to come to Wheaton College in 1992..."

Dark Tower expertise is "seminal"—a strange claim if he has read Lobdell's essay, because Lobdell admits there that he has read *Dark Tower* only twice.[34]

Lobdell seeks to show that the Ransom trilogy would have been better-ordered if Lewis had completed *The Dark Tower* instead of replacing it with *Perelandra*. He readily admits that *Perelandra* is in itself a more memorable book, but for the sake of the series he would have preferred *Dark Tower*. He concludes with a long addendum titled "The Authorship of *The Dark Tower,*" where he gives seven reasons for thinking it genuine:

1. Lewis had no recognizable style until sometime in the 1940s; until then his writing was inconsistent and imitative. (Is there one serious student of Lewis anywhere who believes that Lewis had no recognizable style before 1940?)
2. *The Pilgrim's Regress* (1931) is almost as poorly written as *The Dark Tower* and as dark spirited. (If so, why did Lewis continue to value *Pilgrim's Regress* and encourage people to read it?)
3. The best parts of *Dark Tower* are too superb to be by anyone except Lewis. (What parts are so good that no one but Lewis could have written them?)
4. The dull parts of *Dark Tower* are too dull and unlike Lewis to be the work of a forger. (How can one tell what kind of work an unknown Lewis forger would or wouldn't do?)
5. Lewis tried to make *The Dark Tower* allegorical, and it didn't work. (Isn't this circular reasoning? How does this differ from a forger trying and failing?)
6. Lewis was fascinated by J. W. Dunne. (If that is true, it has no bearing on the forgery issue; but what source is there for this assertion other than Hooper's *Dark Tower* notes?)
7. Because Lewis was not a scientific genius, he could not complete *The Dark Tower*. (How does this differ from a forger being unable to complete the story because the forger was not a scientific genius?)

---

[34] Jared Lobdell revealed in 1994 that in the mid-1960s Hooper asked him whether he should publish C. S. Lewis's unfinished novel or not. "I told him yes."

Lobdell concludes that the whole question of forgery is a nuisance rather than a useful scholarly endeavor, and he ends by recommending John Rateliffe's overwhelmingly hostile 1989 review "The Kathryn Lindskoog Hoax."[35]

On 31 January 1992, on a nationwide radio program, Pastor Jerry Root, co-editor of *The Quotable C. S. Lewis*, portrayed *Hoax* as a tool of Satan.[36] I purchased a recording of the interview and took careful notes. "She seems to imply in her book that Hooper might be a homosexual...and makes it sound like Lewis was a womanizer and a fornicator and so on." Root said my book is full of inaccuracies; my motive seemed to be anger and pride, and my purpose was to sow hatred. "Satan...wants people to doubt Lewis's character, thereby doubt his writing." He claimed that A. N. Wilson drew poisonous charges against Lewis from my book. I wrote to Root in bewilderment. In reply, he informed me that he was preparing a lecture titled "Rescuing C. S. Lewis from the Hoax" to deliver at the 1992 conference of the Evangelical Theological Society.[37] Because the lecture failed to materialize, I suspect that he might have found *Hoax* too difficult to attack. On 30 November 1998 he appeared on the Ray Suarez program on National Public Radio along with Dabney Hart and Michael Aeschliman. After Aeschliman's hearty endorsement of *The C. S. Lewis Hoax* and *Light in the Shadowlands*, Root countered

---

[35] Jared C. Lobdell, "C.S. Lewis's Ransom Stories and Their Eighteenth-Century Ancestry" in *Word and Story in C. S. Lewis*, eds., Peter J. Schakel and Charles A. Huttar (Columbia MO: University of Missouri Press, 1991) 213-31. Lobdell was an early member of the New York C. S. Lewis Society. In his conclusion Lobdell indicates that he was constrained to add "The Authorship of *The Dark Tower*" to his essay and disliked wasting time on such an unworthy topic.

[36] Moody Broadcasting Network's "Open Line" program from Chicago, hosted by Greg Wheatley.

[37] In a letter dated 23 March 1992 Root estimated that *Hoax* is 85 percent false, but he gave no specifics. He revealed that in the 1980s he served for ten years as assistant pastor at College Church in Wheaton, Illinois, where Bob O'Donnell was one of his parishioners. (After that he became a California pastor.) According to Root, O'Donnell tearfully told him that I published untruths about O'Donnell in *The C. S. Lewis Hoax*. I asked Root what I had said falsely about O'Donnell so I could apologize; but the answer was silence.

Root has visited Oxford often, once for six months and seeing Hooper socially two or three times a week. He also knows Douglas Gresham and Barbara Reynolds, and has discussed *Hoax* with her. He is now an instructor at Wheaton College.

with "Although I have the highest respect for Michael and his work, I disagree. I feel like the *Lewis Hoax* is not a very accurate book, and I disagree with its presuppositions...Anyway, I think the debate's died down quite a bit of late."

In 1992 David Downing of Westmont College defended *The Dark Tower* in his book about the Ransom novels, *Planets in Peril*. He says, "Even though 'The Dark Tower' is only about seventy-five pages, it does reveal the mind, and narrative skill, of Lewis." (He doesn't say how the sexually perverse, badly written *Dark Tower* could reveal Lewis's Christian mind and superb narrative skill.) He suspects that the book is based on one of Lewis's nightmares. He devotes a four-page appendix to analyzing it and admits that it is flawed. MacPhee comes near to stupidity, and Ransom lacks the richness of character that he has in *Out of the Silent Planet* and *Perelandra*. He and his colleagues lack the holiness needed to balance the hellish nature of the Stingingman, who is by far the most powerful image; as a result the vision of horror is not balanced by a vision of goodness. "Despite its incompleteness and evident flaws," Downing concludes unflinchingly, "the 'Dark Tower' remains an intriguing piece of work."

Ironically, the first *Dark Tower* reference Downing cites is a review by Julian Barnes in *The New Republic;* but he has the reviewer's name wrong. The reviewer is Ursula Le Guin, and her review is a scathing condemnation of *The Dark Tower*.[38] Although Downing warns readers that the book is dark, he fails to warn them that it is much despised, and he never mentions that its authenticity is questioned. It seems surprising that someone who spent a day in 1989 serving on the Mattson jury would write an entire book about the Ransom novels and fail to include so much as one footnote about the controversy.

In 1992 James Como, editor of *CSL* and leader of the New York C. S. Lewis Society, finally stirred. In 1977 he had warned Hooper about a future battle for *The Dark Tower;* but he didn't take part in it until 1992, and then in a most peripheral way—by praising Hooper's expanded bibliography and thus endorsing its posthumous contents, by identifying Hooper again as Lewis's personal secretary, by seeming to imply that Lewis scholars with evangelical affiliations are cultists, and by claiming for himself the high ground above the fray. He did all this in the new 1992 edition of his *C. S.*

---

[38] Ursula Le Guin, "The Dark Tower," *The New Republic* (16 April 1977).

Lewis at the Breakfast Table. His restraint is surprising in light of his personal interest in *The Dark Tower,* his combative spirit, and his startling animosity toward Clyde Kilby and myself expressed in his letters in the Chapel Hill collection.[39]

Como's restraint in *C. S. Lewis at the Breakfast Table* is especially surprising in light of his expressed gratitude to editor John Ferroni, who was Walter Hooper's editor at Harcourt (where *The Dark Tower* and other posthumous Lewis works are published). On Harcourt stationery Ferroni has called the *Hoax* charges absurd. He told an inquirer he had worked with Father (sic) Hooper for many years and could vouch for him as a man of the greatest integrity. He had not read *The C. S. Lewis Hoax,* nor did he intend to; and he predicted that my ill-conceived (and probably unChristian) charges would blow away.[40]

Como's connection to *The Dark Tower* evidently dates back at least as far as Ferroni's, because Hooper let him preview the story in typescript. On 29 May 1975 he wrote to Hooper that it had really stayed with him. On 12 February 1977 he warned Hooper that of all Lewis's books, *The Dark Tower* is the one which (however unjustly) could most easily be ambushed by "the intellectualoids," such as a certain "idiot" they knew of. On 2 May he wrote to Hooper that *The Dark Tower* was magnificent, what he called a "perfect" gem.

---

[39] On 7 March 1975 Como called another Lewis expert a creep, and then called Kilby resentful, irrational, and libelous. On 2 April 1977 he exclaimed about how wrong Protestants are. On 29 October 1977 he exclaimed about Kilby's possessiveness. On 21 December 1977 he warned Hooper to be on guard for an assault from Kilby, who was old, ill, desperate, and apt to pull something. On 30 December 1977 he wrote in jocular mood that Hooper shouldn't take "no s——" from Wheaton. On 11 February 1978 he wrote about Kilby's false humility. On 25 February 1978 he asked if Kilby was going mad. On 18 March 1978 he warned Hooper to keep his powder dry concerning Kilby; "kick a— and take names later." On 6 May 1978 he wrote "S—— Kilby." On 11 November 1978 he said that the atmosphere at Wheaton College was oppressive and the staff was a disappointing crew not worth suing. On 22 January 1979 he hoped to make plans with Hooper and Eugene McGovern to combat Lindskoog. On 12 February 1979 he wrote that Clarence Walhout of Calvin College must be a co-conspirator with Kilby and Lindskoog. He declared that although Gilbert Meilaender and Sheldon Vanauken have very little intellectual integrity, they are not devoid of intellect; but Terri Williams and Lindskoog lack both.

[40] An unpublished letter from John Ferroni to Paul McCusker, 31 January 1989.

Within a year of *The Dark Tower*'s publication, Como was assembling the first edition of *C. S. Lewis at the Breakfast Table* for editor William Griffin at Macmillan. On 18 March 1978 Como assured Hooper in a letter[41] that he would not include any essays by "Kilbyites." The only way that Kilby himself would ever get into the book, Como boasted, would be by buying a copy and writing his name in it.[42] (Ironically, his genial-sounding dedication to both editions of the book includes the phrase "to the rational opposition of goodwill.")

On the first page of his 1992 preface, Como indicates that his selection of contributors (twenty-four, including Como) forms a providential kind of "Community" protecting Lewis from misuse. "And none—ever—approximates 'cultism' or remotely occasions it in the reader." He does not state here who the perpetrators of Lewis "cultism" are, but he had already excoriated a certain number of us in that vein elsewhere.[43] In Como's view, he and his contributors exemplify the fact that "the way attentive and receptive people speak of one is a reliable guide to one's worth." He warned readers, "Lewis

---

[41] In the Chapel Hill Collection.

[42] As if in extension of his decision to exclude "Kilbyites" from his book, during his entire 1992-2000 tenure as editor of *CSL, Bulletin of the New York C. S. Lewis Society*, the names Lindskoog and Vanauken never appeared, not even upon the death of Vanauken. In contrast, the editors before and after Como, Jerry Daniel and Robert Trexler, were cordial and published Lindskoog articles.

In "The Inner Ring" in *The Weight of Glory* (Grand Rapids: Eerdmans, 1965) 60-62, Lewis says, "But your genuine Inner Ring exists for exclusion. There'd be no fun if there were no outsiders. The invisible line would have no meaning unless most people were on the wrong side of it. Exclusion is no accident: it is the essence." Lewis says that Marx and Freud were wrong: the economic motive and the erotic motive don't account for everything that goes on in human life. Inclusion and social intimacy are as important a lure. The desire to be inside inner rings is one of the great factors in "the world as we know it—this whole pell-mell of struggle, competition, confusion, graft, disappointment, and [public relations]..."

[43] In Volume 10 of the Yale series *Children's Literature*, in 1982 Como condemned "shabby" books on C. S. Lewis "from publishers of religious evangelicalism," citing Clyde Kilby's *Images of Salvation in the Fiction of C. S. Lewis,* Gilbert Meilaender's *The Taste for the Other*, Leanne Payne's *The Real Presence*, and my own *Lion of Judah in Never-Never Land.* "A small company of like-thinking people—in the absence of disinterested and rational opposition—can sneak by almost anything." I suspect that Como never examined these books, or he would realize that Meilaender is not an evangelical, and *Lion of Judah* sneaked by Lewis himself—with high commendation.

does not differ from any famous literary personality. His prominence has occasioned a fair amount of professional jealousy, personal resentment, academic self-aggrandizement, and plain old literary politics."

This scattershot accusation seems to be a veiled reference to my detective work, since Como has attached the terms *Evangelical aggrandizement* and *literary politics* to me elsewhere. [44]

Como indicates in Volume 10 of *Children's Literature* that my work on Lewis is "equivocating, narrow, and not disinterested," and "little more than enthusiastic cartographies." "In short, much current work on Lewis, posturing as scholarship, consists of diatribe, pedantic analysis, or cheerleading formulas." Given that opinion of my serious but noncontroversial early work on Lewis, his opinion of *Sleuthing C. S. Lewis* would be interesting to read. [45] (He once informed a colleague that I'm a cripple and he doesn't intend to answer my letters. In light of his title *C. S. Lewis at the Breakfast Table*, if I wrote again I would be tempted to advise him "Wake up and smell the coffee.")

Thinking a petition might help, in the summer of 1992 I sent out a letter to about a hundred people. It began, "I hope that because of your interest in the integrity of the C. S. Lewis canon you will read and consider signing the enclosed petition. I am sending it to a few writers, editors, academics, religious leaders, concerned members of the reading public, and personal acquaintances of C. S. Lewis. Those who sign do so desiring a resolution to the contradictions and doubts that plague the posthumous C. S. Lewis canon." The last sentence of the petition said, "It is time to get the posthumous Lewis canon into the public forum where evidence, logic, and persuasion can begin to validate it or to correct it."

Eighty people signed, including such luminaries as Arthur C. Clarke (twice winner of the Hugo Award), Katherine Paterson (twice winner of the Newbery Medal), American Poet Laureate Richard Wilbur (winner of the National Book Award and the Bollingen Award, twice winner of the Pulitzer

---

[44] See Como's 22 January 1979 and 12 February 1979 letters to Hooper in the Chapel Hill collection.

[45] In his excellent article "Mere Lewis" on pages 109-117 of the spring 1994 issue of *The Wilson Quarterly*, Como limits his disapproval of Lewis commentators outside his circle to one gentle remark: "A patently uneven industry of anecdotal memoirs, biographies..., and especially commentary continues to flourish."

Prize), Lyle Dorsett (past Wade Center Curator), Algis Budrys (Editor, *Tomorrow: Speculative Fiction*), William Hasker (Editor, *Christian Scholar's Review*), and Christopher Ricks (Co-editor, Oxford's *Essays in Criticism*)[46].

I sent the signed petition with a personal letter[47] to about forty individuals or groups with influence in C. S. Lewis affairs. To the following representatives of the Lewis Estate: Elizabeth Stevens of the Curtis Brown and John Farquharson literary agency in London, Owen Barfield, and Walter Hooper. To the following academic institutions: Mary Clapinson (Keeper of Western Manuscripts at the Bodleian Library in Oxford), Marjorie Lamp Mead (The Marion E. Wade Center Committee, Wheaton College), David K. Winter (President, Westmont College). To the following publishers: Lesley Walmsley (Editor, HarperCollins, London), Jon Pott (Editor, Wm. B. Eerdmans), editors of the Macmillan Publishing Company, John Radziewicz (Senior Editor, Harcourt Brace Jovanovich).[48] To the following C. S. Lewis

---

[46] For the petition and the list of signatories, see Appendix 6.

[47] The letters varied. The following sample is chosen at random.
Dear Dr. Walker:
I am writing for the eighty signatories on the next page, including such internationally famous contemporary authors as Arthur C. Clarke, Katherine Paterson, Richard Wilbur, and Christopher Ricks.
Please read our petition requesting that the C. S. Lewis Centre should now begin to freely address in print the problems of the posthumous C. S. Lewis canon. This emergency call for a public forum is unique in contemporary Christian scholarship.
I assume that in regard to the Dead Sea Scrolls you agree with Hershel Shanks, editor of *Biblical Archeology Review*: "Let us cast our vote for freedom of scholarship. Let us place our faith in the belief that truth will prevail in the marketplace of ideas—if only the competition of ideas remains unfettered." May Lewis studies become unfettered!
Thank you for whatever acknowledgment or response you can send me; I will report responses soon to my Board of Advisors, and later to all the petition signatories.

[48] On 8 November 1992 I sent the following reply to Mr. Radziewicz's response to the petition:
On 1 November 1992 you sent a photocopy of several three-year-old misstatements by A. N. Wilson as your only response to the C. S. Lewis Petition and its signatories.
I had enclosed for your interest a public endorsement from Lyle W. Dorsett, curator of the Marion E. Wade Center: "I think [Lindskoog's] case grows stronger all the time." You countered with A. N. Wilson's claim that

organizations: Stanley Mattson (C. S. Lewis Foundation for Christian Higher Education), Carl Swift (Southern California C. S. Lewis Society), M. J. Logsdon (Salinas Valley C. S. Lewis Society), Art Lindsley (C. S. Lewis Institute of Arlington, Virginia), Andrew Walker (C. S. Lewis Centre for the Study of Religion and Modernity, London), The Inklings—Gesellschaft fur Literatur and Asthetik (Aachen, Germany), Michael Macdonald (C. S. Lewis Institute, Seattle Pacific University), James Como (New York C. S. Lewis Society), The Council of Stewards (Mythopoeic Society), and Paul Blattner (Portland C. S. Lewis Society).

The results were revealing. There was no response at all from Stevens, Barfield, or Hooper. Among Lewis publishers there was no response from HarperCollins, Eerdmans, or Macmillan. Among Lewis organizations there was no response from Mattson's C. S. Lewis Foundation, the C. S. Lewis Centre, the New York C. S. Lewis Society, the Mythopoeic Society, or the German Inklings. Among academic institutions, there were courteous demurrals from Michael Macdonald of Seattle Pacific University; David Winter of Westmont College; and Raymond E. Whiteman of Wheaton College, who spoke for the Wade Center. Negative responses arrived from Harcourt Brace Jovanovich and the Bodleian Library; both insisted that

---

Dorsett once said that Lindskoog had gone too far. In fact, Dorsett denies that and other erroneous allegations made by Wilson.

You answer the Petition itself with A. N. Wilson's erroneous claim "A manuscript of [The Dark Tower] is deposited in the Bodleian Library in Oxford and experts have made it clear beyond doubt that it is written in Lewis's hand." This 1989 claim seems irrelevant for the following reasons:

1. The C. S. Lewis Petition is about 12 possible literary forgeries, not about even one document forgery.

2. No document experts have ever tested the *Dark Tower* document or claimed to do so, and none have vouched for its authenticity.

3. There has been no provenance for the *Dark Tower* document since the alleged provenance was disproved by a letter from Warren Lewis.

4. As Nicolas Barker, Deputy Keeper of the British Library, has pointed out, ink on the 1928 *Dark Tower* document did not exist before 1950.

5. As Alastair Fowler of the University of Edinburgh has pointed out, document authenticity would not in itself prove authorship anyway.

I must regretfully report to the C. S. Lewis Petition signatories and to readers of *The Lewis Legacy* that Harcourt is evidently opposed to attempts at authentication of the posthumous C. S. Lewis canon.

because the handwriting on the Dark Tower document resembles Lewis's, the matter is settled.[49]

I began 1993 by sending the signed petition to a distinguished member of the Mattson jury and the Board of the C. S. Lewis Foundation, who teaches at Westmont College. On 23 January he answered with a fusillade. In his letter he accused me of descending into hell like Wentworth in *Descent into Hell* by Charles Williams. He spoke of my poison pen, my silly suspicions, my trivial obsession, my victims, and my lack of a well-developed understanding of the scholarly endeavor. In the future, he assured me, he will save his time for the work of God's kingdom and destroy unopened any letter from me; and he will not read materials written by me that come to him by other means. He ended with a memorable image: even if my literary views should be vindicated, at the great ongoing banquet of Lewis appreciation, where good meat and strong drink from others is spread on the table, my contribution is no more than a passing of gas [sic]. The academic vehemence and religious zeal of certain of the *Dark Tower* defenders has always amazed me.

Three surprising things happened as if in answer to the petition: the Portland Society issued its own independent statement in October 1992[50], the Southern California *Lamp-Post* accepted an article by A. Q. Morton, and the *Newsletter of the Salinas Valley C. S. Lewis Society* was successfully launched in November 1992. (The society was stillborn, and the title was changed later to the *Salinas Valley Lewisian*.) The Salinas editor was *Dark Tower* defender Michael Logsdon, a friend of Stanley Mattson.

Logsdon's newsletter soon developed what he called a "leisured friendly debate" (not my idea of a debate, especially near the end) about the forgery question. The forgery claims wouldn't go away if they were ignored, he said, and so he would seek to refute them. "I'm also spurred forward by the belief that Walter Hooper since about 1978 has been consistently and wrongly

---

[49] A few years later an innocent inquirer asked Douglas Gresham, spokesman for C S Lewis Pte, for his response to the signed petition displayed at http.//www.discovery.org/lewis/petition.htm. At first Gresham didn't know what she was talking about, but he said later she must mean "the one that Kathryn made up a while back." The only names she cited that Gresham was familiar with, he said, were those of Arthur C. Clarke and Lyle Dorsett; and if she talked to them, Gresham thought, she would find that they have changed their views somewhat.

[50] See Appendix 7.

attacked, and that I find myself in a position of being able to offer some help...Plus, it's fun."[51]

This is the only forum where any defender of *The Dark Tower* has been willing to discuss our differences, and I agree that it was usually fun for both of us; I took Logsdon's outspoken style in good spirit. In Issue 4 he said "dealing with the likes of dear Kay can be a bit frustrating," "ultimately her claims are insignificant," "if she's ignored she won't go away," and "Why, in God's name?!" In Issue 6 he said "*Get real, K!*" and "not good, K, not good." In Issue 7 he said, "My suggestion, K, is that you not bother so much about this question," "K...please. We wrestle with this sort of thing so often," "this goes beyond bad journalism," "it's downright misleading, and does much more harm than good," "not answering your question means nothing more than that," "Please don't make this kind of statement anymore," "maybe, just maybe, you worry about them too much," "It's not worth your or anyone else's time." "hounding the likes of Owen Barfield," and "not worth anyone's time."

In Issue 8 he said, "maybe you shouldn't bother with this angle so much," "of course—*OF BLOODY COURSE!*," "Hoo boy," "needing to pry in that way," "the Lindskoogianly-incorrect idea that Walter has the right to have honest changes of mind," and "you shouldn't bother with them." In Issue 9 he said "The bonfire date question is a dead horse" and "Hammer anything hard enough, K, and you're sure to find some cracks." In Issue 10 he said "Mr Tennyson has put the whole matter to rest" and "You, K, won't accept this, of course."

In Issue 11 he said, "Do you deny that for you Walter's guilt is a done deal?" "by this time things are getting a bit...ahem...vague," "What's the point, K?!," "goodness, K!," "Why, K, do you consider any opinion contrary to you and your claims to be an *ad hominem* attack?," "I must seriously criticise what I perceive to be the unChristian spirit in which you present it," "*judgmentalism*," "you make such a big deal," "good Lord, K, do you believe," "that's no one's business but his" and "doesn't deserve any flack from you." Finally, in Issue 13 he said "I might pull a 'K'-ism on you here."

One of the unusual things that Logsdon's newsletter accomplished was to bring Douglas Gresham out into the *Hoax* discussion for the first time. Not

---

[51] *The Salinas Valley C. S. Lewis Society Newsletter*, 4: 1.

one to mince words, Gresham said "Mind your own business, Kathryn," "a ridiculous scenario," "it doesn't work because it is not honest," "Kathryn's assumptions," "Kathryn v The World debate," "rubbish," "nonsense," "lousy journalism, Kathryn," "the same sort of journalistic misconstruction that we have all become used to from Kathryn." "I disagree with most of what Kathryn writes," and "I have far more important things to do than spend time in the boring pursuit of researching my own writing and letters in order to make absolutely sure that I get everything exactly right, which is, after all, the first duty of a commentator or dialectician."[52] In spite of his exasperation with my methodical emphasis upon factual details, he pointed out the fact that we are on friendly terms. I took it all in good spirit, quietly amused.

Logsdon ended Issue 12 with an article by his best friend, Juan Fajardo (not a Lewisian), accusing me of flagrant intellectual incompetence and possible falsification of sources. I was disappointed when Issue 13 arrived without my rebuttal to Fajedo, announcing that there would be no more issues and, in my opinion, misrepresenting the outcome of our "debate." I commented later that I've never before heard of a debate in which one debater cuts off the debate permanently when he chooses, without giving his opponent a chance to make a closing statement. Reader Martin Ward of Durham, England, replied, "Actually, the last tactic is not unknown, even in a debate. It is called 'surrender'."

In the autumn 1993 an English combatant waged a frontal assault in the Salinas newsletter. Aiden Mackey is an Inklings bookseller and the founding director of the G. K. Chesterton Centre in Bedford. As a friend of Walter Hooper, he says, he cannot possibly believe charges against him, "I have the pleasure, the fun, and the honour to know Walter Hooper fairly well...I have so far refrained from becoming involved with the extraordinary claim that *The Dark Tower*, and other Lewis material, is not by Lewis at all...but I am disappointed that the silly business still drags on."

Mackey took several paragraphs to demonstrate that *ejaculate* is not a pornographic word, under the misapprehension that I think it is. Then he stated that my unworthy accusation should never have seen print, but that in fairness to all concerned, the C. S. Lewis Foundation went to the trouble and

---

[52] An odd position, in light of the fact that Gresham is so often a Lewis commentator.

expense of requesting an authority of great stature to examine the manuscript with other scholars. Their report should have settled the matter once and for all, Mackey concluded. He included the phrases "This is almost beyond belief," "Can it be that K.L. has so little command of the English language," "[she] should never have been granted the dignity of a reply," and "May we not now lay this diversion to rest?"

After my response was published, Mackey fired another volley in the winter 1993 issue:

> Unless something unexpected transpires, this will be my last note on the Lindskoog Fiasco. If people are prepared to indulge her, this correspondence will continue *ad nauseam,* and I have serious work to do...Mrs. Lindskoog claims to be surprised because I wrote that *it appears* (those italics were not in my original) that she based her claim not upon knowledge of forgery, but upon what she saw as internal evidence. Now she tells me she has "a lifelong avocational interest in forgeries and forgery detection," has written a book on the subject and has uncovered more than one forgery. This sort of thing simply won't do in serious discussion among adults...
>
> My response to that opaque nonsense...I have known of people clutching at straws before, but never at straws so patently nonexistent...Now she is running this way and that and dragging in all manner of irrelevancies and side-issues to conceal her discomfiture. If Kathryn Lindskoog wishes to retrieve any vestige of academic credibility, she must at once admit she has been quite wrong, and that she has no evidence (we are uninterested in her instincts or hunches or emotions in the matter) that *The Dark Tower* is other than the work of C. S. Lewis. My intervention in this absurdity is now ended.

Aidan Mackey is one of the four *Dark Tower* defenders who are known to have received Wade Center grants since their inception in 1982. The four are William Griffin (1983), Barbara Reynolds (1986), Paul Ford (1987), and Aidan Mackey (1988). Ford and Griffin first protested my questions about Hooper in the *Los Angeles Times* in 1979. Mackey and Griffin attacked me in print more recently, and Ford and Reynolds were Mattson jury members.

None of the four answered my 1989 letter about the matter.[53] Another grantee said in the question period after his Wade Center lecture that my charge about *The Dark Tower* is "nonsense," and yet another grantee suddenly cut off our friendly contact and told me never to mention her name in print because she can't afford to be associated with me. This makes a total of six grantees opposed in various ways to my attempt to correct the Lewis legacy. So far, not one scholar known to support my efforts has received a grant. This situation has not been lost upon knowledgeable people who would like to receive a grant or who might dream of a future appointment at the Wade Center.[54] I know of at least one professor (not a grantee) who appreciates my efforts but is unwilling to let that be known.

Grantees are chosen informally by the steering committee of the Wade Center, a strictly anonymous group of individuals (not all of them in Illinois) who oversee all Wade Center decisions and policy. I was told shortly after publication of *Hoax* that this committee had three meetings to decide upon a strategy for handling the "problem," and they decided that the best course was institutional neutrality, although individuals might be discretely partisan. Committee member Luci Shaw, who has not read *The C. S. Lewis Hoax*, has very actively supported Stanley Mattson and his efforts to discredit my work. The Wade Center's long, productive friendship with Owen Barfield might have been another factor. In spite of such influences, however, the Wade maintains silence, neither condemning nor encouraging investigation of the authenticity of the suspect posthumous Lewis canon. Christopher Mitchell, the third curator, inherited a sensitive position in that regard.

In the September 1993 issue of *The Lamp-Post*, John Beversluis had lobbed a small verbal missile my way while engaged in a spirited defense of his own book that was under attack for attacking Lewis, *C. S. Lewis and the Search*

---

[53] In 2000 Reynolds and I became friendly correspondents because of our common enthusiasm about her friend Dorothy Sayers and our mutual love of Dante. She still doubted that my charges in *The C. S. Lewis Hoax* were correct, but that was not our focus.

[54] It is commonly said that the grants are strictly reserved for research done at the Wade Center, but that is not always the case. One recipient received a Wade grant for a project involving fifteen standard books by Lewis, powerful computer equipment, and nothing else; every bit of that project was done about 2,000 miles from Wheaton College. There is no written list of qualifications for the grants, there is no way to apply, and winners are not told how they were selected.

for a Rational Religion.[55] "I want to begin by distancing myself as far as possible from various criticisms which have recently [sic] been lodged against Hooper: not only charges of critics like Kathryn Lindskoog—according to whom he almost singlehandedly masterminded a massive 'C. S. Lewis Hoax' by telling outright lies and inventing an elaborate mythology about the extent and intimacy of his associating with Lewis—but also the deflating chatter of milder critics like A. N. Wilson....I have no sympathy—and in fact deplore—these attempts to impugn the integrity of, or otherwise belittle, a man whose biographical research and editorial research and editorial industriousness have placed all Lewis students in his debt."

At the end of 1993 George Musacchio launched a gentle rear guard action to enhance Downing's position as a key defender of *The Dark Tower*. Musacchio wrote a rave review of Downing's *Planets in Peril* for *The Lamp-Post*:

> There is an appendix on *The Dark Tower* in which Downing discusses "its distinctive Lewisian qualities." An admirably knowledgeable reader of Lewis, a veteran of years in the college classroom discussing Lewis with students, Downing concludes, "it does reveal the mind, and narrative skill, of Lewis." [56]

Musacchio is also a staunch defender of Hooper's claim that *A Grief Observed* is fiction.

On 2 December 1994 the world's leading *Dark Tower* defender, Stanley Mattson, brought an amazing new ally into the battle. Timothy Stoen was then a private attorney in his late fifties in Montecito, California,[57] but he

---

[55] John Beversluis, "Did C. S. Lewis Lose His Faith?" *The Lamp-Post of the Southern California C. S. Lewis Society* (September 1993): 17.

[56] *The Lamp-Post of the Southern California C. S. Lewis Society* (December 1993). In his 25 January 1980 letter to Barbara Reynolds in the Chapel Hill Collection, Hooper alleged that George Musacchio told him I quit the Southern California C. S. Lewis Society because I was defeated in an attempt to exclude male pronouns from that journal at its founding. To the contrary, my efforts to influence the journal consisted of my creating its title, designing its logo, and requesting a professional rendition of the logo from mythopoeic artist Tim Kirk. It still bears that title and logo.

[57] Montecito is a scenic town about 200 miles north of San Francisco, best known as Angela Lansbury's fictional Cabot Cove in her television series *Murder, She Wrote*.

was still famous for his bizarre past. Although Stoen grew up in a well-to-do Christian home, graduated from evangelical Wheaton College, earned a law degree at Stanford, and was a conservative Republican who attended Berkeley Presbyterian Church. In 1967 he became enamored of the Black Panthers. Next he joined the Jim Jones communal cult called People's Temple, where he became a Communist.

By 1970 Stoen was Jim Jones's best friend (Jones was literally an atheistic criminal psychopath, drug abuser and sex pervert), and Stoen became assistant leader of the cult. In 1973 he began engineering the group's secret exodus to Jonestown, Guyana. According to published evidence and his own videotaped account, in 1978 Stoen deserted Jones, besieged him, and intentionally precipitated the massacre of over 900 people.[58] The latter features a fifty-four-page chapter titled "Timothy Stoen."[59]

After his Communist years Stoen returned to Republicanism and ran unsuccessfully for office. (In 1998 he would switch parties and run as a Democrat with no better luck.) In 1992 he intended to specialize in representing victims of murderous devil-worshipping cults (a common problem in the United States, in his opinion). In 1994 he became the attorney for the C. S. Lewis Foundation, although he was located 500 miles to the north. On 2 December he threatened the original publisher of *Light in the Shadowlands* with "loss of your consitutional privilege" and "punitive damages" if all copies of the new book were not immediately recalled. On 6 December he followed up with an imaginative list of forty-four purported falsehoods about Stanley Mattson in the book. (Stoen is an advocate of filing nuisance suits in order to drain energy from opponents.) Although Leonard DuBoff, a leading libel authority, studied the case and decided that not one of the libel charges was valid, the nuisance suit threat was so financially intimidating to my small publisher that a newly installed management team put the book on hold. When Hope Publishing House rescued the book months later, Stoen threatened again, this time in vain. And he told a reporter for a

---

[58] Information about Timothy Stoen appears in *Raven: The Untold Story of the Rev. Jim Jones and His People* by Tim Reiterman (Dutton, 1982); *Our Father Who Art in Hell: The Life and Death of Jim Jones* by James Reston, Jr. (Times Books, 1981); and *The Strongest Poison* by Mark Lane (Hawthorn, 1980).

[59] A detailed chronological overview of Stoen's life is available in *The Lewis Legacy*, 64: 15-18.

major newspaper that *Light in the Shadowlands* is "flagrantly false and openly slanderous."

One month after recruiting Timothy Stoen, Mattson recruited yet another *Dark Tower* defender, a California handwriting analyst named Nancy Cole. Three months later, Cole traveled to Oxford to see the *Dark Tower* manuscript and wrote a completely inaccurate, confused, and superficial report, dismissing the forgery charge out of hand. In August she sent a copy to Michael Logsdon, and in January 1996 he began claiming on the Internet that Cole had proved the *Dark Tower* genuine. I promptly contacted Cole in hopes of purchasing a copy of the report, but she declined.

On 15 February 1995 a new *Dark Tower* defender, G. B. Tennyson of UCLA, charged with a flourish onto a safe corner of the field, brandishing as his powerful weapon; a videotape he had made in England. The corner he chose was a meeting of the Southern California C. S. Lewis Society, and his ammunition was billed as a public discussion of the hoax charges by Walter Hooper and Owen Barfield. (Tennyson was a friend of Barfield's and edited *Owen Barfield on C. S. Lewis.*) The video showed Hooper and Barfield (then in his mid-90s) agreeing that Lewis wrote a story about a man born blind in the 1920s. Tennyson appeared on the video explaining that my charge was an "unfalsifiable hypothesis" because of my overall claim that the more genuine a manuscript looks, the more expert a forger it proves Hooper to be. Hooper agreed with Tennyson, and added that most of my followers must feel the need to agree with me on all my charges rather than picking and choosing which charges to agree with. He recalled talking with one of the Lewis Petition signatories and learning that the person had neither examined the manuscripts in question nor read the book in question.

In the discussion following the video, Tennyson pointed out that one of my methods involved a "where were you on the night of..." sort of question, the sort that few human beings can answer without inconsistencies. Someone at the meeting (perhaps Michael Logsdon, who recounted it) stated that with the showing of the video, Tennyson had put the whole matter to rest by showing Hooper and Barfield "so calmly and rationally discussing these issues" with no telltale signs of nervousness.[60] Perhaps Tennyson was the nervous one, however, because that was the last anyone saw or heard of the

---

[60] Michael Logsdon, *The Salinas Valley Lewisian* (Spring 1995) 10:14-16.

video. He chose not to sell, rent, or loan out copies; and when I courteously inquired, he did not answer.

Next, Logsdon became interim editor of the *Lamp-Post*. In March 1997 he triumphantly announced the existence of the Cole report, heaped accolades on it, and featured a four-page promotional article about it by Juan Fajardo. He offered photocopies of the twenty-page report at cost and planned to post it on an Internet website in June. But the tide turned; instead of posting it on a website, without explanation he abruptly stopped providing copies. The summer 1997 issue of *The Lewis Legacy* exposed in detail the secret history of the Cole report, the people involved, and the egregious errors invalidating the report from beginning to end.[61] After being heralded for well over a year with trumpets and banners, the Cole report turned out to be a fiasco. Except for inadvertantly supporting the charges against Hooper's LeFay fragment and "Encyclopedia Boxoniana,"[62] it amounts to no more than its six forerunners: the Marchington report, the Warner report, the Mattson Jury report, the Grant report, the Morrison report, and the Sawyer report.

In 1997 Douglas Gresham backed Michael Logsdon a few times on Internet, dismissing my charges out of hand. (He later revealed that he was paid by C. S. Lewis Pte to further their interests on the Internet. If he is his own employer, that means he was paying himself to further his interests on the Internet.) 1997 is the year when he said, "As a private detective (which is something I spent many years doing) I can tell you that to actually prove that papers containing Jack's handwriting were burnt on this fire in 1960 (the site of it is now under a house) is going to be tantamount to impossible; to prove that they were not, is impossible."

He did not explain what he meant about being a private detective or what he meant about a 1960 bonfire site that is now under a house. And he did not explain what burnt papers he was discussing, since the papers he now defends are those that were rescued, not those that burned.

At Oxbridge in 1998 he expostulated, "Why doesn't she produce the evidence?" In 1998 he and C. S. Lewis Pte began claiming that Lewis wrote

---

[61] See Appendix 10.

[62] For Nancy Cole's samples of the handwriting from the LeFay fragment and "Encyclopedia Boxoniana" and her statements of how they differ from Lewis's normal handwriting, see *The Lewis Legacy* 73, Summer 1997, 15.

The Dark Tower in the late 1950s rather than the late 1930s. (This theory eliminates the problem of the post-1950 ink on the manuscript.) Gresham indicated that I (not Walter Hooper) originated the 1930s date. In interviews he defended *The Dark Tower* by interpreting it as an expression of the darkness Lewis was suffering in the Shadowlands while Joy was dying of cancer. He vouches for the story's authenticity (he says he recognizes Lewis's style) and considers it the first draft of a work of great creative imagination. He repeats the old rumor that I probably made a request of Hooper that he denied, and I thus became fixated and attacked him for simply doing the work of a good editor. "I think Kathryn has added two and two and come up with seventeen." (In our cordial correspondence we have avoided the controversy.) At Oxbridge in 1998 he also attacked Sheldon Vanauken and claimed that Leonard and Molly Miller were corrupted by greed and always stealing things. He even accused them of feeding alcohol to Warren Lewis so they could steal from him. (I suspect that Douglas Gresham's employers find him a useful tool because of his famous name, his speaking talent, his dramatic style, his quick wit, and his naiveté. If he is his own employer, that still holds true.)

The days of triumphal defensive forays with flags and banners seemed to end with the abortive Nancy Cole campaign; but the Tower stands fast, and no major defense has been necessary. Only minor defensive forays occur occasionally.

After *The C. S. Lewis Readers' Encyclopedia* was published in 1998 by Zondervan, in August James Prothero, then editor of *The Lamp-Post*, wrote to several of his fellow *Encyclopedia* contributors that the book was shockingly "Lindskoogian."[63] Walter Hooper warned him, he said, that Lindskoog could now imply to the innocent public that all the contributors agreed with her opinions. A month later Prothero issued a formal but misguided salvo in defense of his friend Hooper (and by implication, of Stanley Mattson and *The Dark Tower*):

---

[63] By the end of 1996, when he first learned about plans for Zondervan's *C. S. Lewis Readers' Encyclopedia*, a spokesperson for C. S. Lewis Pte informally threatened a court case that would include contributors. Two contributors took him so seriously that one backed out completely and the other came close to doing so.

we, the undersigned, declare that we contributed to the recently published volume, *The C S Lewis Readers' Encyclopedia*, without knowledge of the extent of editorial influence exercised on that volume by Ms Kathryn Lindskoog. We do not agree with the allegations Ms Lindskoog has made against Walter Hooper and desire in no way to be mistaken for believing their authenticity.

It was signed by only two of the many contributors: James Prothero and Jerry Root. What these men did not realize was that my only influence on other contributors' entries came if they had read my books or articles. I wielded no editorial influence whatsoever and saw no entries before publication except my own. Prothero's and Root's (and Hooper's) suspicions were mistaken.

In 1999 a new English bookdealer named Ian Blakemore, connected with Aiden Mackey, published a catalog in which he offered a copy of *The C. S. Lewis Hoax*. Mackey inserted the following note about *Hoax*: "A book by a disturbed person whose accusations have been investigated and demolished by the highest independent authorities in Britain and the United States. My impression is that K. L. was a genuine and valuable scholar, but became afflicated by physical illness and other problems which distorted her judgement enormously. I engaged her in dispute over one single issue, but it was like taking a sword to a mist."[64]

In 1999 an English freelance writer named Patricia Batstone published her book *In Debt to C. S. Lewis*. It includes a paragraph in which she says that Walter Hooper rescued the *Dark Tower* manuscript from a bonfire days [sic] after Lewis's death. "For some reason best known to herself, Kathryn Lindskoog, an American academic and former acquaintance of Lewis, decided to scrutinize the story and concluded that C. S. Lewis did not write it

---

[64] A spoken rumor that I am mentally deranged has been circulating since 1978, and I was informed from the beginning that the source was Walter Hooper. In 1998 a professional journalist called me to report that he had just received advice from Hooper urging him not to waste any of his valuable time on Kathryn Lindskoog, a "strange woman" who is "obsessed" with him. I had received a similar report from a *Los Angeles Times* reporter almost ten years earlier because Stanley Mattson had told him off the record that I'm mentally ill. Both reporters were amused by the misinformation, as I was.

but that it was all a big hoax on the part of Walter Hooper...The long-drawn out affair did nothing to help the health of either Hooper or Kathryn Lindskoog and eventually, after some retraction, faded off the scene, leaving a distinctly nasty taste." When contacted about her claims, Batstone referred to her sources as "various reports" and an unidentified newspaper cutting: "...unfortunately, by now, it is not possible to trace chapter and verse.... Let us agree to differ and move on.... At the end of the day I have to ask the question, does it really matter anymore?"

Yes, to some of us truth really matters. And there has been no retraction, nor has the affair faded off the scene as Batstone would like to think. In 1999 *The Guardian* took note of the ongoing battle over *The Dark Tower*. "Few posthumous works have attracted as much controversy as this, purportedly a 1939 follow-up to Lewis's 'interplanetary trilogy' of Christian sci-fi. An American, Walter Hooper, claimed to have rescued the manuscript just as Lewis's brother Warren was about to destroy it in a bonfire. But US literary scholar Kathryn Lindskoog insists the work is a forgery by Hooper, part of a Byzantine hoax that even included the recruitment of a soil analyst to study the site of the alleged bonfire. Unlike the rest of Lewis's elegant fiction, Lindskoog writes, 'The Dark Tower'—which teems with clunky double entendres and embarrassingly naive sexual references—'reads like a winning entry in a bad-writing contest'."[65]

In 1999 a longtime resident of the Dark Tower nonchalantly showed her face at one of its parapets for the first time; her name is Lesley Walmsley. In an article in Ian Blakemore's catalog she said she became an editor at William Collins publishers in 1976 and edited several C. S. Lewis books including *Boxen* and *The Dark Tower*. (William Griffin says *he* edited *The Dark Tower*.) Walmsley says "although the author [C. S. Lewis] was not here to help, he was ably represented by two trustees of the Lewis Estate, Walter Hooper and Elizabeth Stevens, to whom I shall always be indebted and for whom I shall always carry a strong respect and affection. They knew everything, had phenomenal memories, and were unstinting in their time

---

[65] "Deathless prose: literary afterlives" by Oliver Burkeman (*The Guardian*, Friday 26 November 1999). Burkeman comments on five posthumous books: *Sanditon* by Jane Austen (published 1925), *The Mystery of Edwin Drood* by Charles Dickens (1870), *The Dark Tower* by C. S. Lewis (1977), *A Confederacy of Dunces* by John Kennedy Toole (1980), and *The First Man* by Albert Camus (Eng. trans. 1995).

and help." (It seems that Walmsley's own memory is less than phenomenal: Elizabeth Stevens is not on record as ever being a trustee of the Lewis estate.)

In 2000 HarperCollins released its massive *C. S. Lewis: Essay Collection & Other Short Pieces*, edited by Walmsley. In her introduction she writes "For all this background information, as for so much else to do with the works of C. S. Lewis, I am greatly indebted to Walter Hooper, whose *C. S. Lewis: Companion & Guide* gives full details of all Lewis's writings, including of course his essays." Four of Walmsley's 135 selections are the Lewis forgeries "Christian Reunion, An Anglican Speaks to Roman Catholics," "The Man Born Blind," "The Dark Tower," and "Forms of Things Unknown." Each is introduced with Hooper's usual explanation of its origin. It's not as if Walmsely is unaware of the charges against these pieces; she has been well aware since at least as far back as 1992, when she received a copy of the C. S. Lewis Petition with a letter from me.[66]

In 2000 John Rateliff revisited the fray with his essay "*The Lost Road, The Dark Tower*, and *The Notion Club Papers*: Tolkien and Lewis's Time Travel Triad" in a book titled *Tolkien's Legendarium: Essays on The History of Middle-earth*. There he presents good evidence that C. S. Lewis did not write *The Dark Tower* circa 1939, but claims instead that Lewis wrote it in 1946. He adds:

> Some have questioned the authenticity, in whole or in part, of *The Dark Tower*. This is not the place to examine the claims and counterclaims; suffice it to say that I have thoroughly examined the evidence (including consulting the original manuscript) and concluded that there can be no reasonable doubt that the story as we have it is entirely the work of C. S. Lewis. Those interested in investigating the matter further are invited to read my [1989] essay review of *The C. S. Lewis Hoax*...and the [1995] forensic examination by Nancy H. Cole, "An Investigation into the Authorship of *The Dark Tower*: a Work Published Posthumously and Attributed to C. S. Lewis."

---

[66] On 10 October 1992 I sent her a copy of the C. S. Lewis Petition and a request for any kind of response she could give me. (She did not respond.)

In 2000 Colin Duriez published *The C. S. Lewis Encyclopedia*[67] with a commendation by Walter Hooper on the back: "This is one of the most useful books I know. I look for excuses to read it." (Inside, Duriez quotes Hooper as saying, "I like detective work very much. I like details, and I like mysteries." It seems to me that Hooper likes to create details and mysteries.) Duriez's acknowledgments include, among others, Stanley Mattson, Walter Hooper, and Douglas Gresham. Duriez is generally reliable, but he repeats Hooper's claim that he was invited to England by Lewis. His entry on *The Dark Tower* begins "A collection of two unfinished narratives and three short stories...One fragment, 'The Dark Tower,' seems to have been written after *Out of the Silent Planet* and before *Perelandra*, and is about time rather than space travel." He casually dismisses the forgery charge: "Lewis abandoned it as unsatisfactory. Some have doubted the genuineness of the bulk of the text, a view I do not share." He does not elaborate, and I suspect that he cannot. (There are four short stories, not three, in the *Dark Tower* collection; Duriez doesn't name any of them. He seems unaware that two of the short stories have been impugned as forgeries since 1988 along with the Dark Tower fragment.) I suspect that Duriez has been hoodwinked.

In 2001 David Gresham published *We Remember C. S. Lewis: Essays and Memoirs*. On pages 158-59 he claims that several handwriting experts unanimously concluded that C. S. Lewis was the author of *The Dark Tower*. "By the end of 1992 the matter was settled, as evidence for Lewis authenticity was overwhelming, including the admission by Lindskoog that she herself had committed forgery in writing spurious letters to support her claims." Like Duriez, Graham has evidently been hoodwinked by misinformation.

C. S. Lewis admitted that he was easy to hoodwink, and we have all been hoodwinked in one way or another when it comes to C. S. Lewis affairs. As Molly Miller remarked affectionately about Warren Lewis, "He was a bit simple, you know."[68] I think we are all a bit simple—those who deceive others, as well as those who are deceived.

---

[67] This book is an updated edition of Dureiez's 1990 book *The C. S. Lewis Handbook*, which lacked the final sentence of the current preface: "My thanks also to Walter Hooper and to Douglas Gresham for reading through the manuscript (though, of course, any errors are my own)." I wrote to Duriez about *Handbook* twice in 1991 (we had mutual friends) but received no answer.

[68] In his diary once Warren referred to "my own ingenuousness."

We might as well laugh, if we can, when we consider our gullibility. There is a grain of truth in Logan Pearsall Smith's overly optimistic claim: "It is almost always worth while to be cheated; people's little frauds have an interest which more than repays what they cost us." Cheaters do interest us.[69] We tend to be fascinated by forgery and fraud.

I think that's because we have a deep spiritual longing to be ultimately uncheated and undeceived. Much of human life itself is deceptive, and our final enemy is the confidence artist called Death. C. S. Lewis and his brother are now laughing at that cheater, I think. And at all the other pain and loss and defeat that cheated them here in the tragicomic Shadowlands. Where they are now, only reality exists.

> Thanks be to God for a life full-packed,
> with things that matter crying to be done—
> a life, thank God, of never-ending strife against odds.
> Just time enough to do one's best, and then pass on,
> leaving the rest to him.
> —*John Oxenham*

---

[69] "What would Lewis think of what has happened since his death? 'He would be slightly amused,' says Vanauken, 'but he would put things right.'" (K. L. Billingsley, "The Highjacking of C. S. Lewis," *Heterodoxy*, October, 1996.)

APPENDIX 1

AN AFTERWORD

By John Bremer

Reading the preceding chapters is a disturbing, if exciting, experience, for it is hard to forget the fundamental purpose of scholarship, the discovery of the truth. I have never met Kathryn Lindskoog (although we have talked on the phone and exchanged letters many times) but I have come to have unflinching trust in her desire for the truth. In this book, she may have made a mistake of fact or judgment, but I know that if such could be shown she would at once correct what seemed to be wrong. Her desire for truth is matched by the scrupulous procedures she uses to find it.

I wish the same could be said of some of the commentators on C. S. Lewis. Confusion among them abounds, witness the account of C. S. "Jack" Lewis's first book, *Spirits in Bondage*.

George Sayer (in his 1988 biography) reports that in the publisher's advertisement at the back of Heinemann's 1919 edition of *Spirits in Bondage* the author was incorrectly named George Lewis and identified as Lieutenant G. S. Lewis. According to A. N. Wilson, however, Jack "appeared in the Heinemann catalogue as George S. Lewis." The title page of the book actually attributes the poems to Clive Hamilton—the pen name that Lewis, who did not wish to be known in the army as a poet, took; it was made up of his own proper first name and his mother's family name, Hamilton. But according to William Griffin's 1985 biography, Jack had first wanted the pen name of Clive Staples (as he told Arthur Greeves on 12 September 1918) but had changed his mind and preferred Clive Hamilton; Griffin also reports that the publisher's promotional material slipped into the book gives the name of the poet as George Hamilton. Furthermore, Griffin says that the author's name was misspelled on the title page as Glive Hamilton, but this is not borne out by a simple inspection of the book.

There is even more confusion since Sayer reports that one of the poems, "Death in Battle," was selected by John Drinkwater ("the well-known poet, playwright, and literary critic") and published in a literary magazine, *Reveille.*

According to Griffin and Wilson, it was not Drinkwater but John Galsworthy who wanted to publish one of Lewis's poems in *Reveille*. But, says Wilson, Galsworthy first rejected the poem, much to Lewis's chagrin, and "later" (in February 1919, which is not much later, the book being published in March) relented, and it was published in the February 1919 issue. It was supposed to accompany poems by "Robert Bridges, Siegfried Sassoon, and Robert Graves" according to Wilson, but George Sayer reports that it appears with "poems by Robert Bridges (the poet laureate), Hilaire Belloc, and Siegfried Sassoon." It would be interesting to know if both are right.

Another commentator, Walter Hooper, tells us there was no rejection or hesitation by Galsworthy, for Jack "was told that John Galsworthy had read his manuscript and wished to publish 'Death in Battle' in his newly formed magazine *Reveille*. Jack agreed and his first published poem was to appear in the third (February 1919) number of *Reveille.*" (An odd claim because since 1965 Hooper has been listing in his bibliographies "Quam Bene Saturno" as Lewis's first published poem.)

Jack's brother Warren, in his *Letters of C. S. Lewis*, quotes Jack's letter of 27 October 1918 to his father as saying that, indeed, John Galsworthy was the admirer. Unfortunately Warren cannot always be trusted (witness his dating of Jack's letter of 19 September 1918 as 9 September), but in this case he was probably right.

Griffin also made a little joke about Jack's finding a review stuck between the front endpapers of his copy from Heinemann; it complimented him for "a scholarly elucidation of a difficult subject." Griffin explains "the press-cutting agency had sent him a review of 'The Principles of Symbolic Logic' by C. S. Lewis of the University of California." Without wishing to appear too picky, the famous philosopher and logician was C. I. (Clarence Irving)

Lewis—that is fact—and I believe his 1918 book was titled "A Survey of Symbolic Logic." The story seems to have been copied, almost verbatim, from Jack's letter to his father on 25 May 1919. And, moreover, Jack's letter indicates what Griffin obscures, namely, that Jack (not Heinemann) had sent ten shillings to a press-cutting agency and they had sent him only one review—that of C.I. Lewis's not Jack's book. Why Griffin says Jack "found" the review is unclear for he himself must have put it there.

The title of Jack's poems did not fare much better. It started out as "Spirits in Prison," a title taken from 1 Peter 3:19. It modestly cast Jack in the role of Christ who "went and preached unto the spirits in prison."

For reasons unstated Wilson comments that "the lyric cycle is not markedly religious in tone, but it is striking that, even in his 'atheistical' phase, the young poet should have looked to the New Testament for his title." How naive can he be? Jack's choice was pure arrogance—as his poems and comments about them testify. Jack was the savior, telling those in prison of the outworn creed that controlled them.

It was the voracious reader Albert Lewis who pointed out that there was already a novel called "Spirit in Prison" (at least according to Hooper; the name is given elsewhere as "A Spirit in Prison") published in 1908. But the author is named Robert Hitchens by Hooper in *They Stand Together* and again in Preface to the 1984 reprint of Jack's poems. Robert Hichens is the (correct) spelling to be found in Wilson's pseudo-biography.

So the title of the cycle of lyrics had to be changed, and the Willson-imagined piety notwithstanding, Jack used Milton, *Paradise Lost,* and assumed the voice of Satan who tells his followers:

For this Infernal Pit shall never hold
Caelestial Spirits in Bondage, nor th'Abysse
Long under darkness cover. But these thoughts
Full Counsel must mature: Peace is despaird,
For who can drink Submission! Warre then, Warre
Open or understood must be resolv'd

If Jack cannot be Jesus preaching his gospel to the spirits in prison, then he will be the great rebel, exhorting his troops to war against heaven. Wilson's fantasy about Jack's piety is pie-in-the-sky.

The choice of using a nom de plume, and of changing it, together with the change of title for the poems, and the publisher's printing errors, can, perhaps, excuse some confusion but it would not be unreasonable to expect these things to be reported accurately.

It might be argued that these are details of no significance whatsoever, but it is hard to know if they are significant if we do not know what they are. Scholars should be exact. And, as in the case of Wilson, if they are not trustworthy in small things why would we trust them in larger things?

The example of Jack's poems requires no special knowledge—only the courage and persistence to track down every piece of information and to get it right. There is another kind of error that depends upon cultural background. American scholars, not well steeped in English ways, can easily make forgivable errors.

Walter Hooper, an American, tells us that "Albert [Lewis] had reason to be worried about the safety of his sons. Warren had his training at the Royal Military Academy at Sandhurst cut short by Britain's declaration of war on Germany in August (1914). The next month he was posted to Aldershot in preparation for his being sent to France as a second lieutenant in the Royal Army Service Corps."

Warren was able to visit the wounded Jack in April 1918 and he reports that he was greeted with "a cheerful 'Hullo, I didn't know you A S.C. people got as far up the line as this!'" It was, in accordance with infantry regiments' prejudice, unusual for any member of the Army Service Corps (the A S.C., that had been formed only in 1869) to be so close to the actual fighting. But it happened increasingly (and for more important reasons than visiting a wounded brother), and as a result the King conferred the prefix Royal on the A S.C. in November 1918. But in 1914 the Royal Army Service Corps did not exist.

Perhaps not important, but it is the fact and Hooper does not know it. Nor do Kilby and Mead (see pp. 2-3 of *Brothers and Friends*).

Another source of confusion among the Lewis commentators is the difference between being commissioned and being gazetted. Commissions and postings are printed and announced in *The London Gazette*. Being commissioned is one thing; being posted to a regiment or other army unit is another. But apart from the confusion of terminology (again, more excusable in Americans than in British writers or scholars), there are a strange variety of opinions about Jack Lewis and the end of his training course.

Warren Lewis—who was an army man and should have been exact in these matters—tells us that Jack was in Belfast on leave "for a couple of days" in August 1917 (although he missed seeing his brother by a few days), that he was commissioned on 25 September in the Third Battalion of the Somerset Light Lnfantry and given a month's leave. He went to Janie Moore in Bristol and arrived in Belfast on 12 October.

According to Griffin, it was on "September 18th the newly commissioned young men got four weeks' leave. Instead of hurrying to Belfast to visit his father, Lewis decided to accept Moore's invitation to go to Bristol. He brought a cold and a severe sore throat...Lewis arrived home in Belfast on October 12th."

George Sayer manages another date. "After passing a simple exam, he (Jack) was made second lieutenant and attached to the Third Battalion of The Somerset Light Infantry. Before being posted for active service, he was given a month's leave from September 28. He did not go directly to his father's house in Belfast, but accepted an invitation from Paddy Moore to stay at his mother's house...in Bristol. On October 12, he traveled to Ireland, spending only half of his leave at home. Albert was deeply hurt."

Roger Green and Hooper have it as follows. "After a brief leave in Belfast (9-11 August) Lewis was writing to his father..." And later "This was followed by an exam, which seems to have been little more than a formality; and on 25 September 1917 Albert Lewis noted that Clive was 'gazetted to Third Battalion, Somerset Light Infantry,' and on Saturday, 29 September 1917, 'Jacks got one month's leave from this date from officer cadet corps, Oxford. Went to stay with a chum named Moore and his mother. Came home on 12th October.'"

Wilson has fabricated something different "In August, Warnie got a short spell of leave from the Western Front, and Jack was persuaded to go back to Strandtown (Belfast) to spend the week with him. He had reached the point where he could not bear to see his father a deux, but with his still loved brother it was a different matter. On 21 August, Warnie went back to France and Jack returned to Oxford."

This seems to contradict Warnie's statement that he missed Jack and that the latter had only three days leave, returning on 11 August. Furthermore, Warren was never at the Western Front; he was in France but never at the front as Jack's greeting quoted above makes clear. Perhaps the author was Pudd'nhead Wilson.

On the dates of commissioning, gazetting, and of leave, and of Jack's arrival in Belfast, Wilson offers us nothing except "at the end of September."

Hooper does not help much. In *They Stand Together,* however, Jack's letter to Arthur Greeves (dated by Hooper as 4 August 1917) contains the statement: "By the way I have forgotten to tell you any news about leave. It was going to be from next Friday till next Teusday [sic], but that has been changed. It is now going to start on Wednesday 9th and go on till that Sunday midnight. A lot depends on whether I can get any extension for travelling," This is helpful, even though Hooper says in a footnote that Lewis wrote Wednesday in mistake for Thursday.

It would be customary for leave to finish at midnight (23:59, actually) on a Sunday. Three days leave would mean that it consisted of Friday, Saturday, and Sunday, and probably would have begun after duty on Thursday. But Jack refers to "the promised four days leave" in a letter to his father, postmarked 22 July 1917. Did he have three or four days leave? If he had four days leave, then the error noted by Hooper was not that he wrote Wednesday for Thursday but that he put 9th when he meant 8th.

The locus classicus for all of this is in *They Stand Together,* where Hooper states that Jack "was on leave in Belfast from 9-11 August...He was on leave again from 18 September-18 October, and much to his father's chagrin he spent the first three weeks with the Moores in Bristol, not arriving home until 12 October...News arrived while he was at home that he had been gazetted into the 3rd Somerset light Infantry and he joined this regiment in Crown Hill, near Plymouth, on 19 October."

It is impossible to reconcile the above accounts. Did he spend two weeks or three weeks with Janie Moore? The naivete of the commentators should be observed. At least two say that Paddy Moore issued the invitation. How do we know that? In other sections of their accounts Jack is described as arriving sick at Janie Moore's house. Was that true? There is no corroborative evidence, although Griffin knows that "Mrs. Moore took his temperature and when the mercury soared past 100 degrees she swept him under the covers." How does he know that it was a mercury thermometer, and that it not merely passed but soared past 100 degrees, and what happened under the covers? Griffin subtitled his work "A Dramatic Life" but this is going a little far.

Hooper repeats his earlier account in his 1984 Preface to the reprint of "Spirits in Bondage," although it was not "while he was home" that Jack learned of his posting to the Somerset Light Infantry. He learned it *when* he got home because Albert, his father, recorded it on 25 September.

In his latest version, in the Introduction to *All My Road before Me,* Hooper says of Jack's stay in Bristol, "It is evident that Lewis savoured to the full the hospitality afforded by Mrs. Moore. They all knew it could not be like this again for a long time because Lewis had already been gazetted into the 3rd Somerset Light Infantry and Paddy (Moore) into the Rifle Brigade." And yet Hooper tells us elsewhere that Jack learned of his gazetting while at home, which itself is inaccurate and should be when he reached home.

Perhaps we should be grateful that the place to which Jack was posted after his leave has been corrected from the Crown Hill of *They Stand Together* to Crownhill.

The spelling of the Lewis family certainly left something to be desired. Both Jack and Warnie could be very careless if not downright erratic, but it is possible for the commentators to be more thorough. Some of them—not all—are scholars and we can expect and demand accuracy from them.

Another complicating factor is that Jack lived in an English culture and some of his comments need more cultural understanding than other people—even those "separated by a common language"—can easily acquire. And to complicate it still further, Jack, Warnie, and their father, were Ulstermen and we need to know, for example, what the word "cod" meant in one proposed title for "Spirits in Bondage." This was "Metrical Meditations of a Cod," and reportedly, "cod' was equivalent to "an eccentric."

And English culture is not unified, so that different classes have different cultures—or they have some culture in common, but some in separation.

As a final example, consider the discussion of Owen Barfield in the Foreword to *All My Road Before Me* of the parlor game called "Boys' Names." I do not know how Jack and the Moores played that game, but I know how it was played in my own family. I do not believe that Barfield (who was a venerable nonagenarian) remembered the game. This is not the place to give what I believe to be the accurate description of it, but it is permissible to wonder about the validity of what has been said and done, even by friends as close as Sayer and Barfield.

This may seem insignificant, but Barfield was one of Lewis's oldest friends (and also his literary executor) and what he knew and did not know may be important to us. In some ways, Lewis was a very private man, and it is very revealing when Barfield remarks "I find it strange to recall that during those early years I was given no hint of all that household background." This is not true, for Barfield goes on to indicate that he was given hints, but did not consider them as such and remained ignorant of how much time and energy went into cleaning out "the oven in the gas cooker." Barfield—and this is substantively much more important—confesses "to some surprise at finding no reference [in Jack's diary] to his long argument with myself, later referred to in *Surprised by Joy* as 'the great war.'"

Among all the good work that has been done on Lewis, there is much that is not satisfactory. The causes are multiple but corrigible. There is carelessness, complacent repetition from unchecked sources, errors from ignorance, misreadings from unrecognized cultural differences, and so forth, but all these can be corrected by patient work if the sources and resources are freely available.

A second level of unsatisfactory work is produced by people such as A N. Wilson whose so called biography is not a portrait of C. S. Lewis but an impressionistic sketch of what Wilson projects from his own unconscious, a projection that images how a mean, petty, narcissistic man views a truly good man, and who then decides to belittle the goodness (presumably because he cannot believe in it since he does not find it within himself). This can only be done by condescension that is an impertinence. Wilson seems to have wanted a best-selling book about an important thinker (so that he would be enhanced by his subject), who could be shown, by sly innuendo and the ignoring or distorting of facts and downright falsehood, to be less than supposed (thereby establishing the superiority of the author). Egomania is a solitary disease.

A third level of difficulty is that there are those who have interpreted and controlled Jack Lewis and his writings to serve some personal, commercial, or doctrinal agenda, to magnify their own importance, to make money, or to further some cause foreign to Lewis. It appears that Walter Hooper falls into this third category and what Kathryn Lindskoog has revealed is shocking. It is not my business to concern myself with the state of Walter Hooper's soul—he has to live inwardly with what he has done—but we all have to live outwardly with it. A public cleansing is needed.

The trust in any of Jack Lewis's books printed or reprinted after his death in November 1963 has been destroyed. I do not feel able to pick up any such book and read it without comparing it with some pre-1963 original to ensure that it has not been contaminated. The moral character of Jack Lewis carries enormous weight—with me, as with countless others—and nobody can be allowed to use that weight to support words that are not Jack's words.

The world is entitled to know what Jack Lewis wrote in the full, uncompromising, straightforward way in which he wrote it, without the intervention and corruption of a scrivener. Purification of the texts is a major scholarly task, but it should be done, and until it is done, Hooper continues to damage the thought of a singularly good man. Fortunately, the character and opinions of Jack Lewis are too well founded in his goodness to be destroyed, but the interference with the texts diverts attention away from what was of supreme importance to their author, namely, how to live a good life.

John Bremer was born in England has advanced degrees from the University of Cambridge, the University of Leicester, and St. John's College; he came to the United States on a Fulbrigt in 1951. He has also lived in Canada (where he was provincial Commissioner for Education) and in Australia (where he founded the education supplement for *The Australian,* the national daily newspaper). He has worked and written extensively on educational reform, and is best known for the creation of the Parkway Program, the School-without-Walls, in Philadelphia in 1969. He vras Killam Senior Fellow at Dalhousie University and was tenured at the University of Leicester in England. He has written several books, the last being *On Plato's Polity,* translated into six languages, and is author of more than seventy articles. When he wrote this he lived in the Washington, D.C. area and was an editor at *The World and I.*

APPENDIX 2

FACTS ABOUT FORGERY

Two Kinds of Forgery

1. Literary forgery. A bogus work of literature is falsely attributed to another author.[70] It may or may not appear in what pretends to be the penmanship or typing of the purported author. For example, William Henry Ireland could not show people the manuscript of the lost Shakespeare play that he claimed he had discovered. (The fact is that he wrote the play himself and didn't have enough time afterwards to produce a forged document to go along with it.) The play was accepted as Shakespeare's long enough to be performed in a theater. Those who perceived that it was a literary forgery (it didn't sound like Shakespeare) said so without seeing the original manuscript that Ireland claimed he had discovered. They didn't need to see it.

---

[70] "Plagiarists offer as their own what someone else has written. Literary forgers offer as genuine writing of another what they have themselves composed." The motives may be promotion of some scheme or point of view, catering to the market demand, and for the love of the lie itself. "Literary forgeries seem to be numerous in all countries and in all ages. A book of nearly 300 pages by J. A. Farrer gives accounts of many famous literary forgeries, yet, as Andrew Lang says, several additional volumes would be needed to make the account of known forgeries complete." This warning is from *A Handbook to Literature,* originally by Thrall and Hibbard, now by Holman and Harmon. Ironically, the handbook originated primarily at the University of North Carolina at Chapel Hill (alma mater of both Walter Hooper and Stanley Mattson) and is published by Macmillan (publisher of Hooper's Narnia scraps) and Collins (publisher of *The Dark Tower*).

If the Dark Tower story (published in 1977) was not created by the mind of C. S. Lewis, the story is a literary forgery.

2. Document forgery. The content of a bogus document is either copied exactly from a genuine document—like a counterfeit $100 bill—or else invented—like a $150 bill. If William Henry Ireland had eventually produced the artificial Shakespeare manuscript as planned, his opponents would have claimed that the manuscript had to be a document forgery. And they would have been correct. (After his exposure, Ireland confessed to both literary forgeries and document forgeries.)

If the Dark Tower manuscript (donated to the Bodleian Library in 1989) was not written by the actual hand of C. S. Lewis, the manuscript is a document forgery.

Two Kinds of Authentication

1. Preliminary Authentication of a Piece of Literature

1. Provenance: The exact history of the piece of literature from its production to its present disposition should be ascertained in detail, with strong supporting evidence.

(So far no one except Walter Hooper claims to have read or heard the Dark Tower story before 1973. Warren Lewis disbelieved in the story's existence.)

2. Content: Content of a piece of literature should be consistent with the facts of the author's life and the content of his mind.

(Part of the Dark Tower content is semi-obscene, and the author expresses beliefs and attitudes contrary to Lewis's.)

3. Quality of writing: Literary characteristics should be reasonably consistent with the range of writing by the alleged author, allowing for natural fluctuations.

(The Dark Tower quality is amateurish and unlike Lewis's unquestionably authentic writing.)

4. Statistical analysis of words and sentences: Invisible linguistic patterns should match those of the alleged author.

(The 1986 Literary Detective analysis of letter and letter-pair frequencies in Dark Tower passages and the 1991 Cusum Chart analysis of subtle sentence variations both show that language in the Dark Tower does not match C. S. Lewis's language pattern.)

2. Preliminary Authentication of a Document

1. Provenance: The exact history of the document from its production to its present disposition should be ascertained in detail, with strong supporting evidence that the claims are true.

(No one except Walter Hooper claims to have seen the Dark Tower manuscript before 1980.)

2. Handwriting style: Handwriting that looks like that of the purported writer does not prove that a document is genuine, but if the handwriting has characteristics of an inept counterfeit it can prove the document a forgery.

(The Dark Tower manuscript looks like Lewis's penmanship, but it has not been studied by qualified handwriting experts like Charles Hamilton and Kenneth Rendell, who have at times successfully detected handwriting forgeries.)

3. Chemical analysis of paper and ink: The use of appropriate paper and ink does not prove a document genuine, but use of the wrong paper and ink can prove it a forgery.

(Charles Hamilton, America's leading autograph expert, says "A forger would have no trouble finding paper and ink that are 40 years old," but no one has chemically tested the Dark Tower paper and ink, although it was falsely announced that they did so. Nicolas Barker says that he can tell by the shade of blue that some of the ink on that document did not exist before 1950.)

Worth remembering: Most of our literary heritage exists without the survival of original manuscripts. Questions of literary authenticity cannot be decided by the mere existence of documents with imperfect provenance, because when such documents surface they raise questions about their own authenticity. The production of forged documents is far more common, more popular, and more profitable than the production of forged literature.

Motives for Forgery

In 1989 Richard Wilbur reflected upon the motives of forgers, imposters, and similar tricksters:

> I think that we all can understand something about the hoaxing impulse. At its simplest, it is the desire to swindle, to deceive for gain. At another and more complex level, it is the desire to seem, temporarily, more clever and interesting than one is. And perhaps, temporarily, to deceive oneself.
>
> At a still loftier and wickeder level, it is a desire to tamper with the fabric of reality. A colleague at Harvard once told me of a medievalist who, on his deathbed, confessed to his sorrowing students that he had forged such-and-such a manuscript—and then, carried away, *falsely* confessed to having faked many celebrated documents and codices. I suspect that that fellow died laughing. When hoaxers are negligent about making their swindles air-tight, I think it is because their chief motive is not gain or imposture but a heady sense of having shaken up the realm of fact a bit.[71]

Rudyard Kipling wrote a verse once about the creative pleasure of deception, called "The Lie."

> There is pleasure in the wet, wet clay
> When the artist's hand is potting it.
> There is pleasure in the wet, wet lay
> When the poet's pad is blotting it.
> There is pleasure in the shine of your picture on the line
> At the Royal Academy;
> But the pleasure felt in these is as chalk to Cheddar cheese
> When it comes to a well-made Lie.—
> To a quite unwreckable Lie,

---

[71] From a personal letter dated 16 February 1989, and printed with permission in *The Lewis Legacy* Issue 12. Richard Wilbur has been on the faculties of Harvard, Wellesley, Wesleyan, and Smith. He won the Pulitzer Prize for Poetry in 1957, served as second Poet Laureate of the United States in 1987, and in April 1989 won his second Pulitzer for *New and Collected Poems*.

To a most impeccable Lie!

To a water-tight, fire-proof, angle-iron, sunk-hinge, time-lock, steel-faced Lie!

C. S. Lewis Autographs and Documents

One of the easiest ways for forgers to make money is to buy early copies of books by famous authors, autograph them with the authors' names, and sell them for inflated prices. For example, Twain's personal copy of the 1901 Riverdale Edition of *The Writings of Mark Twain* had notes of his pencilled in the margins, and the rare books people at John Wannamaker's priced the set at $5,800. A doctor's wife surprised her husband with this newly-surfaced literary treasure on their anniversary, and because the doctor allowed R. W. Hoag of East Carolina University to study the marginalia, Hoag received a grant to do so.

After months of studying the marginalia, Hoag was horrified to learn from the world's expert on handwritten notes by Twain that these were forged. The expert said, "Please be aware that more than one forger is at work in the production of Twain association items. I encounter two or three every year—usually placed in expensive sets of books to inflate their value." Three of the better-known Twain forgers so far have been Joseph Cosey, Eugene Field II, and Mark Hofmann.[72]

Circa 1994, when this essay was first published, an enthusiastic collector of Inklings material ordered an autographed first edition of *The Silver Chair* from a dealer in England. Another dealer, who was a local friend of the purchaser, took a look at the book and recognized it immediately: he had bought and sold it a few months earlier for a much lower price, because then it had not been autographed by Lewis. (As a dealer, he had left his small identification mark inside the book in case it turned up again.) The purchaser, who didn't want to offend anyone in the book trade, quietly returned the book to the seller and got credit toward future purchases.

There is no way to know how many C. S. Lewis autographs and documents have surfaced (often to be sold or donated to collections for tax

---

[72] "All that Glitters is Not Mark Twain" by R. W. Hoag of East Carolina University appeared in the *Mark Twain Journal* (29:2) in June 1993.

purposes) since his death, but their total market value has to be hundreds of thousands of dollars. There is no clearinghouse for such information. The most expensive Lewis document to surface was probably the 78-page Lewis/Barfield manuscript that Owen Barfield sold through Sotheby's on 18 December 1986.[73] The most expensive Lewis signature to surface was probably the one said to be in a Narnia book belonging to the Tolkien children; the set of seven books including the autographed volume was reportedly priced at $10,000. (At that time a more normal price for first edition Narnia books was $100.) Late in 1991 Walter Hooper revealed a fact he inexplicably left out of his own book about Narnia—that he owns a classical atlas that had belonged to Lewis in his boyhood, with the name "Narnia" underlined on the map of ancient Italy. Such a remarkable collector's item might be worth at least $1,000 to some people.

Three rather awkward 1933 letters from Lewis to a publisher and carbons of two typed replies surfaced more than fifty years after they were allegedly written and were offered to a Wade Center benefactor for $6,000. She eventually paid $3,500 for them and felt they were a historical treasure in spite of the fact that they contained nothing significant and had no known provenance. They are probably genuine, but if they are not they were an easy project for an experienced forger. Compared to that purchase, a brisk four-sentence note that Lewis sent to an acquaintance in the early 1940s was a bargain when a friend of mine purchased it for only £185 (approximately $370).

Buying directly from an original owner is the ideal arrangement for collectors, and a document with meaningful content not already available in print is highly prized. In 1993 Gracia Fay Ellwood sold her only letter from Lewis to collector Ralph Blair for only $800 (earmarked for Spanish-language Lewis books to be donated to literate but bookless peasants in Nicaragua).

Dr. Edwin Brown of Indianapolis trusts the judgment of dealer Peter Jolliffe of Eynsham, England, and purchased several Lewis documents, including a handwritten manuscript of "A Man Born Blind" that surfaced several years ago without provenance.

---

[73] *Clivi Hamiltonis Summae Metaphysices conta Anthroposophos Libri II.* Walter Hooper donated a photocopy of this manuscript to the Bodleian in 1986.

In 1994 dealer Sophie Dupré[74] advertised an unusual scrap of Lewis's handwriting for £950 (approximately $1,900). On one side it had most of the fifth and sixth paragraphs of chapter 5 of *Christian Behavior* (part of *Mere Christianity)* in what appears to be Lewis's handwriting. On the other side it has some incoherent penciled notes such as "Doctrinal. Wing Commander Snooks...(a) Knowledge experience & logic." The piece of paper was folded like a fan and the edge is burned away, which allegedly shows that Lewis used it to light a fire and someone in his household saved it from the flames. This makes the item "excessively rare." Needless to say, with a collection of old paper any skillful forger would find it easy to invent relics like this, reproducing in Lewis's handwriting portions of his published works.

Early in 2000 the daughter of an Oxford gradute brought to the BBC Television program "Antiques Roadshow" two handwritten letters her father had received from Lewis. The one three pages long was appraised at £1500 (approximately $3000), and the one five pages long was appraised at £3000 (approximately $6000).

The Bodleian Library does not reveal its arrangements with finders or with depositors, donors, and sellers of Lewis documents—much less what it pays for purchased documents. But in 1989 Judith Priestman compiled a fifty-seven page catalog titled *A Selective Catalogue of the Papers of C. S. Lewis (1898-1963)* that is not for publication or distribution. According to that catalog, it seems that from 1968 to 1989 Walter Hooper deposited in the Bodleian for safekeeping several bunches of valuable documents that he owns, some typed and others written in what is alleged to be Lewis's handwriting. The following thirty handwritten Lewis documents owned by Walter Hooper have been kept in the Bodleian since 1989 or earlier. (It is always possible for more to have been added.)

FAIR COPIES (the final draft in the author's handwriting)
A Grief Observed
"A Problem about Prayer"
"A Reply to Professor Haldane"
"After Ten Years"
"De Futilitate"

"Forms of Things Unknown"
"Imagery in the last ten Cantos of Dante's *Comedy*"
"Imagination and Thought in the Middle Ages"
"Modern Theology and Biblical Criticism"
"On Criticism"
"On Obstinacy in Belief"
"On Science Fiction"
"Preface" to *Pilgrim's Regress*
"Spenser's Cruel Cupid"
Surprised by Joy (fragment)
"Tasso"
The Dark Tower (donated sometime in 1989)
The Great Divorce (fragment)
"The Language of Religion"
"The Psalms"
"Williams and the Arthuriad"
DRAFTS (not Lewis's final version)
"Encyclopedia Boxoniana"
Letters to Malcolm
"Membership"
"More Studies in Words"
Narnia scraps
Preface to *The Screwtape Letters*...(1961)
That Hideous Strength (fragment)
"The Genesis of a Medieval Book"
"The Man Born Blind"
"We're proud of Finchley Avenue..."
"When the year dies..."

According to the Bodleian, Hooper's manuscript copy of *Letters to Malcolm* is an 89-page draft with additional material on the Bible and fundamentalism, and a different ending to the last chapter. This is especially interesting in light of Hooper's expressed desire to defend Lewis from the kind of mischaracterization purportedly imposed upon him by fundamentalists[75]

---

[75] "C.S. Lewis and C. S. Lewises" in *The Riddle of Joy*, 40-43.

and Hooper's 1 August 1963 attempt to obtain the *Letters to Malcolm* manuscript from publisher Jocelyn Gibb. In his 6 August reply, Gibb explained that the decision was Lewis's to make, not his. Gibb would be happy for Hooper to obtain the manuscript, with Lewis's permission, except for the fact that Gibb preferred for English manuscripts to stay in England.[76]

Hooper does not deposit all his Lewis manuscripts in the Bodleian; for example, he showed "Christian Reunion" to visitors in his home in 1989. He has never disclosed the extent of his collection. The two notebooks and an exercise book full of assorted material by Lewis that Hooper deposited in the Bodleian in 1989 were enigmatically numbered by Hooper: Lewis Mss. Nos. 27, 31, and 46. In response to those high numbers, Joe Christopher remarked in print, "What else, one wonders, does Hooper have?"[77]

In 1990 Hooper revealed that although the entire content of *All My Road before Me* was typed by Warren Lewis into the Lewis Family Papers (and the originals were burned by C. S. Lewis in 1936), the original manuscript of the last section, "Magdalen College Appendix," survived in one of Lewis's old exercise books and belongs to Hooper. But A. Q. Morton tested the text of "Magdalen College Appendix" in 1992, and his test showed that it is not the work of one writer.[78] If Morton's test is correct, it seems likely that Warren took it upon himself to edit or expand the divergent sections as he typed them. If that is the case, however, Hooper's original manuscript in Lewis's

---

[76] This letter from Gibb to Hooper is in the Chapel Hill collection. It is evidence that Hooper was not then expected to become Lewis's permanent secretary in England.

[77] Joe Christopher, "A Catalogue, Two Notebooks, and an Exercise Book," *Mythprint* 163: 4.

[78] The first portrait, of Benecke, is split near the middle. The third section, Craig's portrait, is not by the author of the second part of Benecke's portrait. The fourth section, which includes portraits of Dixon, Hope, Lee, MacKeith, and Parker, is not by the author of the Craig portrait. The fifth section, Segar's portrait, is not by the author of the long previous section. The last portrait, that of Weldon, is not by the author of the Segar portrait. The simplest guess about the multiple authorship of the portraits would be this one:

1. Benecke portrait (part 1) by Lewis
2. Benecke (part 2) —*editing*
3. Craig portrait by Lewis
4. Dixon, Hope, Lee, MacKeith, and Parker portraits—*editing*
5. Segar portrait by Lewis
6. Weldon portrait—*editing*

handwriting should differ from Warren's typed version. Surely a thorough investigation is called for. If Hooper's old exercise book with Lewis's Magdalen portraits in it should prove false, it would cast doubt on all Hooper's valuable handwritten copies of historic Lewis documents.

In 1954, Hooper first ventured to write to C. S. Lewis and Lewis responded on 30 November with a letter of profound spiritual advice, encouraging Hooper to focus on God rather than himself.[79] That happened to be the same year when an excellent little booklet about art forgery was published.[80] In it W. G. Constable advised art lovers that successful forgery is all too easy:

> With a contemporary artist recently dead, his work not yet fully known or catalogued, a vogue for collecting him fanned by a skillful entrepreneur, prices not so high as to provoke critical examination, and with not too many genuine examples accessible for comparison, the forger is in velvet.

If there has been a talented forger of Lewis documents at work behind the scenes since 1964, Constable's words in 1954 have proved prophetic. The forger has been in velvet.

---

[79] In the Chapel Hill collection.

[80] *Forgers and Forgeries* by W.G. Constable (New York: Harry N. Abrams, 1954). An excellent 23-page booklet from the "Art Treasures of the World" series, analyzing the sources and qualities of forgeries, with many examples.

APPENDIX 3

THE MISTRESS OF C. S. LEWIS

By John Bremer

The relationship between C. S. Lewis (or Jack) and Janie Moore (or Minto) began shortly after 7 June 1917 and ended with the death of Janie Moore on 12 January 1951. The relationship undoubtedly changed its character during this period but it is possible to identify certain phases. In considering these phases, it must be born in mind that Janie Moore was twenty-seven years older than Jack. Their respective birthdays were 28 March 1872 and 29 November 1898.

Phase One: In early June 1917, Jack met Janie Moore in Oxford; she was married but had been separated from her Irish husband since 1907. She was in Oxford to be with her son, Paddy, who was in the same cadet battalion as Jack. Jack found in her a substitute for the mother he had lost in 1908, when he was 9 years old. He fell under her spell and was in love with her by August. Jack shared her with her son, Paddy, but soon after he was commissioned in the army on 25 September 1917 the relationship was sexual and Paddy had become irrelevant.

Phase Two: From September 1917 until Jack returned to Oxford in January 1919, they continued their sexual relationship (when this was possible) and wrote each other, seemingly, every day. When Jack was transferred to various army hospitals and posts in England, Janie Moore followed him, with her daughter, Maureen, in tow.

Phase Three: From January 1919 until 28 September 1931, the day of Jack's conversion, Jack and Janie Moore lived together in many different rented apartments and houses in and around Oxford, finally moving into the Kilns, which they purchased with the help of Jack's brother, Warren, in October 1930. Whatever the recent state of their sexual relationship had been (Janie Moore would have been about 58 years old), it was terminated on Jack's conversion, since he would have regarded it as sinful and contrary to God's law.

Phase Four: Jack and Janie Moore continue to live together at the Kilns, with Warren, until, after several years of sickness, she entered a nursing home in April 1950, where she died on 12 January 1951.

A more detailed history of the relationship is set forth in the following chronology.

Pre-Phase One: Jack is a somewhat loutish schoolboy—intellectually precocious, socially limited, emotionally stunted, and sexually prurient.

5-9 Dec. 1916 Jack sits for scholarship at Oxford.

11 Dec. 1916 Jack returns to Belfast.

13 Dec. 1916 Receives scholarship at University College.

20-26 March 1917 Jack to Oxford for Responsions (i.e. university entrance exams). Fails algebra but still acceptable to Univ. Coll. provided he re-takes exams successfully.

26 April 1917 Returned to Oxford after three weeks in Belfast.

28 April 1917 Signs his name in Univ. Coll. book.

30 April 1917 Volunteers for the army and is assigned to a cadet battalion in Oxford.

Over the previous few years Jack had been physically maturing and had felt his sexuality very keenly. Masturbation was a problem for him, but he began to notice members of the opposite sex, not only in fantasy but also as possible companions or friends in real life.

27 May 1917 Jack writes to Arthur Greeves (AG): "Cherry (Robbins) is not pretty unfortunately but she is what I call a really ripping kind of person—an awfully good sort, and (greatest recommendation to us) a lover of books."

3 June 1917 Jack writes again: "The piano too would be a perpetual joy, for Cherry was playing it when she was in here to tea the other day, and says it is quite good...She is a real sportsman, the sort of person I really like. *Quel domage que sa figure n'egale pas son esprit!* Yet after all she is plain in rather

a pleasing kind of way when you get to know her." There follows a short sentence— "Mrs. Robbins I also like immensely"—that foreshadows his judgment of Janie Moore in a 27 August letter (see below).

Phase One:

7 June 1917 Jack drafted into cadet battalion. Moved to Keble College, Oxford and is alphabetically roomed with E.F.C. Paddy Moore.

10 June 1917 Writes AG that "I am in a strangely productive mood at present and spend my few moments of spare time in scribbling verse...During (an anticipated four weeks leave) I propose to get together all the stuff I have perpetrated and see if any kind publisher would like to take it."

10 June 1917 Jack writes AG in same letter about Cherry Robbins, "How sad that so interesting a girl is not beautiful (tho' she is certainly not nearly so plain as I at first imagined)..."

18 June 1917 Jack's first mention of Janie Moore (in letter to his father Albert Lewis (AL): "Moore, my room mate, comes from Clifton and is a very decent sort of man: his mother, an Irish lady, is staying up here and I have met her once or twice." (Clifton is an English public, i.e. private, school, near Bristol.)

8 July 1917 Jack complains to AG in a letter: "Yes, I must say that the society of some interesting person of the other sex is a great anodyne in a life like this—especially if it is one of the very few people who share our own pet tastes—Wagner, Rackham and the rest. Cherry has been away on leave this last week, and I find this causes quite a gap in my routine."

9 August 1917 Jack in Belfast for three days.

27 August 1917 Jack writes father that he is staying with Paddy "at the digs of his mother who, as I mentioned, is staying at Oxford. I like her immensely and thoroughly enjoyed myself."

Phase Two:

25 Sept. 1917 Jack commissioned.

29 Sept. 1917 Four weeks leave on completion of course. AL writes in his diary that Jack stayed with Moore and his mother. Came home on 12th October.

19 Oct. 1917 Posted to Somerset Light Infantry at Crownhill, near Plymouth.

28 Oct. 1917 In a letter to AG: "At last you will say, and I admit I should have written long ago. I am the more sorry to have to begin my letter by saying something rather ungracious. Since coming back and meeting a certain person [i.e., Janie Moore] I have begun to realize that it was not at all the right thing for me to tell you so much as I did. I must therefore try to undo my actions as far as possible by asking you to try and forget my various statements and not to refer to the subject. Of course I have perfect trust in you, *mon vieux*, but still I have no business to go discussing those sort of things with you. So in future that topic must be taboo between us."

15 Nov. 1917 Jack wires AL with news of "48 hours leave—report Southampton, Saturday." Asks for reply at Janie Moore's address in Bristol. AL professes not to understand, asks for letter. Jack writes explaining he is going to France, concluding that he must go and do some shopping—presumably for Janie Moore and an adumbration of his future function.

17 Nov. 1917 Jack crosses to France, without seeing AL.

29 Nov. 1917 Reaches the front line on his 19th birthday.

13 Dec. 1917 Tells AL that he is behind the line, and has finished George Eliot's *Adam Bede.* Writes to AG on 14 December 1917: "...you may perhaps understand how nice and homely it is for me to know that the two people who matter most to me in the world [i.e., Arthur Greeves and Janie Moore] are in touch." The exclusion of Albert Lewis is noteworthy.

26 Dec. 1917 Jack's battalion near Arras, France.

4 January 1918 Tells AL, after his return, that "I have been up in the trenches for a few days...Reading *The Mill on the Floss.*" Jack writes to AG 2 February 1918: "...as for the older days...Perhaps you don't believe that I want all that again, because other things more important have come in: but after all there is room for other things besides love in a man's life." This presumably acknowledges Jack's love for Janie Moore, and ten days later in another letter he writes "However, we may have some good times yet, although I have been at war and although I love someone."

Feb. 1918 Jack sick with trench fever. Spends four weeks in hospital at Le Treport.

28 Feb. 1918 Returns to front.

24 March 1918 Paddy Moore missing? Perhaps later.

15 April 1918 Jack is wounded at Battle of Arras by a British shell that fell short. Shrapnel wounds in three places—leg, hand, and in the chest under the arm. Visited by Warren who reported "wounds not serious." But the wounds were serious enough that Jack was still convalescing in October.

14 May 1918 Jack writes "I expect to be sent across [to UK] in a few days...as a stretcher case..." He also reports that Paddy Moore has been missing for more than a month. Writing to AG on 23 May 1918 Jack says, "You will be surprised and I expect not a little amused to hear that my views at present are getting almost monastic about all the lusts of the flesh."

25 May 1918 At Endsleigh Palace Hospital, London, and Janie Moore present by 29 May. From A. N. Wilson, p.58: "That he fell in love with Mrs Moore, and she with him—probably during the period when she was visiting him in hospital, and frantic with worry about Paddy—cannot be doubted. [They were lovers] probably from the summer of 1918 onwards." (But it can be doubted; see the discussion above.)

30 May 1918 Jack asks AL to visit but his father does not come. Jack writes to AG on 29 May and 3 June 1918: "Yes, after all our old conversations I can feel otherwise about the lusts of the flesh: is not desire merely a kind of sugar-plum that nature gives us to make us breed...and...one thing you may find in me now—a vein of asceticism, almost of puritan practice without the puritan dogma. I believe in no God, least of all in one that would punish me for the lusts of the flesh."

20 June 1918 Jack visits the Kirkpatricks in Little Bookham.

25 June 1918 Jack moved to convalescent home near Clifton, Bristol, chosen by him for proximity to Janie Moore's home.

17 July 1918 Jack writes that he has been preparing poems for publication. In late July/August Jack submits poems to Heinemann.

3 Sept. 1918 Again asks father to visit him, AL remains at home. Letter to AL, ?9 Sept. 1918 (date wrong, see below, probably 19 September): "You are aware that for some years now I have amused myself by writing verses, and a pocket- book collection of these followed me through France. Since my return I have occupied myself by revising them, getting them typed with a few additions, and trying to publish them...accepted by Heinemann."

12 Sept. 1918 Jack writes to AG from Janie Moore's address.

18 Sept. 1918 Jack tells AL that Paddy Moore is confirmed dead.

1 Oct. 1918 AL writes to Janie Moore commiserating on the confirmed death of Paddy Moore.

10 Oct. 1918 Jack remains at Clifton, then is transferred to Ludgershall, near Andover. Wound still troubling and Jack sent to Eastbourne, followed by Janie Moore.

Nov 1918 Jack writes to AG that his book of poems has been discussed with Heinemann [October 25]. Original title taken from St Peter's First Epistle where Christ went and preached unto the spirits in prison. But AL pointed out that there was already a novel called A *Spirit in Prison* so it was changed to *Spirits in Bondage*.

11 Nov. 1918 Armistice declared.

2 Dec. 1918 Jack writes AG about narrative poem, *Dymer*.

27 Dec. 1918 Jack's surprise visit to Belfast, demobilized; Warren there.

Phase Three:

13 Jan. 1919 Back to Oxford. Janie Moore already there.

Feb. 1919 One poem, "Death in Battle," appears in *Reveille* (attributed to Clive Hamilton).

20 March 1919 Publication of *Spirits in Bondage*. Jack writes no more lyric poetry at this time.

Phase Four:

Little needs to be said of this period of more than twenty years. Jack wrote to Arthur Greeves (5 November 1929): "[Barfield] said among other things that he thought the idea of the spiritual world as home—the discovery of homeliness in that wh[ich] is otherwise so remote—the feeling that you were coming back to to a place you have never yet reached—was peculiar to the British, and thought that Macdonald, Chesterton, and I, had this more than anyone else. He doesn't know you, of course—who with Minto, have taught me so much in that way..." This acknowledges Jack's debt to Janie Moore, for she taught him what having a home, and being at home, could mean, and she was considered to be a gracious hostess.

At the same time, she treated Jack abominably and had little consideration for his intellectual work, interrupting his studies with petty demands and wasting his time on niggling household chores. Three months after Janie Moore's death, Jack wrote in a letter: "I have lived most of it [my private life] in a house which was hardly ever at peace for 24 hours, amid senseless wranglings, lyings, backbitings, follies and scares. I never went home without a feeling of terror as to what appalling situation might have developed in my absence. Only now that it is over do I begin to realize quite how bad it was." It might reasonably be wondered why Jack continued the relationship. All that can be said is that he had made a commitment and that he thought it ought to be maintained. As he wrote to his brother in 1930: "I have definitely chosen and I don't regret the choice. Whether I was right or wrong, wise or foolish, to have done so originally, is now only an historical question: once having created expectations, one naturally fulfills them."

Some comments on the above are appropriate. It is obvious from the chronology that Jack wanted a relationship with somebody of the opposite sex and he seems to have been developing an affection for Cherry Robbins who was serving as a nurse (strictly with the V.A.D.) in a military hospital in Oxford. The entries above on 27 May, 3 June, 10 June 1917 show an increasing appreciation of Cherry Robbins and on 8 July Jack complains of her absence on a week's leave. But this is the last mention of Cherry in the published letters and diaries. She vanishes. It would be reasonable to suppose that Janie Moore caused her disappearance.

On 18 June, Jack mentions Janie Moore for the first time (in a letter to his father) and says that he has met her once or twice. Although Jack later became secretive and dissimulating with his father in regard to Janie Moore, it seems unlikely that at this point he had any reason to be either. And even two months later, he tells his father in a letter dated 27 August that he had spent a weekend with Moore "at the digs of his mother who, as I mentioned, is staying at Oxford. I like her immensely and thoroughly enjoyed myself." Again, this seems free of anything in the way of deceit, but it shows that eighteen-year old Jack is aware of forty-five-year old Janie Moore's impact upon him; he innocently reveals his own feelings—he likes her immensely (as he did the mother of Cherry Robbins), but there is no word of Paddy Moore. Incidentally, Warren in his diary, reports after Janie Moore's death, "...J(ack)...mentioned, greatly to my surprise, that 'when he first knew her she didn't get on any too well with her son.' I mention it because of my own ingenuousness, and to show the power of propaganda. All this Paddy-worship business has gone on so long, that I had come to believe—with a liberal discount of course—in the legend of the perfect son and the perfect mother united in the perfect relationship."

Jack was granted four days leave in early August 1917 and since his brother Warren was at home, he went to Belfast for the period 9-11 August. What transpired is not known, but very shortly afterwards Albert Lewis asks for a book he had lent Jack to read on the boat journey to be returned; he is told that "just at present my friend Mrs. Moore has borrowed it." Clearly, Jack had seen her and shortly after his return, at that. When Jack had finished his course he was granted four weeks leave and it appears that he went immediately to Bristol. He wrote to his father "On Monday, a cold (complete with sore throat) which I had developed at Oxford went on so merrily that Mrs Moore took my temperature and put me to bed. It took two weeks for him to recover and he arrived in Belfast on 12 October—much to the chagrin of his father who saw him for only a week. Jack was a truthful person and an honest person in all his dealings and for all of his life, except for matters connected with his relationship to Janie Moore, and particularly where his father was concerned. It is, of course, well known that he never told his father that he lived with Janie Moore and used his paternal allowance to support their household. But that is later.

What is highly probable on 25 September 1917 is that Jack had no intention of going to Belfast, at least, not first. He then writes to say he is sick, and perhaps he was (for he was prone to sickness all his life), but it certainly gave him a most convenient reason for not going home and it is not unreasonable to doubt the truth of his excuse. Moreover, it took him two weeks to get well enough to travel, according to his account—possible but, in the circumstances, certainly convenient. It seems much more probable that it was during this two-week stay in Bristol that the sexual relationship between Jack and Janie Moore began. It is easy enough to understand why Jack would not want to leave, but he had to—so he left it as late as he could, protected by the excuse of his real or feigned illness. There is, incidentally, no independent evidence to corroborate the story of sickness that he told his father.

This beginning of a sexual relationship between Jack and Janie Moore is a surmise and is clear contrary to the biographers—Wilson (who thinks it began in the summer of 1918), Green and Hooper (who imply that it happened but are competely vague about when), and Hooper (who for more than twenty years denied it ever existed, and who now regards it as likely but has nothing to say as to when it began).

Although it is—and will presumably remain a surmise, it has some confirmation from the letter that Jack wrote to Arthur Greeves on 28 October 1917. It is a belated letter—ten days after Jack's return from his leave in Belfast—but in it he tells Arthur that the subject of a certain person and himself is in future taboo. He goes further and asks Arthur to forget his statements—"it was not at all the right thing for me to tell you so much as I did." What did Jack say to Arthur? Clearly, it must have been something that really belonged to both Jack and Janie Moore—something that they shared. Jack realizes that it was not at all the right thing to do. If this is correct, then Jack had not merely reported to Arthur his feelings for Janie Moore or his hopes for their future; he must have reported what took place between them—namely, their lovemaking. Jack was still quite young and he and Arthur had freely shared sexual thoughts and fantasies in the past; perhaps during his October leave he had continued as if that were still possible, but meeting Janie Moore upon his return he realized that it was no longer something to be shared. It was a confidence and an intimacy, but with Janie not Arthur. Jack has no alternative because the episode does not belong to him alone; it also belongs to Janie Moore. This gives him no choice. He must remain silent.

In *Surprised by Joy*, the autobiographical story of his conversion, Jack Lewis reports his return to Oxford after the war: "But before I say anything of my life there I must warn the reader that one huge and complex episode will be omitted. I have no choice about this reticence. All I can or need say is that my earlier hostility to the emotions was very fully and variously avenged. But even if I were free to tell the story, I doubt if it has much to do with the subject of this book."

It is, perhaps, surprising that Janie Moore had nothing to do with his conversion—Jack seems to have found her indispensable, but only in a hermetically sealed capsule. Or perhaps his religious and academic developments were in the capsule. Quite apart from when the sexual relationship began, Jack tells Arthur Greeves in at least three letters (4 December 1917 and 2 and 12 February 1918) that he is in love with Janie Moore.

There is a strange confession that Jack makes three times to Arthur (23 and 29 May and 3 June 1918) about his views getting almost monastic about all the lusts of the flesh. They are not repeated and it is probable that the unaccustomed absence of sexual feelings on Jack's part are connected with the wounds he suffered on 15 April and the sexual suppressants (generically referred to as "bromides") provided routinely in British hospital fare—usually in the tea. They were not used only in hospitals, incidentally.

A final view of the Lewis-Moore relationship may be derived from a consideration of Jack's poems *Spirits in Bondage* published in March 1919, and the extracts from his diaries. The poems, forty in number, contain only two that might remotely be thought to be addressed to a woman—and even then, there is nothing to suggest that if they are addressed to a woman, that that woman is Janie Moore. What is absolutely clear is that Janie Moore and Jack's feelings for her and his sexual relationship with her do not play any significant part in the composition of these poems. Jack's only concern was to write of his equation: matter=nature=Satan, a concern that was not justified by his writings.

In the diaries of 1922-27, Janie Moore is often called Minto, but she is also designated by the letter D in the published text. This is misleading, because Warren, using an old typewriter, transcribed the diaries and she was designated originally by the Greek letter Delta which Warren, having only English characters, replaced with D. The significance of this is that the Greek letter almost certainly stands for a character in Platos famous dialogue on love, *The Symposium*, the priestess Diotima. It was Diotima who, Socrates reports, introduced him to the true nature of love, a nature that was essentially and ultimately spiritual. But we know that one of Jack's tutors at Oxford said that Jack thought that Plato was always wrong and, accordingly, he made the true nature of love physical—not spiritual—and acclaimed Janie Moore as his Diotima, as the woman who introduced him to the pleasures of the flesh.

In *Surprised by Joy*, Jack says that his earlier hostility to the emotions was fully and variously avenged. Janie Moore played a critical role in that avenging, and for the first ten or so years of their relationship it was largely defined by sexual satisfaction and a home-life on Jack's part, while Janie Moore had in Jack a replacement for her dead son, Paddy, and a surrogate for The Beast, her absent husband sequestered in Ireland.

APPENDIX 4

STEALING THE KING'S RING

When I was talking with C. S. Lewis on 20 July 1956, I let slip that something I liked was childish. He corrected me immediately. *Childlike* was the word I wanted, he explained; reserve the word *childish* for misbehavior. I never forgot the difference. Lewis's juvenilia is childlike, and the way it has been handled is childish.

The early juvenilia itself was charming and simple. But it has been turned into a tangle of missing documents, false claims, wrong attributions, contradictions, obfuscations, and outright misinformation, topped off by what looks like a forgery. The very same people who have treated the juvenilia this way control Lewis's adult writings, and the story of the juvenilia is one of great importance.

Although Walter Hooper says he received two childhood notebooks from C. S. Lewis to help him with his research, he has kept them from other Lewis researchers ever since. Even Lewis's chosen biographer never got to see the originals or photocopies. An entire generation of Lewis specialists is aging and dying without access to the early (not late) juvenilia.

Because almost anything written by C. S. Lewis sells prodigiously, *Boxen: The Imaginary World of the Young C. S. Lewis* was published in 1985 and soon spread across the United States, England, and Canada. Store managers wondered whether to place it with books for children, religious books, biography, or adult fiction; but perhaps it belonged in the mystery section instead.

In it Hooper told his January 1964 bonfire all story over again:

Jack and Warnie had been living at the Kilns since 1930. Then, when Jack died on 22nd November 1963, Warnie was afraid he could not afford to go on living there and decided to move into a smaller house. Preparatory to moving into the smaller place where I was to join him, I was living in Keble College with Dr and Mrs. Austin Farrer. One day in January 1964 I went out to see Warnie. I discovered from the gardener, Paxford, that Warnie had been burning various papers on a bonfire for the past three days.[81]

According to Hooper, Fred Paxford asked to be allowed to save some of the papers for Hooper, and Major Lewis answered (unreasonably) that the papers had to be burned unless Hooper happened to visit that very day. Fortunately, Hooper was led to come and rescue many things from the flames, including a notebook and an exercise book full of Lewis's childhood writing. (Unlike loose-leaf or spiral bound notebooks, Lewis's were solidly bound hardcover books similar to ledgers.)

Hooper added this material to the two notebooks of Lewis juvenilia that he had already received as a personal gift from C. S. Lewis six months earlier, when he was visiting Oxford in the summer of 1963. Apparently Hooper means for us to assume that he took the first two gift notebooks home to Kentucky with him at the end of August and then brought them back to England in January 1964 and kept them secret—in his own words, "most tenderly preserved." After his return to England, Hooper finally met Major Warren Lewis in the second half of February 1964, then allegedly obtained more of the early juvenilia at a January 1964 bonfire.

It is a remarkable coincidence that after the Lewis brothers had cherished their childhood material for over fifty years; a brand new friend allegedly obtained much of it within six months, through two entirely unrelated events. This is all the more remarkable in light of the fact that he was in the United States most of that six-month period. It seems that Warren, who took immense interest in the juvenilia and some interest in life's coincidences, was unaware that Hooper had acquired either set of the early material. In his references to the juvenilia in his diary and letters, I have found no sign of Warren's realizing that Hooper had some of it.

---

[81] C. S. Lewis, *Boxen* (San Diego: Harcourt Brace Jovanovich, 1985) 21.

At some point in 1965 Hooper borrowed Lewis materials from Warren's collection. On 14 September 1965 he returned them to Warren at his home on Ringwood Road. But Warren checked and realized that some of the juvenilia was missing. He wrote to Hooper immediately. "Would you let me have it like a good fellow next time you come up this way?" There is no record of what happened. [82]

On 28 February 1969 Warren notified Hooper that Jock Gibb expected him to pick up the Lewis juvenilia at the Kilns and deliver it to his publishing office in London. Gibb would consider publishing it. Warren told Gibb he had great hopes the project would be a success: "Mind, if you lose any of these books, I will return from the grave and make your life a torment!" [83]

Although the Lewis brothers had long ago sentimentally buried in the garden the toys that inspired the stories, and they might have lost some of their juvenilia through the years, Warren carefully preserved most of it in a locked drawer in his bedroom toward the end of his life. His concern about its safety, expressed to Clyde Kilby, might possibly have reflected a sense that some was missing. [84]

Warren willed it all to the Marion E. Wade Center in Wheaton, Illinois, and died in 1973. When Hooper co-authored the 1974 volume *C. S. Lewis: A Biography,* he chose not to tell co-author Green or the public about his private collection of Lewis's childhood productions. According to that official biography, only a few poems—not any stories—survived from Lewis's early knights-in-armor juvenilia. [85] But that was not true. Hooper has a personal collection of Lewis's earliest prose and drawings that I consider more interesting than the set of longer products from Lewis's later childhood. (All of Lewis's juvenilia is commonly referred to as Boxen material. Hence the title *Boxen* for a book which includes a variety of childhood materials.)

A decade after Warren's death, Curator Lyle Dorsett gave Hooper free use of the Wade's juvenilia to prepare his 1985 volume *Boxen,* and Hooper's

---

[82] The letter is part of Walter Hooper's document collection in the library of the University of North Carolina at Chapel Hill.

[83] From the Chapel Hill Collection.

[84] Author's personal conversation with Clyde Kilby.

[85] Roger Lancelyn Green and Walter Hooper, *C. S. Lewis: A Biography* (London: Collins, 1974) 24.

position with the Lewis estate gave him the legal right to publish it. He presented it with great scholarly flourish.

The materials in *Boxen* appear chronologically, which meant starting with the material in Hooper's private collection rather than Wade material. *Boxen* begins with a three-act play titled "The King's Ring," probably written when Lewis was seven years old. Whether one finds it a valuable example of creativity from an unusual child or no more than early practice from an author who became interesting later, some familiarity with it is needed in order to grasp the puzzles involved in *Boxen*.

The First Act of the play begins with this first scene:

KING BUNNY: This wine is good.
BAR-MAN: I shall drink a stiff goblet to the health of King Bunny.
KING BUNNY: For the good toast much thanks.
SIR PETER: Draws near the dinner hour so pleas your Magasty.

In the second scene the mouse named Hit, who had been the barman, visited the King in Pip Castle and tricked him into taking off his ring. Hit disappeared with the ring.

In the third scene Sir Peter announced to some of King Bunny's retinue that the ring was lost. Immediately thereafter, Hit entered and sold the ring to one of the King's friends. Hit had disguised the ring so it would not be recognized.

In the Second Act, Hit had shot one of King Bunny's musicians with an arrow and had fled to Cannon-Town. The King and his friends went to Cannon-town and dubbed Hit a knight in order to get to know him better, because he was their prime suspect.

In the Third Act, the frog named Mr. Big recognized the disguised ring of the King on the hand of a friend and accused him of being the thief. Sir Peter exclaimed, "Who!! Which!! Where!! When!! Why!! How!!" Then wise Sir Goose explained Hit's trickery. Soon Sir Goose captured Hit. The King received his lost ring back and prepared to sail home. The play ends.

KING BUNNY: Now I think we must go back to
Mouse-land. Look the sun hath clove the earth in
2. (Curtain.)
THE END

*The anchient Mice believed that at sunset the sun cut a
hole in the earth for its self.

This simple play has a large cast, and the child Lewis's own cast-of-
characters page is reproduced in the book in all its ink-blotted glory, a clumsy
and extremely ambitious list for a seven-year-old boy, in both printing and
cursive script. It was tidied up a bit in the printed version (Icthus-oress for
ic-this-oress, General for generel), but much of the eccentricity is preserved,
apparently at random.

Most Lewis enthusiasts would have preferred many more facsimile pages
in *Boxen* and photos of the old notebooks Lewis used and treasured. The more
interested one is in children's art and writing, the more questions one has
that *Boxen*, in its present format, does not answer. For example, there is no
hint about the size of Lewis's illustrations or, in many cases, their location.[86]
Scale is one of the factors in the charm of juvenilia. There is no word about
the size and length of the notebooks or the number of pages devoted to a given
project. Readers have no way to get a sense of proportion or position for the
materials.

Readers naturally assume that the four ink drawings illustrating "The
King's Ring" are by Lewis and that they are all we have of his illustrations for
the project. They are wonderful for a seven-year-old boy. Not only is the
perspective and composition advanced, but the boldness, accuracy, and
vitality of the ink drawing is amazing in contrast to Lewis's immature
printing. King Bunny, various mice, and the Golliwog are charming
creatures depicting actual toys in the Lewis nursery. In some scenes the plump

---

[86] Joe Christopher reported in "Publishing Boxen" in the November 1988 *Lamp-Post* that Hooper has shifted some of the illustrations around. In the Wade Center Christopher was unable to discover sources for the map on page 97 and the drawing on page 177, both of which should be at the Wade Center according to Hooper's notes.

mice, clad only in fur and whiskers, perch on their haunches in genuinely mousy style.

Few adults can produce a sketch as complex and charming as the third "King's Ring" illustration, on page 29 of *Boxen*. It includes all of these: Mr. Icthus-oress sitting on a bench with his harp nearby; the wonderful Golliwog next to him with a staff; the mouse Lob in his monk's habit; the mouse Tom behind him with his spinning wheel nearby; playing cards that have fallen on the floor; a barred window; a lighted wall sconce; and a table with a glowing candle on it.

Most of the drawings in *Boxen*, however, are much less exciting. They are the stiff, laborious efforts of a child who grasped perspective very early. They are skillful, clear, and detailed—but not delightful. One might get the impression that Lewis had a flash of artistic precocity when he was seven and that it immediately faded away.

By marvelous good fortune, however, the entire final page of "The King's Ring" is available just as the child Lewis penned it, but shrunk to 2 by 3.5 inches. It does not appear in *Boxen*. It appears on page 98 of an earlier book, *C. S. Lewis: Images of His World* by Clyde S. Kilby and Douglas R. Gilbert (published by the William B. Eerdmans Company in 1973). With a magnifying glass, the page becomes fairly clear. The page is numbered 24 in the upper left corner, and it contains the following:

> hath clov clove
> the earth in 2.*
>
> CURTAIN
> THE END
>
>
> *the ancheint Mice belived
> that at sun-set the
> sun cut a hole in
> the earth for its self.

C.S. Lewis ended the play with an illustration that is edited out of the book *Boxen*. It shows the thief being punished. Sir Peter Mouse and King Bunny pose triumphant over their prisoner, Hit—the mouse that stole the ring. King Bunny, alas, is a rumpled figure who didn't turn out right. Hit is not much more than a stick figure with incredibly long arms. And charming Sir Peter is a tall skinny mouse in a tunic, like a lanky boy with a mouse head.

This fifth picture resembles in an immature way most of Lewis's art in *Boxen*, but it doesn't look like the four previous "King's Ring" illustrations at all. It looks as if the child Lewis had help with the first four. *Great help.* If Warren had been allowed to publish *Boxen*, he might have told us truly that his mother or father drew the first four illustrations for their bright little son, at his request. As it is, readers are being royally fooled.

"The Relief of Murry," on pages 37-38 of *Boxen*, is closely related to "The King's Ring." In his preface to the 1982 book *On Stories and Other Essays on Literature*,[87] Hooper described "The Relief of Murry" without naming it and said it is in the notebook that contains "To Mars and Back," elsewhere called Notebook III. That seems to be an error; Hooper says in *Boxen* that he found "The Relief of Murry" in Notebook I with "The King's Ring." Furthermore, it looks as if the two illustrations for "The Relief of Murry," like the four mature illustrations for "The King's Ring," were done by a Lewis parent. First is a vigorously fluid sketch of a dressed mouse with sword, and second is a troop of chivalrous mice in armor, one on a steed, all setting off to do battle. They are the work of a hastily careless but sure and talented hand. I think we have a precocious young child's story with adult sketches done at his request. (It should be remembered that C. S. Lewis was born with slightly defective hands and lacked full digital dexterity.)

"To Mars and Back," in Notebook III, would be great fun to analyze as a precursor to *Out of the Silent Planet*. In his preface to *On Stories and Other Essays on Literature*, Hooper not only placed it in the same notebook with "The Relief of Murry" (Notebook I), but placed it in Lewis's early childhood, claiming that he wrote it when he was not much more than five or six years old. But the first two pages of the story appear on page 104 of *C. S. Lewis:*

---

[87] C. S. Lewis, *On Stories and Other Essays on Literature* (New York: Harcourt Brace Jovanovich, 1982) x.

Images of His World, and it seems like a much older child's story. It begins with a narrator named Bensin invited to go to Mars in a "vessel" with a chum of his. He has a "mild intrest" in astronomy, but is doubtful about the trip. He decides to go to Southampton and perhaps from there to central Africa and Mars. This is all on the first two pages. That is all we know about it.

What readers have had no way to know until now is that Notebook III includes, along with "To Mars and Back," a story or diary entry in lofty style telling how eleven-year-old Lewis got up one bleak November morning at boarding school in 1909 and washed in icy dormitory water. I propose that "To Mars and Back" was written when Lewis was closer to age ten than age five, placing the story after his mother's death.

Walter Hooper said on page 9 of his lengthy introduction that he regrets that not much of Lewis's earliest work survives, but that "all that has survived is in this book." That is an odd claim, because his accounts contradict it. Besides that, there are five notebook pages of Lewis's earliest surviving work pictured on pages 98 and 99 of *C. S. Lewis: Images of His World,* and they are not included in *Boxen.*

These five pages seem to be located in Hooper's Notebook I with "The King's Ring. " (These pages have rounded corners and 21 ruled lines, and the ratio of their dimensions is approximately 2 by 3.5.) On page 197 of *Boxen* we read that "The King's Ring" is in an account book with stiff black covers—the only one of its kind in the assorted Lewis juvenilia. (It seems to be the only one with rounded corners.)

Clearly, the early material that is being left out of *Boxen* is relevant for anyone who wants to know all surviving details about Lewis's childhood. But the strange circumstances of the ownership and handling of the early childhood material present a literary mystery that is intriguing in its own right. The juvenilia in *C. S. Lewis: Images of His World* has to be noted carefully for this reason.

First there is the important concluding illustration for "The King's Ring." Then there is on the facing page (25) a six-panel cartoon about a similar adventure. In the first panel a burglar mouse in a tunic, with long pipe-stem arms and legs, reaches into a large jar in the treasure room of a castle and says, "Dear me. O someone coming. I'll hide." In the second panel the burglar is down in the jar and says "Ah now I'm safe, hop they no one I'll will see Me."

In the third panel, a servant in a tunic picks up the large jar and says, "I have to take this off—." In the fourth panel the servant is stooping awkwardly on the edge of a bridge saying, "and as there is nothing in it throw it away!!" The jar has fallen into the water below, and a voice comes out saying "Oh!"

In the fifth panel the burglar can be seen inside the jar under the water with fish swimming by; he says, "Oh and I'm sinking." In the sixth panel the burglar, dead or alive, is being hoisted up onto the bridge with a long pole wielded by a mouse in an impressive uniform.

Warren Lewis was reportedly concerned that someone might pilfer his hoard of juvenilia. It is interesting to imagine someone taking part of it and then discovering little C. S. Lewis's stern moral fable about burglary inside.

Another page from Notebook I shows some of the characters from "The King's Ring" in another story. Again a stiff boy-shaped mouse is the thief. It looks as if he is hiding in a large "oile" jar. Sir Big the frog and Mr. Icthyosaurus are sitting in the road, and a truly marvelous Sir Goose is about to disappear over the horizon. The words "Take any ruby" are written across the sky.

Yet another page pictured in Gilbert's book but left out of *Boxen* and left out of Hooper's supposedly complete accounts is the delightful conclusion of a description of some Animal-land geography. It tells that Murry was the capital of Mouse-land and Canon-town was the capital of Rabbit-land. Little Lewis's spelling is brave: "A twon is a large piece of land covered with buildings, most of wich tuch each other. The parts of a town bwetwen the houses are called streets or roads and are used for trafic to travel up and dwon. If a twon is verry small it is called a vilage. Vilgges are more pretty than twons." This essay is followed by a banner that says "Fines" suspended between two funny little buildings with human legs (Lewis meant "Finis," The End).

In addition to all of the above, some of the juvenilia in Hooper's Notebook I that was left out of *Boxen* does not appear in *C. S. Lewis: Images of His World*. It has not been displayed, published, or described anywhere except in *The C. S. Lewis Hoax*. For example, a page marked June 1907 shows a sketch of several people in a severe thunderstorm in a city, with a sign that says "Beware." On the facing page, marked "A Dream," a man with a cane is walking in the sky above a city and his top hat is falling off. On another page, five little men hunt sea creatures underwater, and on the facing page a large deep-sea diver poses in his gear with an ax in his hand. In the upper corner one man in a tunic beheads another with an ax. On another page a neatly diagrammed house features a trunk room and a servant's room in the attic.

Best of all, perhaps, is the page in Notebook I featuring a tidy, circular solar system with "air" inside, "space" outside, and "unknown" under it all. The latter would make a wonderful illustration for the epilogue of C. S. Lewis's serious study *The Discarded Image*.[88] It is a shame that hardly anyone knows about this wonderful design, and no one can see it. The original belongs to Walter Hooper, and the right to publish it belongs to the Lewis Estate.

How did I see it? Fortunately, Douglas Gilbert keeps all his old negatives and proofs on file. He sent me proofs of the Lewis memorabilia that he happened to photograph on his 1972 visit to Oxford. As he recalls, all the juvenilia photos were taken in the Kilns; but I think it possible that he photographed Notebooks I and III in Hooper's apartment.

Gilbert's pictures of Notebook III material include, in addition to the beginning of "To Mars and Back" and the dormitory scene, a page from an illustrated story about Mr. Bull and a red-haired Indian in shiny boots who came in and shook snow on the Turkey carpet. For thirty years, Hooper has kept this story secret. Why?

One can assume that Gilbert wishes he had photographed Notebooks I and III much more completely while they were in his hands. Surely students of Lewis's early life wish he had done so.

Hooper's *Boxen* introduction is long, evasive, and confusing. There is much mystification. For example, Hooper says that the little stories "Manx against Manx" and "The Relief of Murry" form a transition between the modern setting of "The King's Ring" and a medieval setting; but "The King's Ring" is itself medieval. Hooper mentions Lewis's "Tararo," "The Life of Lord John Big," and "Littera Scripta Manet" ("The Written Word Abides"), but says he left them out for the sake of brevity. (They are "most tenderly preserved.") Surely many readers would much prefer the missing juvenilia to

---

[88] C. S. Lewis, *The Discarded Image* (Cambridge: University Press, 1964) 216-23.

ten solid pages of "Encyclopedia Boxoniana" and fifteen solid pages of what could be called Hooperiana.

Hooper says, "Honored as I am in being appointed to edit the stories, I suppose my old friend [Lewis] would, with his usual gaiety, call me that future Boxonologist. He might even have suggested me as the first holder of the Lord Big Chair of Boxonology." He tells how much he enjoyed reading the juvenilia while he lived with C. S. Lewis in 1963. He says that Lewis talked with him about it at some length.

In what is perhaps an effort to make Lewis into a saint, Hooper explains away the claim in his childhood diary that he had a bad temper like his father. According to Hooper, "When Jack spoke of himself...as having his father's 'bad temper' he almost certainly meant that he shared his father's gift for oratory."[89]

Few people force themselves to wade through *Boxen*; and of those who do, few really read "History of Animal-Land" on pages 43-49. By far the most interesting part of this turgid essay is its enigmatic last sentence: "The Archbishop was murdered." Hooper probably expected this to whet the interest of Lewis specialists, because in Lewis's 1938 poem "The Queen of Drum" an old Archbishop is murdered. Early foreshadowing is sometimes genuine, but it is also one of the common ploys of literary forgers.

What is the provenance of this "History of Animal-Land" essay? Hooper does not give the manuscript's location, but he gives its peculiar source. He claims that in 1953 Lewis read a story by Hugh, the eleven-year-old son of his friend Lord David Cecil. Then Lewis loaned Hugh "History of Animal-Land," and Hugh liked it so much that he hand-copied much of it. (Surely no normal eleven-year-old boy would copy out this dull essay of his own free will.) It is Hugh Cecil's fragmentary copy that Hooper rescued from the bonfire and published in *Boxen*.

But on 31 May 1968 Lord David Cecil wrote to Hooper[90] that although C. S. Lewis and Hugh once discussed their rather similar juvenilia about bears, "I do not remember him giving any stories to Hugh." ("A History of Animal-Land" is not about bears.)

---

[89] C. S. Lewis, *Boxen*, 17.

[90] In the Chapel Hill collection.

Nothing can make *Boxen* very interesting, but some of its needless confusion can be sorted out. In addition to the materials in *Boxen* from the Wade Center ("Boxen or Scenes from Boxonian city life,"[91] "The Locked Door and Thankyu," "The Sailor") and the essay allegedly contributed by Hugh Cecil ("History of Animal-land"), *Boxen* contains the following:

1. From Notebook 1, which C. S. Lewis gave to Walter Hooper in the summer of 1963: "The King's Ring, " "Manx against Manx," and "The Relief of Murry."

2. From Notebook II, which Walter Hooper saved from the Lewis bonfire: "History of Mouseland from Stone-Age to Bublish," "The Chess Monograph, Part I," "Life of Little Mr. White," and "How To Make Men Picturesc."

3. From Notebook III, which C. S. Lewis gave to Walter Hooper in the summer of 1963: "The Chess Monograph, Part II," and "The Geography of Animal-land."

4. From a certain exercise book that Walter Hooper saved from the Lewis bonfire: "Encyclopedia Boxoniana."[92]

C. S. Lewis allegedly wrote "Encyclopedia Boxoniana" in September 1927 and April 1928 while visiting his father at the family home.[93] Unfortunately, what we have is both dull and long-winded. Parts of it do not sound at all like C. S. Lewis. (Would the adult Lewis intrusively refer to one king's ring as "the crown jewels of Animalland?")

The mock-scholarly tone appropriate for satirizing poor English is not used with that particular purpose in "Encyclopedia Boxoniana," and so readers are left wondering why Lewis wrote dreadful sentences such as this:

---

[91] In "Publishing Boxen" Christopher reports that in the Wade Center he saw this essay in Lewis's childhood penmanship and that Lewis spelled the key words "Boscen" and "Bosconian."

[92] Joe R. Christopher examined this notebook in the Bodleian Library on August 24, 1992, and has described it in "A Catalogue, Two Notebooks, and an Exercise Book" in *Mythprint* (April 1994): 2-4. He reports that this notebook was deposited (not donated) in January 1989, evidently in response to the charges in *The C. S. Lewis Hoax.* It is labelled "Lewis Ms. No. 27" in Hooper's usual handwriting. On the inside of the front cover there are two sets of initials in pencil: J.R.R.T. and T.S. E. (Do they stand for J.R.R. Tolkien and T.S. Eliot?) "Encyclopedia Boxoniana" is written on the first sixteen pages, followed by apparently random notes on Chaucer, Spenser, Boswell, Jeremy Taylor, and linguistics, plus a quotation from Shakespeare.

[93] In his 5 October 1927 letter to Warren, Lewis mentions beginning such an overview of their juvenilia; but that does not guarantee authenticity of the 1985 essay.

"As regards the configuration of the principle [sic] land masses all the extant maps show a remarkable uniformity, but as regards the scale it is quite impossible to reconcile any of the maps with the distances implied in the texts where journies [sic] are described."[94] Readers are supposed to believe that one of the greatest masters of English in our century wrote this when he was already teaching at Oxford. I don't think he could have written such prose unless he had been delirious with fever.

Lewis is not satirizing his own Boxen materials, and he is not satirizing pompous scholarship, and so the following sentence appears inexplicable: "To draw out all that can be deduced from the texts, to attempt the solution of all problems and the removal of all contradictions in the light of general probability and skilful hypothesis, would have been to anticipate the future Boxonologist rather than to provide him with his tools."[95] Really.

For content as well as style, this grandiose declaration about his childhood creations may be the most unLewisian sentence of all: "And this is a matter of absorbing interest; to trace the process by which an attic full of common-place childrens' [sic] toys became a world as consistent and self-sufficient as that of the Iliad or the Barsetshire novels, would be no small contribution to general psychology.'"[96] Neither the words, the attitude, nor the wrong punctuation of *children's* are true C. S. Lewis, some readers suspect.

A sprinkling of spelling errors in the text might make it look more authentic to readers who know that Lewis was an imperfect speller. But to those who are suspicious it looks like a ploy.

Ironically, when Stanley Mattson appointed handwriting analyst Nancy Cole to attest to the authenticity of *The Dark Tower* manuscript, she did not know of my charge that "Encyclopedia Boxoniana" was an earlier forgery. Therefore, she unguardedly observed that Lewis's handwriting on this manuscript differs from Lewis's usual style because of its more formal look, more vertical slant, and more regular rhythm.

Questioning the validity of "Encyclopedia Boxoniana," which C. S. Lewis supposedly wrote as a mature man, is not to doubt his fondness for his childhood creations. But the most interesting part of *Boxen* is "The King's

---

[94] *Boxen*, 206.
[95] Ibid., 206.
[96] Ibid., 197.

Ring," and from there the book goes downhill to "Encyclopedia Boxoniana." Whether this final essay is by Lewis or not, it is almost unendurable.

Roger Lancelyn Green, who had discussed Lewis's juvenilia with him and who saw how precocious it was, nevertheless admitted frankly in the biography that as literature Boxen was "intensely dull."[97] Dr. Clyde S. Kilby was delighted to place much of the juvenilia in the Marion E. Wade Center, but he felt that it shouldn't be published. If published, he reasoned, it would surely sell because of the name of its author; but it would bore the purchasers. (He had not seen the most boring part, "Encyclopedia Boxoniana.") History seems to bear out Kilby's prediction.

The review praising *Boxen* in the October 1986 issue of *Eternity* magazine[98] gave me the impression that the reviewer had been too bored to read the book. He said that the first section consisted of a group of short plays (it consisted of one short play and some short essays), and that it was apparently written when Lewis was in elementary school (Lewis did not attend elementary school, as the introduction makes clear). For the bulk of the book, the reviewer remarked, "These writings are obviously from the pre-Christian Lewis and reflect his classically romantic mind." This idea seems to reflect a classically sleepy mind.

Inaccurate reviews of *Boxen* will do the world little harm. Even possible additions or omissions in *Boxen* itself are of minimal significance to the reading public. The only two people who cared ardently about the Boxen material are long buried together under a common marker in the Headington churchyard.

Since *Boxen* is of little interest to most readers, what difference does it make whether it is handled scrupulously or not? An answer can be found in "The King's Ring" itself.

Near the end of "The King's Ring," helpful Sir Goose asked Sir Peter Mouse and Sir Big why all this fuss was made about the missing ring when King Bunny could have got a new ring which would have been just as good.

And they answered, "Ah, but this ring was an airloom."

---

[97] Green and Hooper, *C. S. Lewis*, 23.
[98] Philip G. Houghton, "C. S. Lewis's *Boxen*," *Eternity*, (October 1986): 55-56. Houghton observes, "Lewis fans will welcome this book with open arms. Many have been waiting for decades to learn more of Boxen."

That suggests the real reason why some of us are exclaiming like Sir Peter, "Who! ! Which! ! Where! ! When!! Why!! What!! How!!"

When asked "Why all this fuss about what is or isn't correct and genuine in the posthumous C. S. Lewis books, and what difference does it make?" we can echo Sir Peter: "Ah but this was an *airloom* to us." We count Lewis and whatever he created as part of our heritage.

APPENDIX 5

A. N. WILSON ERRATA

Like the delightful cottage that Hansel and Gretel found in the woods, novelist
A. N. Wilson's biography of C. S. Lewis looks wonderful and is easy to feast
upon. Most readers start nibbling, then start gobbling, and exclaim that it's
delicious. I feel like a little bird that chirps a warning to forest travelers. C. S.
Lewis, J.R.R. Tolkien, and Charles Williams would all have loathed this book,
and rightly so.

The good news is that Wilson is dramatic, entertaining, and nimble-
witted; a writer who lightly tosses words and ideas into the air for the fun of
seeing what he can do to please the public while skewering anyone handy. The
bad news is that when illusion is more fun than reality, Wilson chooses
illusion. He claims to be smashing two images of Lewis, but in fact he is
smashing three. And he sets up a brand new Lewis image of his own, one that
makes him look very clever at Lewis's expense.

First, Wilson attacks a Roman Catholic myth about C. S. Lewis's per-
petual virginity. But the existence of that Catholic myth is itself a Wilson
myth based upon a Walter Hooper myth. Hooper's insistence upon Lewis's
celibacy has never been accepted by such Roman Catholic Lewis authorities as
George Sayer, Dom Bede Griffiths, and Sheldon Vanauken. Even Father John
Randolph Willis, in *Pleasures Forevermore: The Theology of C. S. Lewis* from
Loyola University Press, accepts Lewis's account of his marriage in *A Grief
Observed*. But Wilson slays his first strawman with a flourish and makes
Roman Catholics look silly.

Second, Wilson attacks the Protestant myth that C. S. Lewis didn't smoke
and drink. That purported Protestant belief is another Hooper creation, and
Wilson professes to believe in it. Paradoxically, he has to admit that
abstemious Protestants admit that Lewis smoked and drank (Lewis's tankard
and pipes are on display in the Wade Center), but he concludes that in doing
so they fail to take the matter seriously enough. "Evidence is only of
peripheral interest when the idolatrous imagination gets to work." Unlike the

irritatingly tolerant Protestants, Wilson takes smoking and drinking so seriously that he claims against all evidence that Lewis disliked nonsmokers: "Lewis was impatient with puritanism and disliked non-smokers or teetotallers." (Lewis's good friends Roger Lancelyn Green and George Sayer were both nonsmokers, and Lewis tried hard to quit but couldn't.) But Wilson slays his second straw man with a flourish and makes Protestants look silly.

Third, Wilson attacks C. S. Lewis's own portrayal of himself as a reasonably heathy-minded Christian. Wilson reduces Lewis's evangelizing Christianity to a crippled way of coping with life. He claims that Lewis's account of his boyhood frustration with prayer can't be true. Then in one of the most amazing passages in his book (on page 162), Wilson claims to have been considering for twenty years a June 1938 letter from Lewis to Owen Barfield that shows how warped Lewis's thinking was when he began defending Christianity. At that time, Wilson says, Lewis turned against innocent pleasures such as feeling the wind in your hair, walking with bare feet on the grass, and swimming in the rain: Lewis decided these activities were Nazi or would lead to homosexuality. Thus "one must also view with ambivalence his excursion into the realm of religious apologetics." Wilson slays his third strawman with a flourish, and makes C. S. Lewis look silly.

But as anyone can see by reading the passage in *Letters*, Lewis was reporting an idiocy that he overheard from two undergraduates, and he was horrified by it. "Think it over: it gets worse the longer you look at it," he urged Barfield. Wilson now attributes the students' notion to Lewis himself, thus impugning Lewis's common sense and his Christian apologetics.

Fourth, while rejecting the two insubstantial Hooper myths and C. S. Lewis's substantial account of his religious pilgrimage, A. N. Wilson substitutes his own ideological Freudian view of C. S. Lewis. Thus the real C. S. Lewis, he claims, was not a perpetual virgin, not a nonsmoker and nondrinker, and not the genuine Christian believer he wanted to be. He was instead a terrified Oedipal neurotic and a closet misanthrope. The Narnian wardrobe is a symbol of Flora Lewis's private parts. Surely it is disingenuous for a biographer to psychoanalyze an author this way without telling readers what that author wrote about such psychoanalyzing. Wilson doesn't even mention Lewis's trenchant essay "Psycho-analysis and Literary Criticism" and what Lewis says in it. I call that cheating.

The hero of this book is A. N. Wilson, who quickly and easily sees through everything, and who winks at his readers because they are now in on the joke also. In this droll style of writing the joke is never stated clearly; but it is based on the assumption that everyone except the author and his reader is patently absurd. Thus Wilson's show of deference to C. S. Lewis comes across as remarkably generous, an enlightened and refined young man's patient, understanding tribute to a popular but coarse, befuddled, blundering, and self-deluded eccentric of his grandfather's era. It is in that spirit that Wilson alleges that once a year Lewis forced all his embarrassed (male) students to get thoroughly drunk and tell dirty jokes with him. He even recounts what the obnoxiously drunk Lewis said to one of his drunken students (unidentified) at a urinal (location unidentified) about fifty years earlier, without explaining how he could possibly come up with such a story unless he invented it.

Wilson is titillating to read, and he displays such self-assured flash and dazzle that few readers and reviewers stop to ask, "Wait a minute—who is this young man to set himself up as the condescending but gentle judge of C. S. Lewis? He certainly doesn't seem to have read and digested most of Lewis's writing, and many of his facts are wrong." Wilson resorts to simplistic dismissal of Lewis's apologetics and inaccurate summaries of complex philosophical issues. He presumes to call Mrs. Moore 'Minto,' and refers to Albert Lewis by his sons' secret, slightly mocking nickname, "the P'daytabird." These liberties give readers the impression that Wilson is an insider.

His most glaring error of all is an error of omission. Although Wilson is a famous novelist and was once literary editor of *The Spectator,* he seems not to have read or even read *about* Lewis's masterpiece, the profound novel that was Lewis's favorite work and is most highly acclaimed by serious critics: *Till We Have Faces.* Although Wilson spends pages on some of Lewis's other books, he says nothing about this one except that it exists and was dedicated to Joy Davidman.

In his list of periodicals about Lewis, Wilson includes the *Portland Chronicle,* which expired in 1984, but skips others that are active. When he describes the Wade Center in Wheaton, Illinois, he invites readers to chuckle with amused disdain. He pretends that he did significant research there; but in fact he visited for less than three hours, and most of what he says about it is wrong. Like the comic novelist that he is, Wilson poses as a kindly but amused authority on this obviously bizarre and silly place.

Wilson's ideas are sometimes borrowed from other people's books without acknowledgment. His errors, misrepresentations, omissions and fabrications range from subtle to obvious. These are scattered throughout the book, as the following examples illustrate.

(xiii) The Marion E. Wade Center on the upper floor of the college library is devoted to the memorabilia of various Christian writers: George MacDonald, T.S. Eliot, Dorothy L. Sayers, Charles Williams, J. R. R. Tolkien, C. S. Lewis and his brother Warren. *(Wilson leaves out G.K. Chesterton and Owen Barfield, but wrongly includes T.S. Eliot.)*

(xiii)...here the faithful may see Muggeridge's portable typewriter kept, like the body of Lenin, in a glass case. *(Muggeridge's typewriter is not at the Wade Center.)*

(xiv) As Lyle W. Dorsett...concedes, Lindskoog has gone too far in her assaults on Hooper's good name. *(Lyle Dorsett denies having said this.)*

(xvi) Lewis idolatry, like Christianity itself, has resorted to some ugly tactics as it breaks itself into [Protestant and Roman Catholic] factions. *(I have not yet seen this purported Lewis idolatry, much less any sign of the bitter Protestant-Catholic feud with which Wilson spices his introduction.)*

(1) More than most men, [Lewis] was the product of his upbringing and ancestry. *(It is logically impossible for Lewis to be more a product of environment and inheritance than most men.)*

(3) In 1894, Thomas Hamilton at length consented to give his daughter's hand in marriage to a solicitor in the Belfast police courts called Albert Lewis. *(It was Flora who kept Albert waiting, not her father.)*

(10)...the very fact that the doctrine of hell was believed in by decent, amiable people, who enjoyed their beer and their whiskey, made it harder, not easier, for [Lewis's] imagination to absorb. *(Lewis didn't say anything about the decency and amiability of beer and whiskey drinkers or their belief in hell and how this made it harder for his imagination to absorb.)*

(25) He made Capron into a monster. It may very well be the case that the man *was* a monster, but since we may only view him through the creative lens of the Lewis brothers' memory, there is no knowing what he was like in other people's minds. *(But Capron was sued by the parent of one of his pupils,*

and eventually certified insane and locked up. Surely that tells us what others thought of him!)

(29) The passages, for example, where he describes his longing to abandon Christianity because of an over-scrupulous terror that he was not sufficiently concentrating on his prayers, while they may be true in general, are far too specifically recalled to be plausible. The details are too sharp. *(Wilson does not give any reason for disbelieving accounts that are detailed and specific.)*

(52) "Also, unknown at this time to either of his sons, he [Albert Lewis] had started to drink very heavily." *(That may be, but Ruth Hamilton Parker denied Wilson's claim about her uncle's alcoholism when she heard him on a television interview.)*

(56) Before they had been separated and sent off to different regiments, Paddy and Jack had made a pact: in the event of one or the other's death, the survivor would 'look after' the bereft parent of the one who had been killed. *(Wilson fails to mention the massive evidence against this 1978 story and the fact that its only source was Walter Hooper and Mrs. Moore's daughter, the two people motivated to justify Lewis's secret life with Mrs. Moore. After Hooper admitted in 1991 that the relationship was probably sexual, the tale of the two-way promise served little practical purpose.)*

(72) If one wants to know what [Mrs. Moore] meant to the young Lewis one should read....the vision in *The Great Divorce* of a Great Lady surrounded by a procession of angels, children and animals. *(The bitterly atheistic Mrs. Moore was never a heavenly figure to Lewis.)*

(78) His fascination with what he deemed to be Christian literature provided him with a good excuse for taking no apparent cognizance of the fact that a profound change had taken place, during his generation, in the human consciousness, and in Western art and literature. *(Isn't Wilson's "profound change" the very change that Lewis railed against in his inaugural address at Cambridge and in* The Abolition of Man?)

(79) In latter days, he made rather a "thing" of preferring children's books to grown-up literature. *(Simply not true. He loved grown-up books to his death.)*

(92) Minto...began to develop a series of psychosomatic conditions which strengthened the ties binding him to her side...rheumatism... *(Wilson offers no evidence that her arthritic disease was psychosomatic.)*

(93) After years of living with Lewis she still knew but did not know that "a man" could regard reading as the main business of the day and everything else as an interruption. *(What does Wilson mean by "a man," and how does he know what Mrs. Moore "knew but did not know"?)*

(95) I suspect that Mrs. Moore's sense of humour contributed much to the genuine streak of misanthropy in Lewis's nature. *(Lewis was no misanthrope. And if he had been, how could Mrs. Moore's alleged sense of humor have contributed?)*

(110) Lewis continued, throughout his life, to be obsessed not only by his father, but also by the possibility that his life could be interpreted in a purely Freudian way. *(There is no evidence that Lewis was obsessed by his father or Freudianism.)*

(111) He was frightened that hostile readers of his theological work would be able to say that his religion could be "explained" in terms of the Oedipus complex (or perhaps the Hippolytus complex)...So much did he dread that his own was a case of "redemption by parricide" that he emphasized his unwillingness with which he accepted the divine call with language which is exaggerated and almost course. *(Wilson not only fails to support this bizarre claim, but on page 110 he also makes the incongruous suggestion that perhaps Mrs. Moore was a Phaedra, Lewis's father was a Theseus, and Lewis, crossing the channel to Ireland, was Hippolytus.)*

(128) It would be far too glib to suggest that he consciously made the second change, to adopt Christianity, merely to give himself an excuse to abandon sexual relations with Mrs. Moore, whatever the nature of those relations had been. *(Wilson repeatedly uses this backhand device, saying that he won't say something in order to say it. For example, on page 306 he says of J. B. Phillips, "It would be churlish to point out...periodic bouts of lunacy; churlish because irrelevant." Thus Wilson is in fact suggesting to his readers that Lewis's conversion was initially a dishonest maneuver. If Wilson hadn't meant to suggest that, he would not have done so.)*

(139)...by a strange series of chances, the *Lewis Papers* now reside in an air-conditioned cavern in the suburbs of Chicago *(Warren typed them, owned them, and chose to donate them to the Lewis collection in Illinois when Clyde Kilby asked him to do so. How is that a strange series of chances? Since when is a basement a cavern, and why would any Illinois library lack air-conditioning?)*

(141) It is true that [Mrs. Moore] was not academic; this was part of her charm for Lewis. (*Lewis was charmed by intellectual women.*)

(177)... *Screwtape*, it has to be admitted, is a cruel book... (*It is?!*)

(183) It is no wonder that *Perelandra* is an artistic failure. (*Lewis and many critics have judged it an artistic success.*)

(201) Perhaps none of Lewis's portraits is more cruel than that of the figure of Dante himself, who...is represented as a dwarf leading the other part of himself, the Tragedian, round on a chai ...(*The person like Dante in* The Great Divorce *is Lewis, the narrator. George MacDonald is his Virgil. In contrast, the dwarf shows what Dante might have been like if he had been an idolator on his way to hell.*)

(211) The confrontation with Elizabeth Anscombe...drove him into the form of literature for which he is today most popular: children's stories. (*There is no evidence to support this theory.*)

(225) There can be little doubt that the energy and passion of the Narnia stories spring from the intensely unhappy and depleted state through which he had been passing. (*In June 1951 Lewis remarked to Sister Penelope that things were marvelously well.*)

(226) The moment when the Witch "in a loud terrible voice" traps the children underground and tries to persuade them that there is no world above the ground as they supposed, is a nursery nightmare version of Lewis's debate with Miss Anscombe. (*This is a factual misreading of the storyline of* Silver Chair *as well as a cavalier interpretation.*)

(236)...Mrs. Joy Gresham of Westchester, New York... (*Joy was from Duchess County, not Westchester.*)

(237) Devastated by the discovery of yet another of her husband's infidelities six months after Douglas was born, Joy had a religious experience. (*As she and Lyle Dorsett have told the story, she was devastated because her husband called to say his mind was cracking, not because of his infidelities.*)

(238) The death of Minto in January 1951 had provided necessary emotional punctuation in Lewis's life, an opportunity to start again from childhood. (*There was no "necessary emotional punctuation," and he did not regress to childhood in 1951.*)

(252) [*Surprised by Joy*] is really a glorious sort of comic novel. (*An interesting assessment of Christian spiritual autobiography from the viewpoint an unbelieving comic novelist.*)

(256) According to an oral memory of Joy's son Douglas, transcribed in the Marion E. Wade collection at Wheaton College, Illinois, the two of them were already lovers in 1955. Douglas on one occasion came into his mother's bedroom at 10 Old High Street and found it occupied by Jack and Joy in a compromising position. *(According to Lyle Dorsett, Douglas Gresham never told this story at Wheaton and it is definitely not in the Wade collection.)*

(264) In *The Times* the next day [22 March 1957], Jack's oldest friends read with astonishment an announcement of which they had been given absolutely no warning: "A marriage has taken place between Professor C. S. Lewis..." *(This announcement was in The Times 24 December 1956.)*

(295) On 15 June 1963, Lewis had a heart attack and was taken into the Ackland Nursing Home. *[The heart attack was on 15 July 1963.]*

(296) Thus passed the month of August and some of September. Then Hooper went back to the United States, intending to return as Lewis's full-time secretary after Christmas. *(Hooper left before the end of August and was invited to return later for only a brief visit.)*

(306) A good example of this was the brilliant television play *Shadowlands* by Bill Nicholson, subsequently written up by Brian Sibley as a book... *(Brian Sibley reportedly wrote the play and book long before Bill Nicholson rewrote the play from scratch.)*

(311) Most surviving Lewis manuscripts, however, both of his literary productions and of his letters, are preserved in the Bodleian Library at Oxford... *(According to the Wade Center, more letters are preserved there than at the Bodleian.)*

(325) *Wilson leaves George Sayer's biography* Jack: C. S. Lewis and His Times, *the best one to date, out of his "Select Bibliography."*

In conclusion, A. N. Wilson is a highly skilled professional writer of the gymnastic type (cartwheels, tightropes, and trapezes), and we can be grateful when any long, serious-looking book with intellectual pretensions turns out to be as twinkling and energetic as a tabloid. But we shouldn't assume too quickly that Wilson really understands C. S. Lewis or that we really understand A. N. Wilson. He said in *Publisher's Weekly* (15 May 1987) that his novels could be called cruel, that his frequent appearance in British gossip columns is probably a distraction to his British readers, and that he doesn't know what he believes. "I mean, I don't know from month to month or year to year." On page 236 of C. S. *Lewis* he remarks breezily, "In books it does not really matter where fantasy ends and reality begins..."

I suspect that Wilson is highly amused by his antics, and his old friends at the *Spectator* seem to think so too. On 10 February 1990 they joshed him in a column about the new poison-pen Lewis biography by "Ann Wilson." "Ever the busy bee, Ann has been diligent in grubbing around in the mud...Such prurience in a biographer is to be roundly condemned." The column went on to reveal that the next Lewis biography will reveal his affair with Marilyn Monroe and his secret life as a part-time cabaret artiste in London's risqué Pussy Galore Club (where along with a couple of other friends, Charles Williams played keyboards and Professor Tolkien played double-bass and kazoo). One of their songs was:

> Oh, we think things
> 'Cos we're the Ink-lings
> And we're always wink-ing
> Yes, we're the I-N-K-L-I-N-G-S
> — INKLINGS !!!!

APPENDIX 6

C. S. LEWIS PETITION
AND SIGNATORIES

We the undersigned are concerned about the apparent irregularities in the posthumous C. S. Lewis canon, first investigated in a computer study by C.F. Jones of the University of Florida in 1986, described by Kathryn Lindskoog in *The C. S. Lewis Hoax* in 1988, and confirmed in 1991 by A. Q. Morton of the University of Glasgow, leading forensic authority on literary forgery. We are concerned because both the complex "Literary Detective" alphabetical analysis by C. F. Jones and the vastly more complex cumulative sum chart sentence analysis by A. Q. Morton refute the authenticity of *The Dark Tower*. We are also concerned because of A. Q. Morton's report that the central forty percent of the 1990 C. S. Lewis essay "Christian Reunion" clearly matches the statistical pattern of Walter Hooper's writing rather than that of C. S. Lewis.

We are concerned about Kathryn Lindskoog's unanswered charge that the following posthumous works published from 1966 to 1991 have faulty provenance, and we are also concerned about the charge that they all exhibit unLewisian style, taste, beliefs, or values.

1. "Forms of Things Unknown" (*Of Other Worlds*. London: Collins, 1966.)

2. Narnia fragments ("Past Watchful Dragons" by Walter Hooper in *Imagination and the Spirit* by Charles Huttar. Grand Rapids: Eerdmans, 1971.)

3. "The Dark Tower" (*The Dark Tower*. London: Collins, 1977.)

4. "The Man Born Blind" (*The Dark Tower*. London: Collins, 1977.)

5. LeFay fragment (*Past Watchful Dragons* by Walter Hooper. New York: Macmillan, 1979.)

6. "Preface to 'Screwtape Proposes a Toast'" (*The Screwtape Letters*. New York: Macmillan, 1982.)

7. "History of Animal Land" (*Boxen*. San Diego: Harcourt Brace Jovanovich, 1985.)

8. "Encyclopedia Boxoniana" (*Boxen*. San Diego: Harcourt Brace Jovanovich, 1985.)

9. "Modern Man and His Categories of Thought" (*Present Concerns*. San Diego: Harcourt Brace Jovanovich, 1986.)

10. "Christian Reunion" (*Christian Reunion*. London: Collins, 1990.)

• If even half of these twelve [99] posthumous works are not genuine, the Lewis corpus is seriously contaminated. We urge those responsible—the anonymous owner(s) of the C. S. Lewis literary estate, Walter Hooper, Owen Barfield, Stanley Mattson, the Curtis Brown Literary Agency, HarperCollins, Harcourt Brace Jovanovich, Macmillan, and Eerdmans—to begin to ask and answer questions. We suggest that it is time for a variety of influential readers, writers, editors, scholars, and C. S. Lewis societies to begin to freely address the topic in print. We suggest that the anonymous directors of the Marion E. Wade Center at Wheaton College in Illinois include this subject in their sponsored lectures and that they support related research with some of their annual grants in C. S. Lewis studies. We urge the Bodleian Library staff to consult A. Q. Morton and to seek unbiased cumulative sum chart authentication of all posthumous Lewis holdings, both published and unpublished.

---

[99] Thanks to new information, two items on the list of suspect literature were removed after the petition was signed. They are "Dr. Easley fragment" and "Magdalen College Appendix." For information about these pieces, see Chapter 5, "The Most Substantial People," and Appendix 2, "Facts about Forgery." If the petition were circulated again today four others would replace those two items: Lewis's Tolkien obituary, "Introductory Letter," "A Pageant Played in Vain," and "Finchley Avenue."

• We believe that more delay would be inappropriate; Walter Hooper and his defenders have refused to answer questions in 1988 and 1989, refused Kathryn Lindskoog's invitation to public debate in 1990, and refused Professor Don Cregier's invitation to co-sponsor document analysis in 1991. *It is time to get the posthumous Lewis canon into the public forum where evidence, logic, and persuasion can begin to validate it or to correct it.*

C. S. LEWIS PETITION SIGNATORIES

AWARD-WINNING AUTHORS

Lloyd Alexander, winner of the Newbery Medal.

Arthur C. Clarke, three-time winner of the Nebula Award, twice winner of the Hugo Award. (See below.)

Katherine Paterson, twice winner of the Newbery Medal, twice winner of the National Book Award.

Tim Powers, twice winner of the Philip K. Dick Memorial Award, winner of the World Fantasy Award.

Robert Siegel, past fellow of National Endowment for the Arts. (See below.)

Richard Wilbur, second Poet Laureate, winner of the National Book Award and the Bollingen Award, twice winner of the Pulitzer Prize.

Gene Wolfe, twice winner of the Nebula Award, winner of the World Fantasy Award, British Fantasy Award, and Prix Apollo.

AUTHORS OF BOOKS ABOUT C. S. LEWIS

Michael D. Aeschliman, author of C. S. *Lewis and the Restitution of Man.* (See below.)

Corbin S. Carnell, author of *Bright Shadow of Reality: C. S. Lewis and the Feeling Intellect.* (See below.)

Joe R. Christopher, co-author of C. S. *Lewis: An Annotated Checklist;* author of C. S. *Lewis* (Twayne's English Authors Series). (See below.)

Lyle Dorsett, author of *And God Came In.* (See below.)

Carolyn Keefe, author of C. S. *Lewis, Speaker and Teacher.*

Kathryn Lindskoog, author of C. S. *Lewis: Mere Christian, The Lion of Judah in Never-Never Land, Around the Year with C. S. Lewis and His Friends,* and *The C. S. Lewis Hoax.*

Gilbert Meilaender, author of *The Taste for the Other: The Social and Ethical Thought of C. S. Lewis*. (See below.)

EDITORSHIPS

Algis Budrys. Editor, *Tomorrow: Speculative Fiction*.

Vickie Danielsen, Editor, *Ponderings*, Adventist Women's Institute, Englewood, CO.

Leonard G. Goss, Editor, Crossway Books, Wheaton, IL.

William Hasker, Editor, *Christian Scholar's Review*. (See below.)

Walter R. Hearn, Editor, *American Scientific Affiliation Newsletter*, Berkeley, CA.

Rodney Morris, Editor, Multnomah Press, Questar, Sisters, OR.

Ben Patterson, Contributing editor, *Leadership, Christianity Today*. (See below.)

Christopher Ricks, Co-editor, Oxford's *Essays in Criticism*. (See below.)

Thomas A. Tenney, Editor, *Mark Twain Journal*. (See below.)

MINISTRIES

D. M. Baumann, Rector, Blessed Sacrament Episcopal Church, Placentia, CA.

Richard Becker, Director of Religious Education, Sacred Heart of Jesus Church, Boulder, CO.

Ralph Blair, Founder of Evangelicals Concerned, New York, NY.

Reverend Albert G. Cohen, Campus Minister, California State University at Los Angeles, CA.

Dr. Kenneth C. Harper, Senior Pastor, First Presbyterian Church, Westminster, CA.

Ben Patterson, Dean of the Chapel, Hope College, Holland, MI.

Larry Repass, Salvation Army Officer, Guatemala City, Guatemala.

Steven Shoemaker, Ph.D., Pastor, McKinley Presbyterian Church, Champaign, IL.

ACADEMIC APPOINTMENTS

Michael D. Aeschliman, Ph.D. Lecturer in English Literature, University of Virginia, Charlottesville, VA.

Alice R. Bergel, Ph.D. Adjunct Professor of Foreign Languages, Chapman University, Orange, CA.

Kurt Bergel, Ph.D. Professor of History, Chapman University, Orange, CA.

Richard W. Bohrer. Professor of Journalism, Liberty University, Lynchburg, VA.

Charles P. Busch, Ph.D. Associate Professor of Philosophy, Arkansas Tech University, AK.

Corbin S. Carnell. Professor of English, University of Florida, Gainesville, FL.

Joe R. Christopher, Ph.D. Professor of English, Tarleton State College, Stephenville, TX.

David G. Clark, Ph. D., Chair, Division of Religion, Southern California College, Costa Mesa, Calif.

Arthur C. Clarke, Commander of the British Empire. Chancellor of the University of Moratuwa, Sri Lanka.

David G. Clark, Chair of the Division of Religion at Southern California College, Costa Mesa, CA

John C. Cooper, Ph.D. Professor of Religion, Eastern Kentucky University, Richmond, KY.

The Rev. Lawrence N. Crumb. Reference Librarian (Associate Professor), University of Oregon, Eugene, OR.

Don M. Cregier, Ph.D. Professor of History, University of Prince Edward Island, Canada.

Sharon E. Cregier, Ph.D. Sessions Lecturer, Library Skills, University of Prince Edward Island, Canada.

Lyle Dorsett. Professor of Educational Ministries and Evangelism, Wheaton College.

Gracia Fay Ellwood. Past instructor in the Department of Religion, California State University at Long Beach, CA. (Past editor, *Mythlore*.)

Ronald Enroth, Ph.D. Professor of Sociology, Westmont College, Santa Barbara, CA.

Robert O. Evans, Ph.D. Professor Emeritus of English and Comparative Literature, University of Kentucky and University of New Mexico.

William Geiger, Ph.D. Professor of English, Whittier College, CA.

David W. Gill, Ph.D. Professor of Applied Ethics, North Park College, Chicago, IL.

W. Fred Graham, Ph.D. Professor of Religious Studies, Michigan State University, East Lansing, MI.

William Hasker, Ph.D. Professor of Philosophy, Huntington College, IN.

Virginia K. Hearn. Adjunct Professor, New College for Advanced Christian Studies, Berkeley, CA.

Sandra Kay Heck. Adjunct Faculty, East Tennessee State University, TN

Ron Henderson. Professor of English, Cincinnati Bible College, OH.

Elias D.S. Medeiros. Professor of Missiology, Reformed Theological Seminary, Jackson, MI.

Gilbert Meilaender, Ph.D.. Professor of Religion, Oberlin College, OH.

Dale J. Nelson. Assistant Professor of English, Mayville State University, ND.

Dorothea J. Nelson. Instructor of Library Science, Mayville State University, ND.

Gary Jackson Oliver, Ph.D. Visiting Associate Professor of Marriage and Family Counseling, Denver Seminary, CO.

Nancy-Lou Patterson. Professor Emerita of Fine Arts, Waterloo, Ontario, Canada.

Richard V. Pierard, Ph.D. Professor of History, Indiana State University, Terre Haute, IN.

Cornelius Plantinga, Jr. Professor of Systematic Theology, Calvin Theological Seminary, Grand Rapids, MI.

Bernard Ramm, Professor Emeritus, Eastern Baptist Theological Seminary.

Dr. Paulo Ribeiro. Professor of Engineering, Dordt College, Sioux City, IA.

Christopher Ricks. Professor of English, Boston University, MA.

Robert Siegel, Ph.D. Professor of English, University of Wisconsin, Milwaukee, WI.

Thomas A. Tenney, Ph.D. Professor of English, The Citadel, Charleston, SC.

Doreen Anderson Wood, Ph.D. Instructor in Humanities, Tulsa Junior College, OK. (Founder, Tulsa C. S. Lewis Society.)

W.R. Wortman, Professor of English, Baylor University, Waco, TX

OTHERS

Margaret R. Barkley, B.A., B.Ed, Ottowa, Ontario, Canada

Fay M. Blix, Attorney at Law, Irvine, CA.

Paul H. Borcher, Student, Medieval and Renaissance Studies and Linguistics, University of Michigan, Ann Arbor.

Mary V. Borhek, Author, Bethlehem, PA.

Marian Flandrick Bray, Author, Santa Ana, CA.

Anne Le Brun Burnett, Santa Rosa, CA.

Willard J. Dickerson, Executive Director, Association of Logos Bookstores

Nancy J. Doman, Garden Grove, CA.

Brenda Griffing, Freelance Editorial Consultant, Fort Lauderdale, FL

Douglas Hackleman, President, Business & Pleasure Productions, Grand Terrace, CA. (Past editor, *Adventist Currents.)*

Margot Lawrence, Author, Secretary of the Prayer Book Society, London, England.

Larkette Lein, Convener of Integrity/Southland, Fullerton, CA.

Phil Lollar, Creator of Adventures in Odyssey, Glendora, CA.

James Long, Ph. D., P.E., Consulting Engineer, Sunnyvale , CA

Lynn M. Maudlin, Council of Stewards, Mythopoeic Society, Altadena, CA.

Paul McCusker, Playwright, Colorado Springs, CO

Jan Pendergrass, English teacher, Whittier, CA

Ken Pendergrass, Music teacher, Whittier, CA

Dean C. Picton, Hollywood, FL

Bebe E. Picton, Hollywood, FL

George Prell, Principal Engineer, Fluor Daniel, Irvine, CA

Louise Prell, Vice-president, Opera Pacific Volunteers Guild , Costa Mesa, CA.

Serena Powers, Santa Ana, CA.

Faith A. Sand, Director of Hope Publishing House, Pasadena, CA.

Chuck Schechner, Former owner of Logos Bookstore, Dallas, TX.

Carol R. Smith, Placentia, CA.

Jeff Taylor, Georgetown, KY.

Carolyn L. Vash, Ph.D., Author, Altadena, CA.

Richard D. Vash, Altadena. CA.

Carl S. Weisman, Herndon, VA.

Max Weremchuk, Albsheim, Germany

John G. West, Ph.D., Fellow of the Discovery Institute, Seattle, WA.

J. Seth Williamson II, Public Radio producer, Roanoke, VA.

Patrick Wynne, Mythopoeic illustrator, Fosston, MN.

APPENDIX 7

THE PORTLAND STATEMENT

OCTOBER 3, 1992

The Portland C. S. Lewis Society is a discussion group which has been meeting once a month for over twenty years. One of our purposes, as expressed in the charter, is "to publicly respond...to public mention or criticism of C. S. Lewis or his ideas, with the intention of presenting to the public the clearest and most accurate image possible." We, the board members, firmly believe that the posthumously published *The Dark Tower* is not by Lewis. It is inconceivable that he could have written something so amateurish in style and vacuous in content.

Time has removed other suspect posthumous works of Lewis (e.g., "Preface to 'Screwtape Proposes a Toast'", "Christian Reunion," Narnia fragments in *Past Watchful Dragons*) as they have gone out of print, but *The Dark Tower* remains, as does "Encyclopedia Boxoniana" of Boxen. The self-important "Encyclopedia" is on the level of *The Dark Tower*.

We have no guarantee against more shoddy writing being attributed to Lewis in the future. Walter Hooper, literary adviser of the Lewis estate and editor of his posthumously published works, claims that there was a bonfire of Lewis's papers after his death and that he salvaged *The Dark Tower*, "Encyclopedia Boxoniana," etc. These manuscripts had no witnesses for their existence before Hooper disclosed them.

Mr. Hooper has not only attributed un-Lewisian works to Lewis, but has also made other claims which are equally suspect. Lewis's supposed dialogue with Hooper in Hooper's introductions, the Green-Hooper biography, and "C. S. Lewis and C. S. Lewises" is clichéd and out of character. Although Hooper spent at most two weeks helping the dying Lewis with his correspondence, the blurbs of the books edited by Hooper persistently identify him as his secretary.

It is time to re-establish a genuine Lewis canon. We are urging the Lewis estate as well as the publishing firms of Macmillan, Harcourt Brace Jovanovich, Collins, and Eerdmans to cease publishing spurious works and to ensure the strict veracity of the editing.

SIGNED BY
Sue-Ann Bishop
Paul Blattner
Jim Childs
Barbara Eng
Tim Nelson
Rachel Sullivan
Brownie Talbot

SENT TO
Owen Barfield
Walter Hooper
Macmillan Publishers
Harcourt Brace Jovanovich Publishers
Sheridon House for Collins
William Eerdmans Publishers
Bodleian Library
Marion E. Wade Center
C.S. Lewis Centre, London
Seattle Pacific C. S. Lewis Studies
C.S. Lewis Foundation
New York C. S. Lewis Society
Southern California C. S. Lewis Society
Tulsa C. S. Lewis Society
Oxford C. S. Lewis Society
Milwaukee C. S. Lewis Society

Stephen Schofield
Mythopoeic Society
Inklings Gesellschaft
Inklings—Jahrbuch fur Literatur und Asthetic
Eagle and Child Reading Group
Other Hands
Vinyar Tengwar
John West
Terri Williams
Gary Oliver
Charles Colson
Pather George Gray
Multnomah Press
Christianity Today
National Review
New York Times
The New Oxford Review
The Living Church

APPENDIX 8

LETTER TO *LA PAZ*

In August 1990 when the June issue of Westmont College alumni paper *La Paz* went out to 8,000 friends and alumni its first two pages were devoted to an article titled "Is There a C. S. Lewis Hoax?" It was a report from Religious Studies Professor Tom Schmidt and English Professor David Downing disparaging *The C. S. Lewis Hoax* and endorsing Mattson's jury trial ("colloquium") that had condemned it. The following note followed their article from the editor: "Please write and tell us what you think about articles in *La Paz.* We'll print what you send!"

I immediately sent the following to *La Paz* and a copy with a cover letter to Westmont College President David Winter:

> You can imagine how surprising it was for me—after cherishing Westmont College for 37 years—to see the first two pages devoted to an erroneous attack upon my character and scholarship. The last time I visited Westmont College I spent a wonderful evening with Dr. and Mrs. Arthur Lynip. I spoke in chapel the next morning and noticed a strange restlessness in the audience. As soon as I finished, students kindly informed me that the correct microphone was missing and the substitute microphone had made it impossible for them to understand me beyond the first few rows. (I would have done better with no microphone at all.) When I read your article I had a feeling of *deja vu.* My words have been distorted beyond recognition again.

Here are some much-needed corrections for readers of *La Paz*:

1. "She wrote the whole book without checking with the Bodleian Library where [Hooper's Lewis manuscripts] are housed." To the contrary, I visited the Bodleian in 1984 and was accurately informed that Hooper's manuscripts there were his private property and not available to researchers. In 1989, in response to my book, Hooper suddenly donated his *Dark Tower* manuscript to the Bodleian, where it can now be seen.

2. "Brown told us she said, 'Hooper is a lot more ingenious than I thought...'" Mr. Brown called me as a stranger on the telephone once, and during our conversation I said nothing at all like the quotation attributed to me in your article.

3. "A lot of her allegations are based on the implication that she has an *unerring* ability to detect Lewis' style." I do not have an *unerring* ability, but C. S. Lewis wrote to me in 1957, "You know my work better than anyone else I've met." For demonstration of my knowledge of the art of writing, including Lewis's, I offer my tenth book, new from Zondervan's Academie line—*Creative Writing for People Who Can't Not Write.*

4. "She claims the fragment 'The Dark Tower,' a short story, 'The Man Born Blind,' parts of the 'Juvenilia' and some letters were forged." The last two items are wrong. I charged that the adult essay "Encyclopedia Boxoniana" in the book *Boxen* was forged, but it is not part of the juvenilia. I did not charge that some letters were forged. I did charge that Hooper's Narnia scraps are forged, however, and don't want that charge to be overlooked.

5. "Mrs. Lindskoog believes Hooper forged it because its literary style is inferior. This is the basis for all her accusations of forgery." To the contrary, there are three elements that form the basis for my charges of forgery: style, content, and provenance. Faulty provenance is usually the first clue that literature is bogus. I consider faulty content more significant than faulty style.

6. "Mrs. Lindskoog relies on the rather embarrassing conclusion that the works published posthumously are not as good as the ones he submitted for publication to prove that the former are forgeries." I never said that the works published posthumously (there are many) are not as good as the others, and I never relied on that idea to prove that the former are forgeries. I am much more specific in my charges.

7. "A man in the audience, Ed Brown, who collects Lewis memorabilia, became very excited and asked to be recognized." The audience consisted of six observers selected in advance. The excited man came all the way from Indiana in order to tell about his "Man Born Blind" manuscript; the impression of spontaneity here is misleading.

8. "Lewis recognized [The Man Born Blind's] inferior literary style or he wouldn't have revised it before he sent it off." Unfortunately for that theory, the purportedly revised version is almost identical to the other version and no better. Furthermore, no one is willing to say where the allegedly revised version was for over fifty years, until Eynsham bookdealer Peter Jolliffe sold it to Edwin Brown a couple of years ago.

9. "Lewis didn't always write brilliantly." That is the claim of Walter Hooper's defenders. In the August 11 issue of *Times Literary Supplement* Yale professor Claude Rawson claims that some of Lewis's most brilliant statements can be found in the casual letters that he dashed off to friends and strangers. I agree.

10. "Why would Hooper forge something that was only a fragment?" "Her only answer is that people do things like this to see if they can pull it off." I don't know where Dr. Schmidt got this idea of how I would answer if I were asked. As readers of *The Dark Tower* have often observed, Lewis (or another writer) apparently got stuck in the hopeless narrative and gave up. The writer couldn't finish it.

11. "Mrs. Lindskoog claims that Paxford (who is dead) denied this [bonfire] story to a couple named Miller who were Lewis' neighbors." Anyone who reads my book can see that I have a signed, dated letter from Fred Paxford verifying the report that I got first in a signed, dated letter from Leonard Miller. Incidentally, the Millers were not just Lewis's neighbors; she was the Lewis housekeeper, and after C. S. Lewis's death the Millers became Warren Lewis's living companions in his last years. One can read his high opinion of them in his diary.

12. "However, a recent book by Douglas Gresham, Lewis' stepson, discredits the Millers and accuses them of stealing from Lewis..." Fortunately, I have a tape-recorded 1973 telephone conversation with Wheaton College professor Robert Bartell (the brother-in-law of Westmont's past chaplain Robert Ohman) in which he describes in detail the orderly disposition of items [supposedly] stolen by the Millers in 1973. It is not

surprising that the characters of Warren Lewis and the Millers were attacked once it was known that they are witnesses against Walter Hooper.

13. **"If you examine the ink, you can tell what year it was purchased."** Counter to the implication here, there has been no chemical analysis of Hooper's documents to prove that they are not forgeries. The documents were supposedly analyzed for Stanley Mattson in the Bodleian Library in January 1989, as reported in the *Sunday Times* on January 29. But when I contacted committee member Dennis Porter of the Bodleian about the the alleged analysis, he wrote that he had not seen the *Sunday Times* article, had served on no committee, and didn't even know there was a committee.

14. **"...her insinuation that Hooper is a homosexual because he titled the book of letters between Lewis and Arthur Greeves *They Stand Together...*"** I never assumed that it was Walter Hooper who chose that title or the homosexual symbol that appeared under it on the original Collins edition of the book. Hooper's new 1988 British edition of Lewis's letters has bolder homosexual symbolism on the cover, but I have no explanation for that fact. I don't consider that any of my business. My business is our contaminated Lewis legacy.

15. **"'They stand together in the midst of a silent world.' That is where the title comes from, and she knows it, but didn't include it in the book."** Neither I nor any other Lewis scholar I know of had ever noticed the occurrence of the common phrase "they stand together" in this sentence buried deep in *The Four Loves.* (It is a phrase that would be noticed, of course, by someone who knew its homosexual meaning.) Those who chose this phrase as the title of Lewis's letters to Arthur Greeves thought so little of its occurrence in *The Four Loves* that they did not mention its source. After a few years, they mysteriously removed it as the title of the Greeves letters, and I suspect that they removed it because of its double meaning.

16. **"...it was simply a matter of preserving Warren Lewis' feelings until he died. She had a clear explanation of why these letters were withheld, but she apparently suppressed it."** To the contrary, Hooper gave no explanation for witholding the letters that he was supposed to deliver to the Bodleian. For the facts about Warren Lewis's feelings, read his diary and *Hoax.*

17. **"Hooper also held up some of the letters written to Greeves for infrared analysis to recover passages Greeves had inked out."** As I stated clearly in my book, these Greeves letters went right to the Wade Center.

Hooper sent friends there to photograph the deleted passages about pederasty and sado-masochism. These letters were never witheld by Hooper or anyone else.

18. "...when Hooper published the 1980 edition of *The Weight of Glory* he wrote a preface in which he corrected the misrepresentations [about his relationship with Lewis]. Here we are in 1989, but she is making many of the same accusations nine years after he set the record straight." In 1989 Hooper is still publishing his old misrepresentations. In the obscure 1980 preface to *The Weight of Glory* he not only failed to set the record straight, but he added some new exaggerations to his story—such as claiming that he was not only Lewis's personal secretary, but also his literary assistant.

19. "Barfield has maintained a dignified silence about the book." In 1979 Owen Barfield published a vitriolic letter castigating me for daring to question any of Walter Hooper's claims. In 1980 Barfield's legal firm threatened to sue me if I revealed any more about Walter Hooper. In 1989 his firm wrote to Multnomah claiming that experts had disproved my book. In 1989 he sent a letter to Mattson's [jury] stating that "The Man Born Blind" is really by Lewis. In my opinion there is not a shred of dignity in Barfield's past performance as executor of the Lewis estate or in his present position. This is sad.

20. "Nobody expected Lewis' estate to be substantial or expected his books to sell so well after his death." Nobody? I don't believe that Dr. Clyde Kilby and I were the only observers of the scene in the 1960s who saw a hint of what was coming. The trend looked obvious.

21. "I believe there is a lot of sloppy Lewis scholarship in the book..." I have sincerely asked some of my critics to point out the errors they claim to see, and they have not yet done so.

22. "She accuses Hooper of forgery, theft, and habitual lying, and she hasn't even done the kind of thorough scholarship such charges require." I spent much time ever since 1975 working hard to uncover and piece together the unpleasant material that is now distilled in *The C. S. Lewis Hoax* . Multnomah Press spent an entire year studying and debating the matter before deciding to publish the book. What more could anyone ask of an investigative writer?

23. "...Mrs. Lindskoog's book accuses him of serious misconduct as a literary executor, so we felt it was important to investigate the truth of her

allegations..." "On the whole, the colloquium found that Mrs. Lindskoog has not adequately supported her allegations and concluded that there was no evidence of wrongdoing on the part of Walter Hooper." These dignified statements imply that the "colloquium" was reasonably well-organized—*balanced, above-board, informed, thorough,* and *accurate.* That was not at all the case.

a. *Imbalance:* The [trial] (held on 21 April) was a last-minute idea, and participants were still being recruited on 19 April. To the best of my knowledge, eleven [jury] members happen to be directly or indirectly associated with Walter Hooper or Owen Barfield, and the twelfth was [to be] employed by Stanley Mattson. The agenda was announced beforehand: to clear Walter Hooper's name. The meeting ended when everyone including Stanley Mattson cast a secret ballot, to be counted later. I think that in the excitement of the event the illogicality and impropriety of the proceedings did not dawn upon the participants.

b. *Secrecy and lack of accountability:* This was a closed meeting, although references to an "audience" imply that it was open. I requested permission to attend, at least as an observer or a (much-needed) resource person, but my request was denied. Stanley Mattson sent out a press report about the "colloquium"; but when I asked him for a copy of the press report he refused, and I have never seen it. He promised several people a tape-recording or transcript of the proceedings, but he changed his mind. Then he promised a summary report, but month after month passed and hope waned. In the meantime, however, Walter Hooper...has been giving out...two pages [purportedly from the summary report], and they include both a closing event that did not really occur at the colloquium and a foolish quotation from me about document authentication, completely fabricated and the opposite of my position.

c. *Lack of preparation:* The twelve "colloquium" members had failed to familiarize themselves with my documentation. Most of them have never laid eyes upon the easily available *Boxen,* for example, and at least one had never seen my book itself until three days before the meeting. Hardly any of them have seen Walter Hooper's film "Through Joy and Beyond." Neither that film nor any of the vast body of published evidence that I cited was provided in advance or at the [trial]. As a result, some of my most easily verifiable statements of fact that I documented in footnotes, such as Walter Hooper's production of Lewisian script, were dismissed as "unproved."

d. *Haste:* One prospective "colloquium" member who declined the invitation thought that the meetings would take several days and would be too hasty at that; he was startled to learn later that it all took place in one day. Given the brevity of the meeting and the complexity of the material, in addition to the fact that most of the [jury members] had not read the C. S. Lewis literature under discussion, the approach had to be extremely superficial.

e. *Inaccuracy:* I must agree with critics of the Mattson 'colloquium" who point out that a one-day meeting of a one-sided group called to vote on a very complex book is no route to truth. The number of errors in the *La Paz* interview with two highly respected Westmont professors shows the level of fallibility at the "colloquium" where they received their information.

In conclusion, let me present twelve of the people who have spontaneously and independently voted the opposite of the twelve at the Mattson colloquium. In the arena of secular literature, my book has been commended by oustanding authors Ursula Le Guin, Arthur C. Clarke, Lloyd Alexander, and Richard Wilbur (1987 Poet Laureate and 1989 Pulitzer winner). In the arena of Christian literature it has been commended by outstanding authors Walter Wangerin, Frederick Buechner, Katherine Paterson, and Philip Yancey. In the arena of religious studies it has been commended by noted author Robert Ellwood, Director of the School of Religion at the University of Southern California. In the arena of Lewis's personal friendships it has been commended by noted authors Dom Bede Griffiths, Sheldon Vanauken, and Roger Lancelyn Green—Lewis's chosen biographer.

What more can I say? I long for my friendship with Westmont College to continue the same as always. I challenge you to show your students and alumni how Westmont will promptly and thoroughly redress an inadvertant wrong once it is brought to your attention. Thank you.

I followed this letter to Nancy L. Wentzel, Editor of *La Paz,* with a short, friendly letter expressing my confidence in her good intentions. One month later I received her refusal to publish my corrections. Instead, she offered to consider publishing a one-paragraph response from me, which would be followed by a rebuttal. In response, I warmly urged her to come to meet me because I was physically unable to travel to Santa Barbara to meet her. She ignored my invitation.

In the meantime, I wrote again and again to President Winter, expressing my dismay about the published falsehoods and my eagerness to meet any Westmont staff members who could come to Orange. He finally answered on 17 October that *The C. S. Lewis Hoax* was not the focus of their article "Is There Really a C. S. Lewis Hoax?" and that he was baffled by my desire to influence their publications.

In January 1990 my three-sentence response to "Is There Really a C. S. Lewis Hoax?" was published in the letters section of *La Paz*, followed by this Editor's Note: "Professors Downing and Schmidt stand by their statements and dispute the existence of factual errors in the article."

APPENDIX 9

THE JULIUS GRANT REPORT

"As near as possible therefore
a precise comparison was possible [sic]."
—*Julius Grant*

Identity of Julius Grant: An octogenarian paper chemist who shared an interest in sailing with Stanley Mattson. According to Mattson, Julius Grant was the author of a report proving that the Dark Tower manuscript is genuine. Grant is not on record as having any background or interest in handwriting analysis, and although Mattson promised to make the report public, he never did so. Grant died at 89 in 1991.

Grant's Stated Motivation: To confirm for Stanley Mattson that the handwriting comparison performed earlier by other friends of Mattson's who reported that certain questioned Lewis handwritings were authentic. "I subsequently received a good deal of information from Dr. Mattson, which disclosed the complicated situation arising from certain persons who were not prepared to accept the above experts' Report; or who objected to it on some other, often irrelevant and somewhat specious grounds."

Content of Grant's Report: Cursory description of Grant's brief 26 June 1990 examination of two documents in the Bodleian Library in Oxford. The librarian's health is described, but identity of the documents is not revealed. According to Mattson, the report is about the Dark Tower document.

Date of Grant's Report: 5 July 1990, sent by fax and post to Stanley Mattson

Letterhead Paper: Analytical and Consulting Chemists, in Croydon, England

Description of the questioned manuscript (A):

"Five pages of handwriting (unbound) on lined foolscap paper, with writing on the lined side. *[Grant is mistaken; the paper was lined on both sides, and the first two pages had handwriting on the back.]* These pages were numbered 1 to 5 and interleaved between the plain white sheets of a rather larger book which served to protect them *[irrelevant description of storage materials].* On the ruled side *[both sides are ruled]* (lines 8 mm. apart) were written neatly, a rather abstract philosophical subject. *[Written on these pages was a narrative fiction, with characters and conversation.]* The documents were not dated *[pages of a novel are not dated],* but on Page 1 (written in pencil) *[page 1 was written in ink]* was 'D.W. Hooper 1989'. This may assist you in identifying them, or their significance. *[Grant clearly failed to realize that he was examining the first five pages of* The Dark Tower, *and he never mentions* The Dark Tower *in his report.]* Dr. Priestman *[librarian]* stated that this writing, which is part of a set totaling at least 64 pages *[exactly 62 pages, not at least 64 pages],* is questioned as to the authenticity of its authorship."

Description of authentic material by Lewis (B):

"Two large, brown covered books, enclosing numerous authentic writings of C. S. Lewis. These were very miscellaneous indeed, but I was able to select samples which were similar in style and date *[similar to each other?],* and therefore suitable for comparison with the writing in 'A'. As near as possible therefore a precise comparison was possible....It should be noted that Item (B), comprising two volumes marked 'letters of C. S. Lewis', had the contents tabbed and dated, and they had writing on the lines of the paper used *[where else would the writing be, if not on the lines of the paper used?].* They were of an extremely miscellaneous nature. As the Exhibit contained the actual letters, in most cases they could be dated. This was useful *[how?]* although (A), the questioned sheets, were not dated."

Selection of documents for comparison:

"For the experimental comparisons I carried out, I took the last of the sheets comprising Exhibit (A), as I assumed it was likely to be the most recent, although I do not know the exact date *[or decade]:* against sheets *[how many?]* from the authentic Exhibit (B) which were tabbed and dated for the 1940's to the 1960's. I took one of the *latter* so as to obtain a recent sample." *[This seems to indicate that for his "experimental comparisons" Grant used only page 5 of the* Dark Tower *manuscript (allegedly written by Lewis in 1938 or 1939) and one page from an unidentified letter dated sometime between 1960 and 1963.]*

How did Grant compare handwriting on page 5 of the Dark Tower manuscript with that on a page from an unidentified 1960s letter?

"I first took each written letter of the alphabet *[the entire alphabet does not appear on p. 5 of the Dark Tower document],* in turn, and compared it thoroughly under high-illumination magnification using the corresponding letters from document (A) and (B). I...can say without hesitation that I have never seen such a close resemblance of individual letters and their structures *[in letters written by one person, or in letters written by that person and his forger?];* this also applied to the connecting links with the letters following and preceding them, where these existed...[T]he approaches to and finishings of individual letters are, in most cases, unusual and highly characteristic. It might be argued that this indicates the work of a 'super-forger'. However, the individualities are so characteristic, and the joins with adjacent letters are very nearly identical in the two letters on the different documents being compared, that I feel that I must rule out the likelihood of forgery in this particular comparison. *[Why?]*...It should also be noted in these comparisons that I have been comparing documents that were probably made as much as 5 or 6 years apart in date. *[If genuine, as Grant assumes, they were made over 20 years apart.]* The close resemblance recorded is, therefore, all the more remarkable *[all the more suspicious, according to Grant's own reasoning]*."

"I also extended my examination to the capital letters, with much the same results — but [with a less definite conclusion]. This is likely to be expected, since capital letters normally have no useful preceding connecting links, being used mainly for proper names. *[False. On page 5 of the manuscript in question, there are 58 capital letters; 22 are used for proper names, and 36 are not.]* Nor did I find any indication of the common devices of forgery such as tracing from an original." *[How could a forger trace a 62-page literary forgery from an original that doesn't exist?]*

Grant's Conclusions:

"I concluded that the writings under comparison were in fact likely to have made [sic] by the same person, and the question of forgery did not arise."

"To sum up:

1) It is highly probable that (A) and (B) were written by the same person. *[That is the impression created by all good forgeries.]*

2) The similarity is too close for them to have been written even by a forger of experience. All letters of the alphabet were examined *[not true: all 26 did not appear on the two pages being compared]*, some in two forms (where there were capitals) *[only 17 letters of the alphabet appeared as capitals on page (A), and there is no way to know which of those appeared also on page (B)]*; and if it was the work of a forger, I have never encountered one so competent." *[What competent handwriting forgers did Grant ever encounter? His obituary in the* Times *in 1991 extolled at length his various accomplishments, but failed to mention that he ever had any connection with handwriting analysis.]*

Lindskoog's Conclusions:

Julius Grant was 88 years old when he wrote this embarrassing report, and he died one year later. (Some of the most embarrassing parts are left out of this synopsis because they are irrelevant to his purpose.) Therefore it is reasonable to assume that his mental powers were under a cloud in 1990. Such confusion is understandable.

But in 1994 Stanley Mattson was in the prime of life and presenting himself to potential donors as an "Intellectual Historian" who is founding an important college on the campus of one of America's great universities. Mattson's attorney Timothy Stoen was also in the prime of life and had been practicing law for over 30 years. Therefore it is difficult to imagine why on 2 February 1995 Stoen sent the Grant Report to libel expert Leonard DuBoff of Portland, Oregon, claiming that this document is "overwhelming evidence *directly refuting* the author [Kathryn Lindskoog]." And it is hard to imagine why he also enclosed as supporting documentation an irrelevant 1990 letter from Stanley Mattson to Julius Grant, plus an equally irrelevant 1995 letter from Bodleian librarian Judith Priestman.

APPENDIX 10

THE NANCY COLE REPORT

"What is worth making clear is how important Nancy's report truly is. [Of all reports about The Dark Tower], Nancy's is the cream of the crop."—Michael Logsdon, *The Lamp-Post*, Winter 1996/1997

1. THE SECRET HISTORY

October 1988: Publication of Kathryn Lindskoog's *The C. S. Lewis Hoax*, a challenge to the authenticity of much of Walter Hooper's posthumous C. S. Lewis literature, especially *The Dark Tower*.

January 1989: J. Stanley Mattson, a California public relations expert, launched a campaign to discredit *The C. S. Lewis Hoax* in order to defend Walter Hooper and his questionable claims.

21 April 1989: Stanley Mattson orchestrated a closed-door one-day trial of *The C. S. Lewis Hoax*. His hand-picked jury of twelve included Jennifer Larson, a rare books dealer. As jury foreman and judge, at the end of the day Mattson pronounced *Hoax* all wrong. Although publicized afterwards as an unbiased and responsible deliberation, the trial had devoted an average of less than ten minutes to each of its forty key issues. This astounding agenda meant that there could be absolutely no defense at the trial, no witnesses, no evidence, no argument, and no examination or cross-examination. There was not even any transcript, and so the proceedings remain secret.

23 April 1989: Walter Hooper donated his Dark Tower manuscript to the Bodleian, making it available to researchers for the first time. (After allegedly finding the story at a January 1964 bonfire, he had waited until the early 1970s before showing even a typed copy to friends. Then at an undisclosed date before 1984 he had placed his valuable handwritten copy in his private cache in the Bodleian.)

Fall 1989: Jury member Jennifer Larson met a document examiner named Nancy Cole and attended a party given by Cole.

12 April 1990: Nancy Cole wrote to Professor Don and Dr. Sharon Cregier of the University of Prince Edward Island, offering them her professional services. (A mutual acquaintance had notified her that the Cregiers were concerned about authenticity of certain C. S. Lewis documents.) Cole's credentials impressed the Cregiers, who assumed that "document examination" meant much more than handwriting analysis. They also assumed that Cole would be unbiased and objective, with no hidden affiliations or conflict of interest.

April 1990: Sharon Cregier and Nancy Cole began corresponding about possibile examination of the Dark Tower manuscript. Cole expressed enthusiasm and cited her hourly fee. The Cregiers had Lindskoog mail her a copy of *The C. S. Lewis Hoax.*

Circa May 1990: Jennifer Larson talked to Nancy Cole about Mattson's April 1989 trial of *The C. S. Lewis Hoax,* and Cole was favorably impressed with Larson.

20 May 1990: Don and Sharon Cregier wrote to Stanley Mattson suggesting that he co-sponsor with them an examination of the Dark Tower manuscript by an unbiased, well-qualified professional document examiner such as Nancy Cole. (Mattson's participation was needed to demonstrate the good faith and evenhandedness of the project.)

7 June 1990: Expecting Stanley Mattson to accept their offer, Don Cregier sponsored Nancy Cole for a reader's ticket to the Department of Western Manuscripts in the Bodleian Library, so she could examine the Dark Tower manuscript and other C. S. Lewis documents during a trip to England for a conference sometime later that year.

24 July 1990: Nancy Cole wrote to the Cregiers inquiring pointedly about the status of the proposed investigation. Cregiers were still waiting for a response from Stanley Mattson, and so the co-sponsored project seemed increasingly unlikely. Cole never communicated with Cregiers again, and communicated with Mattson instead.

27 August 1990: Sharon Cregier sent Stanley Mattson a letter restating the invitation to co-sponsor an unbiased examination. He never answered, and has never corresponded with Cregiers. But he did correspond with Nancy Cole in 1990, and the nature and extent of their communication has never been revealed. In her 1995 essay Cole would thank Mattson for his help.

21 December 1990: Walter Hooper wrote a letter to Nancy Cole. The nature of that letter has never been revealed. In her 1995 essay Cole would thank Hooper for his help.

December 1992: Michael Logsdon, a friend of Stanley Mattson, began publishing the *Salinas Lewisian,* a quarterly newsletter focused on defending Walter Hooper and assuring readers there are no forgeries in the Lewis canon.

October 1994: In late October Kathryn Lindskoog published a greatly expanded, updated version of *The C. S. Lewis Hoax,* titled *Light in the Shadowlands: Protecting the Real C. S. Lewis.*

1 November 1994: Michael Logsdon, who had first learned about Nancy Cole in 1994, wrote to Don Cregier about their co-funding a forensic study of the Dark Tower manuscript. Cregier agreed but said he would want to be consulted about the methods and the choice of analysts; by then he thought there should probably be more than one investigator, without previous familiarity with the controversy. Logsdon did not reply.

2 December 1994: Stanley Mattson's lawyer threatened Lindskoog's publisher with a nuisance suit.

Circa 3 January 1995: Stanley Mattson presided over a dinner party for six in a Berkeley restaurant, with Nancy Cole and Jennifer Larson as special guests from Palo Alto. The purpose of the meeting was defense of Walter Hooper and opposition to the idea that the Dark Tower document might be forged.

January 1995: According to the strong implication in a footnote in Nancy Cole's essay, it was in January that she made her journey from Palo Alto, California, to Oxford, England, to examine the handwriting on the Dark Tower document. Odd as it seems, that was the only hint in her essay about when the examination took place.

4, 5, 6 April 1995: Nancy Cole visited the Department of Western Manuscripts in the Bodleian to look at C. S. Lewis documents. (A researcher located these dates in a registry at the Bodleian.)

August 1995: Nancy Cole read her essay about the Dark Tower document at a forensics conference and sent a copy to Michael Logsdon. She declared that the Dark Tower manuscript could not possibly be a forgery because the handwriting looks just like Lewis's. Although Cole and Lindskoog are strangers, Cole repeatedly scoffed at Lindskoog's character, personality, and intelligence. She ended her essay with a sentiment that Stanley Mattson had expressed in writing in January 1989 — that Lindskoog owes Hooper an apology for questioning the authenticity of "The Dark Tower."

18 January 1996: An Internet web page about Lewis included an item from Michael Logsdon and news that Nancy Cole had published an essay proving the Dark Tower manuscript genuine. (Because Michael Logsdon, Nancy Cole, Stanley Mattson, Jennifer Larson, and Walter Hooper are all connected in an informal web of overlapping friendships, it is reasonable to assume that they keep abreast of some of each other's ideas and activities.)

30 January 1996: Thanks to the Internet announcement, Kathryn Lindskoog learned there was a Nancy Cole essay and faxed her a request to purchase a copy with a query about the content. Cole replied that the essay had been submitted to a journal, and when it was published it would speak for itself. (It was never published.)

April 1996: Michael Logsdon suddenly discontinued the *Salinas Lewisian* without announcing there the news about Nancy Cole's essay. Instead, he announced that there is "nothing really new." He devoted three pages of his last issue to an erroneous article by his friend Juan Fajardo, accusing Lindskoog of intellectual incompetence and possible falsification of sources.

Mid-1996: Michael Logsdon, who had moved to Northern California, became temporary editor of *The Lamp-Post*, quarterly journal of the Southern California C. S. Lewis Society.

Late March 1997: In *The Lamp-Post* Michael Logsdon announced his news about Nancy Cole's essay and featured a four-page promotional article about it by Juan Fajardo. Logsdon praised Cole's essay and Fajardo's article and urged readers to order copies of the full essay from him at cost. Although he did not say so in *The Lamp-Post*, he had already decided not to publish any detailed rebuttals to the allegations in Fajardo's article and Cole's essay.

Early April 1997: Nancy Cole's essay arrived at the homes of *Lamp-Post* readers who had ordered it. There Cole presented a misleading version of events. (See Lindskoog, "Errors in Nancy Cole's Essay.") Cole claimed that four (sic) years after her correspondence with Cregiers, "[her] attention was brought to *Light in the Shadowlands.*" She says she independently decided, "to pursue the examination myself." Readers would never guess that Cole "pursue[d] the examination" three months after an important 1995 dinner meeting with Stanley Mattson and Jennifer Larson. In fact, from her account readers would not guess that Cole knew Mattson and Larson.

April-May 1997: Logsdon posted Internet "advertisements" (his term) for the Cole essay, praising it and urging people to order copies.

18 April 1997: Jill Farringdon wrote to Nancy Cole about her misunderstanding of A. Q. Morton's method.

21 May 1997: Don Cregier sent a letter for publication in *The Lamp-Post*. (Michael Logsdon informed him that it would not appear there.)

June 1997: Michael Logsdon's announced target date for launching an Internet web page for Nancy Cole's essay.

16 June 1997: Kathryn Lindskoog began asking Michael Logsdon for the exact dates of Nancy Cole's 1995 examination of the Dark Tower document. He passed the question on to Cole, with no result.

23 June 1997: Michael Logsdon suddenly notified Kathryn Lindskoog that he was dropping out of the controversy.

30 June 1997: Although Kathryn Lindskoog had not communicated with Nancy Cole since early 1996, in response to Jill Farringdon's forwarded open letter to her, Cole faxed a warning that she would not enter a correspondence "regarding TDT or related research."

2. ERRORS IN NANCY COLE'S REPORT

"An Investigation into the Authorship of *The Dark Tower*" by Nancy H. Cole, M.A., 701 Welch Road, Suite 2214, Palo Alto, CA 94304. Phone (415) 325-3440, Fax (415) 325-1603

This is Kathryn Lindskoog's analysis of Nancy Cole's unpublished 20-page essay written in 1995 and first circulated in manuscript form in March 1997. Section 6 is the most amusing section and the most important.

Nancy Cole is a California member of the Association of Forensic Document Examiners. She begins her essay by thanking the staff of the Bodleian Library for enabling her to see documents there. "I am also indebted to Dr. J. Stanley Mattson, President of the C. S. Lewis Foundation, Redlands, CA, and to Mr. Walter Hooper of Oxford, U.K." Her list of acknowledgments ends with Michael Logsdon, editor of *The Lamp-Post of the Southern California C. S. Lewis Society* (who in 1997 heaped accolades on her report and offered copies of the essay to readers at cost).

Cole's Section 1: "Scope of this paper"

Here Cole states the assumption behind her report: "questions raised concerning authorship [of *The Dark Tower*] could be answered by visual inspection [of the manuscript]." She does not try to explain or defend this assumption, which flies in the face of today's balanced forgery detection procedures.

Cole's Section 2: "Background"

After identifying C. S. Lewis and *The Dark Tower* in her first three paragraphs, Cole launches into a series of errors.

1. She says *The Dark Tower* is a sequel to the science fiction trilogy. But it is a sequel only to *Out of the Silent Planet*.

2. She claims that authenticity of *The Dark Tower* was disputed shortly after publication. But it was first disputed in 1988, not 1977.

3. She claims that the dispute was "partly due to the fervid devotion of Lewis fans to whom he had become almost a cult figure." But she does not identify those legendary fans and does not explain how their fervid, almost cultish devotion contributed to the authenticity dispute.

4. She adds, "There were and are numerous Lewis societies, not only in the U.K. and the United States, but also throughout Europe, in Canada, and in Asia—all of them peopled by vocal fans." If that were true it would be irrelevant to her subject, but it is an exaggeration.

5. "One of the loudest and most fervent of these voices is that of...Kathryn Lindskoog." My authorial voice has been commended for its civility, its friendly wit, and its pleasant tone. In contrast, a "loud" authorial voice from a female is assumed to be strident, overbearing, and even bombastic.

6. "She first expressed this view [that *The Dark Tower* is not by C. S. Lewis] in an article in 1979..." Cole is evidently referring to a 1978 article unrelated to *The Dark Tower*, and she is confusing it with the 1988 book where I first expressed this view.

7. "She reiterated her theories and expanded upon them in the far more strident volume, *Light in the Shadowlands.*" By calling *Light in the Shadowlands* "strident" Cole contradicts the judgment of Richard Wilbur printed on the third page: "I much admire the tone of humane amusement..." Wilbur is the second United States Poet Laureate, twice winner of the Pulitzer Prize, and winner of the National Book Award and the Bollinger Award.

8. "An entire volume, *Fakes, Frauds, and Other Malarkey* (Grand Rapids, Michigan: Zondervan, 1993,) sets forth her theories..." To the contrary, in that book there is not one reference of any kind to *The Dark Tower* or to my forgery charges. The book does not even mention my opinion that there are deceptions in Lewis affairs.

9. "Ah, [Lindskoog] replies...she will go back to her special knowledge of what Lewis *could* have done or might have included in content. If she considers an inclusion 'not like Lewis,' it *can't* be his." Cole has a right to resort to the rhetoric of sarcasm if she chooses, but this grotesque caricature flatly contradicts both my position and my sentiments.

10. "TDT is a handwritten manuscript. Has Mrs. Lindskoog seen it? No, she says she requested it in 1984 at the Bodleian and was told she could not have access to it. Dr. Judith Priestman, the Keeper of the Keys at the Bodleian, says that she never requested it." During the noon hour on June 22, 1984, Dennis Porter, Keeper of Western Manuscripts, informed me that I could not see the Dark Tower manuscript because it was the personal property of Walter Hooper and not available to researchers. Bodleian records prove that Porter's claim was true and that Hooper did not allow researchers to see the manuscript until 1989. (For me to see the manuscript in 1984 would have been pointless anyway, because as I explained in *Light in the Shadowlands,* the idea that the story was forged never crossed my mind until 1986. Since then I have seen the manuscript in photocopy and discovered an atypical letter *I* near the beginning.)

11. "Since no one except Gervaise [sic] Mathews [sic], a friend of Lewis who had died before TDT's publication, may have seen the work prior to publication, Lindskoog thinks this proves it didn't exist during Lewis's lifetime." Cole goes on to remind readers that there is no reason to think Lewis always read his work aloud to friends. But Cole is confused; it is clear in *The Dark Tower* and in *Light in the Shadowlands* that Hooper claims that

Gervase Mathew heard Lewis read a portion of *The Dark Tower* at an Inklings meeting, not that he saw the handwritten manuscript. And I have never thought that anything about this proves anything about *The Dark Tower*.

12. "No agreement was reached [about Cregiers' attempt to co-sponsor an objective analysis of the Dark Tower manuscript], nor was the matter of my investigation pursued. Four [sic] years later, after my attention was brought to *Light in the Shadowlands,* I decided to pursue the examination myself, and the result is this paper." The idea that an agreement was attempted is an error; Stanley Mattson refused to acknowledge or respond to the 1990 letters from Cregiers proposing unbiased manuscript analysis. Five years later he had dinner with Nancy Cole in an upscale Berkeley restaurant to discuss his opposition to *Light in the Shadowlands.* As a result, she prepared and submitted for publication an essay defending the Dark Tower manuscript. This is not what her statement "I decided to pursue the examination myself" means to most readers.

The predominance of error in Cole's section called "Background" does not bode well for the rest of her essay. It could get better, but it's going to get worse.

Cole's Section 3: "Examinations and reports"

Nancy Cole says that before she examined the Dark Tower manuscript it was necessary for her to discover all the previous examinations and reports. She does not say why this was necessary, why she never looked at some of the most important ones, and why she devotes well over one-tenth of her essay to inconsequential data about most of them. Therefore I summarize all of Section 3 in the order she follows.

1. First Cole sought information about the much-publicized Warner Report, commissioned by Stanley Mattson and signed on 24 January 1989, by Francis Warner and R. E. Alton. The two affirmed the manuscript's authenticity, but Cole found their written report devoid of meaningful information. When she interviewed Mr. Alton for details, he resolutely declined to give any information about the examination except to reveal that the two men did not lay out the Dark Tower manuscript next to

unquestioned Lewis documents to compare the handwriting as the report seemed to indicate. He would not say what they did instead; he told Cole he would reveal that only in a court case. Cole inexplicably changes Dr. Alton's name to Dr. Wood in the midst of her account, and concludes, "the thrust of the Warner report remains hidden."

Cole neither examined nor mentioned the first report commissioned by Stephen Schofield in 1991, from a Cheshire detective named Pearson.

2. Next, Cole examined the second report commissioned by Stephen Schofield in 1991, the one by Jacqueline Sawyer of Bristol. Sawyer was in favor of the manuscript's authenticity, but Cole found her report unprofessional, "cursory, and a little silly."

3. Next, Cole mentions Stanley Mattson's 1990 "colloquium." In fact, this bizarre "trial" was neither an examination nor a report, and it took place in April 1989, not in 1990. Cole summarizes it as "[a colloquium] which found TDT genuine and which, of course, Lindskoog discounts for various reasons." This use of "of course" as a rhetorical device indicates erroneously that my critical analysis of the Mattson jury proceedings was reflexive rather than reasoned.

4. Next, Cole examined Stanley Mattson's report from Julius Grant written in June 1990. (She seems to think it was dated 1989.) Grant was in favor of the authenticity of the Dark Tower manuscript, but his report was completely confused and insubstantial. Cole theorizes that Grant was saving his information for a possible court case in the future, but that idea seems untenable. Grant was 88 years old, and no court case was ever considered anyway.

5. Next, Cole considers the opinion of Nicolas Barker, Keeper of the British National Library, who looked at the manuscript in 1989 and considered it authentic. All she says at this point about Barker's findings is that he found some post-1950 ink on the manuscript. She notes that perhaps the manuscript was written in 1950 or later rather than in 1938 as otherwise indicated.

6. Finally, Cole considers the two formal examinations that provide evidence against the authenticity of *The Dark Tower*. She fails to point out that these two examinations have nothing to do with her subject area, which is authentication of physical documents. (Instead, they are products of the discipline of ascertaining authorship of texts directly, and no original documents are involved in that task.)

First Cole dismisses Carla Faust Jones's published 1986 computer analysis of letter and letter-pair frequencies in Lewis texts by claiming that it "only proves what the average reader could discern" about style. This statement shows that Cole has not read Jones's article, which is readily available and clear, and if she read about it she thoroughly misunderstood what she read.

Next, Cole dismisses A. Q. Morton's 1991 cusum analysis of the *Dark Tower* by claiming that although Morton's complex statistical technique of author identification is admissible in British courts, it only works on everyday speech (as in written confessions), not on literary compositions. But that is like claiming that fingerprints only identify people in everyday clothes, not those dressed in their Sunday best or costumes. Cole seems unaware that most of Morton's cusum analysis work is in the field of literature (including ancient Greek texts as well as old and modern English texts). The significance of Morton's method of analyzing works of literature is indicated by the fact that the £6000 1997 Calvin & Rose Hoffman Memorial Prize was awarded to Morton's friend Jillian Farringdon for her essay "Attributing Shakespeare and Marlowe." (Her results demonstrated that Marlowe did not write certain Shakespeare material.)

Cole's Section 4: "Weight of Handwriting Opinion"

Cole begins this section with a personal slur: "One cannot, of course, hope to convince Kathryn Lindskoog that an identification of the writer of TDT would hold any water at all." She mistakenly claims twice that TDT fills "64 long pages." (It fills 62 pages.)

Next, she states that my case against *The Dark Tower* is based upon a fallacy. After mentioning my "lack of understanding of a document examiner's discipline" (a major error in itself), Cole explains the fallacy underlying my forgery charge:

A) Hooper could write like Lewis (at least his signature)

B) TDT looks like Lewis writing

C) TDT must have been written by Walter Hooper

(I'm not making this up; it is her exact words.) My fallacy, she continues, is much like that of the schoolchild who states:

A) Harry has hair

B) horses have hair

C) Harry is a horse

At this point Cole mentions the unresolved dispute about whose writing hand appeared in Hooper's 1979 film "Through Joy and Beyond." She says that I insist the hand signing Lewis's name was Hooper's. But the hand was writing a poem rather than signing Lewis's name, and I was in no position to insist. I was able to show that Hooper's hand was not too bony and hairy in 1978 to be the one in the film (as he claims) and that he refuses to identify anyone else as owner of the writing hand.

Next, Cole refutes my claim that successful forgeries are not unusual. "[Lindskoog] fails to note that the ones she cites (the Hitler diaries, the Mormon papers, the Hughes will, etc.) have all been exposed at the time of her writing." She seems to believe that no matter how much a forger gains and how many people he fools, or for how long, once the forgery has been exposed it can't be counted as a successful forgery. (And until it has been exposed, it can't be counted as a forgery at all.) Needless to say, this unusual approach turns the term "successful forgery" into an oxymoron. Document authenticators like Cole can always assure the public that no such thing exists if they define the term away.

Cole tries to estimate how long it would take a forger to produce the suspect Lewis manuscripts. She does not say if she is imagining a gifted master forger at work or an average person without much skill. Her estimate is staggering: "A forger would have had to have been locked in a room for years to turn out the body of painstaking work that Lindskoog attributes to Hooper." But the main part of that work, the Dark Tower manuscript, is only 62 pages long; and Konrad Kujau's forged Hitler diaries were 64 *volumes* long. An array of handwriting experts vouched for the diaries, along with the German FBI, the former head of forensic services in Zurich, historian H. Trevor Roper, and the world's foremost Hitler scholar, Gerhard Weinberg of the University of North Carolina at Chapel Hill (alma mater of Walter Hooper and Stanley Mattson). Weinberg reasoned as Cole does; the diaries looked genuine, and it seemed implausible that anyone would forge so much. Thus handwriting examiners can be fooled by long, daring forgeries. I suspect that Cole wildly overestimates the time it takes an accomplished forger to create such a product.

Cole concludes this section by referring to evidence about style, content and provenance as "nearly weightless arguments" in contrast to handwriting analysis. (She prefers the term "document examination," but handwriting is all she includes in her report.) Perhaps her statement "document examination produces demonstrable evidence that cannot and should not be dismissed out of hand" is understandably defensive. In the *University of Pennsylvania Law Review* (summer 1989), law professor Michael Saks pointed out that there is no academic training for handwriting experts, no evaluation of their competence, and no certification. When the Forensic Sciences Foundation gave proficiency tests to handwriting specialists, only 45 percent of the test cases were correctly analyzed. Saks has found no evidence that handwriting experts can do what they claim.

Cole's Section 5: "Materials Examined"

Cole's list of 14 items is amazing, in that she travelled all the way from California to the Bodleian Library in Oxford, England, and did not look at even one of the many, many genuine Lewis documents there. All four that she chose to see were on Lindskoog's list of forgeries, yet Cole listed three of them as her chosen exemplars of genuine Lewis handwriting.

An intriguing item on her list is K-6, "Letter to Nancy Cole from Walter Hooper, typed with signature and four line handwritten note. Dated '21 December 1990.'" This is the only indication that Cole and Hooper had such a long association. She fails to mention the nature of the letter and how or why she used it.

Cole's Section 6: "Examination and Findings"

On page 11 of her report Cole states that although Lewis's handwriting was remarkably consistent throughout his career, it varied sometimes according to its content. "When Lewis was translating a classical poem, for instance, his writing assumed a more formal look, a more vertical slant and exhibited an even more regular rhythm." Unfortunately, Cole does not reveal when or where she saw "a classical poem" that Lewis had translated into English using this alternative style of penmanship, so there is no way to check on its provenance (or its existence).

Fortunately, however, she includes in her report a photocopy of three lines of this alternative penmanship; it is from an essay that Walter Hooper allegedly rescued from the 1964 manuscript bonfire, published in 1985 as "Encyclopedia Boxoniana." This is one of the documents that I have challenged and that Nancy Cole is defending. The thrust of her defense is that the challenged documents display typical Lewis handwriting, and yet she openly admits that the handwriting on this one is atypical. She gives no indication that she notices the contradiction. (In my opinion the overly neat "Encyclopedia Boxoniana" document appears to be an early example of forged Lewis handwriting, before practice made it perfect.)

On page 12 Cole says "The closest Lewis exhibits to a careless scrawl was found in the 'LeFay fragment'." Again she provides a three-line sample. Like "Encyclopedia Boxoniana," the "LeFay fragment" is a document I consider an early forgery. For some reason Cole seems to consider these divergences from Lewis's normal penmanship as evidence that the documents in question are genuine rather than as evidence that they are early forgeries.

On page 13 Cole describes the appearance of the Dark Tower manuscript, including the writing on the backs of pp. 1 and 2 in post-1950 ink: "the odd bits of Narnia and, I believe, Boxonian commentary that appear on the verso pages..." But there is nothing remotely connected to Boxen on those pages, and there are no "odd bits of Narnia." There is an alternative opening paragraph of *The Lion, the Witch and the Wardrobe* (already published in 1950) and a very peculiar opening paragraph for Lewis's autobiography. These are clear on the manuscript Cole examined in the Bodelian and clearly described in the book she is refuting, *Light in the Shadowlands*.

On the left side of p. 15 Cole displays photocopies of 16 handwritten words from the Dark Tower manuscript, and on the right she displays 34 words from "known" Lewis documents to show how well key letters match. But 11 words on the right are from documents on the forgery list, and Hooper provided 15 others. The other 7 are from copies of unidentified Lewis letters. Few readers will get out magnifying glasses to try to decipher Cole's miniscule, carelessly scribbled notes that reveal what a farce the illogical comparison is. (Why didn't Cole use unquestioned sources and identify them?)

On p. 16 Cole says, "Lewis makes his commas backwards. Find another author who has this habit and another forger clever enough to notice and replicate it!" One might wonder what kind of forgers Cole is used to dealing with if they are not clever enough to spot distinctive characteristics and replicate them. That is usually assumed to be the very nature of forgery.

Cole devotes the culmination of her report, pp. 13-17, to showing exactly what everyone has always agreed upon: that if the Dark Tower manuscript is a forgery it is an extremely good one, and that Walter Hooper's usual handwriting differs from Lewis's. (Perhaps Cole assumes that people think a forger's usual handwriting does not differ from that of the person he forges. Surely she herself doesn't really believe that, although she actually implies that she does.)

On page 17 she states as her conclusion the same premise with which she began, that it would be impossible for anyone to be such a talented forger. She says she is sure Walter Hooper could not have produced these documents, that there is no base for such a charge. (I consider this begging the question.)

Cole concludes that if I had engaged the services of a handwriting analyst before making charges of literary forgery, a great deal of grief could have been avoided. Whose, she does not say.

3. The Cregier Response to Nancy Cole

Prof. D.M. Cregier (Ret.)
Department of History
University of Prince Edward Island
Charlottetown, P.E.I., Canada C1A 4P3
Fax: 902 838-2882
E-mail: DCregier@UPEI.CA

May 21, 1997

Mr. M. J. Logsdon
Editor, The Lamp-Post
2294 North Main Street, #48
Salinas, CA 93906

Dear Mr. Logsdon:
I am responding to some comments by Juan R. Fajardo and yourself in the Winter 1996-7 issue of your journal, *The Lamp-Post of the Southern*

California C. S. Lewis Society. These concern the involvement of Dr. Sharon Cregier and myself in a proposed forensic examination of the novel fragment, *The Dark Tower*, attributed to C. S. Lewis.

Mr. Fajardo correctly states that Sharon Cregier and I wrote Dr. J. Stanley Mattson in 1990 suggesting that *The Dark Tower* "be scrutinized by a well-qualified professional document examiner" (quotation from my May 20, 1990, letter to Mattson). We offered to co-sponsor and help pay for such a study. Mr. Fajardo, however, goes on to say "the matter was dropped when no agreement was reached." I must point out that Dr. Mattson did not reply either to my letter of May 20, 1990, or to a reminder from Dr. Sharon Cregier on August 27, 1990. "No agreement was reached" because there were no negotiations.

A few observations are also in order about our connection with forensic document examiner Nancy H. Cole. Mr. Fajardo writes that we "sought out [Ms. Cole] to perform [the] analysis" of *The Dark Tower*. This is not strictly accurate. My recollection is that Ms. Cole's name was suggested to us by a mutual friend. However, the earliest document in our file is a letter from Ms. Cole, dated April 12, 1990, in which *she* offers *us* her services.

On the basis of Ms. Cole's impressive credentials, we recommended her to Dr. Mattson. In anticipation that our offer to Dr. Mattson would be accepted, on June 7, 1990, we sponsored Ms. Cole to Dr. Judith Priestman of the Department of Western Manuscripts, Bodleian Library, for a reader's ticket to examine "the 'Dark Tower' MS and other documents relating to C. S. Lewis" (quotation from the "Form of Recommendation for Admission to the Bodleian Library").

Dr. Sharon Cregier and Ms. Cole corresponded between April and July 1990. Although at first very enthusiastic about studying the Lewis material, in late July 1990 Ms. Cole seemed to lose interest, possibly because by that date a remunerative commission was unlikely. In her letter of July 24, Ms. Cole inquired pointedly whether we intended to proceed with the Lewis investigation. This is the last letter from Ms. Cole in our file of correspondence.

What further immediate steps, if any, Ms. Cole took respecting *The Dark Tower* are not known by us. However, in her copyrighted August 1995 conference paper, "An Investigation into the Authorship of *The Dark Tower*...," there is a reference (p. 9) to a "Letter to Nancy Cole from Walter

Hooper...dated '21 December 1990.'" This reference appears to indicate that Ms. Cole and Mr. Hooper, purported discoverer of *The Dark Tower*, were in contact as far back as 1990.

In 1991—as Kathryn Lindskoog notes in her *Light in the Shadowlands* (pp. 246-7)—Dr. Sharon Cregier and I underwrote a computerized stylistic analysis of *The Dark Tower* by forensic expert A. Q. Morton. The Morton Analysis, as Mrs. Lindskoog writes, showed that *The Dark Tower* was a composite work by more than one author. This finding, while extremely interesting and suggestive, did not resolve the authorship question.

As you will recall, Mr. Logsdon, you wrote me in November 1994 offering to help fund another, and presumbably more holistic forensic study of *The Dark Tower*. I replied that Dr. Sharon Cregier and I would be "pleased to contribute something to the cost of such a study" but would want to be consulted about the methods and the choice of analysts. I stated that I thought the investigators—"probably more than one"—should be "completely divorced from C. S. Lewis studies" and "be previously unfamiliar with the controversy over the posthumous 'Lewisiana.'" You did not continue the correspondence.

Nancy Cole, in a footnote on page 4 of her 1995 report, states that Dr. Sharon Cregier contacted her in 1991 [actually 1990], that no agreement was reached, and that "four years later," after reading Lindskoog's *Light in the Shadowlands*, she decided "to pursue the examination myself." In 1990, at our request, Mrs. Lindskoog mailed Ms. Cole a copy of her earlier work, *The C. S. Lewis Hoax*. If Ms. Cole read the *Hoax*, she was familiar with the details of the Lindskoog claims long before 1995.

Ms. Cole's revived interest in *The Dark Tower* controversy would appear to have occurred about the time that you wrote me requesting my cooperation in another forensic analysis of *The Dark Tower*. As neither you nor Mr. Fajardo mention any connection between your inquiry to me and Ms. Cole's decision in 1994 or 1995 to investigate the manuscript, I presume there was none. Confirmation (or dissent) from you on this point would, of course, amplify the record.

Finally, a few words about Ms. Cole's paper, a copy of which you were kind enough to send us recently when we requested it. Her conclusion, that *The Dark Tower* MS is unquestionably in Lewis's handwriting, must be weighed alongside the findings of A. Q. Morton and other investigators.

Unfortunately, Ms. Cole's analysis—beginning effectively on page 8 of her 18-page paper—is significantly flawed by factual errors and imprecision throughout the paper, as well as by her gratuitous censure of Kathryn Lindskoog in pages 1 through 8 and on page 18. The errors, some of which could have been avoided by careful editing, naturally weaken the paper's overall credibility. The unnecessary castigation of Mrs. Lindskoog invalidates any claim by Ms. Cole to neutrality.

We are left, therefore, with a need—as I wrote you on November 12, 1994—for a "comprehensive investigation into the authenticity of the posthumous 'Lewisiana' [which] must include analysis, *by impartial experts* [my emphasis], of the provenance, linguistic patterns, and manuscript features (paper, ink, handwriting) of the various documents." As I further remarked at the time, such experts must be "selected by persons acceptable to all parties in the field of Lewis scholarship."

Yours truly,
Don M. Cregier

P.S. I request that you publish this letter, in its entirety, in *The Lamp-Post.* If you cannot do so, please use the enclosed SASE to return the letter along with any comments you would like to make.

Michael Logsdon declined to publish this letter in the Lamp-Post.

4. Farringdon Response to Nancy Cole

Dr. Michael and Jill Farringdon
Ariel Cottage, 8 Hadland Terrace West Cross
Swansea SA3 5TT, Wales

April 18th, 1997.
Dear Ms. Cole,
My attention has been drawn to your essay "An Investigation into the Authorship of The Dark Tower", in which you write that although Andrew Morton's "complex statistical technique of author identification is admissible

in British Courts, it only works on everyday speech (as in written confessions) not on a literary composition..." As the author of *Analyzing for Authorship* (University of Wales Press, 1996), a text-book and research study into the technique's literary and linguistic applications, copiously illustrated, it falls to me to correct several misapprehensions in your quotation above:

1. The technique is not "complex". As a learned Judge remarked in the Central Criminal Court, Dublin, during the longest-running trial in Irish history, "You could do this with an abacus" (instead of a computer). To which the reply was a "True, my Lord, but it would take somewhat longer."

Please note that the method of cusum analysis is always swiftly grasped by members of an ordinary jury with no expertise in statistics. It can be carried out by anyone (including you yourself) with the motivation to learn how to do it.

2. QSUM has been used in evidence not only in British but in Irish, Australian and Canadian courts, and also used in a Jamaican case. In British justice, its most recent vindication has come with the release (Feb. 1997, the Carl Bridgwater case) of three men who had been wrongfully convicted and spent 18 years in prison: Andrew Morton was not only able to discredit the 'confession', but to match the statement to its real author.

3. Your assertion that the technique works only for everyday speech is massively incorrect (where did you acquire such misinformation?). My recent book gives analyses of natural utterance, both written and spoken, including my own written utterance in samples from 1953-1995

- edited text
- translated work
- children's writing
- dialect
- disputed texts

My most recent research has shown definitively that cusum analysis works on the poetry/prose of Shakespeare and Marlowe (separating each from the other), as well as matching samples of Sylvia Plath's poems and prose (indistinguishable by QSUM).

I trust that clarifies the facts as regards Morton's technique, and it is proper here to emphasise his lifetime's work on attribution of the Greek text of the New Testament - Gospels, Acts, Pauline Epistles, and Revelations (his most recent publication is *Gathering the Gospels,* Mellen Press, 1997). The N.T. can hardly be called "everyday speech", as you mistakenly state.

However, wearing my other hat, as a literary critic and poetry book reviewer (published in national newspapers, *Poetry Wales, Planet, The Anglo-Welsh Review,* and *The New England Review* and *Bread Loaf Quarterly*), perhaps I might be permitted to give my own literary response to *The Dark Tower.* My reading of pp. 29-36, with the description of 'the Man' and the 'sting in his forehead' which is 'like a unicorn's horn' seems to me pure homosexual fantasy. After all, we all know what the unicorn's horn represents! Whatever else Lewis was - fornicator, adulterer, penitent sinner - he was not, I think, homosexually inclined.

Jill Farringdon

APPENDIX 11

WHO OWNS C.S. LEWIS?

by

"Nat Whilk"

Who receives the royalties from the sale of books by C.S. Lewis? And who ultimately controls the rights to Lewis's literary works?

For more than two decades, the answers to these questions have been shrouded in mystery. No one seems to know who owns the rights to Lewis's works—or who is benefiting from the millions of dollars of royalties generated by his books and related products. In 1999 a researcher launched a wide-ranging investigation to track down the mysterious owners of Lewis's literary estate. The results of that investigation, reported here for the first time, reveal the existence of a tangled network of business enterprises that spans the globe and may involve large-scale tax evasion.

In his will, C.S. Lewis left his brother Warren a life interest in the income derived from his writings. After Warren's death in 1973, the rights to C.S. Lewis's literary works went to C.S. Lewis's stepsons David and Douglas Gresham. Many people assume that David and Douglas Gresham continue to own the rights to the works of their stepfather. But Walter Hooper stated in 1998 that the Greshams sold the rights to anonymous investors in the late 1970s who formed C.S. Lewis Pte. Ltd. to manage the publication of Lewis's works. Douglas Gresham has made a similar claim. Gresham says that he is currently employed by C.S. Lewis Pte. Ltd. as an advisor. Asked in 1998 who owned C.S. Lewis Pte. Ltd., Douglas Gresham insisted that he did not know—and that he did not care as long as they continued to pay him.

So what do we know about the shadowy entity called C.S. Lewis Pte. Ltd.? The company was set up in Sinagpore seven years after Warren Lewis's death. In 1981 the firm purchased the copyright of the works of C.S. Lewis for a little more than $2.25 million. C.S. Lewis Pte. Ltd.'s sole business activity appears to be handling the royalties from C.S. Lewis's literary works and related merchandise. The royalties have been considerable. According to financial statements filed with the government of Singapore over the past two decades, from 1982 to 1998 C.S. Lewis Pte. Ltd. earned royalties of more than $14.6 million ($25.6 million in Singapore dollars).Whether these royalty figures accurately represent the full amount of royalties earned on C.S. Lewis's works during this period is open to question, because the auditors who prepare the financial statements for C.S. Lewis Pte. Ltd. have repeatedly issued disclaimers about the basis of the figures reported. Touche Ross, the accounting firm that prepared the company's financial statements for several years, regularly stated in its reports that it "could not obtain direct confirmation from the licensees of royalty received."

While C.S. Lewis Pte. Ltd. is the official recipient of royalties from C.S. Lewis's books, the firm pays no taxes in Singapore because none of the money earned actually goes into Singapore. If the money does not go to Singapore, where does it go? Presumably to the mysterious shareholders of C.S. Lewis Pte. Ltd. And who are they? According to records on file in Singapore, C.S. Lewis Pte. Ltd. has only two shareholders, both of which are companies: Aministralanstalt and Consilium Treuhand AG. Both firms are located in the Swiss Alps in the tiny principality of Liechtenstein.

With bank secrecy laws that exceed Switzerland's in strictness, Liechtenstein is one of the world's premier tax havens for people who want to cheat on their taxes. Under Liechtenstein law, it is a crime for a member of a Liechtenstein financial company to reveal to anyone the owners of anonymous trust accounts and foundations set up within the country, making it virtually impossible for the tax authorities of other countries to track down the income of citizens who choose to hide their money in Liechtenstein.

Both Administralanstalt and Consilium Treuhand AG specialize in setting up trusts, foundations, and other legal arrangements for customers who want to shelter their earnings. Toendury & Partner, which was created out of Consilium Treuhand AG and two other companies in 1992, assures potential customers on its website that "current laws make it virtually impossible for unauthorized persons or authorities to obtain information about Liechtenstein Foundations, Trusts and Companies or bank accounts." The website goes on to say that "foreign currencies may be brought into Liechtenstein freely and Liechtenstein Foundations, Trusts and Companies are not subject to any exchange controls or reporting requirements." (Readers wishing to learn more about the two companies that handle the secret accounts for the owners of C.S. Lewis Pte. Ltd. can go to the firms' websites. Administralanstalt can be found at http://www.administral.li, while Toendury & Partner's address is http://www.toendury.com.)

Dividends from C.S. Lewis Pte. Ltd. are split equally between Administralanstalt and Consilium Treuhand AG, suggesting that the rights to Lewis's writings are owned by two different investors (or two groups of investors). The possibility of two equal owners of C.S. Lewis Pte. Ltd. is further suggested by the fact that since the firm's inception there always have been two main board members who have seemed to exercise equal authority in directing the company. (See below for a complete listing of primary board members since 1984.) From the mid to late 1990s the two key board members were Melvin Adams and Rudolf Sieber. In 1999 Adams and Sieber were replaced by Hans Eggenberger and Gerhard Meier, accountants who are managing partners in the Liechtenstein firm of Toendury & Partner. Assuming that the $14.6 million in royalties from Lewis's works have been reinvested wisely during the last decade and a half, any owners of Lewis's literary rights should be multi-millionaires several times over by now.

The fact that the owners of C.S. Lewis's works are funneling their profits into accounts in Liechtenstein may explain why their identities have been kept as a closely guarded secret for so long. If the owners are trying to avoid taxes in their countries of origin, then they cannot afford to publicly acknowledge that they own Lewis's works. As long as their identities are kept secret, they can fail to report their income from the sale of Lewis's works on their tax returns because there is no way that their governments can find out their real incomes. However, if the owners of Lewis's works were to publicly acknowledge their assets, they would open themselves up to investigations by the tax authorities in their home countries.

It is of course possible that the owners of the rights to Lewis's works have been reporting their full incomes to their own governments all along, but people do not usually set up foreign trust accounts in tax havens unless they are trying to hide their income. Considering C.S. Lewis's reputation as a Christian writer whose ethics were above reproach (and who gave away much of his income to charity during his own lifetime), the possibility that the current owners of Lewis's works may be engaging in large-scale tax evasion on income derived from his books seems ironic to say the least.

The financial statements supplied by C.S. Lewis Pte. Ltd. raise some interesting questions about the role played by Douglas Gresham in business activities related to C.S. Lewis. Gresham says that he is employed by C.S. Lewis Pte. Ltd. Yet the financial statements issued by C.S. Lewis Pte. Ltd. for the years 1996 to 1998 do not seem to allow for any payments to him. According to the profit and loss statements for those years, the only remuneration and fees paid by C.S. Lewis Pte. Ltd. were to its auditors, its board of directors, and "to firms in which the directors are partners" (i.e., Administralanstalt, Consilium Treuhand AG, and the accounting firm that prepares the company's financial statements). According to records on file with the Singapore government, Douglas Gresham is not one of the members of the board of directors of C.S. Lewis Pte. Ltd. Nor is he a financial auditor. Where, then, does the money come from to pay him? Perhaps he is actually an employee of a "firm in which the directors are partners," but if this is the case, why does he say that he is employed by C.S. Lewis Pte. Ltd. rather than by the firm that actually employs him?

In 1999 the activities of the Lewis literary estate gained another layer of complexity with the establishment of the C.S. Lewis Company in England. According to the company's annual return filed with the British government, the business activity of the C.S. Lewis Co. is the "publishing of books." The shareholders of the new entity? Administralanstalt and Consilium Treuhand AG, the same firms that own C.S. Lewis Pte. Ltd. The board members of the C.S. Lewis Company are Melvin Adams and Rudolf Sieber, who until recently had been the primary board members of C.S. Lewis Pte. Ltd. By the end of 2000 it was still unclear what the precise division of duties was between the C.S. Lewis Co. in England and C.S. Lewis Pte. Ltd. in Singapore.

ROYALTY INCOME REPORTED BY C.S. LEWIS PTE. LTD., 1982-1998
(According to financial statements filed with the government of Singapore.)

Year	In Singapore $	In American $
1982	678,822	319,046
1983	549,763	258,389
1984	413,597	194,391
1985	917,007	412,653
1986	647,423	297,815
1987	973,998	457,779
1988	977,392	459,374
1989	2,269,937	1,157,668
1990	1,321,855	727,020
1991	1,447,664	839,645
1992	1,819,653	1,109,988
1993	1,240,050	756,431
1994	1,575,185	960,863
1995	2,535,316	1,546,543
1996	3,348,863	2,042,806
1997	2,191,303	1,631,698
1998	2,708,536	1,468,213
Total:	25,616,364	14,640,322

LIST OF PRIMARY DIRECTORS OF C.S. LEWIS PTE. LTD., 1984-2000
(According to financial statements filed with the government of Singapore.)
Trever Peter Batkin (1984-1989)
Conrad Joseph Brian Alcantra (1984-1989)
Colin Martin Batty (1989-1992?)
Francis Harry Plaistowe (1989-1992?)
Hans Eggenberger (1992?-1993?; 1999-)
M. Marc Mascetti (1992?-1993?
Rudolf Sieber (1993-1999)
Melvin Adams (1993?-1999)
Gerhard Meier (1999-)

APPENDIX 12

THREE LETTERS FROM C. S. LEWIS

14/12/50
Dear Mr. Vanauken,

My own position at the threshold of Xianity was exactly the opposite of yours. You wish it were true; I strongly hoped it was *not*. At least, that was my conscious wish: you may suspect that I had unconscious wishes of quite a different sort and that it was these finally shoved me in. True: but then I may equally suspect that under your conscious wish that it were true, there lurks a strong unconscious wish that it were not. What this works out to is that all the modern thinking, however useful it may be for explaining the origin of an error which you already know to be an error, is perfectly useless in deciding which of two beliefs is the error and which is the truth. For (a.) One never knows all one's wishes, and (b.) In very big questions, such as this, even one's conscious wishes are nearly always engaged on both sides. What I think one can say with certainty is this: the notion that everyone would *like* Xianity to be true, and that therefore all atheists are brave men who have accepted the defeat of all their deepest desires, is simply impudent nonsense. Do you think people like Stalin, Hitler, Haldane, Stapledon (a corking good writer, by the way) wd. be pleased on waking up one morning to find that they were not their own masters, that they had a Master and a Judge, that there was nothing even in the deepest recesses of their thoughts about which they cd. say to Him "Keep out! Private. This is *my* business?" Do you? *Rats!* Their first reaction wd. be (as mine was) rage and terror. And I v. much doubt whether even you wd. find it *simply* pleasant. Isn't the truth this: that it wd. gratify some of our desires (ones we feel in fact pretty seldom) and outrage a good many others? So let's wash out all the wish business. It never helped anyone to solve any problem yet.

I don't agree with your picture of the history of religion—Christ, Buddha, Mohammed and others elaborating on an original simplicity. I believe Buddhism to be a simplification of Hinduism and Islam to be a simplification of Xianity. Clear, lucid, transparent, simple religion (Tao *plus* a shadowy, ethical god in the background) is a late development, usually arising among highly educated people in great cities. What you really start with ritual, myth, and mystery, the death & return of Balder or Osiris, the dances, the initiations, the sacrifices, the divine kings. Over against that are the Philosophers, Aristotle or Confucius, hardly religion at all. The only two systems in which the mysteries and the philosophies come together are Hinduism & Xianity: there you get both the Metaphysics and Cult (continuous with primeval cults). That is why my first step was to be sure that one or the other of these had the answer. For the reality can't be one that appeals either only to savages or only to high brows. Real things aren't like that (e.g. matter is the first most obvious thing you meet—milk, chocolates, apples, and also the object of quantum physics). There is no question of just a crowd of disconnected religions. The choice is between (a.) The materialist world picture: wh. I can't believe. (b.) The real archaic primitive religions; wh. are not moral enough. (c.) The (claimed) fulfillment of these in Hinduism. (d.) The claimed fulfillment of these in Xianity. But the weakness of Hinduism is that it doesn't really merge the two strands. Unredeemable savage religion goes on in the village; the Hermit philosophizes in the forest: and neither really interfaces with the other. It is only Xianity which compels a high brow like me to partake of a ritual blood feast, and also compels a central African convert to attempt an enlightened code of ethics.

Have you ever tried Chesterton's *The Everlasting Man*? The best popular apologetic I know.

Meanwhile, the attempt to practice Tao is certainly the right line. Have you read the Analects of Confucius? He ends up by saying, "This is the Tao. I do not know if anyone has ever kept it." That's significant: one can really go direct from there to the Epistle of the Romans.

I don't know if any of this is the least use. Be sure to write again, or call, if you think I can be of any help.

Yours sincerely
C. S. Lewis

23 Dec. 1950
Dear Mr. Vanauken
    The contradiction "we must have faith to believe and must believe to have faith" belongs to the same class as those by which the Eleatic philosophers proved that all motion is impossible. And there are many others. You can't swim unless you can support yourself in water & you can't support yourself in water unless you can swim.

    Or again, in an act of volition (e.g. getting up in the morning) is the very beginning of the act itself voluntary or involuntary? If voluntary then you must have willed it, . . you were willing it already, . . it was not really the beginning. If involuntary, then the continuation of the act (being determined by the first movement) is involuntary too. But in spite of this we *do* swim, & we *do* get out of bed.

    I do not think there is a *demonstrative* proof (like Euclid) of Christianity, nor of the existence of matter, nor of the good will & honesty of my best & oldest friends. I think all three (except perhaps the second) far more probable than the alternatives. The case for Xianity in general is well given by Chesterton; and I tried to do something in my *Broadcast Talks*. As to why God doesn't make it demonstratively clear; are we sure that He is even interested in the kind of Theism which wd. be a compelled logical assent to a conclusive argument? Are we interested in it in personal matters? I demand from my friend a trust in my good faith which is *certain* without demonstrative proof. It wouldn't be confidence at all if he waited for rigorous proof. Hang it all, the very fairy tales embody the truth. Othello believed in Desdemona's innocence when it was proved: but that was too late. "His praise is lost who stays till all commend." The magnanimity, the generosity which will trust on a reasonable probability, is required of us. But supposing one believed and was wrong after all? Why, then you wd. have paid the universe a compliment it doesn't deserve. Your error wd. even so be more interesting & important than the reality. And yet how cd. that be? How cd. an idiotic universe have produced creatures whose mere dreams are so much stronger, better, subtler than itself?

Note that life after death which still seems to you the essential thing, was itself a *late* revelation. God trained the Hebrews for centuries to believe in Him without promising them an afterlife, and, blessings on Him, he trained me in the same way for about a year. It is like the disguised prince in a fairy tale who wins the heroine's love *before* she knows he is anything more than a woodcutter. What wd. be a bribe if it came first had better come last.

It is quite clear from what you say that you have conscious wishes on both sides. And now, another point about *wishes*. A wish may lead to false beliefs, granted. But what does the existence of the wish suggest? At one time I was much impressed by Arnold's line "Nor does the being hungry prove that we have bread." But surely tho' it doesn't prove that one particular man will *get* food, it *does* prove that there is such a thing as food! i.e. if we were a species that didn't normally eat, weren't designed to eat, wd. we feel hungry? You say the materialist universe is "ugly." I wonder how you discovered that! If you are really a product of a materialistic universe, how is it you don't feel at home there? Do fish complain of the sea for being wet? Or if they did, would that fact itself not strongly suggest that they had not always been, or wd. not always be, purely aquatic creatures? Notice how we are perpetually *surprised* at Time. ("How time flies! Fancy John being grown-up and married! I can hardly believe it!") In heaven's name, why? Unless, indeed, there is something about us that is *not* temporal.

Total humility is not in the Tao because the Tao (as such) says nothing about the Object to which it wd. be the right response: just as there is no law about railways in the acts of Q. Elizabeth. But from the degree of respect wh. the Tao demands for ancestors, parents, elders, & teachers, it is quite clear what the Tao wd prescribe towards an object such as God.

But I think you are already in the meshes of the net! The Holy Spirit is after you. I doubt if you'll get away!

Yours,
C. S. Lewis

17/4/51

Dear Vanauken

My prayers are answered. No: a glimpse is not a vision. But to a man on a mountain road by night, a glimpse of the next three feet of road may matter more than a vision of the horizon. And there must perhaps be always just enough lack of demonstrative certainty to make free choice possible: for what could we do but accept if the faith were like the multiplication table?

There will be a counter attack on you, you know, so don't be too alarmed when it comes.

The enemy will not see you vanish into God's company without an effort to reclaim you.

Be busy learning to pray and (if you have made up yr. mind on the denominational question) get confirmed.

Blessings on you and a hundred thousand welcomes. Make use of me in any way you please: and let us pray for each other always.

Yours,

C. S. Lewis

APPENDIX 13

A SHADOWLANDS CHRONOLOGY

(• = Famous forgeries and unlikely Lewis literature)

1920s

1926
• "The Man Born Blind" written by Lewis in the late 1920s, according to
  Barfield
1927
"The Most Substantial People" novel begun by Lewis circa 1927
1928
• "Encyclopedia Boxoniana" allegedly started by Lewis in September
1929
• "Encyclopedia Boxoniana" allegedly finished by Lewis in April

1930s

1930
Purchase of the Kilns by the Lewis brothers and Mrs. Moore
1931
Walter Hooper born March 27 in Reidsville, North Carolina
C.S. Lewis and Warren Lewis separately embrace Christianity
1934
• Master forger Thomas J. Wise, England's "Prince of Bibliographers,"
  exposed
Kathryn Lindskoog born on December 27 in Petaluma, California

1938

Out of the Silent Planet published

• *The Dark Tower* allegedly written by Lewis as sequel to *Out of the Silent Planet*

1940s

1942

Publication of *The Screwtape Letters* makes Lewis a popular author

1944

David Gresham, future heir of Lewis's literary estate, born 27 March

Lewis delivers warning, "The Inner Ring"

1945

Douglas Gresham, future heir of Lewis's literary estate, born 10 November

1947

• "Mussolini's diary" forgery fools the *Sunday Times*

1949

Publication of *C. S. Lewis, Apostle to Skeptics* by Chad Walsh (first Lewis study)

1950s

1950

• Lewis allegedly writes "Finchley Avenue"

Joy Davidman Gresham's first letter to Lewis

1951

Lewis invites Roger Lancelyn Green to write his future biography

1952

Mrs. Hooker poses as Lewis's wife

1954

Hooper receives his B.A. and enters the United States army

Hooper's first letter to Lewis, expressing appreciation

Lewis accepts chair at University of Cambridge, departs University of Oxford

Lindskoog discovers Lewis and begins honors research project on him

1955

Lewis's first year at University of Cambridge

Birth of Anthony Marchington

1956

Civil marriage of C. S. Lewis and Joy Davidman Gresham in April

Hooper leaves the army and begins graduate studies

Lindskoog meets C. S. Lewis, begins graduate studies

Joy's cancer strikes

1957

Lewis's bedside marriage in March, Joy's gradual recovery

Hooper receives M. A., enters seminary

Lindskoog receives M. A., begins teaching

Hooper's second letter to Lewis, hoping to meet Lewis someday

Lewis's letter to Lindskoog saying "you know my work better than anyone
else I've met"

1958

"Forms of Things Unknown" idea appears in the *Saturday Evening Post*
story "Island of Fire" and on the cover of *Fantastic Universe*, both
American magazines

1959

Hooper leaves Virginia Episcopal Seminary, teaches in a boys' boarding
school

1960s

1960

† Death of Joy Davidman Gresham Lewis

1961

A Grief Observed published

Hooper begins teaching at the University of Kentucky

1962

Hooper's third and fourth letters to Lewis, requesting 1963 meeting

1963

• Lewis allegedly writes "Introductory Letter" for poetry collection

Hooper meets Lewis 7 June lives at Exeter College during six-week summer
program

Lewis's near-fatal heart attack 15 July that temporarily deranges him

Hooper begins helping Lewis with correspondence

Lewis allegedly tells Hooper *A Grief Observed* is fiction, allegedly gives him
juvenilia

Hooper sorts through Lewis's papers alone in Cambridge in mid-August

Hooper returns to Kentucky in late August, resumes teaching

Hooper arranges to visit Lewis between semesters in January 1964

† Death of C. S. Lewis on 22 November

1964

In January Hooper moves to England with leave of absence from University of Kentucky

In January Hooper allegedly saves trunkloads of Lewis manuscripts from three-day bonfire

In mid-February Hooper meets Warren Lewis for the first time

Hooper begins editing C. S. Lewis's posthumous books, beginning with poetry

• Publication of *Poems*, in which half are altered and Hooper introduces himself as Lewis's personal secretary

1965

Clyde S. Kilby starts Wheaton College C. S. Lewis collection (later called the Marion E. Wade Center)

Hooper is ordained an Angican priest in Oxford by a diocese in Kentucky

Lindskoog/Hooper correspondence begins (1965-1977)

• Someone places "Preface to Screwtape Proposes a Toast" in publisher's files

1966

• Hooper includes "Forms of Things Unknown" in *Of Other Worlds*

• Hooper includes "On Criticism" in *Of Other Worlds*

• Hooper reveals existence of *The Dark Tower* in preface to *Of Other Worlds*

Light on C. S. Lewis (U.S.) incorrectly says Hooper met Lewis in 1956, lived with the brothers

Clyde Kilby meets Warren Lewis for the first time

1967

Hooper founds C. S. Lewis collection at the Bodleian Library

Glen GoodKnight founds Mythopoeic Society (source of the journal *Mythlore)*

1968

Warren twice challenges Hooper about *The Dark Tower*'s existence

1969

Warren protests Hooper ascendancy in Lewis affairs

Henry Noel founds New York C. S. Lewis Society (source of the bulletin *CSL)*

1970s

1970

Hooper becomes Co-Trustee of Lewis Estate

1971

• Hooper publishes photos of handwritten Narnia scraps in *Imagination and the Spirit*

• Clifford Irving forgery of Howard Hughes documents exposed

1972

Terri Williams and Carole Sperou found Portland C. S. Lewis Society (source of *The Chronicle)*

1973

† Death of Warren Lewis

† Death of J.R.R. Tolkien

• Anonymous Tolkien obituary in London's *Times* (later copyrighted by Lewis Estate)

Wade Center inherits Warren Lewis's diary and family papers

Tony Marchington enters Brasenose College in Oxford to study science

The Thirsks buy the Kilns

• Bodleian luminary Sir Edmund Backhouse (1873-1944) exposed as criminal forger

1974

Green/Hooper biography C. S. *Lewis* (includes first description of *Dark Tower* story)

After publication of biography, Green sees Hooper's claims in final chapter, disapproves

• "Forms of Things Unknown" praised by Hooper in biography

• Colin Hardie and others preview *Dark Tower* in typescript

1975

Tony Marchington visits North Carolina with Hooper

Hooper says in tape-recorded lecture that he learned to forge Lewis penmanship

Hooper visits California, tells of 1964 bonfire for the first time

1976

Paul Ford founds Southern California C. S. Lewis Society (source of *The Lamp-Post)*

Anonymous alleged purchase of the Lewis Estate from David and Douglas Gresham
* **Death of Molly Miller** (Lewis friend and housekeeper, who, with her husband Leonard, became living companions of warren Lewis.)

1977
* *The Dark Tower* title story published and explained by Hooper
* "The Man Born Blind" published in *The Dark Tower*
Fred Paxford denies bonfire story in signed letter

1978
Publication of *They Stand Together* (Hooper's attack upon Warren Lewis and *double entendre* cover)
Filming of "Through Joy and Beyond"
Lindskoog publishes "Some Questions in C. S. Lewis Scholarship" in *Christianity & Literature*
Tony Marchington's chemical soot analysis hoax prepared on Hooper's typewriter
Timothy Stoen, future C. S. Lewis Foundation attorney, knowingly triggers the Jonestown massacre of over 900 people

1979
Hooper's "Through Joy and Beyond" film and seminar tour, February-April
Stephen Schofield launches *Canadian C. S. Lewis Journal* in Surrey, England
* Publication of Hooper's Narnia scraps in *Past Watchful Dragons*
Hooper's "A Bibliography of the Writings of C. S. Lewis" in C. S. *Lewis at the Breakfast Table*

1980s

1980
Seven launched at Wade Center with Barbara Reynolds as editor
Hooper places 1200 letters in collection at Chapel Hill
Hooper's and Barfield's attorney warns Lindskoog not to probe any farther in print
Centaur's Cavern charity for Mother Teresa prohibited by Lewis Estate

1982
* First publication of "Preface to Screwtape Proposes a Toast"
Annual Wade Center grants begin
Founding of Oxford C. S. Lewis Society

1983

Douglas Gresham visits the Wade Center as a guest speaker

Robert Cording begins to launch Kilns Partnership

Stanley Mattson moves to Redlands, California, as a fundraiser

• Konrad Kujau's "Hitler diaries" forgery fools *Sunday Times*

1984

Lindskoog visits the Bodleian, denied view of Hooper's *Dark Tower* manuscript

C. S. Lewis stained glass window installed in Monrovia, California

Purchase of the Kilns from the Thirsks by the Kilns Partnership

• Mark Hofmann exposed as America's most notorious document forger

1985

"Shadowlands" BBC film success

• Publication of "Encyclopedia Boxoniana" (in *Boxen*)

1986

• Publication of "Modern Man and His Categories of Thought" (in *Present Concerns*)

Mattson launches C. S. Lewis College Foundation charity

Kilns Partnership becomes Kilns Association charity

C. F. Jones's "Literary Detective" computer study shows *Dark Tower* differs from Lewis's prose

† Death of Clyde S. Kilby ("dean of American Lewis specialists")

1987

Roger Lancelyn Green reads and approves *C. S. Lewis Hoax* manuscript

† Death of Roger Lancelyn Green (Lewis's chosen biographer)

1988

Mattson becomes president of Kilns Association, links it to his own C. S. Lewis Foundation

Hooper converts to Roman Catholicism

The C. S. Lewis Hoax published

1989

Bogus Mattson authentication of *Dark Tower* fools *Sunday Times* in January

Lewis Legacy newsletter launched in February

Mattson stages 12-man jury trial of *The C. S. Lewis Hoax* in April Hooper donates *Dark Tower* manuscript to the Bodleian

"Shadowlands" stage play success

† Death of Richard Hodgens (*Dark Tower* expert)

1990s

1990

• Publication of "Christian Reunion" (in *Christian Reunion and Other Essays*)

Mattson announces nonexistent chemical analysis of *Dark Tower* document

Mattson announces bogus Julius Grant report

1991

A. Q. Morton tests *Dark Tower* and "Christian Reunion," both of mixed authorship

† Death of Chad Walsh (first American Lewis specialist)

1992

C. S. Lewis Petition calls for open forum on posthumous Lewis canon

Hooper's "Supplement to Bibliography" (in C. S. *Lewis at the Breakfast Table*)

M. J. Logsdon launches *The Salinas Lewisian* newsletter

† Death of Ruth Pitter (distinguished poet, special friend of Lewis)

1993

† Death of Dom Bede Griffiths (old friend of Lewis, dedicatee of *Surprised by Joy*)

† Death of Jerry Daniel (editor of *CSL*)

† Death of Stephen Schofield (editor of *Canadian C. S. Lewis Journal*)

1994

"Shadowlands" film success increases Lewis's popularity

Roger Stronstad turns *Canadian C. S. Lewis Journal* into a formal journal

• *Collected Poems of C. S. Lewis*

Light in the Shadowlands published

Stanley Mattson engages Timothy Stoen to quash *Light in the Shadowlands*

† Death of John Wain (student and friend of Lewis, Oxford Professor of Poetry)

1995

Arthur C. Clarke calls for a *Dark Tower* probe

Nancy Cole's bogus examination of *Dark Tower* manuscript

1996

† Death of Sheldon Vanauken (old friend of Lewis, author of *A Severe Mercy*)

Nancy Cole's bogus examination first publicized

1997

† **Death of Maureen Moore,** Lady Dunbar of Hempriggs (Lewis's "foster sister")

Nancy Cole's bogus examination briefly distributed, then permanently withdrawn

1998

C. S. Lewis Centenary celebrations, conferences, memorials

Publication of *The C. S. Lewis Reader's Encyclopedia*

† **Death of Owen Barfield** (old friend of Lewis, his attorney and the trustee of his estate)

1999

† **Death of John Lawlor** (student of Lewis at Oxford, author of *C. S. Lewis: Memories and Reflections*)

2000s

2000

Theodore Sherman turns *Mythlore* into a formal journal

Groundbreaking for the new Wade Center at Wheaton College

2001

† **Death of Elizabeth Anscombe** (philosopher who debated Lewis.)

- Revelation that Lewis's massive posthumous royalties all go to Liechtenstein, a tax haven.

Just as this book was going to press, a stunning announcement appeared in the April 29 issue of London's *Sunday Times*. It seems to confirm my speculations in Chapter 11, "The Business of Heaven," about the Gresham brothers secretly owning and controlling the Lewis literary estate. And it is definitely an addendum to Appendix 11, "Who Owns C. S. Lewis?" The article, "Narnia reborn in The Lion, the Witch and new stories" was by Richard Brooks, Arts Editor. Here are the second and third paragraphs of his article:

The original work, first published in 1950 before the six other Narnia books, was chosen as the most influential children's book of the 20th century last year by parents, teachers and librarians. It has been adapted for television, video and the stage.

Ever since Lewis died 40 years ago his estate has guarded his work with care as his books achieved worldwide sales of 65m. Now Douglas and David Gresham, his stepsons, and the C S Lewis Company, which looks after the rights, are to cooperate with the publisher HarperCollins to bring out new Narnia novels and picture books for younger children.

(The article failed to mention that Simon Adley is the leader of the C. S. Lewis Company, hence the gatekeeper. He derailed Carol Hatcher's documentary, which led to an article on the first page of Sunday's *New York Times* on June 3 about the secularization of Narnia.)

In the June 16 issue of *World* magazine, Douglas Gresham appears to finally acknowledge that he and his brother David are the real owners of the Lewis estate after all, now saying that "the estate is made up of two trusts benefiting the families of C.S. Lewis's stepsons." At the same time, he insists that he is only "one of several" voices determining how Lewis's works are managed. However, he declines to identify who those other voices are, or what authority they have to make decisions involving Lewis's works. So mystery remains about who is in final control.

INDEX

Adams, Don, 167n
Adams, Melvin, 226–227, 389–391
"After Ten Years" (Lewis), 80n
All My Road Before Me (Lewis), 84, 92n, 126, 128n–129n, 129–132, 299, 310–311
"All or Nothing" (Lewis), 6, 91n–92n
Aministralanstalt, 388–390
Anscombe, Elizabeth, 114–115, 343, 407
Argue, Randy, 80–81
"Arthurian Torso, The" (Lewis), 66
authentication, types of, 303–304

Barfield, Owen
  compares CSL to MacDonald and Chesterton, 317
  and *Cretaceous Perambulator* material, 117, 117n
  defends bonfire story, 48
  "dignified silence" of, 360
  dismisses bonfire story, 168n
  extent of knowledge about CSL, 299–300
  "Great War" of with CSL, 133
  handles CSL's finances, 223–224
  handles W. Lewis's finances, 216–217
  meets Lindskoog, 191
  objects to W. Lewis publishing CSL juvenilia, 121
  proposes Hooper as CSL's executor, 198
  reviews *They Stand Together* favorably, 210–211
  said by Hooper to remember bonfire, 47
  sells CSL/Barfield mss., 307
  tells Vanauken that *Grief Observed* is nonfiction, 159
  threatens to sue Lindskoog for writings about Hooper, 167–168, 168n, 360
Barker, Nicolas, 108–109, 228, 228n, 261, 304, 376
Bartell, Robert, 358–359
Batstone, Patricia, 288–289
Baylis, Robert, 57n
Baynes, Pauline, 147n
Beversluis, John, 282–283
Bide, Peter, 152
Blake, Mrs. Leonard. *See* Moore, Maureen
Blakemore, Ian, 288

Bodleian Library, 16, 16n, 39n, 208, 308–310
bonfire story
  CSL's poems featured in, 93, 93n, 192
  date of, 52–54
  defended by Barfield, 48
  defended by Marchington in hoax letter, 48–52
  denied by Miller, 47
  denied by Paxford, 47–48
  omitted from *C. S. Lewis, Companion and Guide* (Hooper), 47
  outline of, 41–44
  plausibility of, 54
  told by Hooper, 41f, 43n, 46–47, 322–323
Boxen, 83, 121–123, 196, 215–216, 322–336
Bramlett, Rev. Perry C., 4n, 6
"Break, Sun, My Crusted Earth" (Lewis), 95
Brothers and Friends (W. Lewis), 62n, 64n
Brown, Ed, 357–358
Browning, Robert. *See Dark Tower, The,* title of
Business of Heaven, The (Lewis), 83

C. S. Lewis, A Biography (Green and Hooper)
  contradictory views of CSL's marriage in, 154
  Dark Tower described in, 17–18
  delayed by Hooper till after W. Lewis's death, 201, 201n–202n
  Hooper's numerous appearances in, 202
  Kilby infuriated by (Hooper says), 70
  origin of *Screwtape Letters* muddled in, 75
  states wrongly that no CSL juvenilia exist, 46, 46n
C. S. Lewis: A Companion and Guide (Hooper), 47, 159
C. S. Lewis: Collected Letters, Vol. I, 85–89
C. S. Lewis: Images of His World (Kilby and Gilbert), 97, 327, 329
C. S. Lewis: Readings for Meditation and Reflection, 84
"C. S. Lewis and C. S. Lewises" (Hooper), 115–116, 155–157, 219

C. S. Lewis at the Breakfast Table (misc. authors), 274–275. *See also* Como, James

C. S. Lewis Company, 390, 407

C. S. Lewis Foundation, 233–249, 284

C. S. Lewis Hoax, The (Lindskoog)
　anticipates attack by Wilson on CSL, 66
　approved of by Harris, 16–17
　charges that Hooper forges CSL's handwriting in film, 175
　criticized by
　　Barker, Nicolas, 228, 261
　　Beversluis, John, 282–283
　　Ford, Paul, 234
　　Griffin, William, 252–255
　　Hart, Dabney, 256
　　Marlin, George, 256
　　Mattson committee, 238–241, 361–362, 368
　　Piret, Michael, 255
　　Purtill, Richard, 259
　　Rateliff, John D., 255–256, 290
　　Root, Jerry, 271–272
　　Stoen, Timothy, 283–285
　　Walker, Andrew, 260–261
　　Warner Report, 236–238
　　Wilson, A. N., 257–258
　Dark Tower mss. made publicly available after release of, 38, 357
　Lindskoog begins writing, 28, 255n

C. S. Lewis Institute(s), 3–4, 233, 2442

C. S. Lewis Pte Ltd, 37, 198n, 225–228, 387–391

Carpenter, Humphrey, 1–2, 21, 67, 117, 152, 162

Centaur's Cavern, The (author unknown), 8–9, 80, 403

Christian Reflections (Lewis), 82

"Christian Reunion" (essay), 84, 119–121, 263–264, 290, 310, 347, 353

Christianity, case for by CSL, 392–396

Christopher, Joe, 326n, 333n, 348

Christopher, John, 144n, 148n

Clapinson, Mary, 238

Clarke, Arthur, 29–30, 29n, 275, 348, 406

Cole, Nancy, 111, 123, 243, 285, 290, 334, 368–386

Collected Poems of C. S. Lewis, The, 84, 96–99

Collmer, Robert G., 52

Como, James, 48, 57n, 72n, 160n, 167n, 272–275

computer analysis of authorship. *See* cusum analysis; Literary Detective computer program

Consilium Treuhand AG, 388–390

Cording, Robert, 230–232

Cregier, Don and Sharon, 262, 369, 381–384

Cretaceous Perambulator, A (booklet), 116–117

cusum analysis, 36, 262–264, 262n–263n, 269, 310, 377, 384–386

Dante, 133n

Dark Tower, The
　computer analyses of, 28–29, 29n, 30–31, 255n, 262–264
　date of composition of, 20, 24, 32, 37
　defended by Purtill, 259–260
　Hooper's preface to, 82, 103n, 107
　literary style of, 30–37, 353
　mss. of
　　access to restricted until 1989, 16, 16n, 357, 374
　　descriptions of, 20, 20n, 365, 380
　　examined by
　　　Cole, 111, 123, 243, 285, 290, 334, 368–386
　　　Grant, 242–243, 364–367
　　　Griffin, 254
　　　Morrison and Sawyer, 266, 266n
　　placed in Bodleian, 79, 368
　　shown by Hooper to friends, 79, 368
　possible literary models for, 24–27
　provenance of, 36, 357
　release of, 13, 19
　rescue of from bonfire. *See* bonfire story
　reviewed by
　　Brady, Charles, 23n
　　Downing, David, 272
　　Fowler, Alistair, 23
　　Glover, Donald, 23–24
　　Green, R. L., 17–19
　　Hannay, Margaret, 24
　　Hardie, Colin, 21n–22n
　　Hodgens, Richard, 23, 23n
　　LeGuin, Ursula K., 22, 272
　　Lobdell, Jared, 269–271
　　Nancy Cole, 111, 123, 243, 285
　　Walsh, Chad, 23

sexual overtones of, 21–22, 32, 386
title of, from Robert Browning, 13n, 18n
Dart, John, 112, 169
Davidman, Joy
  ambitious for her sons, 224n
  epitaph for by CSL, 97–98
  marriage of to CSL, 67–68, 148–153
  papers of, said to be destroyed, 218–219
  writing career of, 160
document forgery, definition of, 303
Dorsett, Lyle, 39, 231
Downing, David, 239, 241, 283, 356
Doyle, Arthur Conan, 27–28
Dunbar, Lady. *See* Moore, Maureen
Duriez, Colin, 291
Dymer (Lewis), 147

Eggenberger, Hans, 389, 391
Eliot, T. S., 77, 92
Ellwood, Gracia and Robert, 72–73
"Encyclopedia Boxoniana" (essay), 122–123,
    332–335, 347, 353, 357, 379–380, 397
Evans, Robert, 168–170, 170n, 178
Ewart, Lily, 197, 209

Fajardo, Juan, 280, 286, 381–382
Fakes, Frauds, and Other Malarkey
    (Lindskoog), 374
Farrer, Austin and Kay, 43, 174, 177, 187,
    188
Farringdon, Jill, 377, 384–386
Faust, Carla, 255n
feminism, Hooper and, 114–117
Fern-seed and Elephants (Lewis), 82
Ferroni, John, 273
"Finchley Avenue" (poem), 100–101, 398
Finlay, Virgil, 106
First and Second Things (Lewis), 83
Fleetwood Correspondence, The (Griffin), 80,
    80n
Ford, Paul, 169–170, 231, 234, 239, 281, 402
forgeries, famous, 237, 266–267, 302–311,
    378
"Forms of Things Unknown" (short story),
    103–107, 290, 346, 399–400
Four Loves, The (Lewis), 214, 216, 359

Gebbert, Vera, 217n
Gibb, Jocelyn, 89, 89n, 143n, 184, 215, 324
Gilbert, Douglas, 97, 217, 331

God in the Dock (Lewis), 82, 86, 91
Grant Report on *Dark Tower*, 242–243,
    364–367
Great Divorce, The (Lewis), 21, 131n, 133,
    135n–136n, 139–140, 222n–223n
Green, Roger Lancelyn
  biography co-authored by. *See C. S. Lewis,
    A Biography*
  borrows Lewis Papers from W. Lewis, 215,
    217
  denies having been shown *Dark Tower*
    mss. by Hooper, 16
  letter to from Jocelyn Gibb, 143n
  reviews *C. S. Lewis Hoax*, 29, 37, 404
  reviews *Dark Tower*, 17–19
  said by Hooper to have lied about *Grief
    Observed*, 158
  says Boxen literature is dull, 335
  tells Lewis about Lunar Hoax, 37–38
Greeves, Arthur
  letters to from CSL
    about sex, 142–143, 210, 313–314,
      313–315, 320–321, 359–360
    first, 66n
    during period of military service, 298,
      314–317
    sent to W. Lewis after Greeves's death,
      196, 359
  meets Leo Baker, 130n
  never told by CSL about Hooper, 183
Gresham
  David, 225, 225n, 227, 407
  Douglas
    attacks American school system,
      78n–79n
    claims *Dark Tower* was written not in
      '30s but in '50s, 286–287
    conversion to Christianity of, 247
    criticizes Millers, 224, 224n–225n, 287,
      358–359
    criticizes Vanauken, 88–89, 287
    describes chronology of CSL's life, 62n
    as Honorary Vice Chairman of Kilns
      restoration committee, 242
    joins debate about *C. S. Lewis Hoax*,
      279–280
    publishes photo of CSL poem in *Lenten
      Lands*, 98
    said by Como to have ordered Hooper to
      change book, 160n

says CSL was century's greatest mind,
    149
sells share of Lewis estate, 225–227, 387
sent with Hooper to clear CSL's rooms,
    111, 111n–112n, 192
as shareholder and employee of C. S.
    Lewis Pte Ltd., 227–228, 247–248, 286,
    387, 390, 407
as spokesman for C. S. Lewis
    Foundation, 246–248
states that handwriting experts validate
    Dark Tower, 291
states that mother's marriage was
    consummated, 68, 344
unimpressed by Lindskoog petition, 278n
Joy Davidman. See Davidman, Joy
Grief Observed, A (Lewis), 10, 156–159,
    180–181
Griffin, William, 80, 169–170, 252–254, 281,
    294–295, 298
Griffiths, Dom Bede, 19, 21n, 29, 89, 153,
    224n
Guardian, The (garbled account of Dark
    Tower controversy in), 289

Haldeman, Joe, 39–40
Handbook to Literature, A (Farrer), 302n
handwriting
    analysis of Dark Tower
        by Cole, 111, 123, 243, 285, 290, 334,
            368–386
        by Grant, 242–243, 364–367
        by Morrison and Sawyer, 266, 266n
    CSL's forged by CSL (Hooper says), 117
    CSL's forged by Hooper (Hooper says),
        173
    of "Encyclopedia Boxoniana," 123, 286n,
        334
    Hooper's, compared to CSL's, 174–176
    of Lefay Fragment, 111, 286n
    limitations of analysis of, 236n, 378–279
    style, importance of, 304
Hardie, Christian, 21, 21n
Hardie, Colin, 21n
HarperCollins (publisher), 228, 407
Harwood, A. C., 158, 193–194, 200
Havard, Robert E., 223
Hearn, Walter, 50n–51n
Hemingway, Ernest, 16, 16n, 39–40, 112
"History of Animal-Land" (essay), 332, 347

Hodgens, Richard, 105–106
Holbrook, David, 258n
Holmes, Sherlock, 27–28
Hooper, Walter, 21n–22n
    anecdotes about CSL told by, 69, 77–78,
        81–85, 119, 124, 167, 187n, 206
    announces Dark Tower's existence, 15, 24n
    appointed executor of CSL's estate, 198
    attitude of toward women and feminism,
        114–116
    becomes Anglican priest, 176–179
    bonfire story told by, 41–44, 46–47,
        322–323, 402. See also bonfire story
    converts to Catholicism, 118, 179
    correspondence of with
        Cole, 370, 379
        CSL, 188, 311, 399–400
        Lindskoog, 44–45, 44n, 114–115, 154,
            193, 201n–202n, 214, 229, 261n–262n
        W. Lewis, 15–16, 53, 198
    criticized by W. Lewis, 197–199, 218–219
    criticizes W. Lewis, 89, 204–209
    and CSL's juvenilia, 322–336
    as CSL's secretary, 186–189, 191, 199–200,
        241n
    defends CSL against Anscombe, 114
    defends CSL against feminists, 115–116
    deposits materials in Bodleian Library,
        15n, 16, 16n, 38–39, 79, 92–93, 111,
        264, 307n, 308–310
    discrepancies in claims of, 165–173,
        176–179, 186–187, 198n, 202–203,
        211–212, 212n, 329–330
    editorial errors by, 90, 294–299
    edits CSL's poetry, 93–96
    employment of by C. S. Lewis Pte Ltd.,
        198n, 227–228
    English and Lewisian mannerisms of,
        72–73, 72n, 164–165
    gives W. Lewis's royalties from tapes to
        Barfield, 216
    introductions by to Lewis books, 81–85,
        115n, 122, 126, 155, 205, 331–332, 360
    invents anecdote about Lincoln's funeral,
        166
    leaves Virginia Theological Seminary in
        1959, 177
    links Out of the Silent Planet to Dark
        Tower, 20

and Mattson jury on *C. S. Lewis Hoax*, 239, 239n
meets Colin Hardie, 21n–22n
meets Pope John Paul II, 61, 118
meets W. Lewis, 53
moves in with W. Lewis, 191
orchestrates Warner Report on *C. S. Lewis Hoax*, 236n
plans film *Through Joy and Beyond*, 56–58
prays to CSL, 189
relationship of to CSL, 68–69, 68n, 171–172, 174
restricts access to CSL letters, 87
reverses views of CSL's sexual history, 66–67, 154–159, 319–320
schooling of supported by Bloomfield, 177–178
Screwtape Letters altered by, 76–78
Screwtape Letters's origin garbled by, 73–76, 74n
Screwtape-style letter by, 75n, 104n
sells papers to UNC at Chapel Hill, 147n
sent with Gresham to clear CSL's rooms, 111, 111n–112n, 192
states that
   C. S. Lewis
      asked him to become secretary permanently, 186–187
      believed in Papal Infallibility, 118–121
      called him "the son I should have had," 171, 203
      destroyed own manuscripts, 46n
      dictated poems to him, 92–93
      forged own boyhood handwriting, 117
      never had secretarial help before Hooper, 173
      would have converted to Catholicism, 121
   did not consummate marriage, 155–160
   found *Dark Tower* in a drawer, 112
   he corrected hundreds of W. Lewis's editing errors, 90
   he inherited CSL's papers in 1963, 162
   he learned to forge CSL's handwriting, 173, 402
   he observes strict editorial standards, 90–91
   he showed *Dark Tower* mss. to W. Lewis et al., 16
he was CSL's live-in secretary and literary assistant, 165n
he was editing *Dark Tower* in 1975, 40n
he writes 1,500–2,000 letters per year to inquirers, 172
Lindskoog sought to ban male pronouns from *Lamp-Post*, 283n
many readers like *Dark Tower*, 19
manuscripts he saved from bonfire were "scorched," 43
Thirsks intended to chop up the original Wardrobe, 46n–47n
W. Lewis stole letters to Greeves from CSL, 208–209
told to destroy CSL's literary scraps, 111–112
tours U.S.A. to promote film, 58–59
typewriter owned by used by Marchington for hoax, 51–52
warned by Como against Kilby, Lindskoog, et al., 273, 273n
warns Lindskoog about Vanauken, 71n
warns Reynolds and Walsh about Kilby and Lindskoog, 70–72
Hopkins, Anthony, 161–162
"Humanitarian Theory of Punishment" (Lewis), 86

Imagination and the Spirit (anthology), 110–111
ink, blue, in purported CSL manuscripts, 108–109, 108n, 304, 376
Inklings, the, 21, 21n, 180, 375
"Inner Ring, The" (Lewis), 274n, 398
Invaders from Mars (movie), 25

Joliffe, Peter, 108
Jones, Carla Faust, 28–29, 28n, 346, 377, 404
Jones, Jim, 284

Kelley, H. N., 58–59, 58n, 164–165
Kerwin, Joseph, 19
Key, Tom, 9–10
Kilby, Cyde S.
   asks W. Lewis about unknown CSL space novel, 15
   asks W. Lewis to bequeath Greeves letters to Wheaton College, 208
   infuriated by publication of CSL biography (Hooper says), 70

meets W. Lewis, 195
prevented from hinting that Hooper
    should correct record, 219–220
tribute to CSL by, 11–12
withholds W. Lewis diary for several years,
    204
writes to Lindskoog saying Hooper will
    edit CSL manuscripts, 190
Kilns, the, 2–3, 229–232, 242n, 244–246,
    248–249, 313
Kilns Association, 231–232, 234
Kipling, Rudyard, 305–306
Kreeft, Peter, 1n

La Jetée (movie), 25
La Paz, letter from Lindskoog to, 356–363
Larson, Jennifer, 368–369
Lawlor, John, 36, 407
Lefay fragment, 111, 347, 380
LeGuin, Ursula K., 22, 29, 272
L'Engle, Madeleine, 24–26, 55
Lenten Lands (Gresham), 98, 224n, 247
Letters of C. S. Lewis, 44–45, 53, 64n, 66n, 84,
    89–91, 195
Letters to an American Lady (Lewis), 174, 187
Letters to Children (Lewis), 8n
Letters to Malcolm (Lewis), 93, 101, 309–310
Lewis, Albert, 63–64, 143–144, 295, 314–317,
    341
Lewis, C. S.
    attitude of toward Catholicism, 118–121
    attitude of toward money, 221–223
    autographs and documents attributed to,
        306–311
    books, etc. about, 5–6, 9–10
    copes with madness of John Askins,
        128–133
    correspondence of with
        Hooper, 188, 311, 399–400
        Lindskoog, 222n
        Pitter, 147
        Vanauken, 181, 392–396
    death of, 221, 223
    estate of, 225–229, 387, 407. *See also* C. S.
        Lewis Pte Ltd.
    harassed by a Mrs. Hooker, 144–145
    instructs Hooper to destroy his literary
        scraps, 111–112
    juvenilia of, 46, 46n, 121–123, 322–336,
        357

love of poetry, 92
marriage of, 149, 151–155
military service of, 296–299, 313–317
obituary for Tolkien allegedly by, 117–118,
    347
poems of, 92–102, 332
relationship of with J. Moore, 63–67,
    312–321. *See also* Moore, Jane
sexuality of, 63–68, 89, 142–144, 312–321,
    337, 386
societies devoted to, 3–4
stained-glass portrait of, 2
will of (viewable online), 224n
works by. *See* Narnia; *also specific titles*
writing process of, 35–36
Lewis, Jack (American author), 55
Lewis, Joy. *See* Davidman, Joy
Lewis, Sinclair, 127–128, 128n
Lewis, Warren
    alcoholism of, 191, 197, 204–207, 213
    alleged to have destroyed Lewis Papers
        originals, 44n
    asks Hooper if unpublished Ransom novel
        exists, 15–16
    bequeaths papers to Wheaton College,
        45–46, 70n, 76, 125, 196, 204, 324
    bonfire admitted by (per Hooper), 43n.
        See also bonfire story
    criticized by Hooper, 89, 204
    criticizes Hooper, 197–199, 218–219, 401
    as CSL's secretary, 68, 173, 221
    death of, 218
    diary of, 194–199, 219–220, 318–319
    disapproves of CSL's relationship with J.
        Moore, 63–64, 143–144, 318–319
    generosity of to Hooper, 207, 216
    leaves £5,000 to M. Miller, 193–194
    letters from to Hooper, 15–16, 53, 198
    letters from to Lindskoog, 44–45, 44n
    lives at Kilns with CSL and J. Moore, 313
    meets Hooper, 53
    portrayal of in *Through Joy and Beyond*, 68
    protests Hooper's accounts of living with
        Lewises, 183–185
    says that *Grief Observed* is nonfiction, 159
    solicits CSL letters for collection, 44
    veneration for CSL manuscripts, 45–46
Lewis Papers, 44n, 126
Liechtenstein, 388–389

Light in the Shadowlands (Lindskoog), 29, 284–285, 374–375, 406
Light on C. S. Lewis (misc. authors), 89n, 123–124, 183
"Lilies that Fester" (Lewis), 113
Lindskoog, Kathryn
  begins investigating *Dark Tower*, 28
  bombards Schofield with obvious hoaxes, 266–268
  challenges Hooper in *Christianity & Literature*, 167–168, 403
  correspondence of with
    CSL, 222n
    Hooper, 44–45, 44n, 114–115, 154, 193, 201n–202n, 214
    W. Lewis, 44–45, 44n
    Wilson, 257n
  forbidden to use CSL letter in booklet, 87–88
  invites her critics to debate, 261–262
  letter to *La Paz* from, 356–363
  meets
    Barfield, 191
    CSL, 2, 149–151, 322
    Millers in 1975, 197
  not allowed to see *Dark Tower* mss. in Bodleian, 16, 374, 404
  petition for clarification of CSL canon, written by, 275–278, 276n–277n, 346–352
  responds to Cole, 372–381
  responds to Griffin, 254n–255n
  said by Mattson to be mentally deranged, 241
  sister of meets M. Miller at Kilns, 190–191
  threatened with lawsuit by Barfield, 168, 168n
  visited by Mattson, 234–235
  visits Hooper at Oxford, 40n
  visits Thirsks at Kilns, 46n–47n, 230
  works by. *See specific works*
Lion, the Witch and the Wardrobe, The (Lewis)
  dedication of to Lucy Barfield, 150
  scrap of in purported CSL manuscript, 109–110
  versions of, 5, 11, 11n
Literary Detective computer program, 28–29, 255n, 404
literary forgery, definition of, 302

Logdson, Michael, 278–280, 285–286, 370–372, 384
Long, James, 30
Lunar Hoax, 37–38

MacDonald, George, 101, 317
Mackey, Aiden, 280–281
MacLean, Alastair, 228, 228n–229n
"Magdalen College Appendix" (attributed to Lewis), 310–311, 347n
"Man Born Blind, The" (short story), 107–109, 126, 285, 290, 307, 347, 357, 397
Man Who Created Narnia, The (Coren), 10n
Marchington, Anthony
  appearance in *Through Joy and Beyond* of, 59–61
  appears in rowing garb with Hooper, 172–173
  credentials of, 51n
  hoax letter to *Christianity & Literature* by, 48–52
  lives and collaborates with Hooper, 56–59
  thanked by Hooper in *They Stand Together*, 211
  visits North Carolina with Hooper, 402
Marion E. Wade Center at Wheaton College, 1–2, 45, 76, 125, 208, 281–282, 344, 401
Maritain, Jacques, 77
Marlin, George, 35
Mathew, Gervase, 21
Mattson, Stanley. *See also C. S. Lewis Hoax,* criticized by Mattson committee
  appoints Cole to certify *Dark Tower*'s authenticity, 111, 334, 368–372, 382
  challenged to cosponsor analysis of *Dark Tower* mss., 259
  chronology of involvement of, 404–406
  cited approvingly by Marlin, 256
  opposition of to *C. S. Lewis Hoax,* 230–249, 359–364
McGovern, Eugene, 48, 168
Meier, Gerhard, 389, 391
Mere Christianity (Lewis), 83, 119, 308
Miller, Leonard
  accused by Gresham of robbing W. Lewis's corpse, 224n–225n
  denies bonfire story, 47
  letters to from Lindskoog, 47

states that Hooper did not visit W. Lewis as
  often as claimed, 198n
states that Hooper never lived at Kilns, 68n
Miller, Molly
  death of, 403
  as friend of W. Lewis, 195–196, 217, 358
  meets Lindskoog's sister in 1964, 190–191
  praise Hooper, 188–189
  states that Lewis never said Hooper was
    "son I should have had," 203
  states that W. Lewis left Kilns because of
    grief, 190
"Ministering Angels" (short story), 103
Minto. *See* Moore, Jane
"Miserable Offenders" (Lewis), 91–92
"Modern Man and His Categories of
  Thought" (essay), 112–113, 116, 347,
  404
Moody, Bishop William R., 178, 178n
Moore
  Jane, 63–67, 129, 143–144, 298–299,
    312–321
  Maureen (Lady Dunbar of Hempriggs),
    64–65, 129, 229, 242, 312, 406
  Paddy, 63–64, 154, 312, 314–316, 318–319,
    341
Morton, A. Q., 262–264, 269, 278, 310, 346,
  377, 383
"Most Substantial People, The" (Lewis),
  125–141, 397
Moynihan, Martin, 59
Musacchio, George, 283

Narnia. *See also specific Narnia books*
  fragments, 109–110, 346, 353, 402–403
  marketed on Internet by HarperCollins,
    110n
  sales of books about, 7
  spinoffs from, 5–7, 9, 11, 407
"Narnian Suite" (Lewis), 94, 94n
Narrative Poems (Lewis), 82
Nellie (Nelly), definition of, 32
Noel, Henry, 113, 401

O'Donnell, Bob, 56–58, 57n, 210, 223n
"Of Other Worlds" (Lewis), 1
Of Other Worlds (Lewis), 19, 38, 81, 103, 127
On Stories and Other Essays (Lewis), 83
Out of the Silent Planet (Lewis), 14, 20, 26,
  263, 328, 373, 398

"Past Watchful Dragons" (Hooper), 111,
  346–347, 403
Paxford, Fred, 41, 47–48, 190, 224n, 225,
  323, 358
Payne, David, 10
Perelandra (Lewis), 14, 106–107, 263
petition for clarification of CSL canon,
  275–278, 346–355
Pilgrim's Regress, The (Lewis), 85–86, 93,
  118n, 128n, 270
Pitter, Ruth, 94, 146–148, 150n, 153,
  153n–154n
Pleasures Forevermore (Willis), 118–119
Poems (Lewis), 81, 92, 191, 347n
Pope John Paul II, 61
Porter, Dennis, 238, 238n, 359
Portland Statement, 353–355
Powers, Tim, 118, 348
Present Concerns (Lewis), 83, 112
Problem of Pain, The (Lewis), 26, 223n
Prothero, James, 287–288
provenance, definition of, 303

QSUM analysis. *See* cusum analysis

Rateliff, John, 255–256, 290
Reveille (periodical), 294
Reynolds, Barbara, 69–70, 115, 239, 281
Robins, Cherry, 313–314, 318
Rowse, A. L., 16–161

Sambrot, William, 106
Sayer, George
  alters opinion of CSL's relationship to J.
    Moore, 65
  describes CSL's attitude toward
    Catholicism, 120
  describes CSL's funeral, 189–190
  opinion of *Dark Tower* of, 24
  regarding details of publication of *Spirits in
    Bondage,* 293–294
  speculates that CSL might have married
    Pitter, 153
  visits W. Lewis, 198
Schmidt, Tom, 239, 241, 356
Schofield, Stephen, 71, 118, 224n, 230, 242,
  264–268, 376
Screwtape Letters, The (Lewis)
  altered Lord & King edition of, 76–78

comics version of, 81
continuation of by Griffin, 80
CSL's preface to, 139
Hooper's introduction to, 82
origin of, 73–76, 74n
popularity of, 14
screen rights to, 80–81
"Screwtape Proposes a Toast" (Lewis), 78–80, 347, 353, 404
Selected Literary Essays (Lewis), 82
Shadowlands (book, movie, play), 3, 10–11, 160–162, 244, 247, 344, 404
"Shoddy Lands, The" (short story), 103, 103n
Sieber, Rudolf, 226–227, 389–391
Silver Chair, The (Lewis), 48, 306
Singapore, 388–391
Skeleton in the Wardrobe, The (Holbrook), 258n
Spirits in Bondage (Lewis), 83, 293–296, 317, 321
Stoen, Timothy, 283–285
Studies in Medieval and Renaissance Literature (Lewis), 81–82
Surprised by Joy (Lewis), 42, 64, 116n, 121, 132, 320
Sustins, Nigel, 170
Swann, Donald, 153

That Hideous Strength (Lewis), 15, 18, 32n, 108n
They Asked for a Paper (Lewis), 113
They Stand Together (Lewis and Greeves), 44n, 83, 142, 155, 205, 209–215, 298, 359, 403
Thirsk, Mr. and Mrs. J. W., 46–47, 230
Through Joy and Beyond (book), 60–61, 155
Through Joy and Beyond (movie)
contents of, 59–63
CSL-like handwriting in, 175–176, 377–378
errors in, 62–68, 73–74
genesis of, 56–57
Till We Have Faces (Lewis), 14, 150, 222
Time Travelers, The (movie), 26
Timeless at Heart (Lewis), 84
Toendury & Partner, 389–390
Tolkien, J. R. R., 14, 117–118, 152
Traupman, John C., 85–86
Twain, Mark, forgeries of, 306

Una Gioia Insolita (Lewis), 84–85
United Media, 6–7

Vanauken, Sheldon
dislikes *Dark Tower*, 19
doubts bonfire story, 54n
doubts Hooper's Lewis anecdotes, 81n, 171–172
doubts that CSL wanted Anglicans to unite with Catholics, 119
interview with, 179–183
letters to from CSL, 392–396
Lindskoog warned by Hooper about, 71n–72n
opinion of *C. S. Lewis Hoax* of, 29
proposes scenario for *Dark Tower*'s origin (joke), 26
questions scene in film *Through Joy and Beyond*, 60
receives CSL's permission to publish letters, 87
states that *Grief Observed* is nonfiction, 159, 180–181
states that CSL's marriage was consummated, 180
unpopularity of with Lewis estate, 88
Voyage of the Dawn Treader, The (Lewis), 8–9, 110–111

Wade Center. *See* Marion E. Wade Center
Wakeman, Jean, 183–184
Wall, Barbara, 21, 21n
Walmsley, Lesley, 289–290
Walsh, Chad, 23, 57n, 68n, 71–72, 155, 222
Ward, Michael, 101
Warner Report, 236–238, 375
"We Have No 'Right to Happiness'" (Lewis), 140–141, 182
Weight of Glory, The (Lewis), 83, 274n, 360
West, John, 157–159
Wheaton College. *See* Marion E. Wade Center at Wheaton College
"Who's Cribbing?" (J. Lewis), 55
Wilbur, Richard, 93n, 275, 305, 348
Willis, John Randolph, 118–119
Wilson, A. N.
converts to atheism, 258n
criticizes *C. S. Lewis Hoax*, 144–146, 151, 247–258

describes St. Stephen's as a "high camp"
    world, 66, 176
  errata of, 258, 297, 300, 316, 337–345
Wilson, Angus, 252n
Wrinkle in Time, A (L'Engle), 24–25, 36, 55
Wrong, Charles, 19